尾田栄一郎

The ball always winds up in the bunker when you're trying not to hit it there. In fact, I'd bet you'd have more luck avoiding the sand trap if you actually aimed for it. My favorite iron...is the five iron. Something's just not right with my putter these days...

Actually, *I've never golfed in my life!!!* I want to try golfing one day when I'm all grown up. Here comes volume 65!! Nice shot*!!*

-Eiichiro Oda, 2011

E iichiro Oda began his manga career at the age of 17, when his one-shot cowboy manga **Wanted!** won second place in the coveted Tezuka manga awards. Oda went on to work as an assistant to some of the biggest manga artists in the industry, including Nobuhiro Watsuki, before winning the Hop Step Award for new artists. His pirate adventure **One Piece**, which debuted in **Weekly Shonen Jump** in 1997, quickly became one of the most popular manga in Japan.

ONE PIECE VOL. 65
NEW WORLD PART 5

SHONEN JUMP Manga Edition

STORY AND ART BY EIICHIRO ODA

Translation/Stephen Paul
Touch-up Art & Lettering/Vanessa Satone
Design/Fawn Lau
Editor/Alexis Kirsch

Printed in the U.S.A.

Published by VIZ Media, LLC
P.O. Box 77010
San Francisco, CA 94107

10 9 8 7 6 5 4 3 2 1
First printing, November 2012

SHONEN JUMP MANGA

ONE PIECE

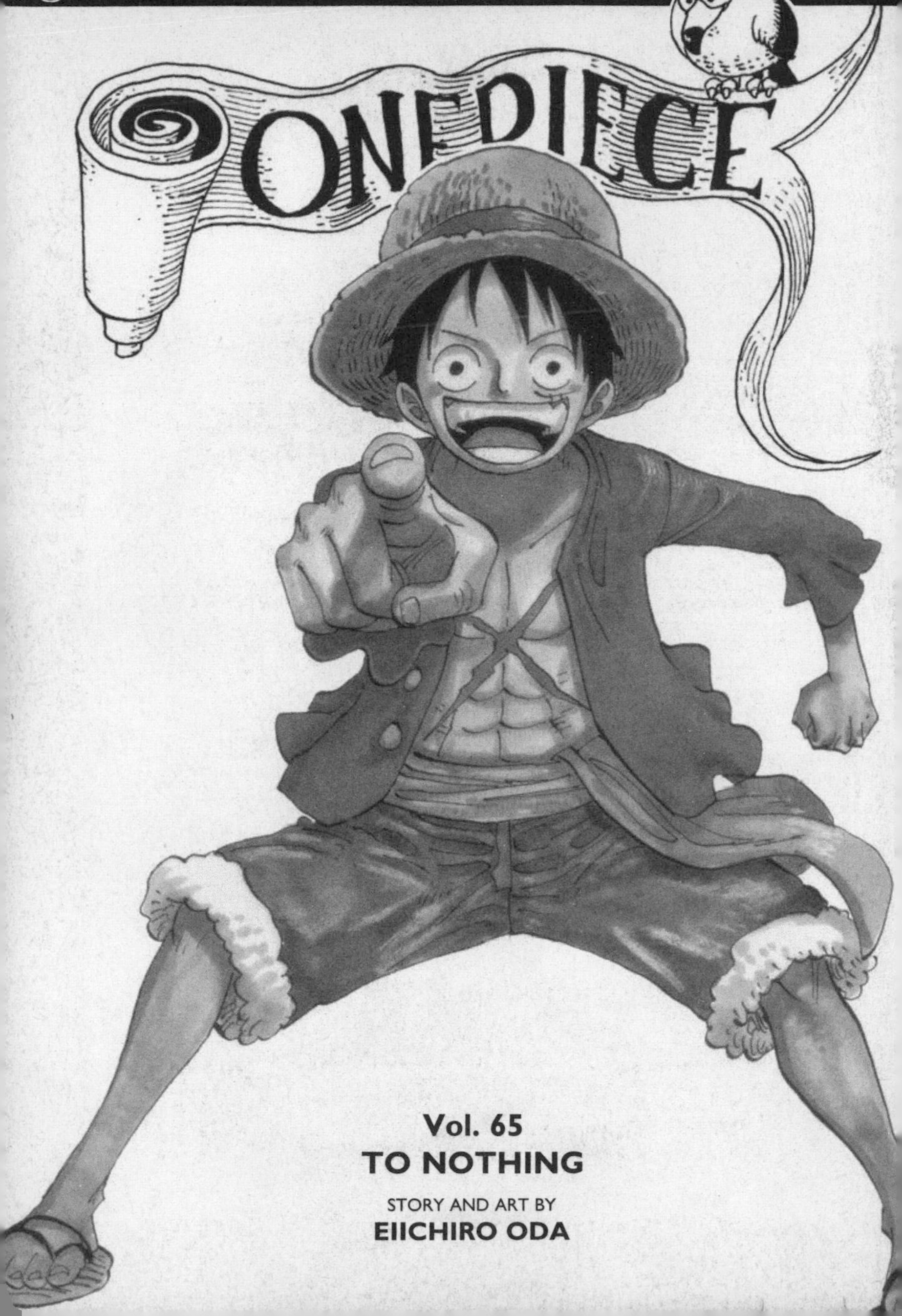

Vol. 65

TO NOTHING

STORY AND ART BY

EIICHIRO ODA

The Straw Hat Crew

Monkey D. Luffy

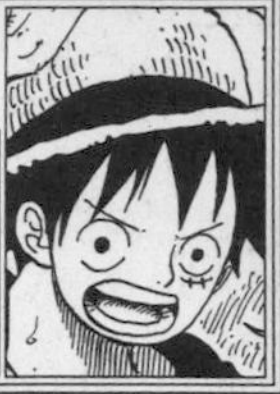

A young man who dreams of becoming the Pirate King. After training with Rayleigh, he and his crew head for the New World!

Captain, Bounty: 400 million berries

Roronoa Zolo

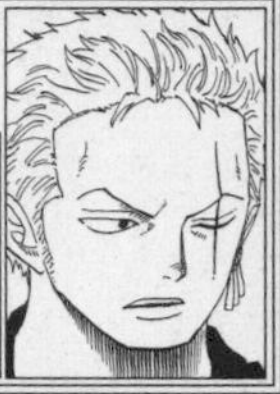

He swallowed his pride and asked to be trained by Mihawk on Gloom Island before reuniting with the rest of the crew.

Fighter, Bounty: 120 million berries

Tony Tony Chopper

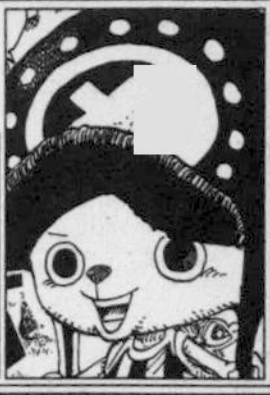

After researching powerful medicine in Birdie Kingdom, he reunites with the rest of the crew.

Ship's Doctor, Bounty: 50 berries

Nami

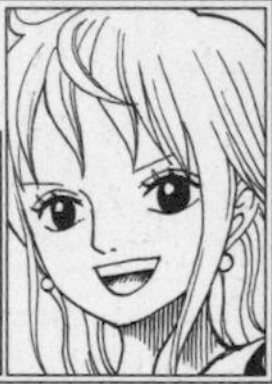

She studied the weather of the New World on the small Sky Island Weatheria, a place where weather is studied as a science.

Navigator, Bounty: 16 million berries

Nico Robin

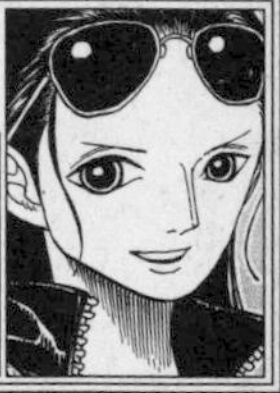

She spent her time in Baltigo with the leader of the Revolutionary Army: Luffy's father, Dragon.

Archeologist, Bounty: 80 million berries

Usopp

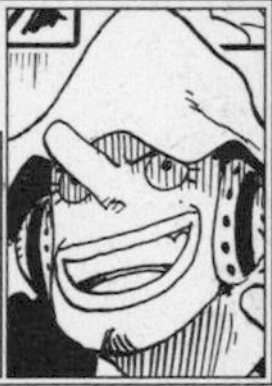

He trained under Heracles at the Bowin Islands to become the King of Snipers.

Sniper, Bounty: 30 million berries

Franky

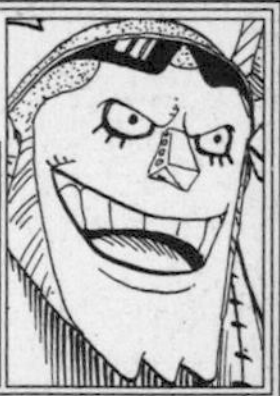

He modified himself in Future Land Baldimore and turned himself into Armored Franky before reuniting with the rest of the crew.

Shipwright, Bounty: 44 million berries

Sanji

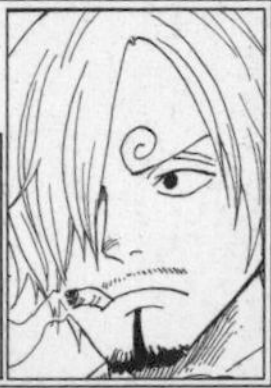

After fighting the New Kama Karate masters in the Kamabakka Kingdom, he returned to the crew.

Cook, Bounty: 77 million berries

Brook

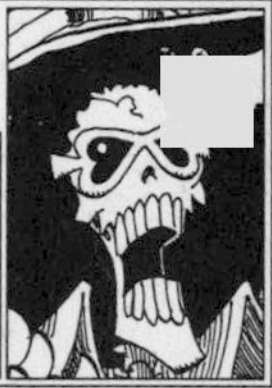

After being captured and used as a freak show by the Longarm Tribe, he became a famous rock star called "Soul King" Brook.

Musician, Bounty: 33 million berries

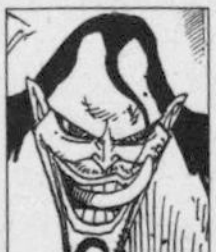

Wet-Haired Caribou

Captain of the Caribou Pirates

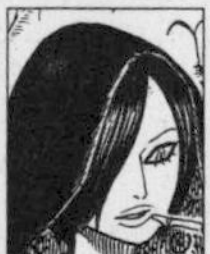

Madam Sharley

Owner of the Mermaid Café

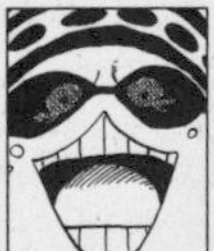

Pappagu

The Designer/President of the Criminal brand

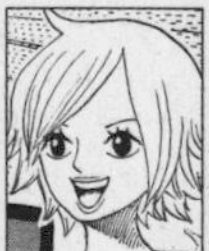

Camie

Works at the Mermaid Café

The story of ONE PIECE 1»65

Shanks

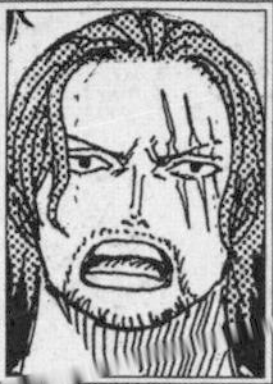

One of the Four Emperors. He continues to wait for Luffy in the second half of the Grand Line, called the New World.

Captain of the Red-Haired Pirates

Jimbei

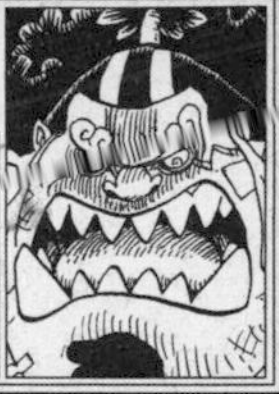

Reunited with Luffy at Fish-Man Island, where he tries to stop Hody's plot.

Former Warlord of the Sea

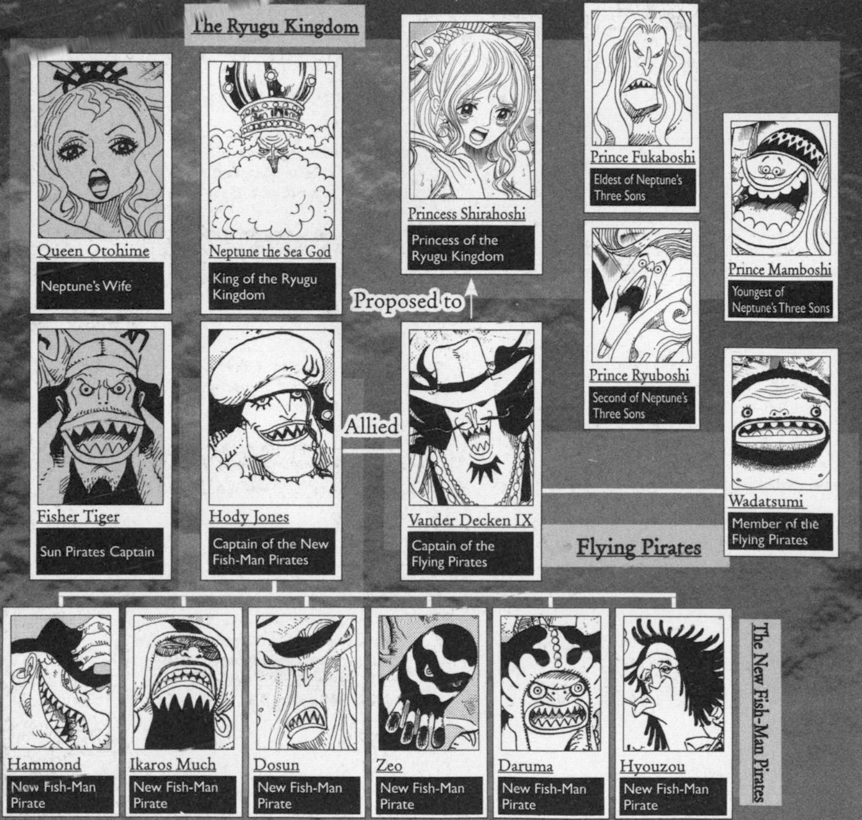

The Ryugu Kingdom
Queen Otohime
Neptune's Wife
Neptune the Sea God
King of the Ryugu Kingdom
Princess Shirahoshi
Princess of the Ryugu Kingdom
Prince Fukaboshi
Eldest of Neptune's Three Sons
Prince Mamboshi
Youngest of Neptune's Three Sons
Prince Ryuboshi
Second of Neptune's Three Sons
Proposed to
Fisher Tiger
Sun Pirates Captain
Hody Jones
Captain of the New Fish-Man Pirates
Allied
Vander Decken IX
Captain of the Flying Pirates
Flying Pirates
Wadatsumi
Member of the Flying Pirates
Hammond
New Fish-Man Pirate
Ikaros Much
New Fish-Man Pirate
Dosun
New Fish-Man Pirate
Zeo
New Fish-Man Pirate
Daruma
New Fish-Man Pirate
Hyouzou
New Fish-Man Pirate
The New Fish-Man Pirates

Story

Having finished their two years of training, the Straw Hat crew reunites on the Sabaody Archipelago. They set sail more determined than ever to reach The New World!

The Straw Hats finally reach Fish-Man Island but are quickly ambushed by the New Fish-Man Pirates. Their hatred of humans was caused by a long and terrible history of oppression. Now Hody Jones has sworn to destroy the Ryugu Kingdom, become the new king of Fish-Man Island and eliminate anyone who hopes for peace with humankind!! Princess Shirahoshi and her brothers want peace, and they stand up to Hody with Luffy's help!! A massive battle is about to engulf the entirety of Fish-Man Island...

NEW WORLD ONE PIECE

Vol. 65
To Nothing

CONTENTS

Chapter 637:

THE ANCIENT ARK

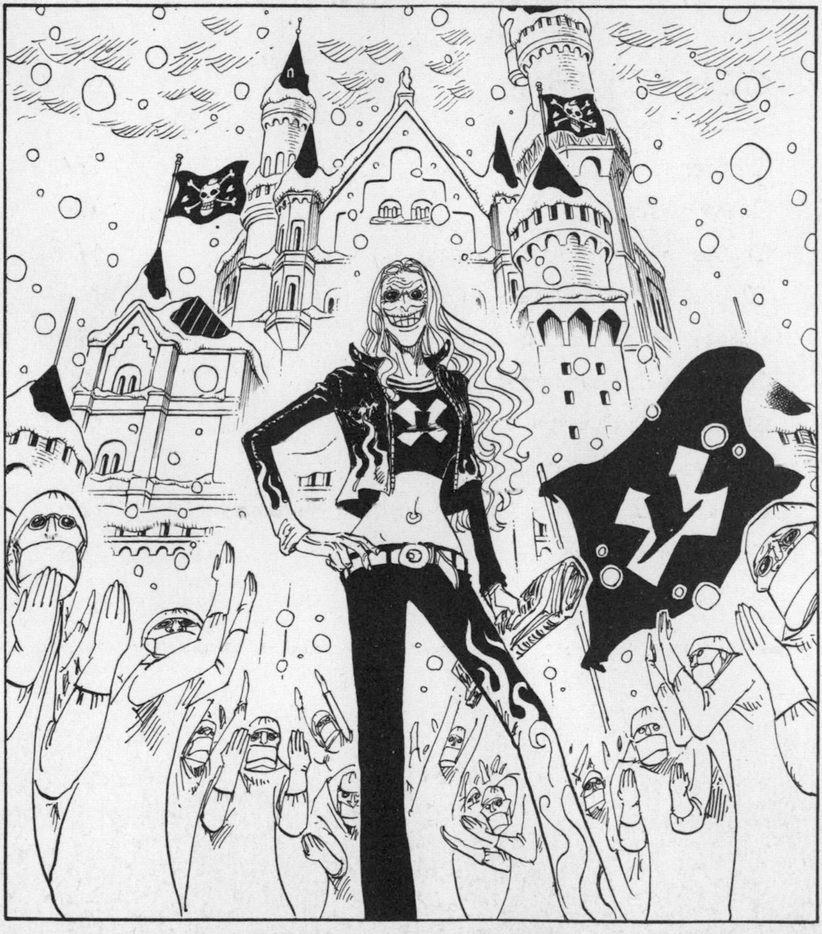

DECKS OF THE WORLD, VOL. 21: "DRUM ISLAND—THE MEDICAL CENTER, HUNDRED DOCTORS"

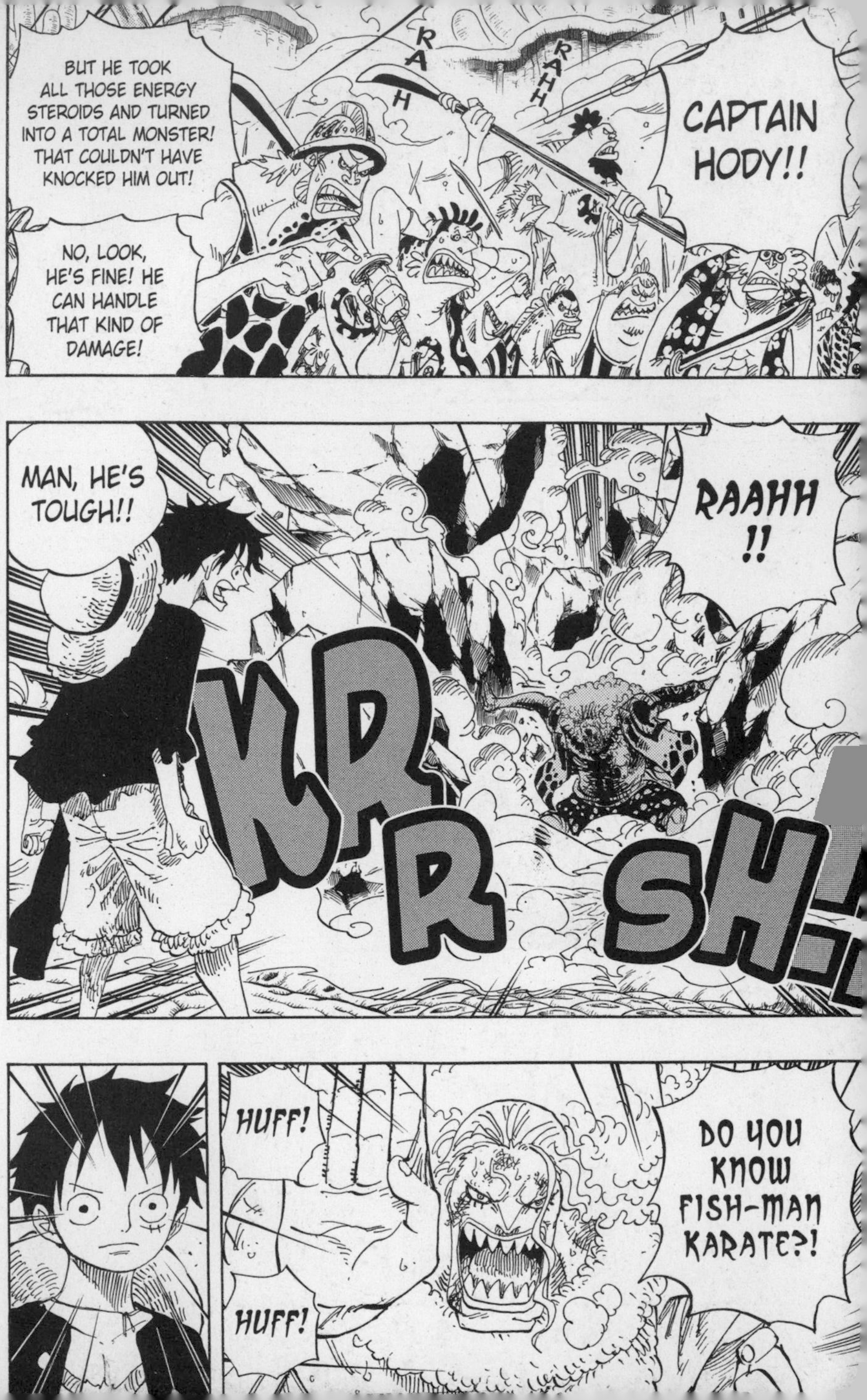
RAHH
RAH
CAPTAIN HODY!!
BUT HE TOOK ALL THOSE ENERGY STEROIDS AND TURNED INTO A TOTAL MONSTER! THAT COULDN'T HAVE KNOCKED HIM OUT!
NO, LOOK, HE'S FINE! HE CAN HANDLE THAT KIND OF DAMAGE!
RAAHH !!
MAN, HE'S TOUGH!!
KR R SH
DO YOU KNOW FISH-MAN KARATE?!
HUFF!
HUFF!

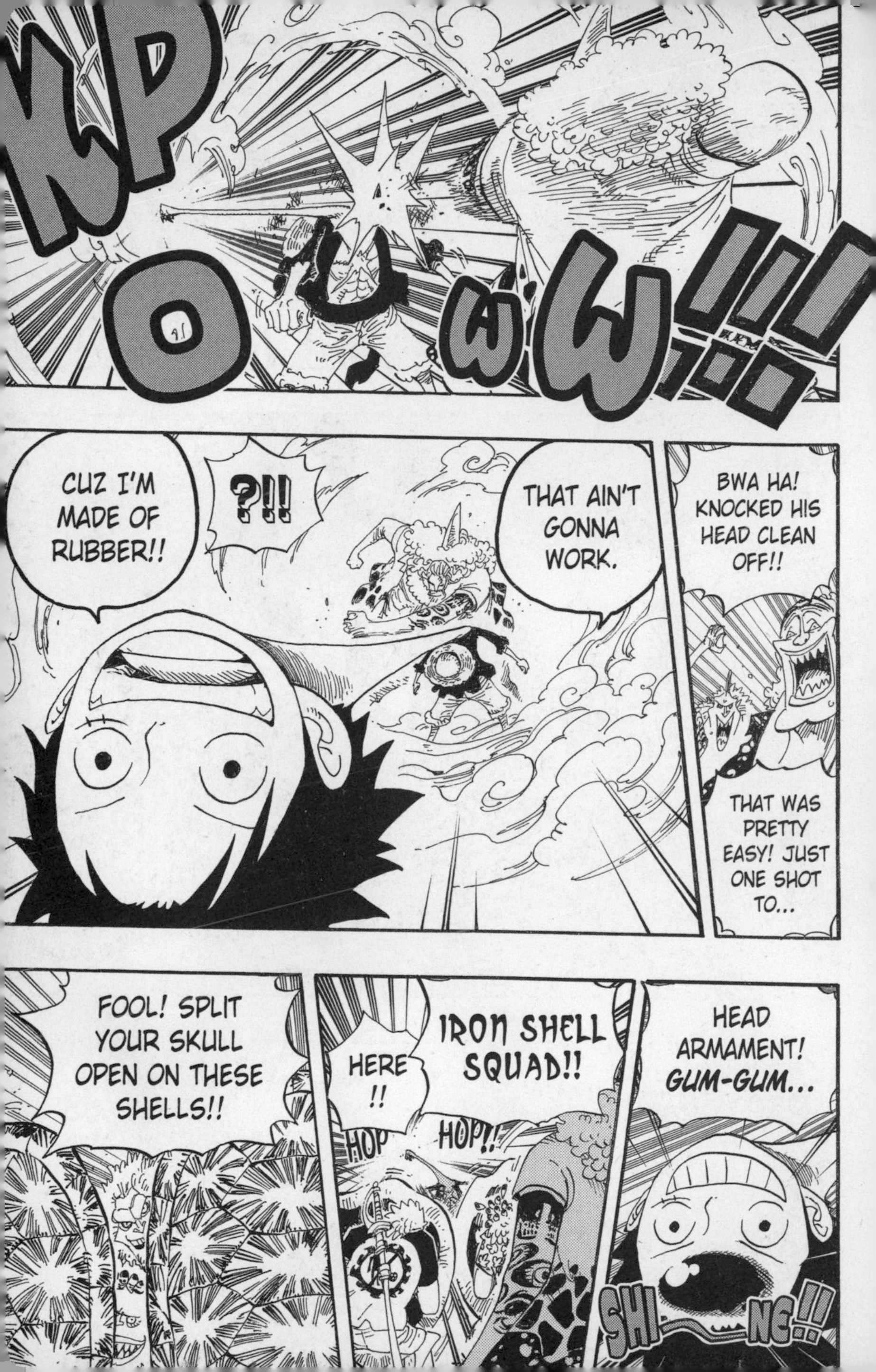
BWA HA! KNOCKED HIS HEAD CLEAN OFF!!
THAT WAS PRETTY EASY! JUST ONE SHOT TO...
THAT AIN'T GONNA WORK.
?!!
CUZ I'M MADE OF RUBBER!!
HEAD ARMAMENT! GUM-GUM...
SHI NE!!
IRON SHELL SQUAD!!
HERE !!
HOP!!
HOP
FOOL! SPLIT YOUR SKULL OPEN ON THESE SHELLS!!

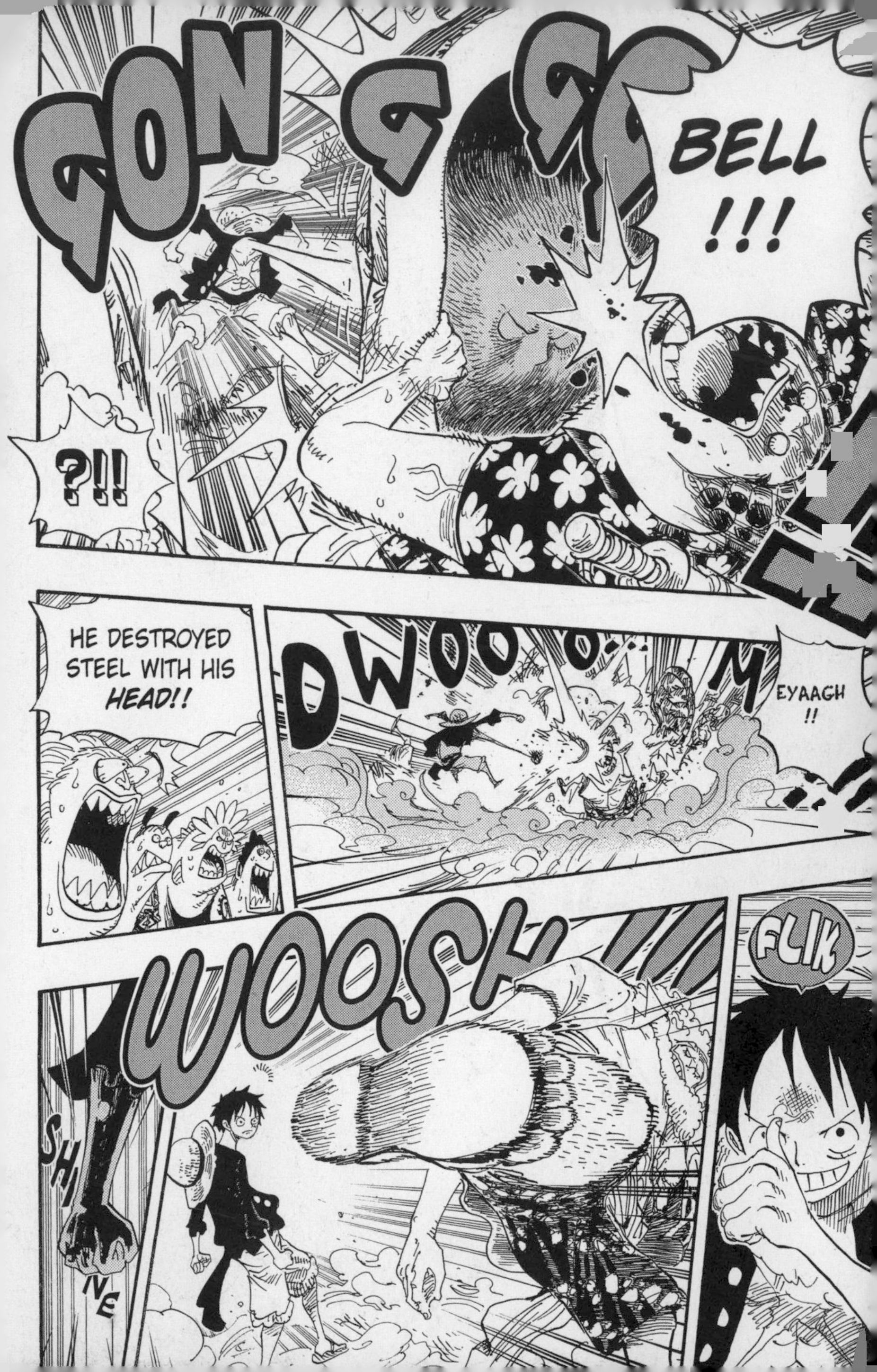
BELL !!!
GON G G
?!!
EYAAGH !!
DWOO...M
HE DESTROYED STEEL WITH HIS *HEAD!!*
FLIK
WOOSH !!
SHI INE

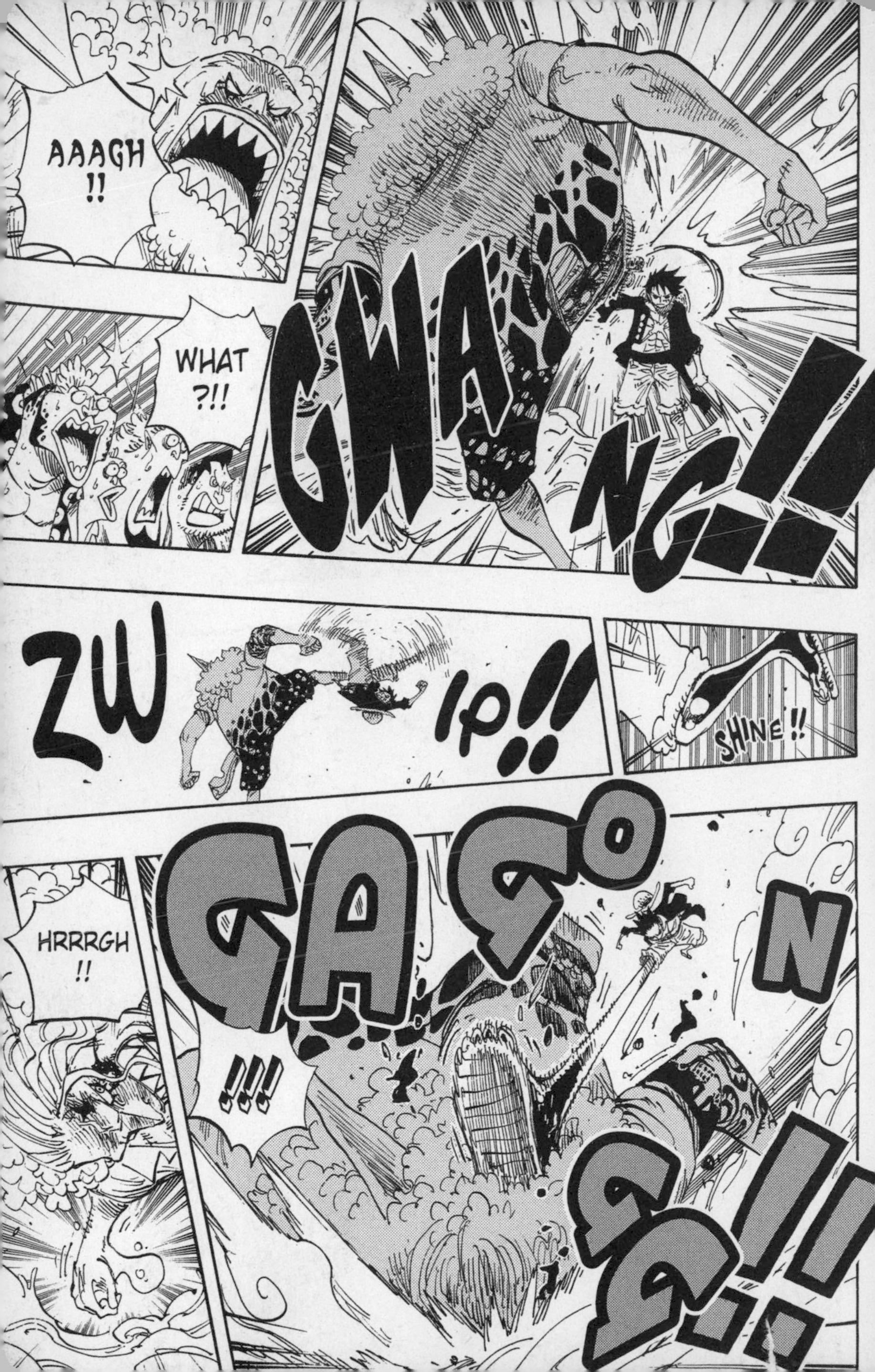
GWANG!!
AAAGH!!
WHAT?!!
SHINE!!
ZWIP!!
GAGON!!
!!!
HRRRGH!!

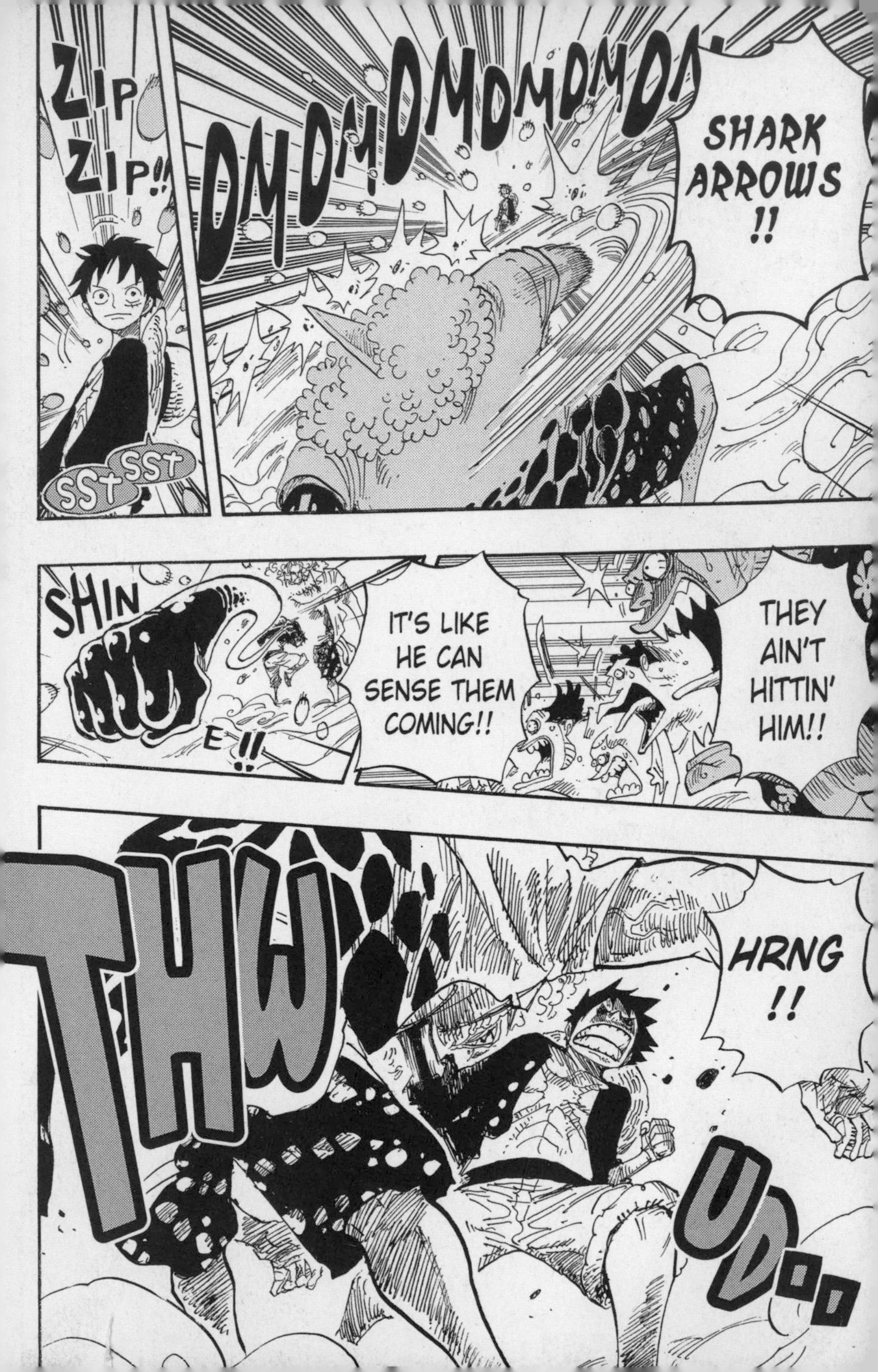
SHARK ARROWS!!
DMDMDMDMDMDMDMDM
ZIP ZIP!!
SST SST
THEY AIN'T HITTIN' HIM!!
IT'S LIKE HE CAN SENSE THEM COMING!!
SHIN
E!!
HRNG!!
THWUD

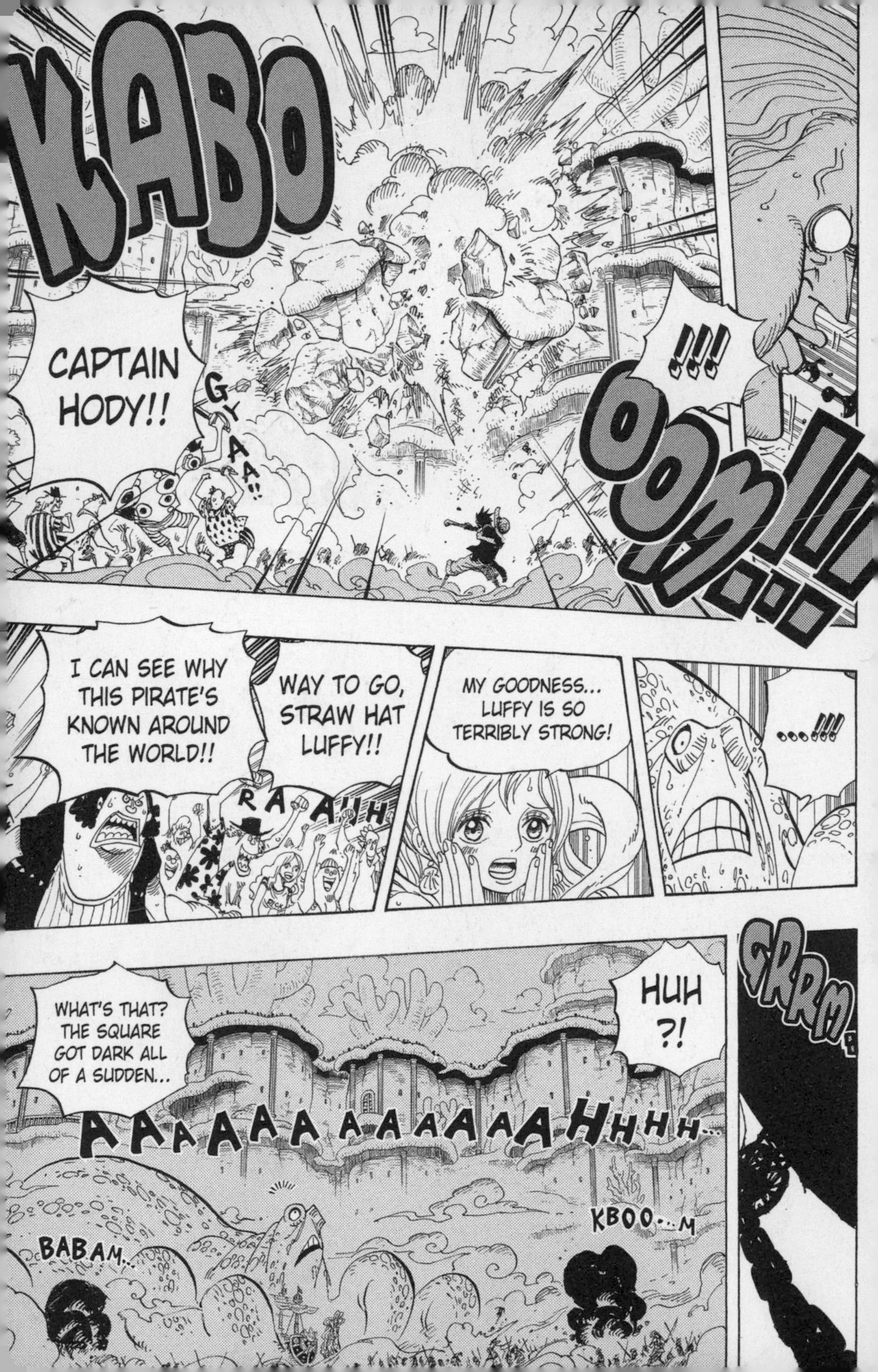

!!!
KABO
OOM!!!...
CAPTAIN HODY!!
GYAA!!
...!!!
MY GOODNESS... LUFFY IS SO TERRIBLY STRONG!
WAY TO GO, STRAW HAT LUFFY!!
I CAN SEE WHY THIS PIRATE'S KNOWN AROUND THE WORLD!!
RAAAH
GRRM...
HUH?!
WHAT'S THAT? THE SQUARE GOT DARK ALL OF A SUDDEN...
AAAAAAAAAAAHHHH...
KBOO...M
BABAM...

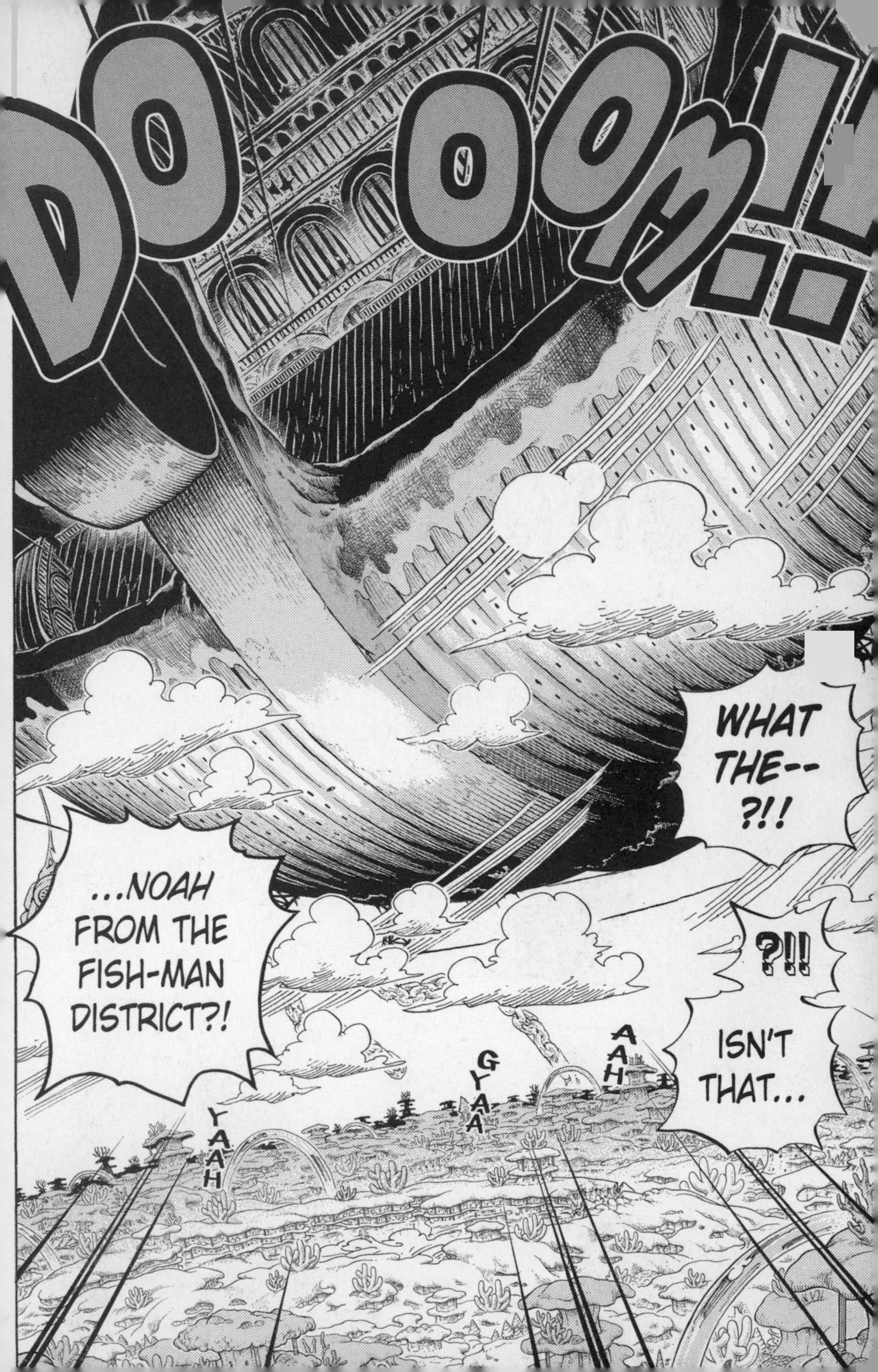
DOOOM!!
WHAT THE--?!!
?!!
ISN'T THAT...
AAH
GYAA
YAAH
...NOAH FROM THE FISH-MAN DISTRICT?!

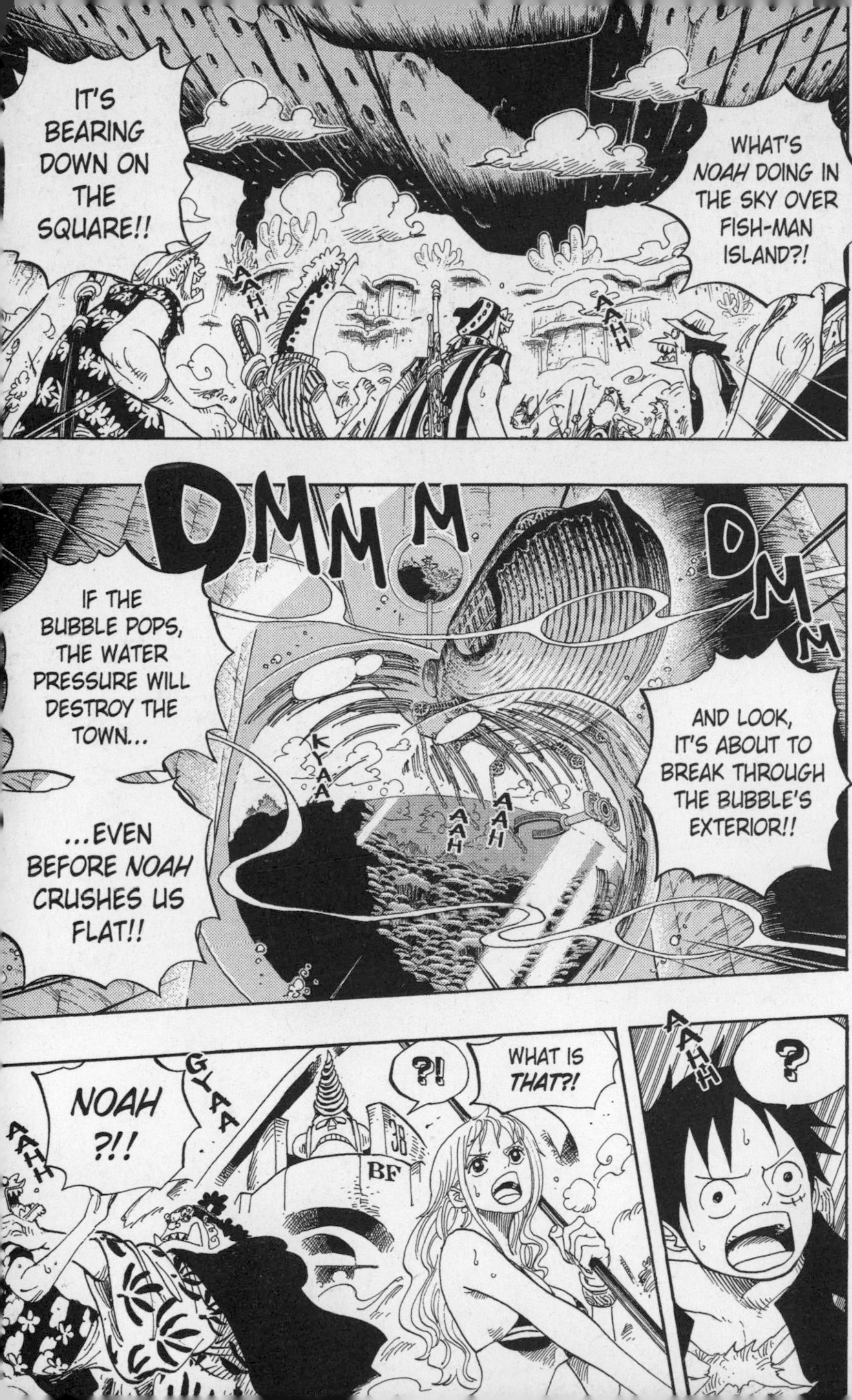
WHAT'S NOAH DOING IN THE SKY OVER FISH-MAN ISLAND?!
AAHH
AAHH
IT'S BEARING DOWN ON THE SQUARE!!
DMMM
AND LOOK, IT'S ABOUT TO BREAK THROUGH THE BUBBLE'S EXTERIOR!!
DMMM
AAAH
AAH
KYAAA
IF THE BUBBLE POPS, THE WATER PRESSURE WILL DESTROY THE TOWN...
...EVEN BEFORE NOAH CRUSHES US FLAT!!
AAHH
?
WHAT IS THAT?!
?!
GYAA
NOAH ?!!
AAHH

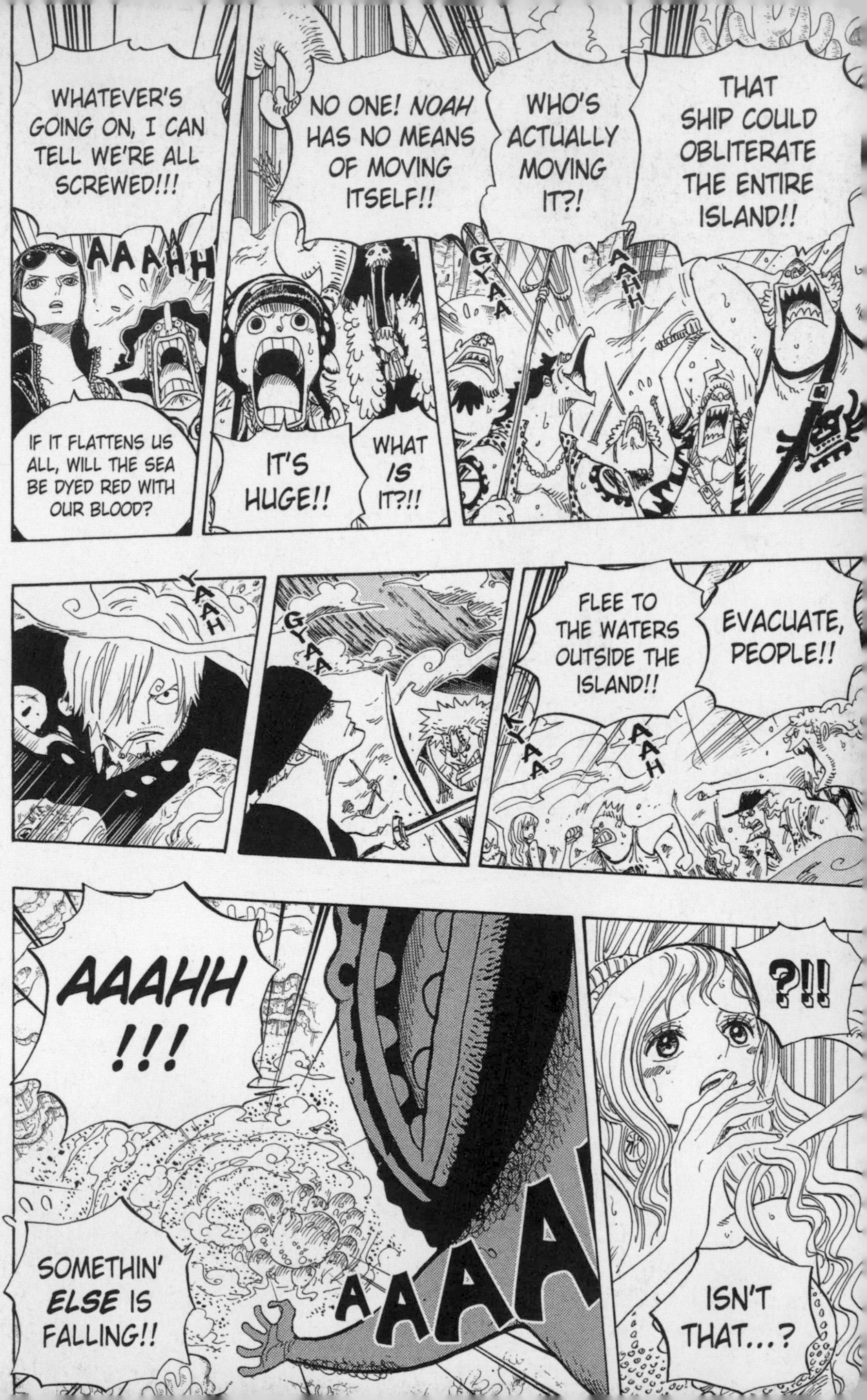
THAT SHIP COULD OBLITERATE THE ENTIRE ISLAND!!
WHO'S ACTUALLY MOVING IT?!
AAHH
GYAA
NO ONE! NOAH HAS NO MEANS OF MOVING ITSELF!!
WHAT IS IT?!!
IT'S HUGE!!
WHATEVER'S GOING ON, I CAN TELL WE'RE ALL SCREWED!!!
AAAHH
IF IT FLATTENS US ALL, WILL THE SEA BE DYED RED WITH OUR BLOOD?
EVACUATE, PEOPLE!!
FLEE TO THE WATERS OUTSIDE THE ISLAND!!
AAH
KYAA
GYAA
YAAH
?!!
ISN'T THAT...?
AAAHH !!!
AAAA
SOMETHIN' ELSE IS FALLING!!

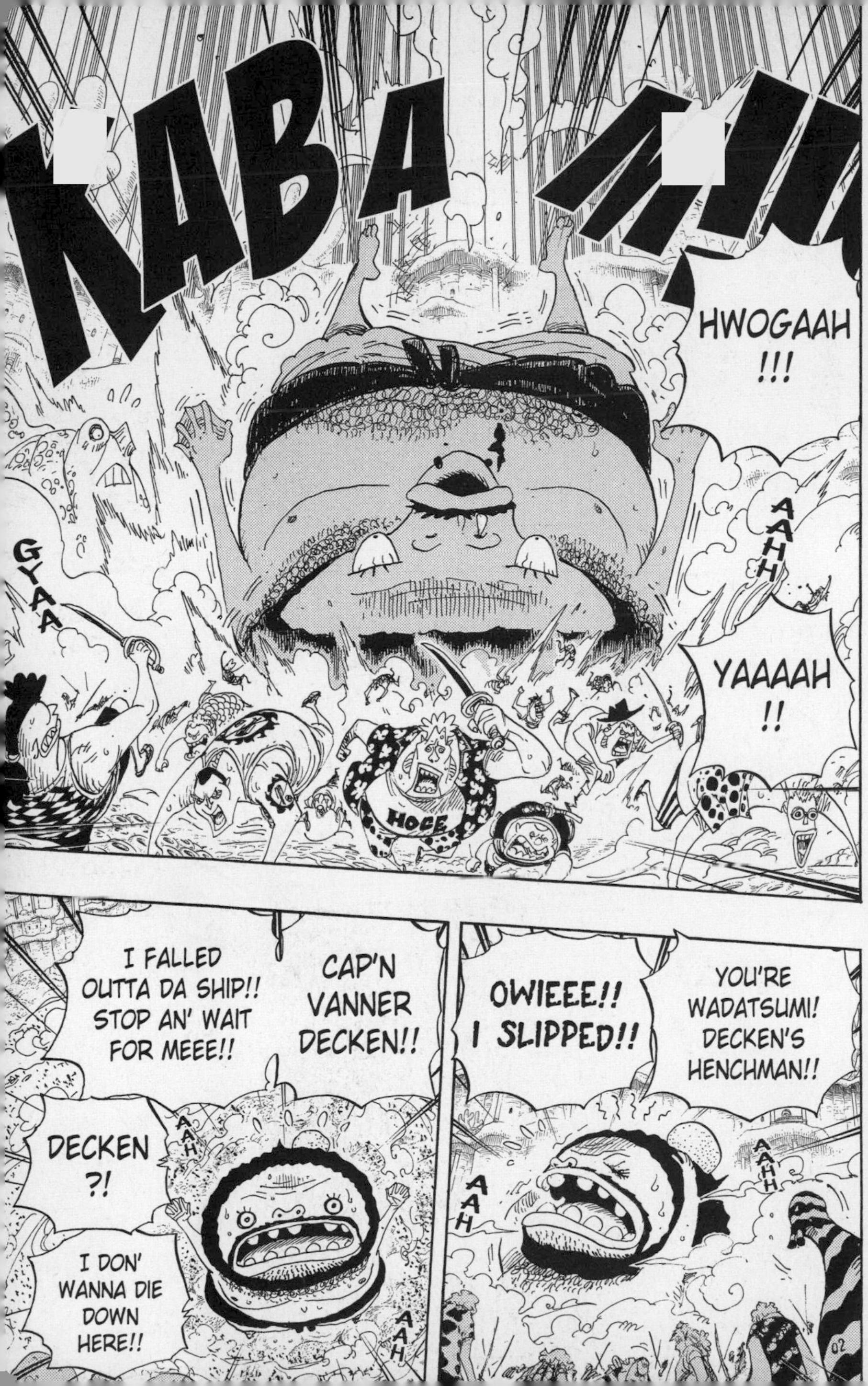
KABA
HWOGAAH !!!
AAHH
YAAAAH !!
GYAA
YOU'RE WADATSUMI! DECKEN'S HENCHMAN!!
OWIEEE!! I SLIPPED!!
AAHH
AAH
CAP'N VANNER DECKEN!!
I FALLED OUTTA DA SHIP!! STOP AN' WAIT FOR MEEE!!
AAH
DECKEN ?!
I DON' WANNA DIE DOWN HERE!!
AAH

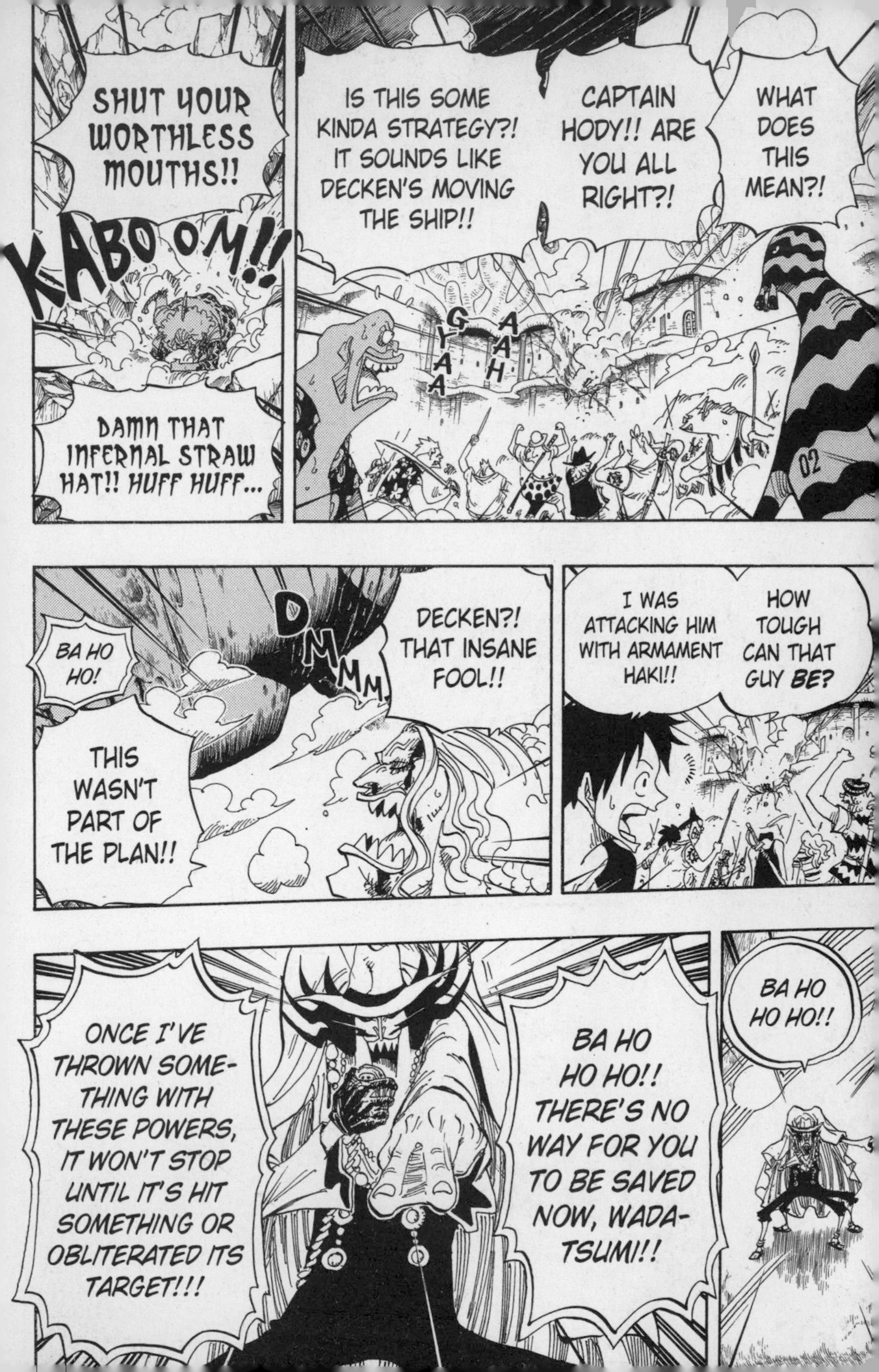
WHAT DOES THIS MEAN?!
CAPTAIN HODY!! ARE YOU ALL RIGHT?!
IS THIS SOME KINDA STRATEGY?! IT SOUNDS LIKE DECKEN'S MOVING THE SHIP!!
GYAAAAAH
SHUT YOUR WORTHLESS MOUTHS!!
KABOOM!!
DAMN THAT INFERNAL STRAW HAT!! HUFF HUFF...
HOW TOUGH CAN THAT GUY *BE?*
I WAS ATTACKING HIM WITH ARMAMENT HAKI!!
DECKEN?! THAT INSANE FOOL!!
DMMMM
BA HO HO!
THIS WASN'T PART OF THE PLAN!!
BA HO HO HO!!
BA HO HO HO!! THERE'S NO WAY FOR YOU TO BE SAVED NOW, WADA-TSUMI!!
ONCE I'VE THROWN SOME-THING WITH THESE POWERS, IT WON'T STOP UNTIL IT'S HIT SOMETHING OR OBLITERATED ITS TARGET!!!

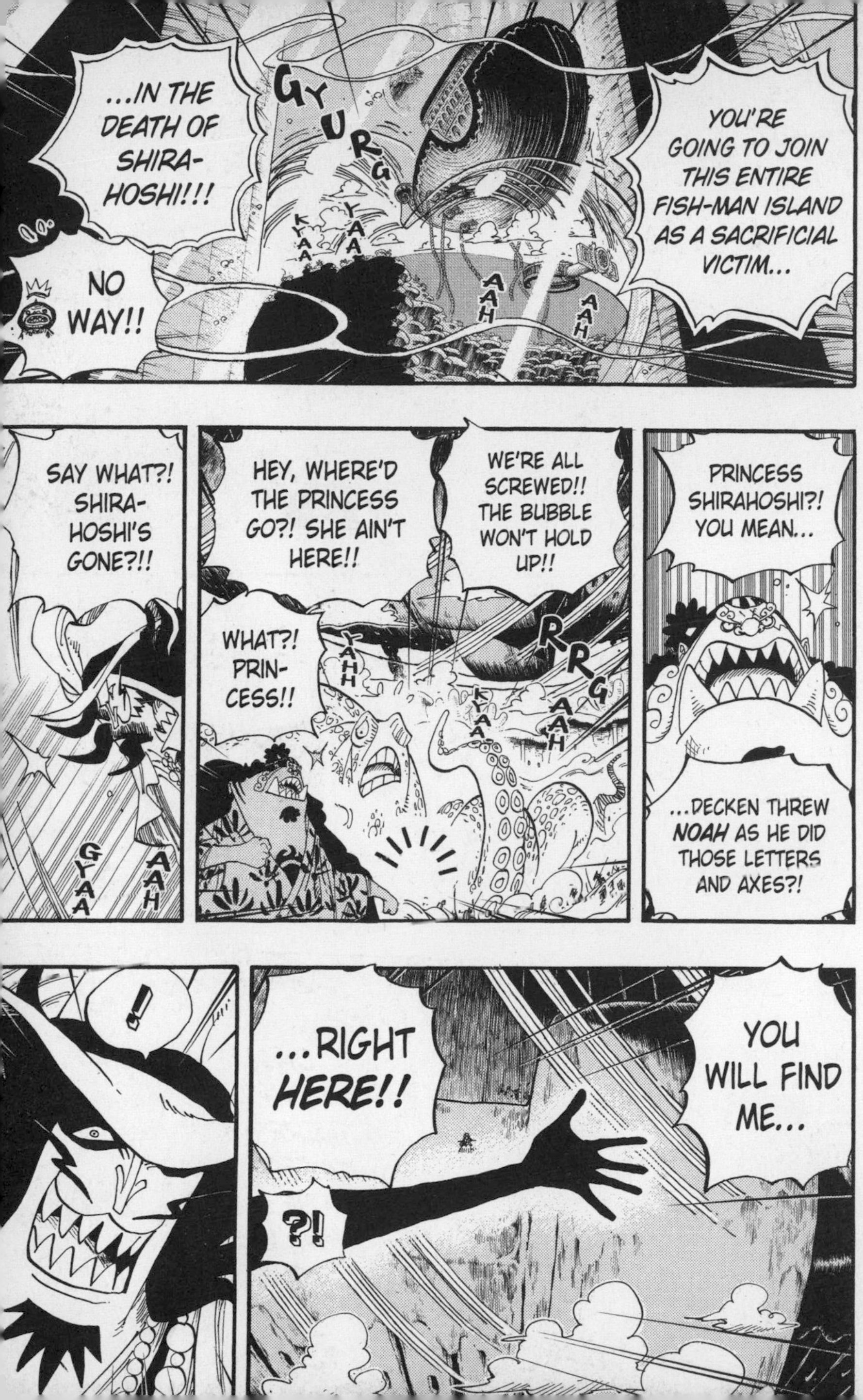
YOU'RE GOING TO JOIN THIS ENTIRE FISH-MAN ISLAND AS A SACRIFICIAL VICTIM...
...IN THE DEATH OF SHIRA-HOSHI!!!
GYURRG
YAA
KYAA
AAH
AAH
NO WAY!!
PRINCESS SHIRAHOSHI?! YOU MEAN...
...DECKEN THREW *NOAH* AS HE DID THOSE LETTERS AND AXES?!
WE'RE ALL SCREWED!! THE BUBBLE WON'T HOLD UP!!
HEY, WHERE'D THE PRINCESS GO?! SHE AIN'T HERE!!
RRRG
AAH
KYAA
YAHH
WHAT?! PRIN-CESS!!
SAY WHAT?! SHIRA-HOSHI'S GONE?!!
AAH
GYAA
YOU WILL FIND ME...
...RIGHT *HERE!!*
?!
!

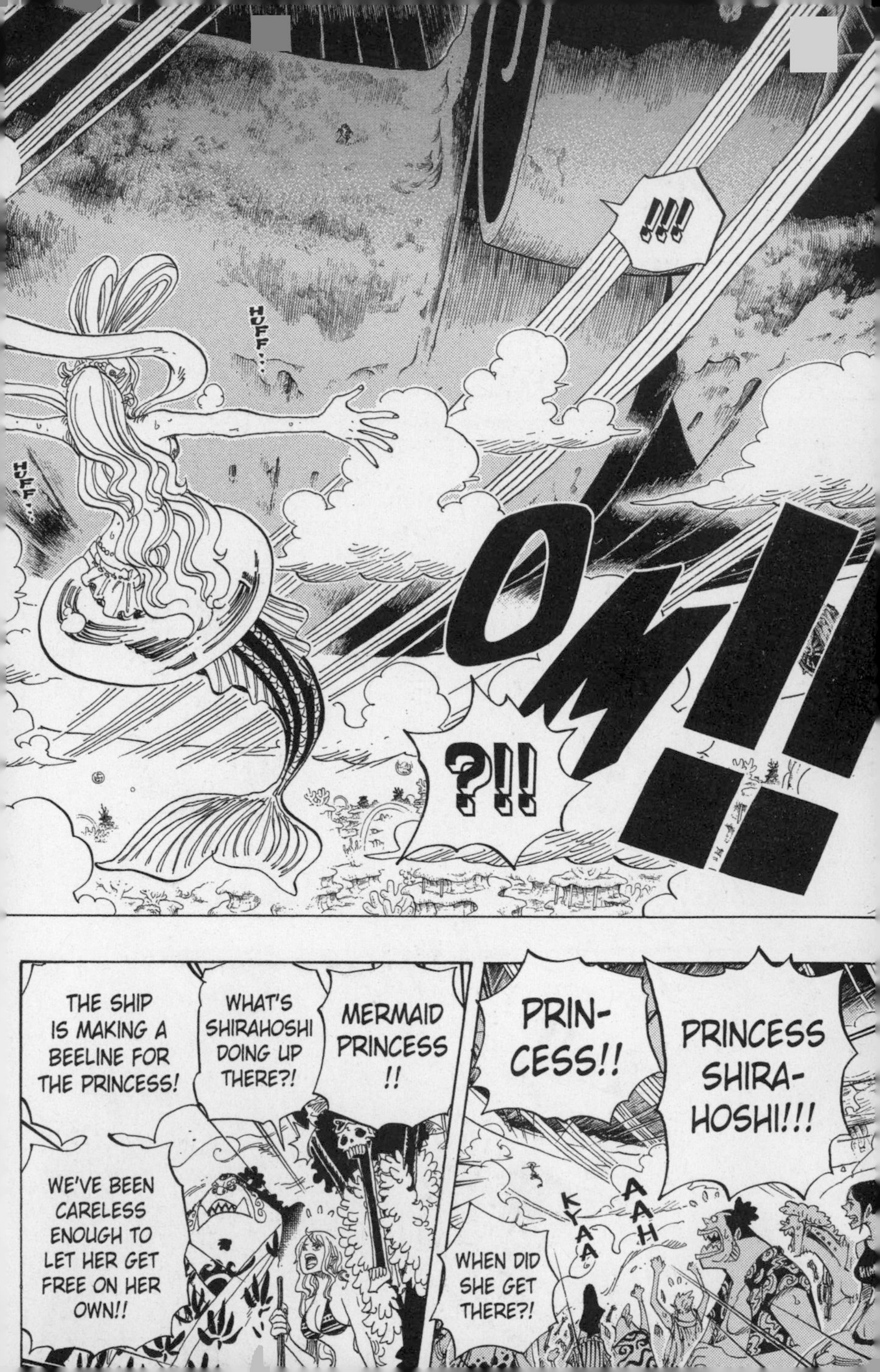
!!!
OM!!
?!!
HUFF...
HUFF...
PRINCESS SHIRA-HOSHI!!!
PRIN-CESS!!
AAH
KYAA
WHEN DID SHE GET THERE?!
MERMAID PRINCESS !!
WHAT'S SHIRAHOSHI DOING UP THERE?!
THE SHIP IS MAKING A BEELINE FOR THE PRINCESS!
WE'VE BEEN CARELESS ENOUGH TO LET HER GET FREE ON HER OWN!!

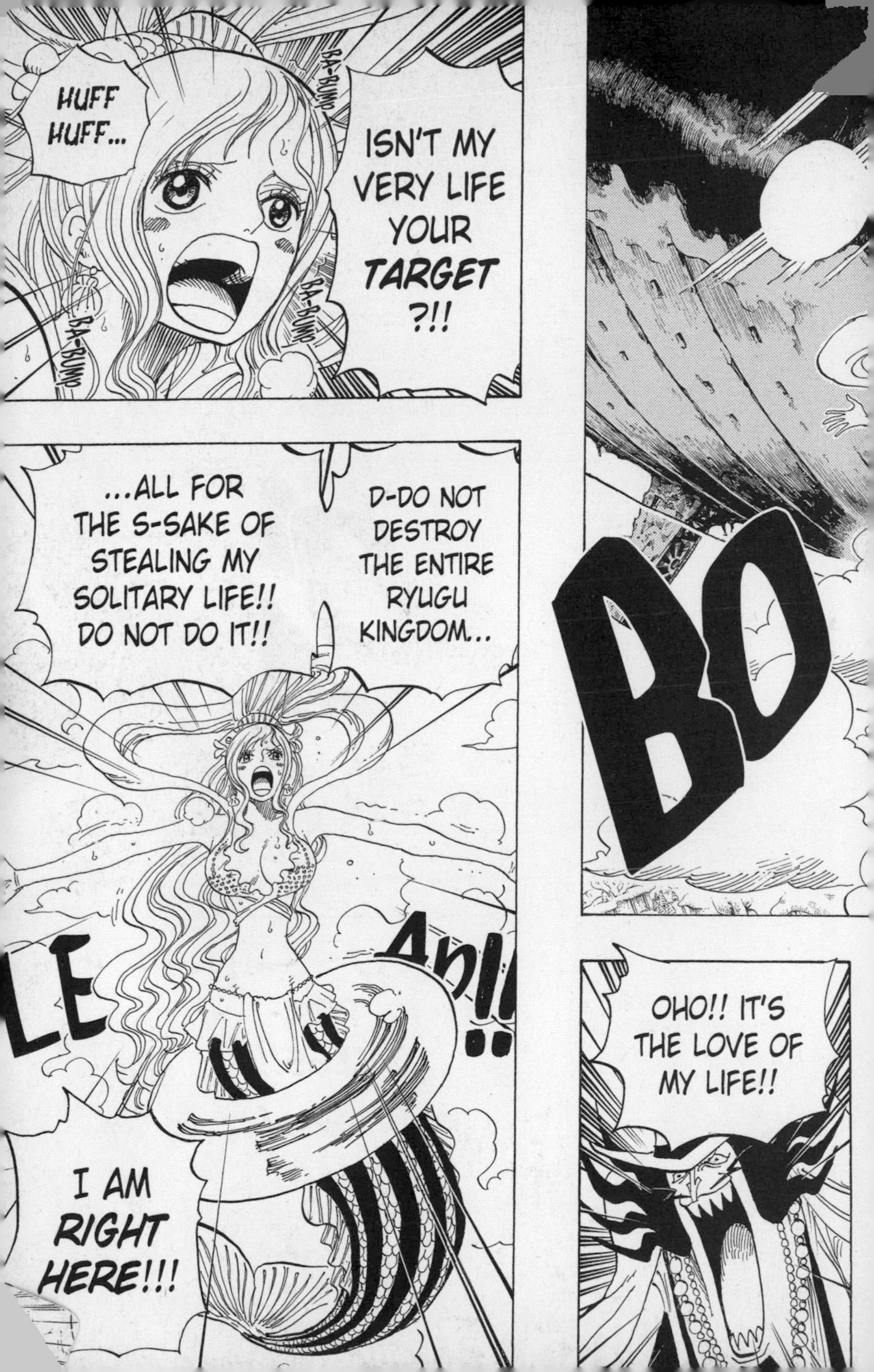
BO
HUFF HUFF...
BA-BUMP
BA-BUMP
BA-BUMP
ISN'T MY VERY LIFE YOUR TARGET ?!!
D-DO NOT DESTROY THE ENTIRE RYUGU KINGDOM...
...ALL FOR THE S-SAKE OF STEALING MY SOLITARY LIFE!! DO NOT DO IT!!
AN!!
LE
I AM RIGHT HERE!!!
OHO!! IT'S THE LOVE OF MY LIFE!!

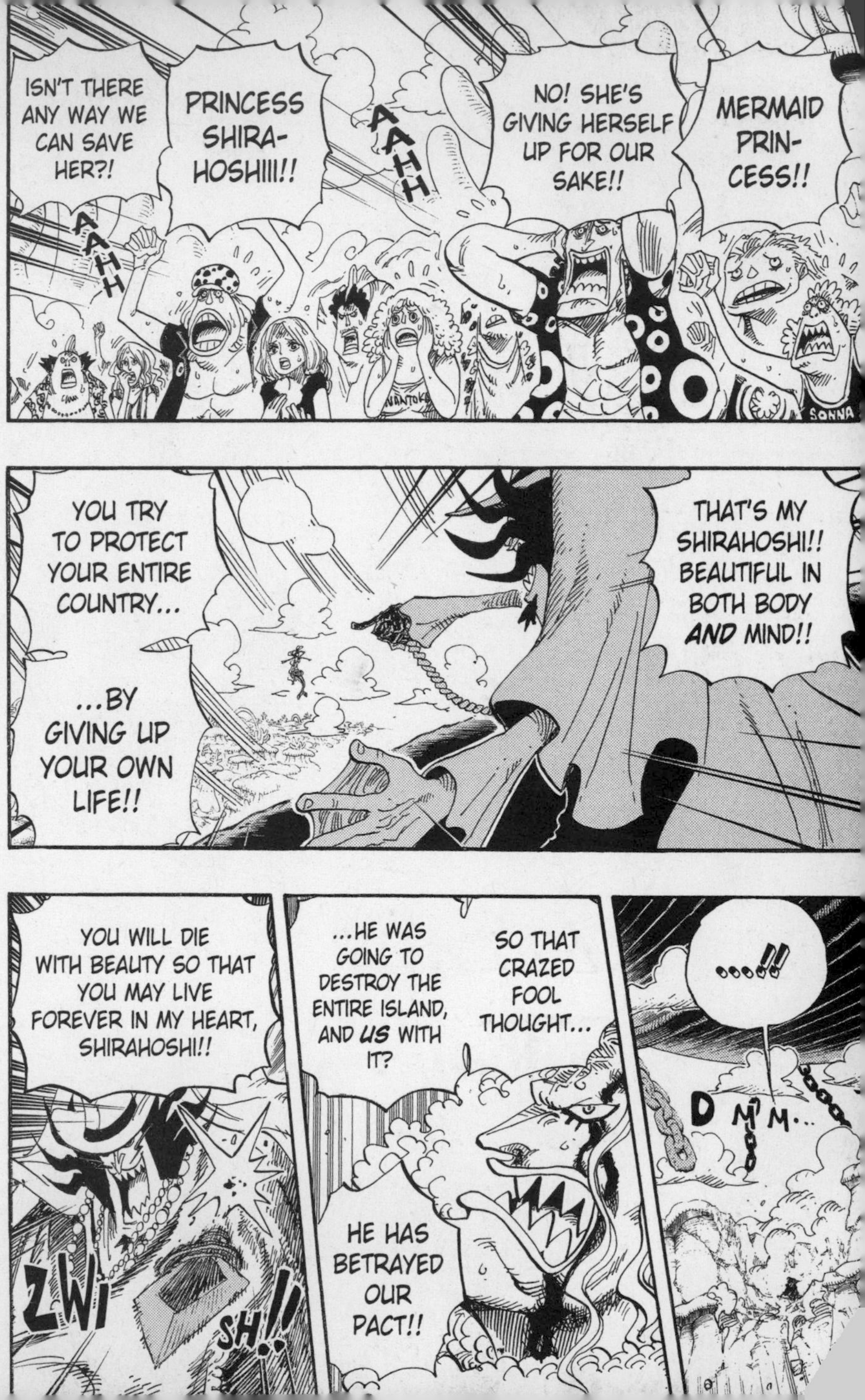
MERMAID PRIN-CESS!!
NO! SHE'S GIVING HERSELF UP FOR OUR SAKE!!
AAHH
PRINCESS SHIRA-HOSHIIII!!
ISN'T THERE ANY WAY WE CAN SAVE HER?!
AAHH
SONNA
NANTOKO
THAT'S MY SHIRAHOSHI!! BEAUTIFUL IN BOTH BODY AND MIND!!
YOU TRY TO PROTECT YOUR ENTIRE COUNTRY...
...BY GIVING UP YOUR OWN LIFE!!
...!!
DMM...
SO THAT CRAZED FOOL THOUGHT...
...HE WAS GOING TO DESTROY THE ENTIRE ISLAND, AND US WITH IT?
HE HAS BETRAYED OUR PACT!!
YOU WILL DIE WITH BEAUTY SO THAT YOU MAY LIVE FOREVER IN MY HEART, SHIRAHOSHI!!
ZWISH!!

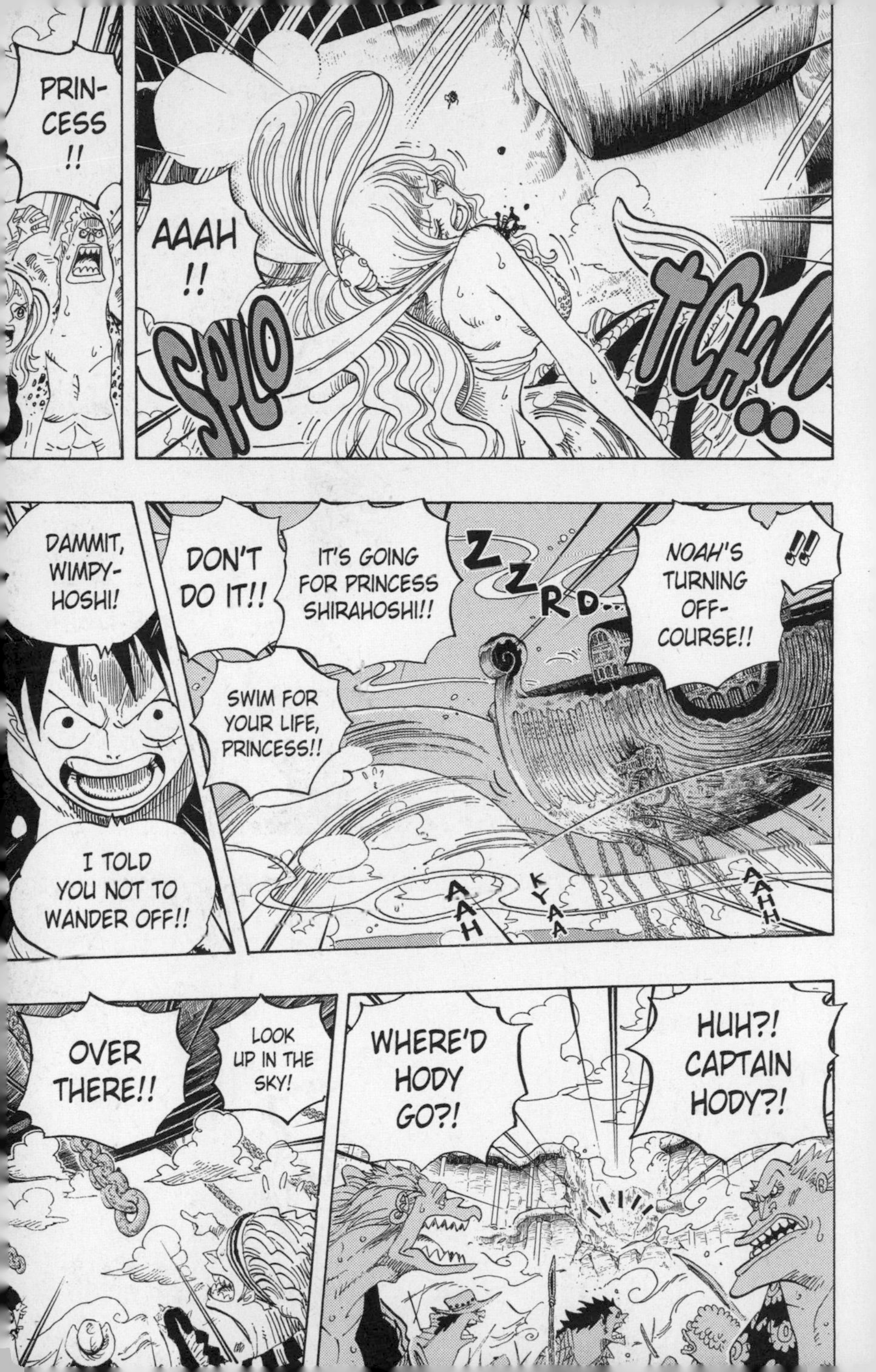
AAAH!!
SPLO
TCH!!
PRIN-CESS!!
NOAH'S TURNING OFF-COURSE!!
!!
ZZZRD..
IT'S GOING FOR PRINCESS SHIRAHOSHI!!
DON'T DO IT!!
SWIM FOR YOUR LIFE, PRINCESS!!
AAHH
KYAA
AAH
DAMMIT, WIMPY-HOSHI!
I TOLD YOU NOT TO WANDER OFF!!
HUH?! CAPTAIN HODY?!
WHERE'D HODY GO?!
LOOK UP IN THE SKY!
OVER THERE!!

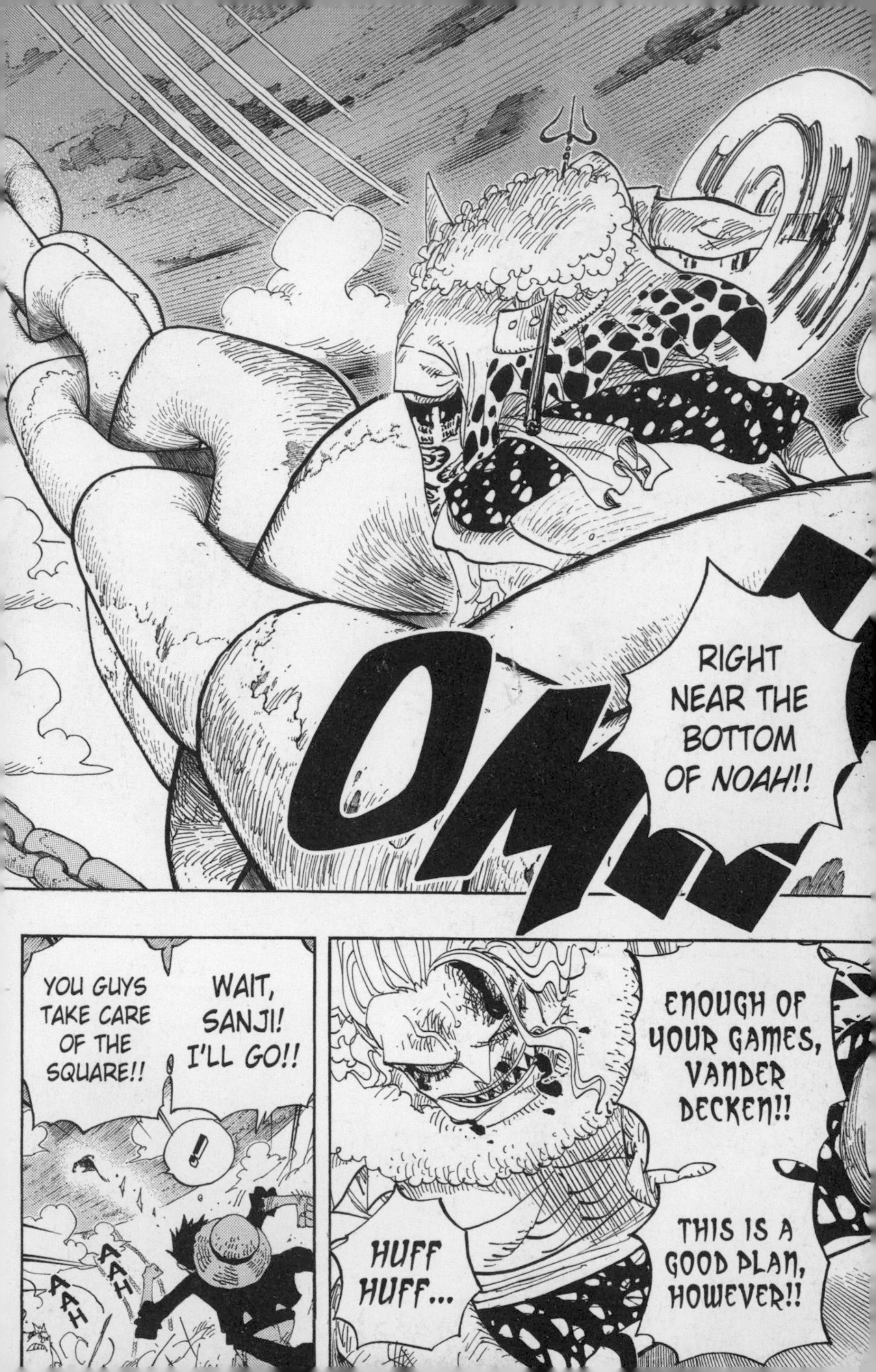
RIGHT NEAR THE BOTTOM OF NOAH!!
ENOUGH OF YOUR GAMES, VANDER DECKEN!!
THIS IS A GOOD PLAN, HOWEVER!!
HUFF HUFF...
WAIT, SANJI! I'LL GO!!
YOU GUYS TAKE CARE OF THE SQUARE!!
!
AAH
AAH

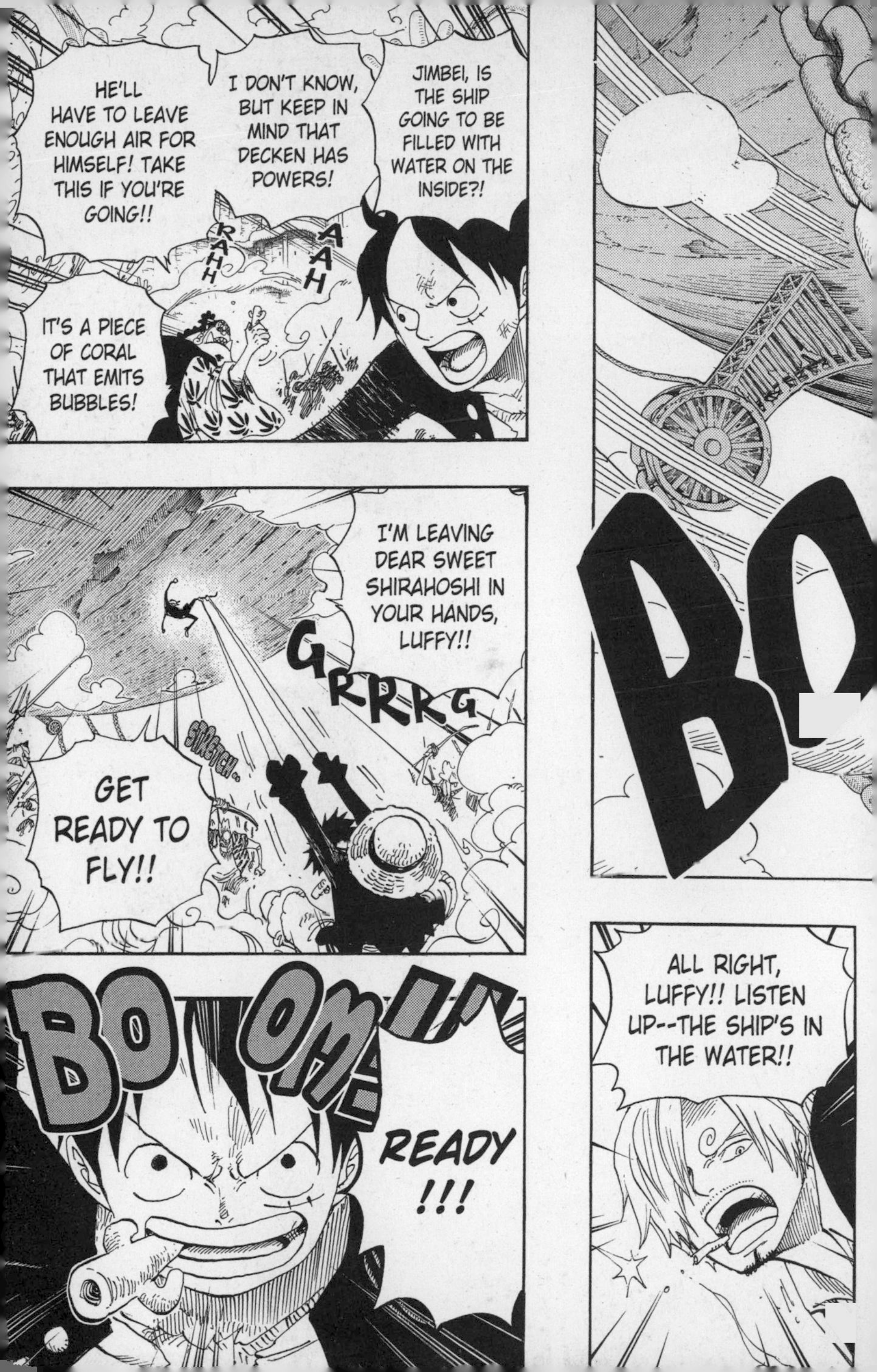
BO
ALL RIGHT, LUFFY!! LISTEN UP--THE SHIP'S IN THE WATER!!
JIMBEI, IS THE SHIP GOING TO BE FILLED WITH WATER ON THE INSIDE?!
I DON'T KNOW, BUT KEEP IN MIND THAT DECKEN HAS POWERS!
HE'LL HAVE TO LEAVE ENOUGH AIR FOR HIMSELF! TAKE THIS IF YOU'RE GOING!!
AAAH
RAHHH
IT'S A PIECE OF CORAL THAT EMITS BUBBLES!
I'M LEAVING DEAR SWEET SHIRAHOSHI IN YOUR HANDS, LUFFY!!
GRRRG
STRETCH
GET READY TO FLY!!
BOOM
READY !!!

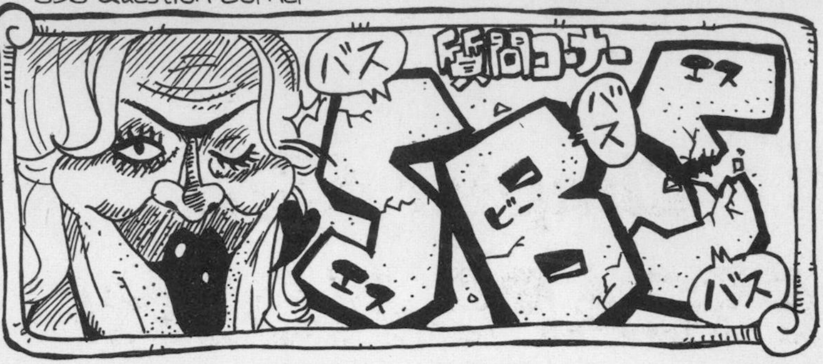
質問コーナー
エス
バス
ビー
バス
エス
バス

(Snowman, Okinawa)

Q: Umm, hey Odacchi. I noticed that your readers always say "Start the SBS" before you have a chance to. I love that about you!! So, here goes.

"Start the SB..."

--Noriaki S.

A: Huh? You mean I can really say it? You left the final letter just for me? Oh my gosh... This means so much to me. Ready? Here I go! "Z." **Oops, I said the wrong letter!!!**

Q: Panties panties panties panties panties panties panties panties panties panties panties panties panties panties panties panties

--Count the panties

A: Stop, stop. Stop...stop stop stop stop **stop!!!**
Huff, huff... It's the curse of the panties again. Three postcards full. Covered with 3,787 panties!! (we counted) You're not getting in the SBS next time! There wasn't even a question! And some of them were weird words like "penties" and "pontees"!!

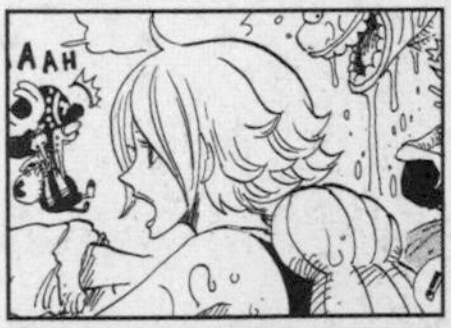
AAH

Q: I'm in fourth grade and I love Fisher Tiger. I can't wait for the newest chapter every week. Here's my question, Mr. Oda. What's in Camie's bag?

--Acerola #1

A: Hmm. Dreams, I bet. Also soy sauce and butter. (for eating clams with)

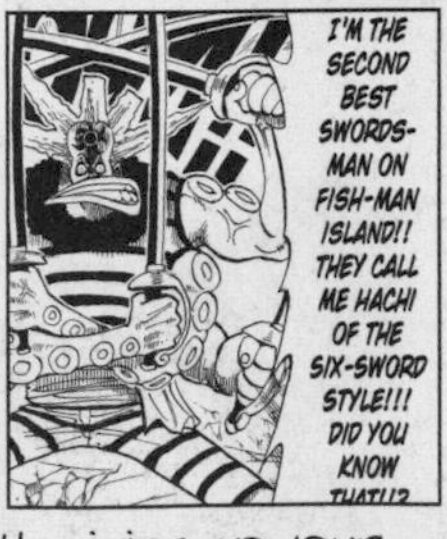
I'M THE SECOND BEST SWORDS-MAN ON FISH-MAN ISLAND!! THEY CALL ME HACHI OF THE SIX-SWORD STYLE!!! DID YOU KNOW

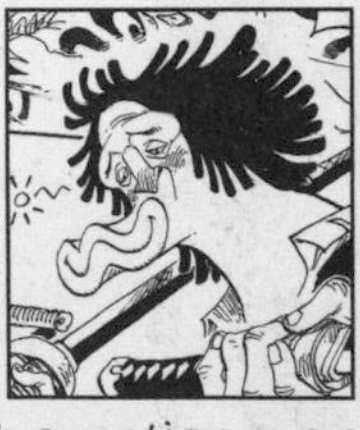

Q: Back in Volume 10, Hachi claimed that he was the "greatest sword user, aside from one man back on Fish-Man Island." Would that *one man* happen to be Hyouzou? If I'm wrong, please kill me.

--Euroclydon

A: Actually, you're right! Was that question worth giving up your life over?! They went to the same dojo for swordsmen, and Hyouzou would beat him every time.

Chapter 638:
ESCAPE-HOSHI

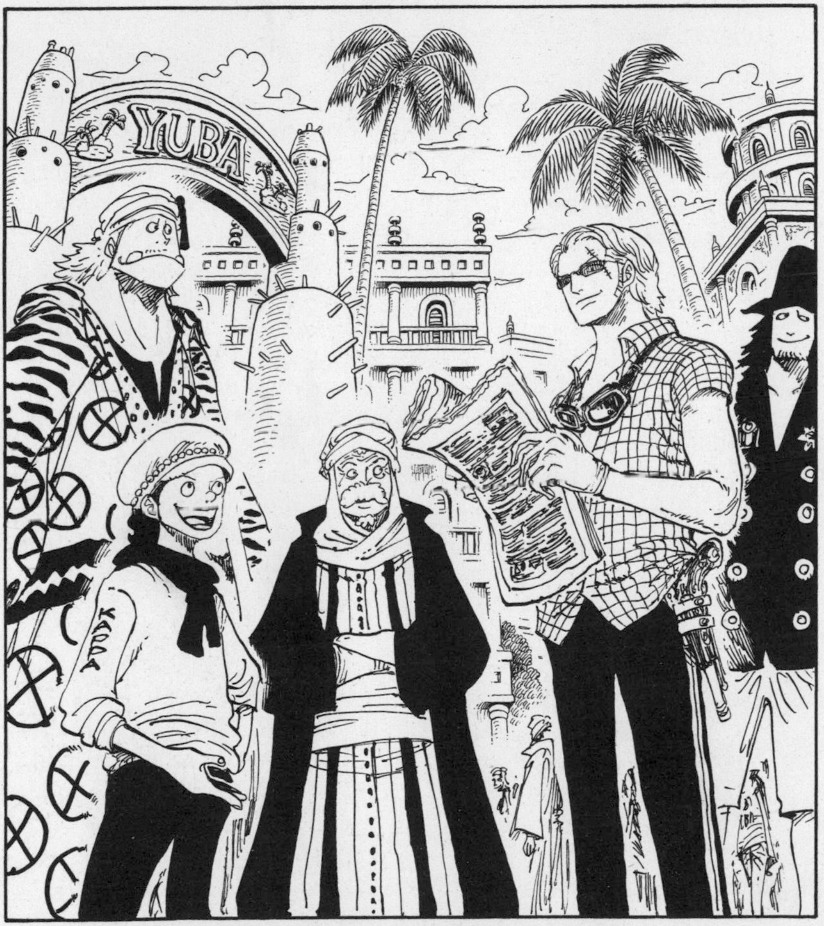
YUBA

DECKS OF THE WORLD, VOL. 22:
"ALABASTA—KOZA, ROYAL ENVIRONMENTAL MINISTER"

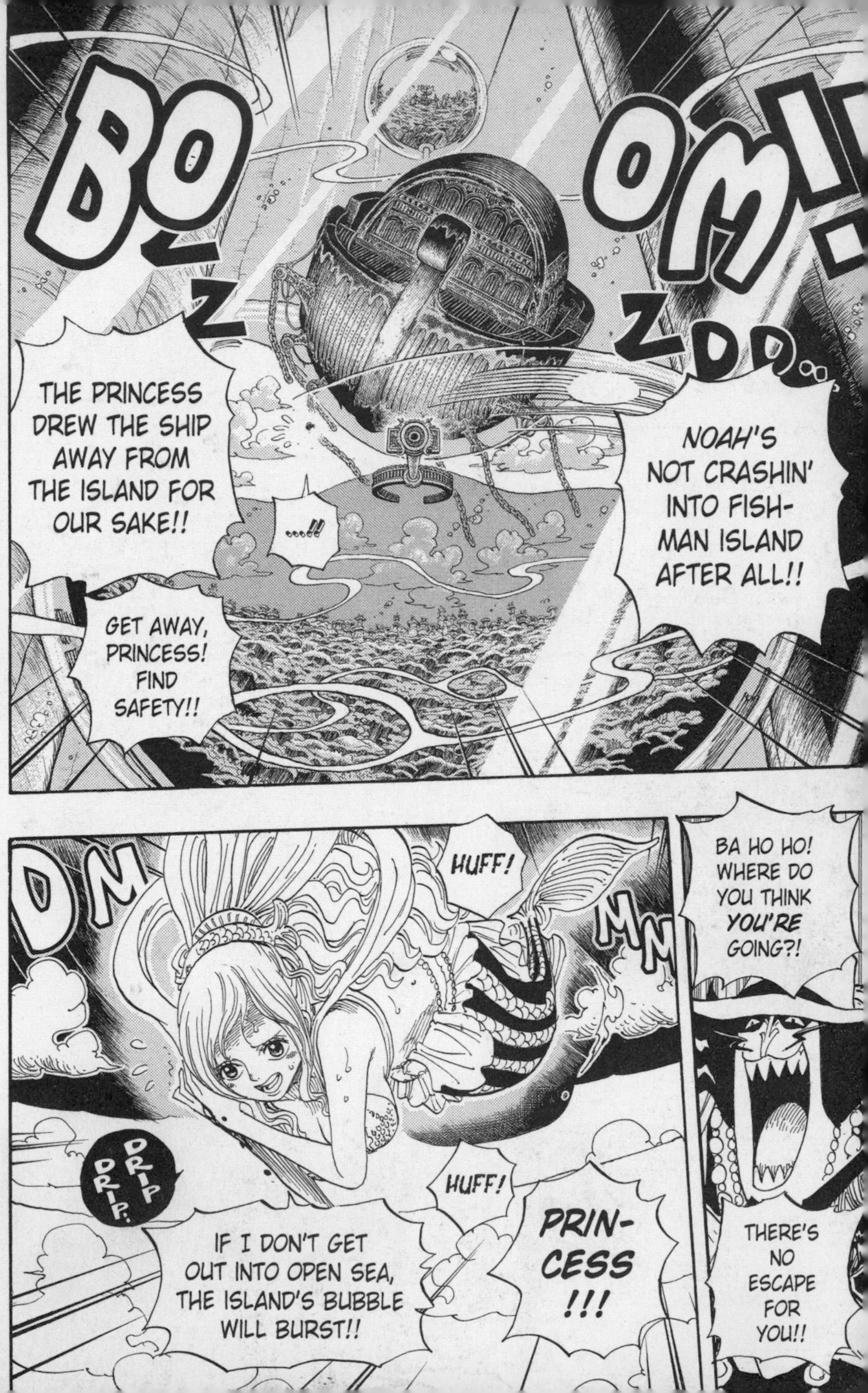
BOOM!!
ZDD
NOAH'S NOT CRASHIN' INTO FISH-MAN ISLAND AFTER ALL!!
THE PRINCESS DREW THE SHIP AWAY FROM THE ISLAND FOR OUR SAKE!!
...!!
GET AWAY, PRINCESS! FIND SAFETY!!
BA HO HO! WHERE DO YOU THINK YOU'RE GOING?!
THERE'S NO ESCAPE FOR YOU!!
HUFF!
PRIN-CESS!!!
HUFF!
IF I DON'T GET OUT INTO OPEN SEA, THE ISLAND'S BUBBLE WILL BURST!!
DRIP DRIP DRIP

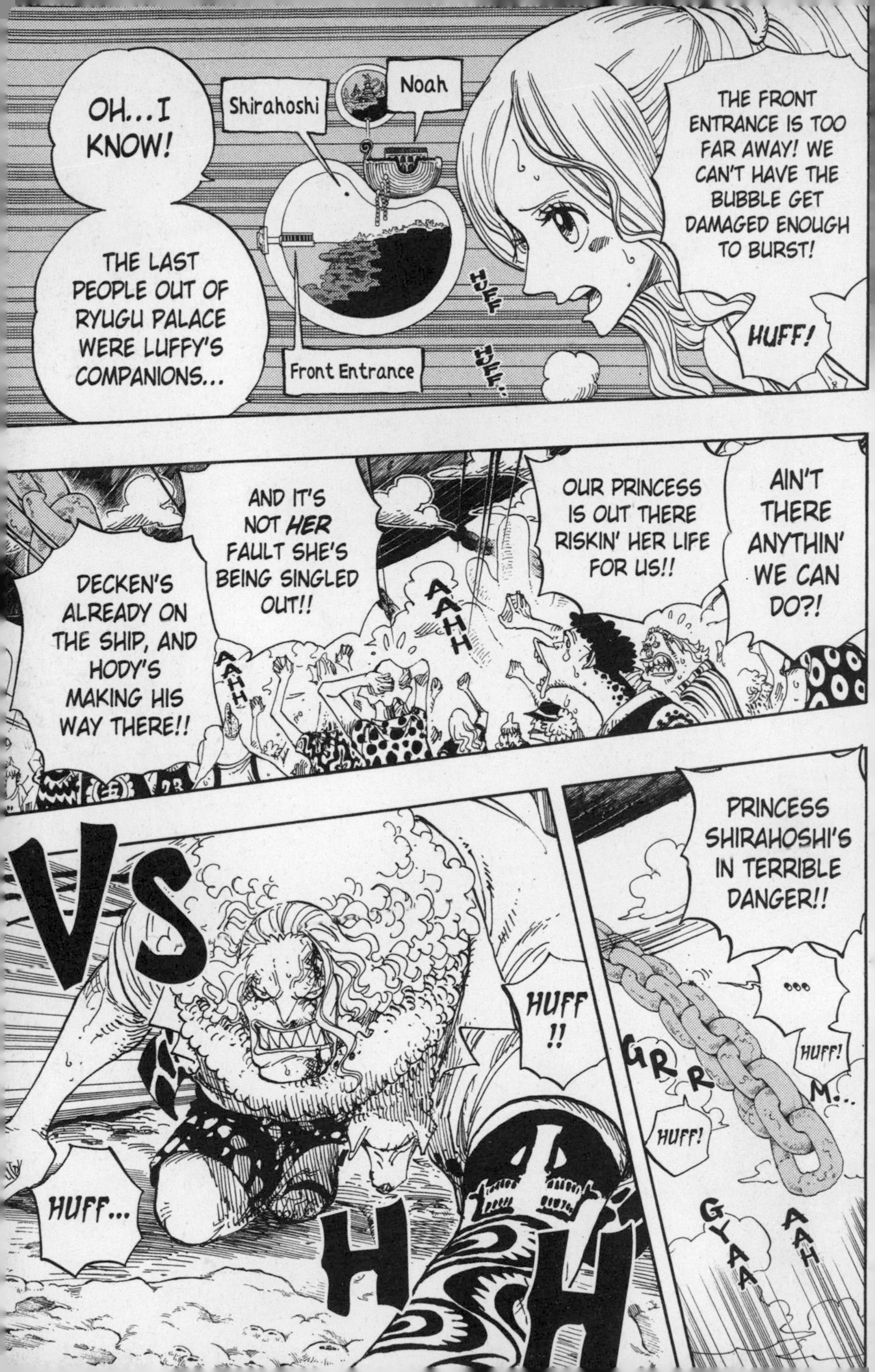
THE FRONT ENTRANCE IS TOO FAR AWAY! WE CAN'T HAVE THE BUBBLE GET DAMAGED ENOUGH TO BURST!
HUFF!
HUFF
HUFF...
Noah
Shirahoshi
Front Entrance
OH...I KNOW!
THE LAST PEOPLE OUT OF RYUGU PALACE WERE LUFFY'S COMPANIONS...
AIN'T THERE ANYTHIN' WE CAN DO?!
OUR PRINCESS IS OUT THERE RISKIN' HER LIFE FOR US!!
AAHH
AND IT'S NOT *HER* FAULT SHE'S BEING SINGLED OUT!!
DECKEN'S ALREADY ON THE SHIP, AND HODY'S MAKING HIS WAY THERE!!
AAHH
PRINCESS SHIRAHOSHI'S IN TERRIBLE DANGER!!
...
HUFF!
M...
GRR
HUFF!
GYAA
AAH
VS
HUFF !!
HUFF...

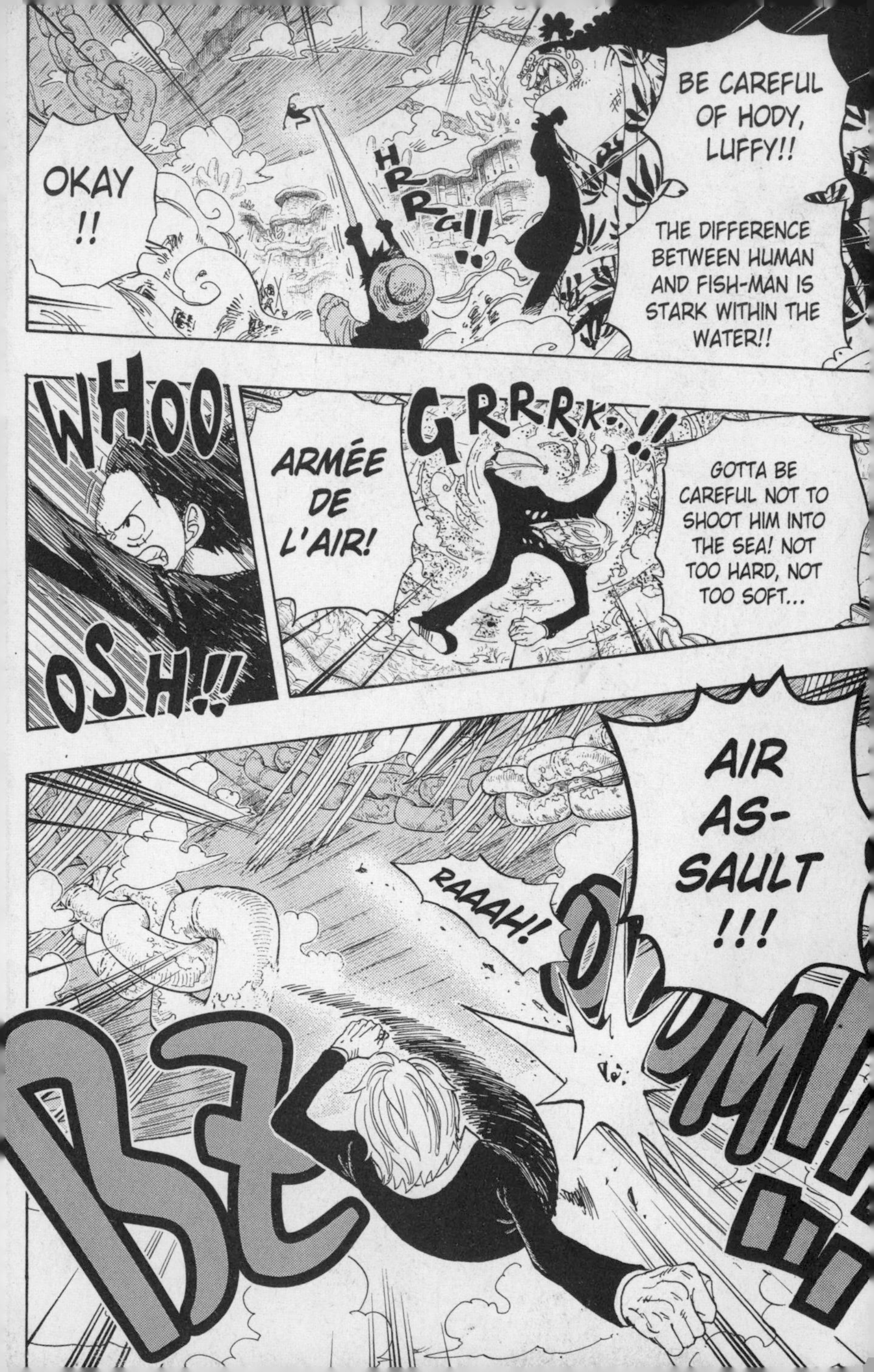
BE CAREFUL OF HODY, LUFFY!!
THE DIFFERENCE BETWEEN HUMAN AND FISH-MAN IS STARK WITHIN THE WATER!!
HRRRG!!
OKAY!!
GOTTA BE CAREFUL NOT TO SHOOT HIM INTO THE SEA! NOT TOO HARD, NOT TOO SOFT...
GRRRRK..!!
ARMÉE DE L'AIR!
WHOOOSH!!
AIR AS-SAULT!!!
RAAAH!

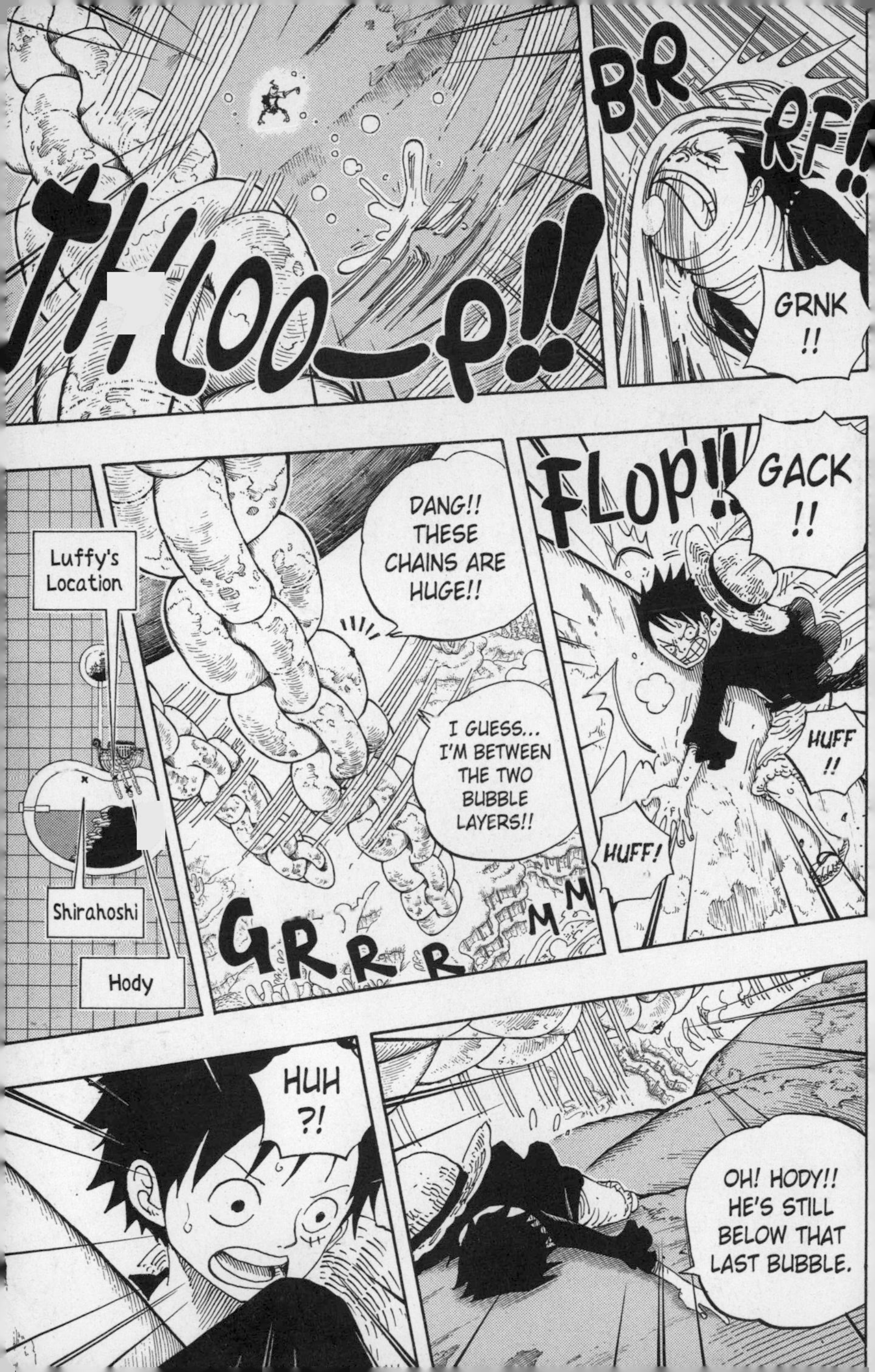
BR RF!!
GRNK!!
THLOO—P!!
FLOP!!
GACK!!
HUFF!!
HUFF!
DANG!! THESE CHAINS ARE HUGE!!
I GUESS... I'M BETWEEN THE TWO BUBBLE LAYERS!!
GRRRR
MM
Luffy's Location
Shirahoshi
Hody
OH! HODY!! HE'S STILL BELOW THAT LAST BUBBLE.
HUH?!

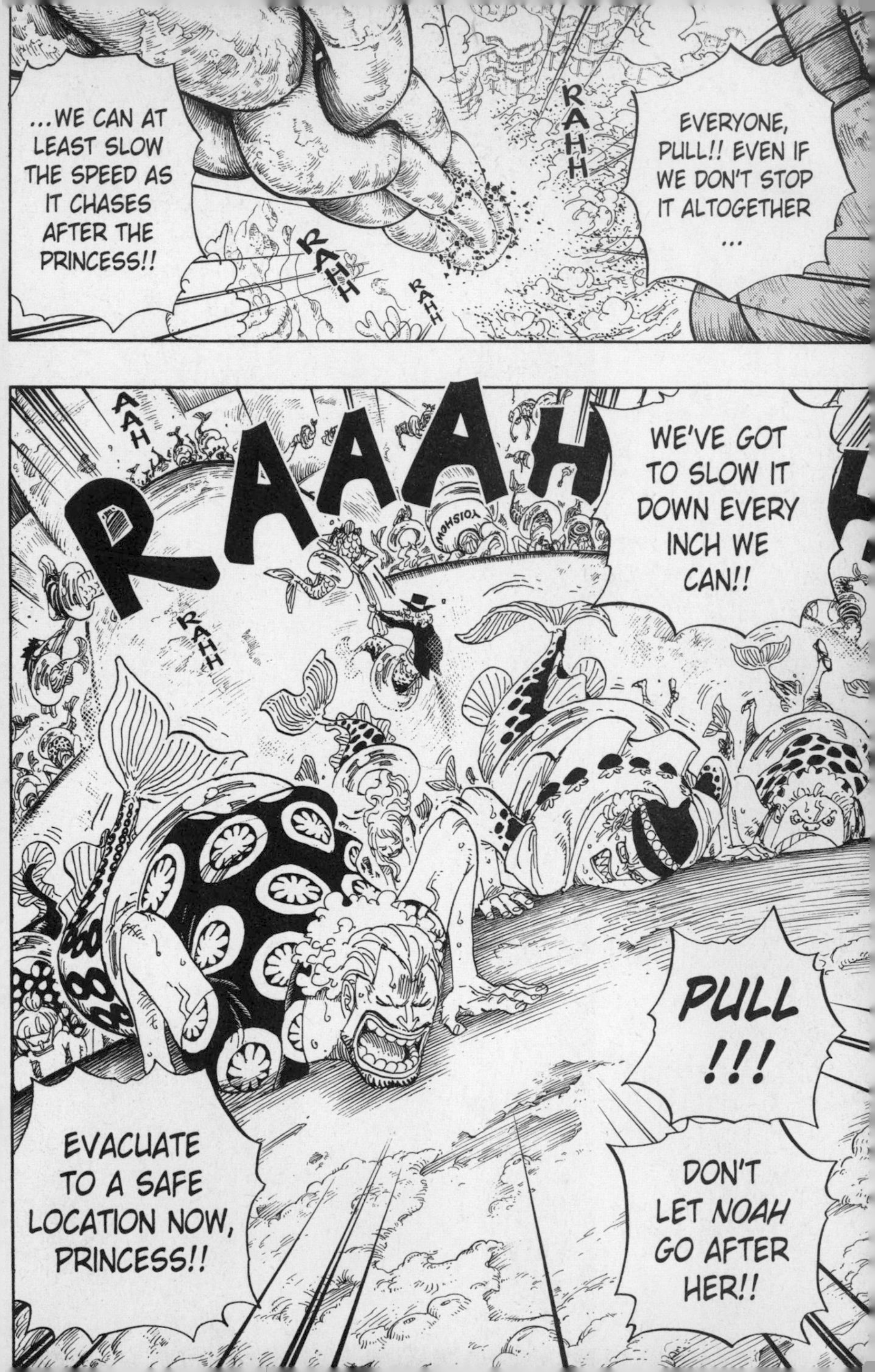
EVERYONE, PULL!! EVEN IF WE DON'T STOP IT ALTOGETHER ...
RAHH
RAHH
RAHH
...WE CAN AT LEAST SLOW THE SPEED AS IT CHASES AFTER THE PRINCESS!!
RAAAH
WE'VE GOT TO SLOW IT DOWN EVERY INCH WE CAN!!
AAH
RAHH
PULL!!!
DON'T LET NOAH GO AFTER HER!!
EVACUATE TO A SAFE LOCATION NOW, PRINCESS!!

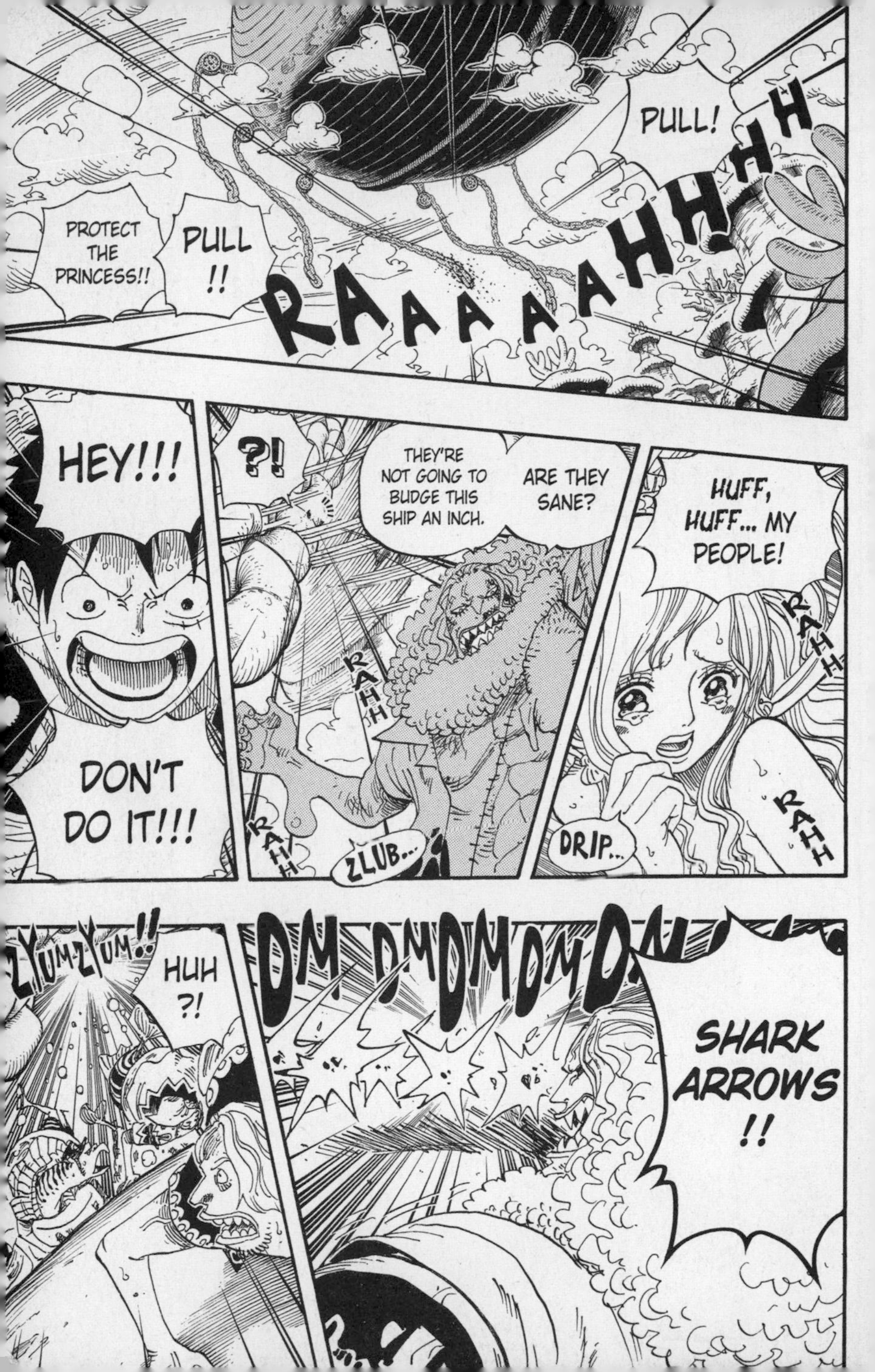
PULL!
RAAAAAHHHHHH
PULL !!
PROTECT THE PRINCESS!!
HUFF, HUFF... MY PEOPLE!
RAHH
RAHH
DRIP...
ARE THEY SANE?
THEY'RE NOT GOING TO BUDGE THIS SHIP AN INCH.
?!
RAHH
RAHH
ZLUB...
HEY!!!
DON'T DO IT!!!
DM DMDMDMDM
SHARK ARROWS !!
ZYUM-ZYUM!!
HUH ?!

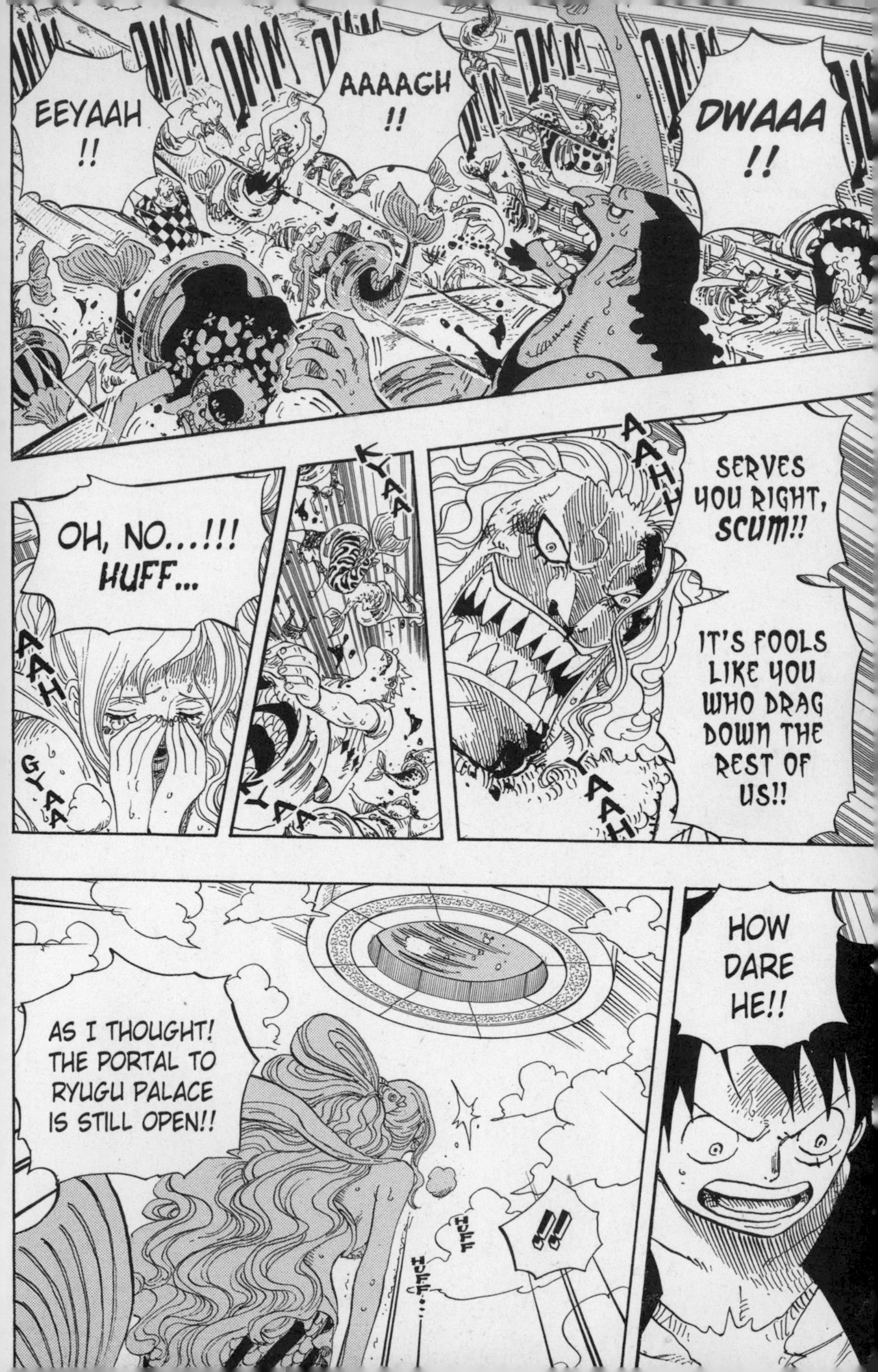
DWAAA!!
AAAAGH!!
EEYAAH!!
AAHH
SERVES YOU RIGHT, SCUM!!
IT'S FOOLS LIKE YOU WHO DRAG DOWN THE REST OF US!!
YAAAH
KYAA
KYAA
OH, NO...!!! HUFF...
AAH
GYAA
HOW DARE HE!!
AS I THOUGHT! THE PORTAL TO RYUGU PALACE IS STILL OPEN!!
HUFF
HUFF...
!!

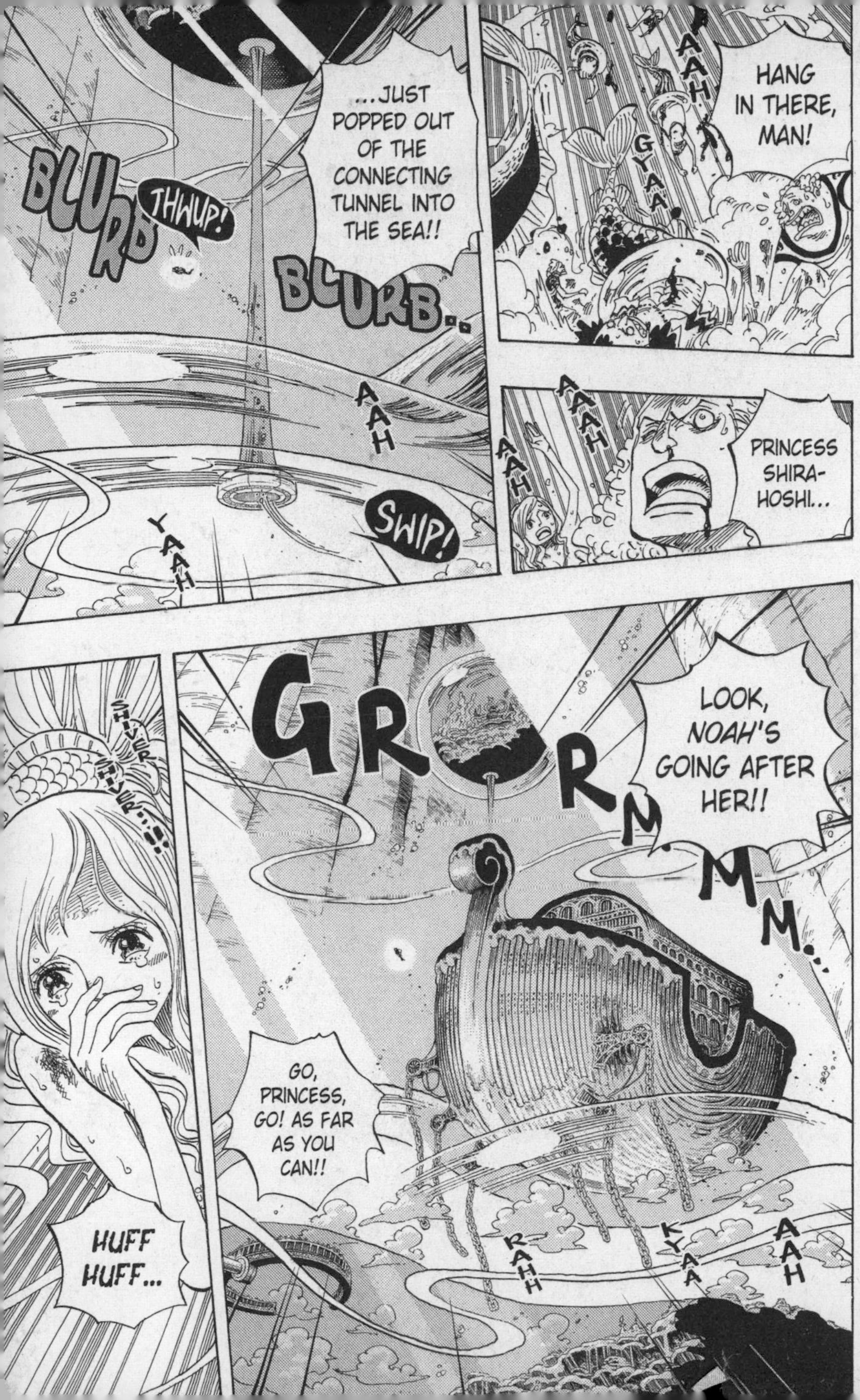
HANG IN THERE, MAN!
AAAH
GYAAA
PRINCESS SHIRA-HOSHI...
AAAH
AAH
...JUST POPPED OUT OF THE CONNECTING TUNNEL INTO THE SEA!!
BLURB
THWUP!
BLURB..
AAH
SWIP!
YAAAH
LOOK, NOAH'S GOING AFTER HER!!
GRORMMM...
GO, PRINCESS, GO! AS FAR AS YOU CAN!!
AAH
KYAA
RAHH
SHIVER SHIVER...!!
HUFF HUFF...

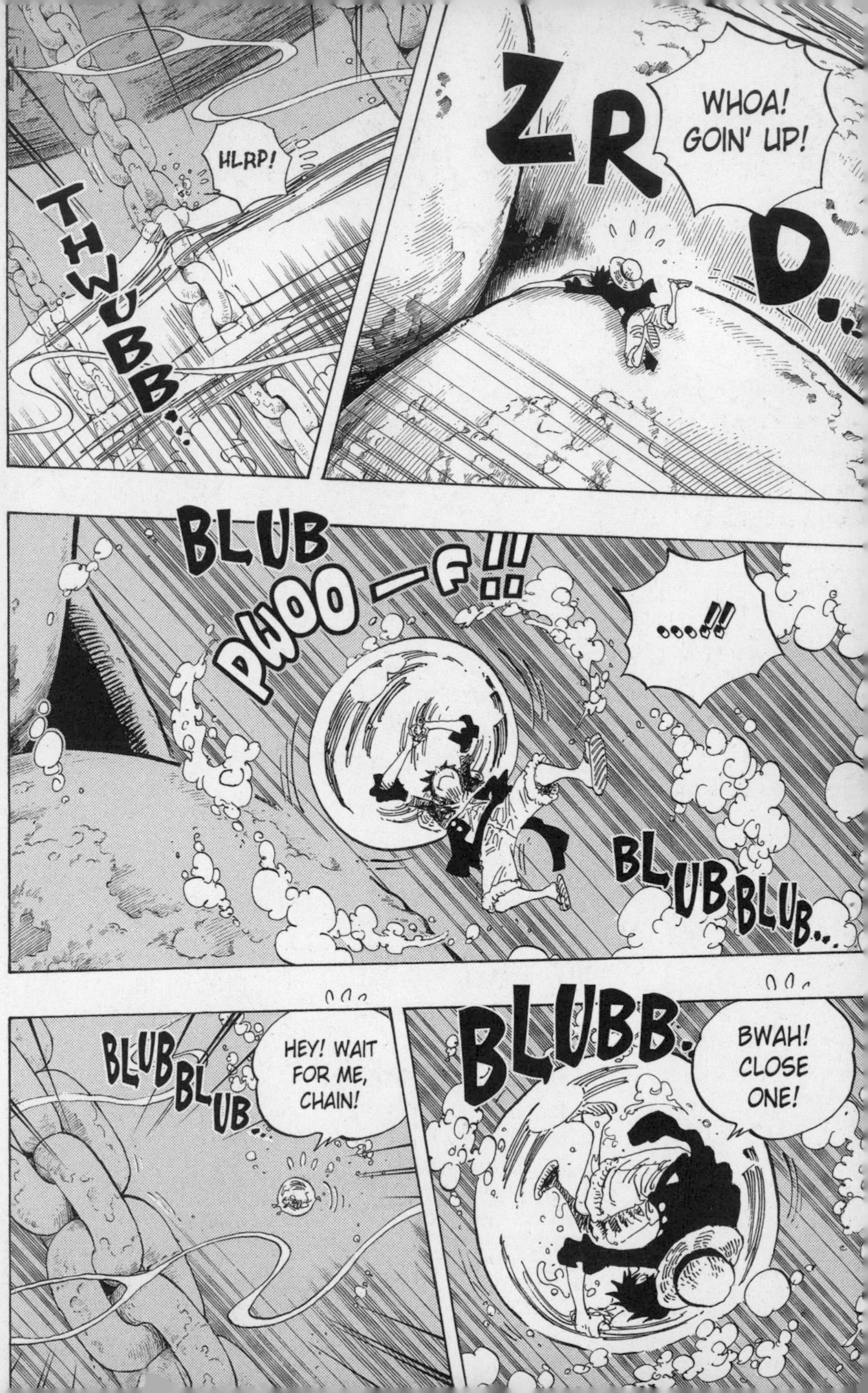
ZRD...
WHOA! GOIN' UP!
HLRP!
THWUBB...
BLUB
PWOO—F!!!
...!!
BLUB BLUB...
BLUBB..
BWAH! CLOSE ONE!
BLUB BLUB..
HEY! WAIT FOR ME, CHAIN!

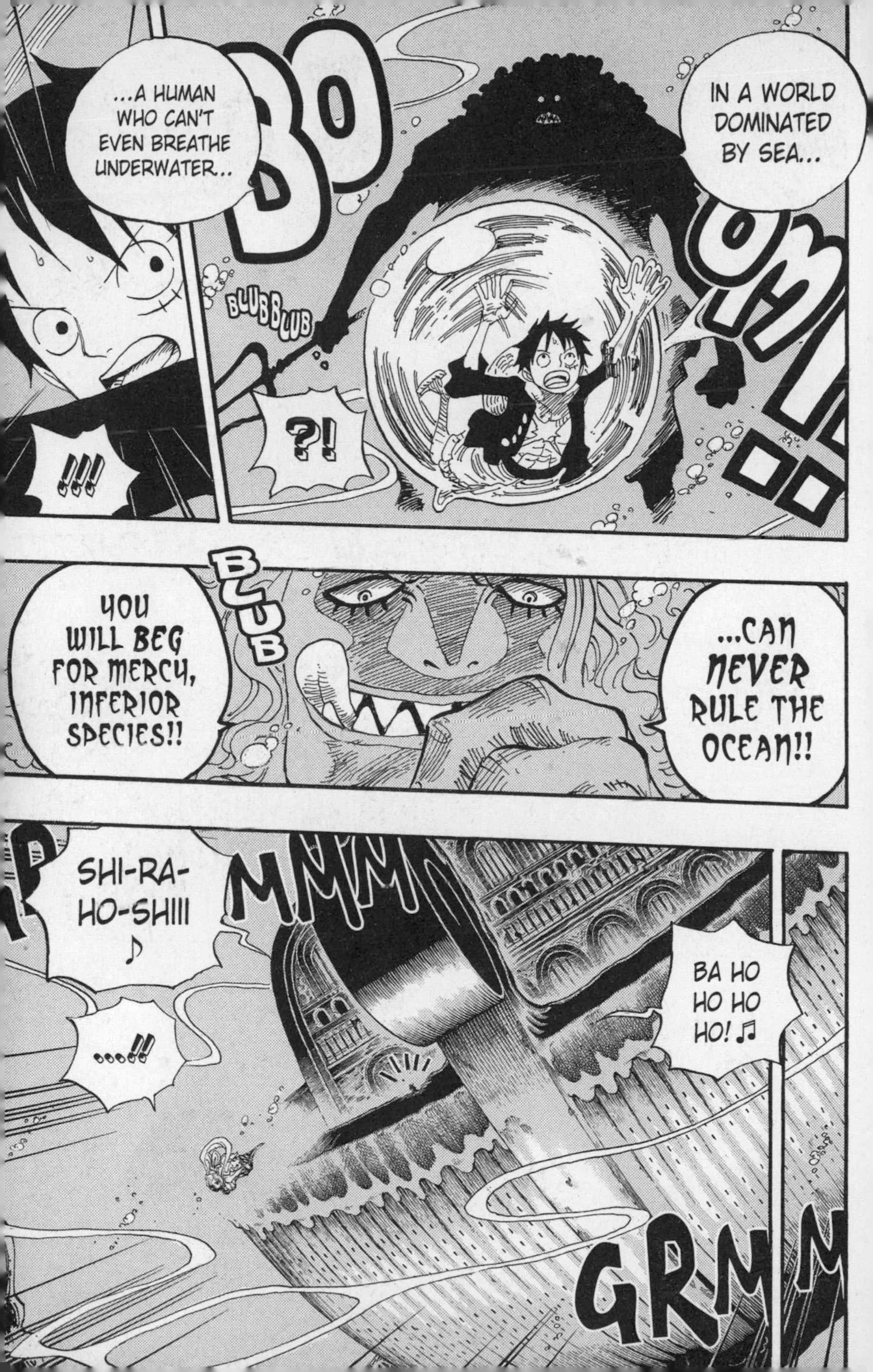
IN A WORLD DOMINATED BY SEA...
?!
BLUBBLUB
...A HUMAN WHO CAN'T EVEN BREATHE UNDERWATER...
!!!
...CAN NEVER RULE THE OCEAN!!
BLUB
YOU WILL BEG FOR MERCY, INFERIOR SPECIES!!
BA HO HO HO HO! ♫
SHI-RA-HO-SHIIII ♪
...!!
GRMM

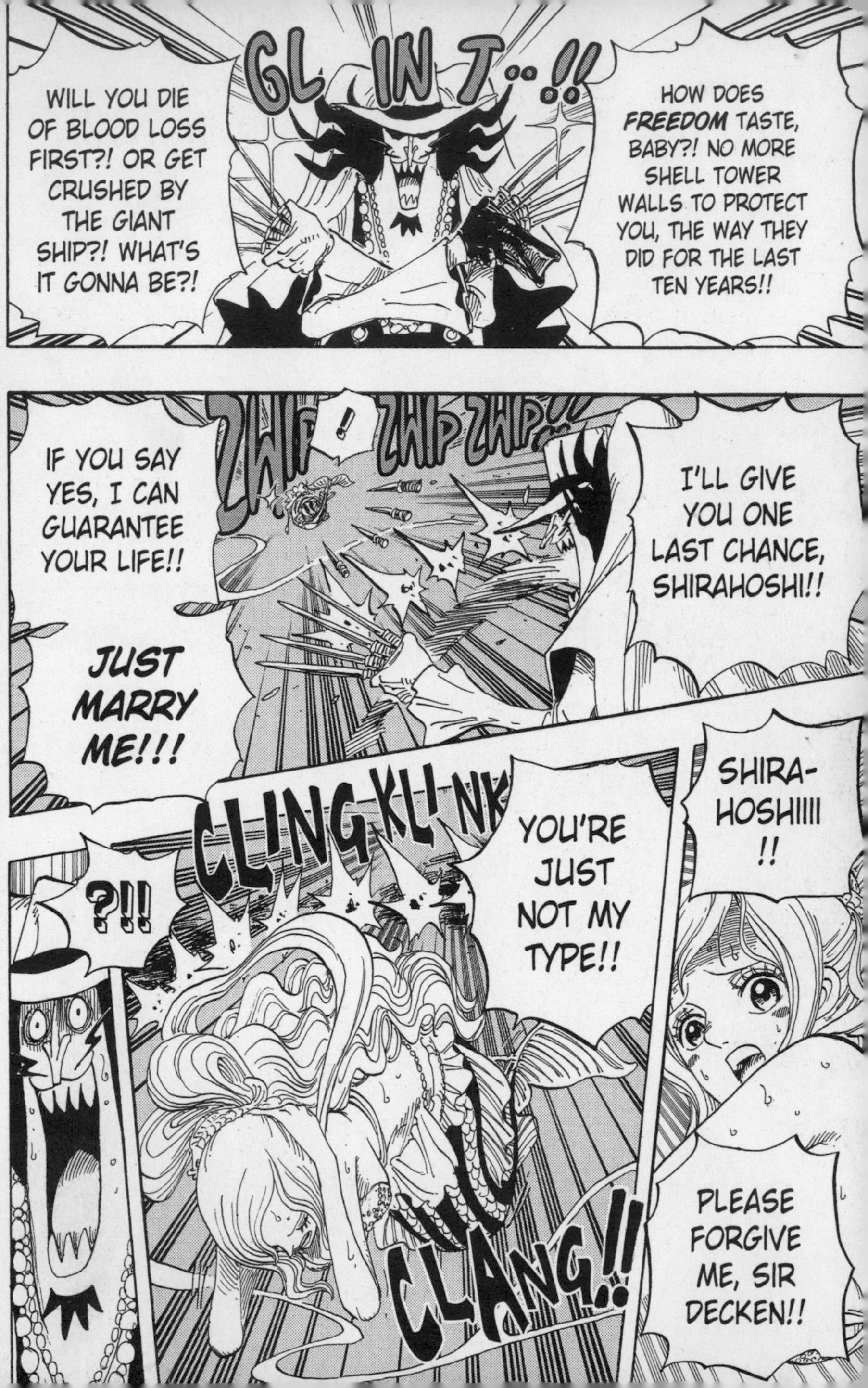
GLINT..!!
HOW DOES FREEDOM TASTE, BABY?! NO MORE SHELL TOWER WALLS TO PROTECT YOU, THE WAY THEY DID FOR THE LAST TEN YEARS!!
WILL YOU DIE OF BLOOD LOSS FIRST?! OR GET CRUSHED BY THE GIANT SHIP?! WHAT'S IT GONNA BE?!
I'LL GIVE YOU ONE LAST CHANCE, SHIRAHOSHI!!
ZWIP ZWIP ZWIP
!
IF YOU SAY YES, I CAN GUARANTEE YOUR LIFE!!
JUST MARRY ME!!!
SHIRA-HOSHIIIII !!
YOU'RE JUST NOT MY TYPE!!
CLING KLINK
?!!
PLEASE FORGIVE ME, SIR DECKEN!!
CLANG!!

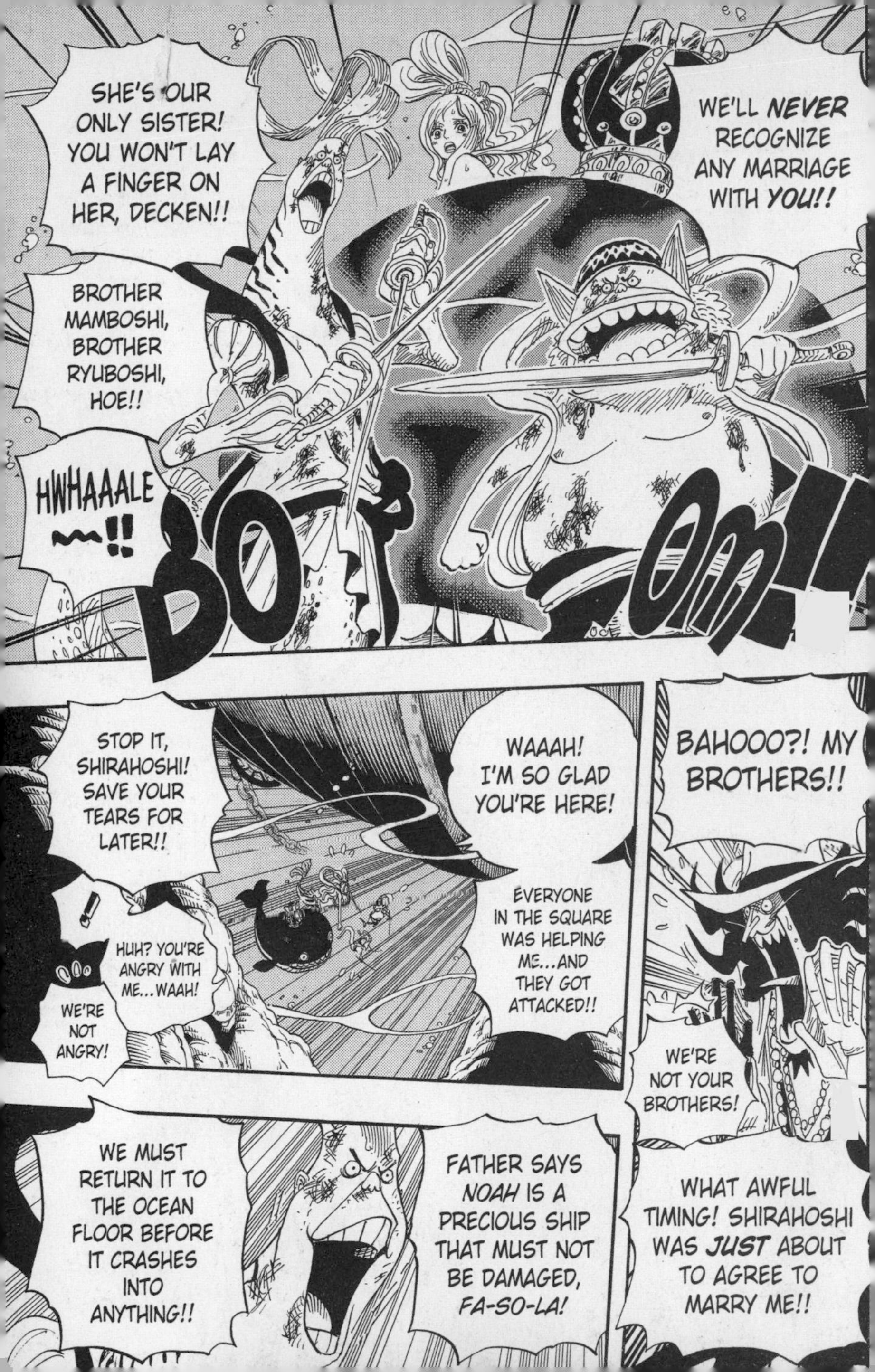
WE'LL NEVER RECOGNIZE ANY MARRIAGE WITH YOU!!
SHE'S OUR ONLY SISTER! YOU WON'T LAY A FINGER ON HER, DECKEN!!
BROTHER MAMBOSHI, BROTHER RYUBOSHI, HOE!!
HWHAAALE~!!
BOOM!!
BAHOOO?! MY BROTHERS!!
WE'RE NOT YOUR BROTHERS!
WAAAH! I'M SO GLAD YOU'RE HERE!
EVERYONE IN THE SQUARE WAS HELPING ME...AND THEY GOT ATTACKED!!
STOP IT, SHIRAHOSHI! SAVE YOUR TEARS FOR LATER!!
!
HUH? YOU'RE ANGRY WITH ME...WAAH!
WE'RE NOT ANGRY!
WHAT AWFUL TIMING! SHIRAHOSHI WAS JUST ABOUT TO AGREE TO MARRY ME!!
FATHER SAYS NOAH IS A PRECIOUS SHIP THAT MUST NOT BE DAMAGED, FA-SO-LA!
WE MUST RETURN IT TO THE OCEAN FLOOR BEFORE IT CRASHES INTO ANYTHING!!

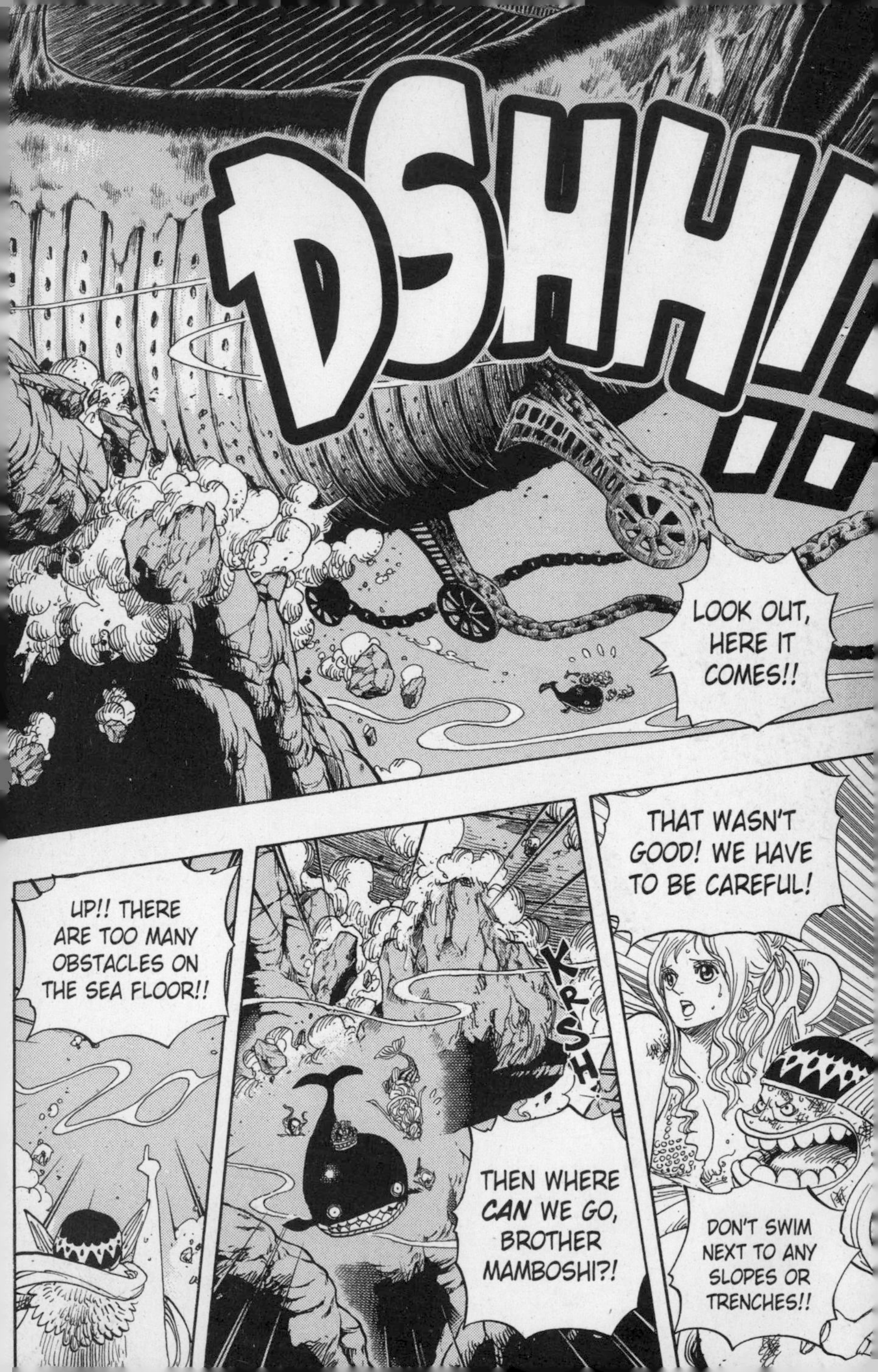
DSHH!!
LOOK OUT, HERE IT COMES!!
THAT WASN'T GOOD! WE HAVE TO BE CAREFUL!
DON'T SWIM NEXT TO ANY SLOPES OR TRENCHES!!
KRSSH
THEN WHERE *CAN* WE GO, BROTHER MAMBOSHI?!
UP!! THERE ARE TOO MANY OBSTACLES ON THE SEA FLOOR!!

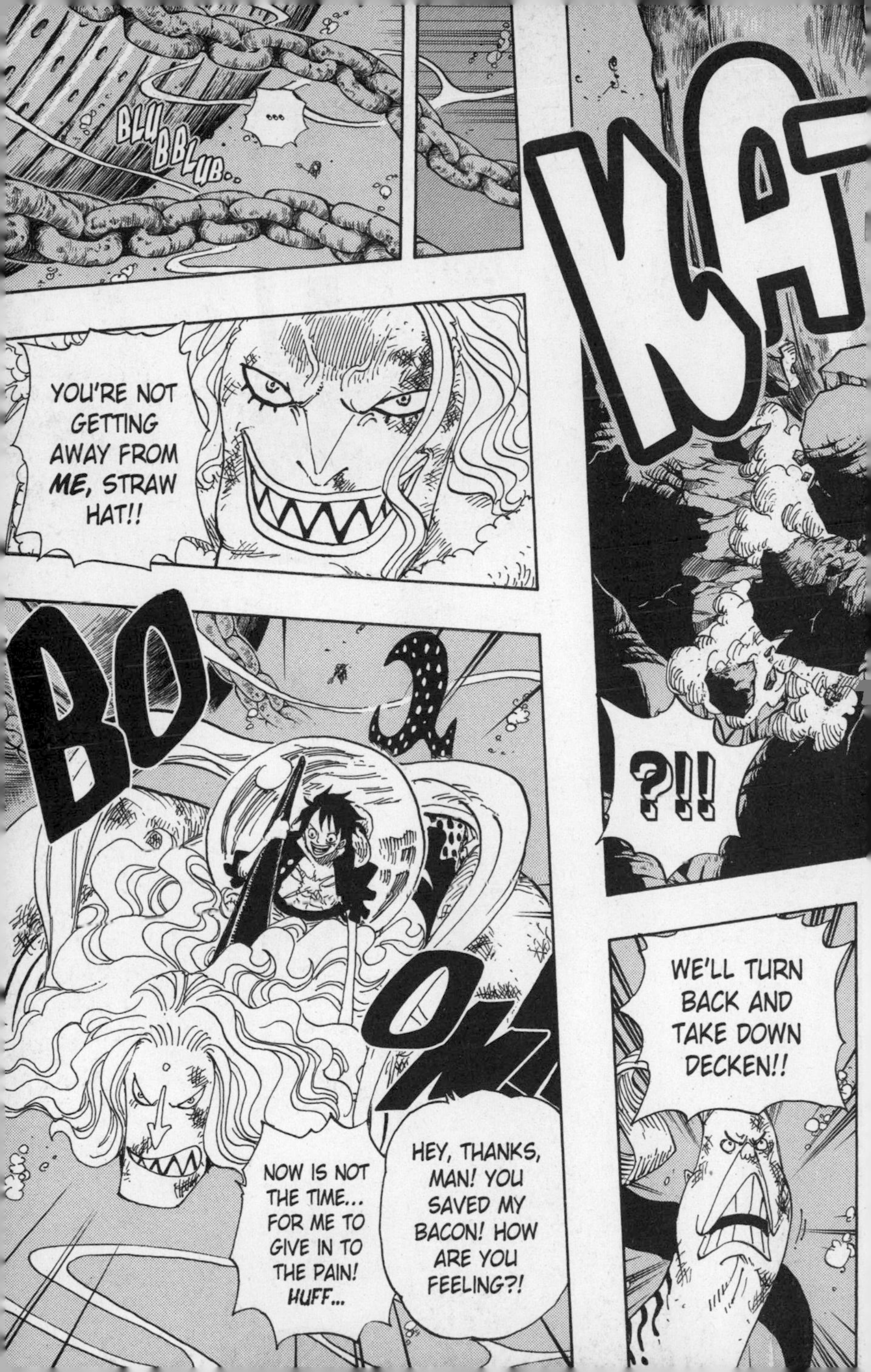
KA
?!!
WE'LL TURN BACK AND TAKE DOWN DECKEN!!
BLUBBLUB...
...
YOU'RE NOT GETTING AWAY FROM *ME*, STRAW HAT!!
BOOM
HEY, THANKS, MAN! YOU SAVED MY BACON! HOW ARE YOU FEELING?!
NOW IS NOT THE TIME... FOR ME TO GIVE IN TO THE PAIN! HUFF...

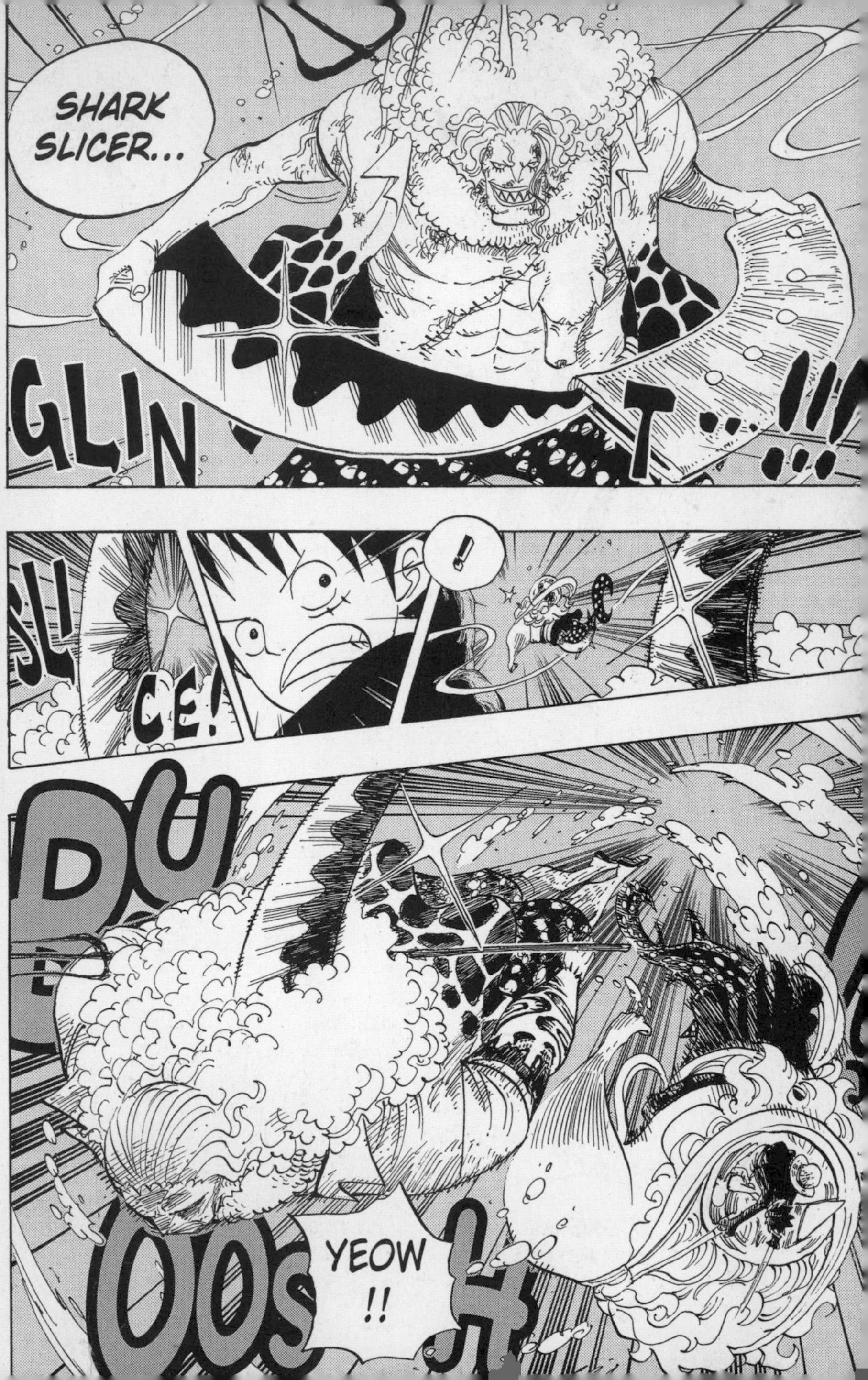
SHARK SLICER...
GLINT...!!!
!
SLICE!
DUOOSH
YEOW !!

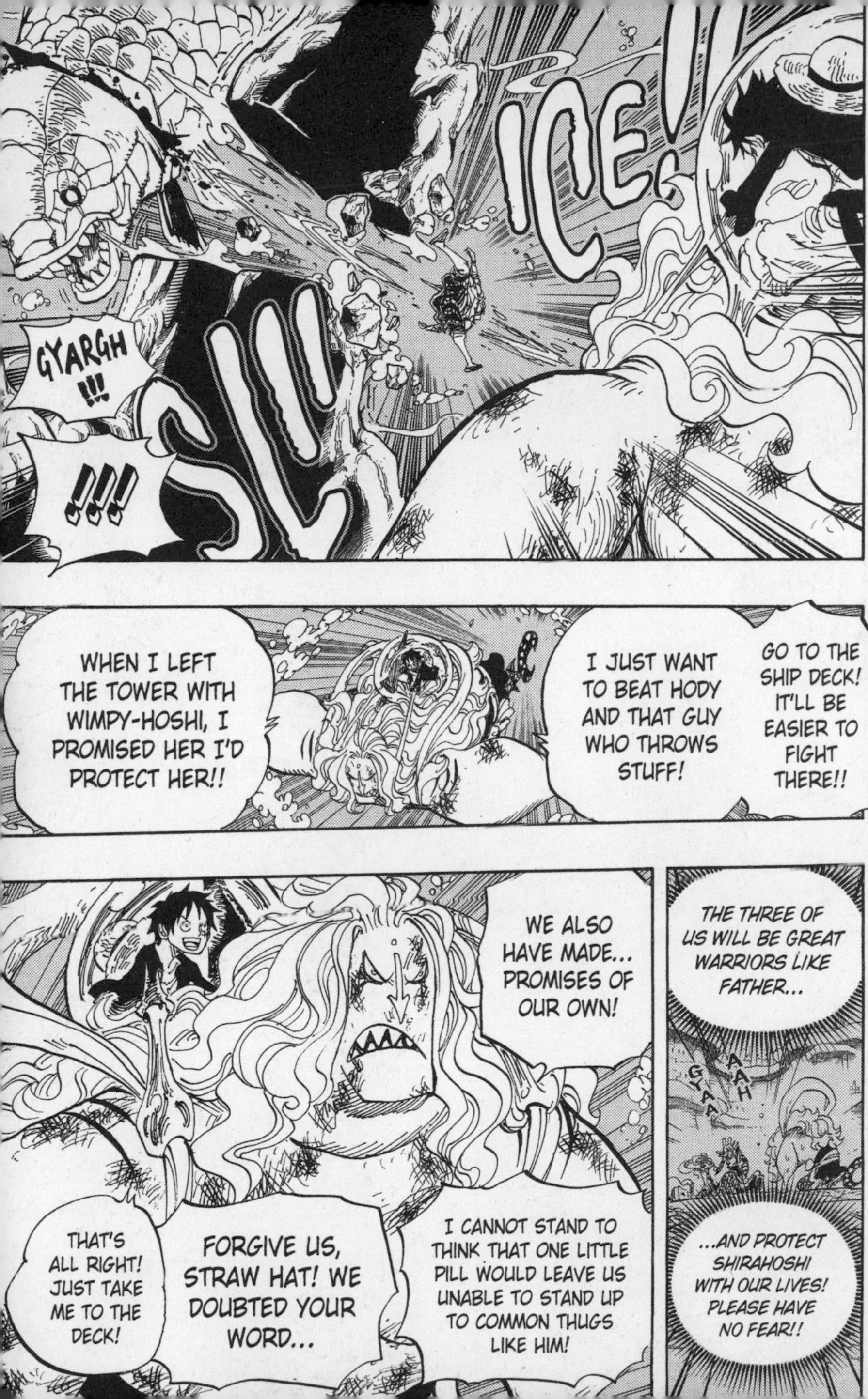
ICE!!
GYARGH !!!
!!!
GO TO THE SHIP DECK! IT'LL BE EASIER TO FIGHT THERE!!
I JUST WANT TO BEAT HODY AND THAT GUY WHO THROWS STUFF!
WHEN I LEFT THE TOWER WITH WIMPY-HOSHI, I PROMISED HER I'D PROTECT HER!!
THE THREE OF US WILL BE GREAT WARRIORS LIKE FATHER...
GYAAAAH
...AND PROTECT SHIRAHOSHI WITH OUR LIVES! PLEASE HAVE NO FEAR!!
WE ALSO HAVE MADE... PROMISES OF OUR OWN!
I CANNOT STAND TO THINK THAT ONE LITTLE PILL WOULD LEAVE US UNABLE TO STAND UP TO COMMON THUGS LIKE HIM!
FORGIVE US, STRAW HAT! WE DOUBTED YOUR WORD...
THAT'S ALL RIGHT! JUST TAKE ME TO THE DECK!

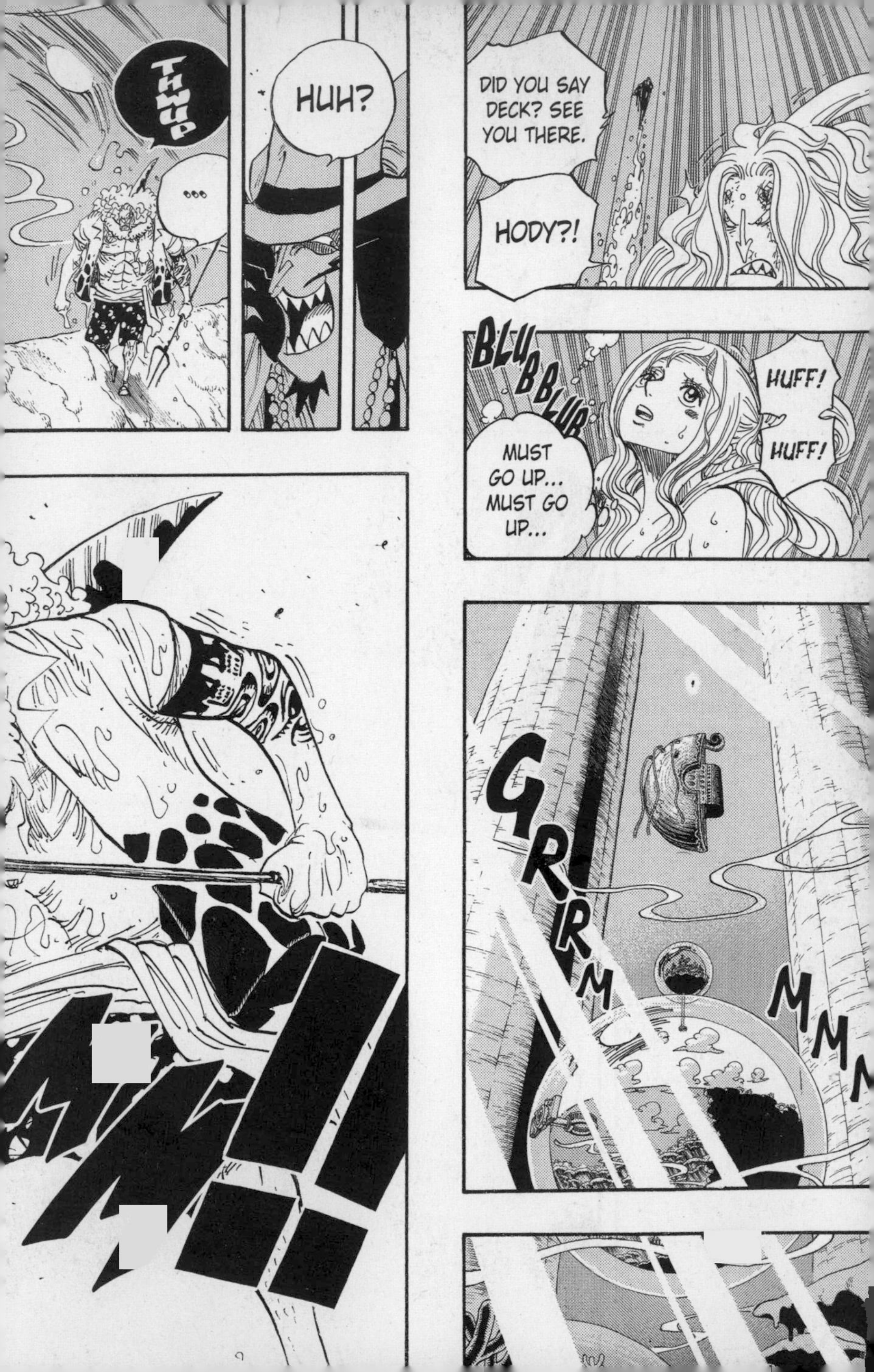
DID YOU SAY DECK? SEE YOU THERE.
HODY?!
HUH?
THWUP
...
HUFF! HUFF!
BLUB BLUB
MUST GO UP... MUST GO UP...
GRRRM
MMM

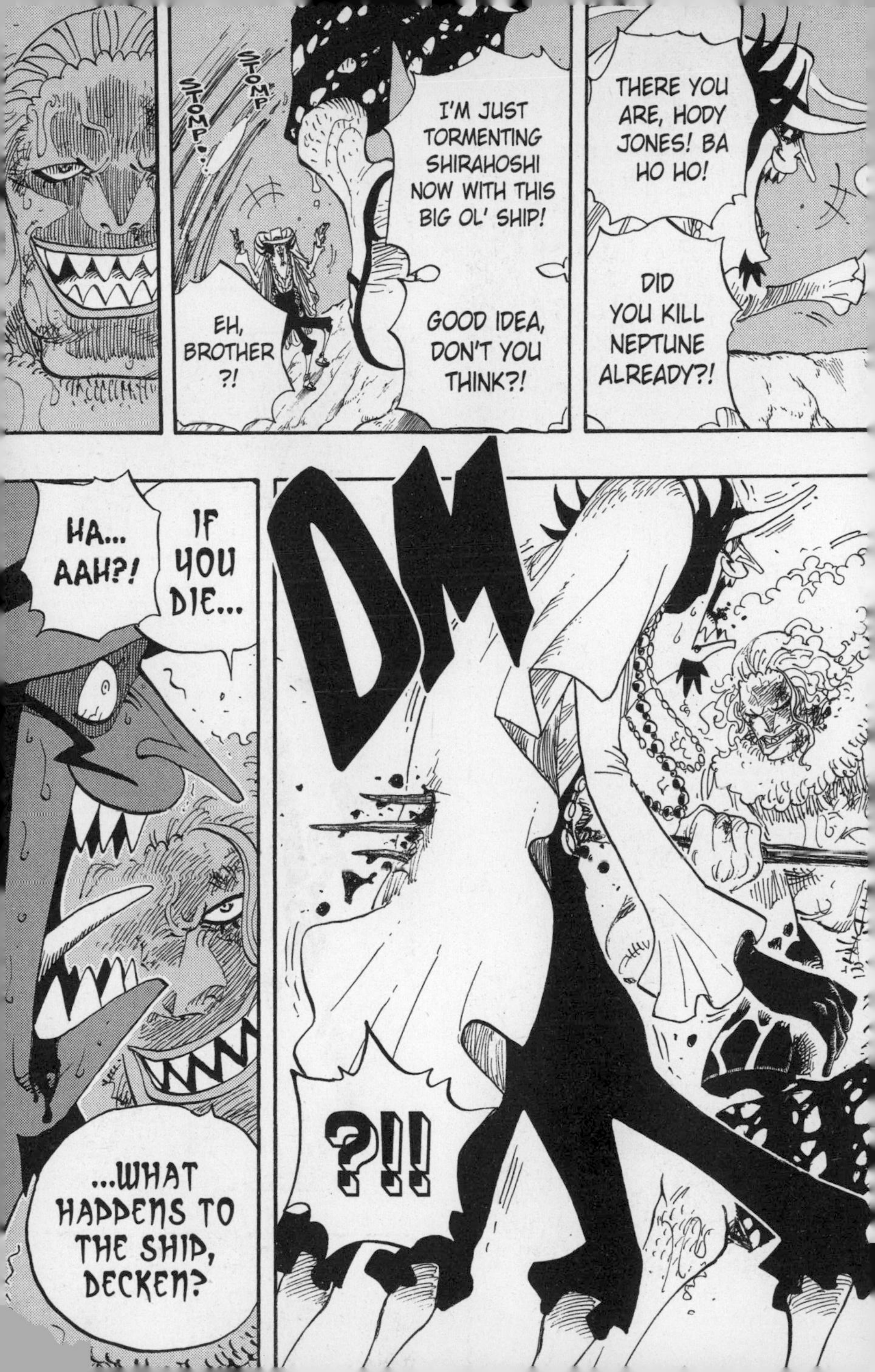
THERE YOU ARE, HODY JONES! BA HO HO!
DID YOU KILL NEPTUNE ALREADY?!
I'M JUST TORMENTING SHIRAHOSHI NOW WITH THIS BIG OL' SHIP!
STOMP STOMP...
GOOD IDEA, DON'T YOU THINK?!
EH, BROTHER?!
DM
?!!
HA... AAH?!
IF YOU DIE...
...WHAT HAPPENS TO THE SHIP, DECKEN?

(Nan Ko, Tokyo)

Q: Ahh, yes, I see!! (Boom.)

I wasn't actually asking, though!! Ha ha!!

--Setobyun

A: And I didn't even say anything. Ha ha ha! (I pulled a prank on you)

Q: I have a serious question! You know how the Straw Hat Pirates each have their own Jolly Roger?? Have you come up with new designs for them, two years later?!

--M-Hyu, age 22

A: As a matter of fact, I had these done fairly early on. The merchandising companies would come to me with new designs, asking if they could use them, and I would say, "No!!" and fix them up. So these are the official new logos. Hey, it's hard to do that merchandising stuff. So here they are.

© Eiichiro Oda / Shueisha / Fuji TV / Toei Animation

Q: Lately in *One Piece,* it seems like Luffy runs across a whole parade of enemies with stronger and stronger powers. In most manga and anime, the hero has the best and most ultimate powers of all, so why did you choose something as weak-sounding as rubber for Luffy?

--Hang in There, Japan

A: Ha ha, good question. It is strange that he'd have that one, when there are so many cool powers out there. The answer is simple: I chose the goofiest power I could think of. I probably couldn't handle drawing a straightforward, cool, tough hero for this long. No matter how serious and dark the story gets, Luffy's still stretching and inflating and so on. He always gives me the chance to lighten the mood. That's the kind of manga I wanted to draw.

Chapter 639:

PROTECT EVERYTHING

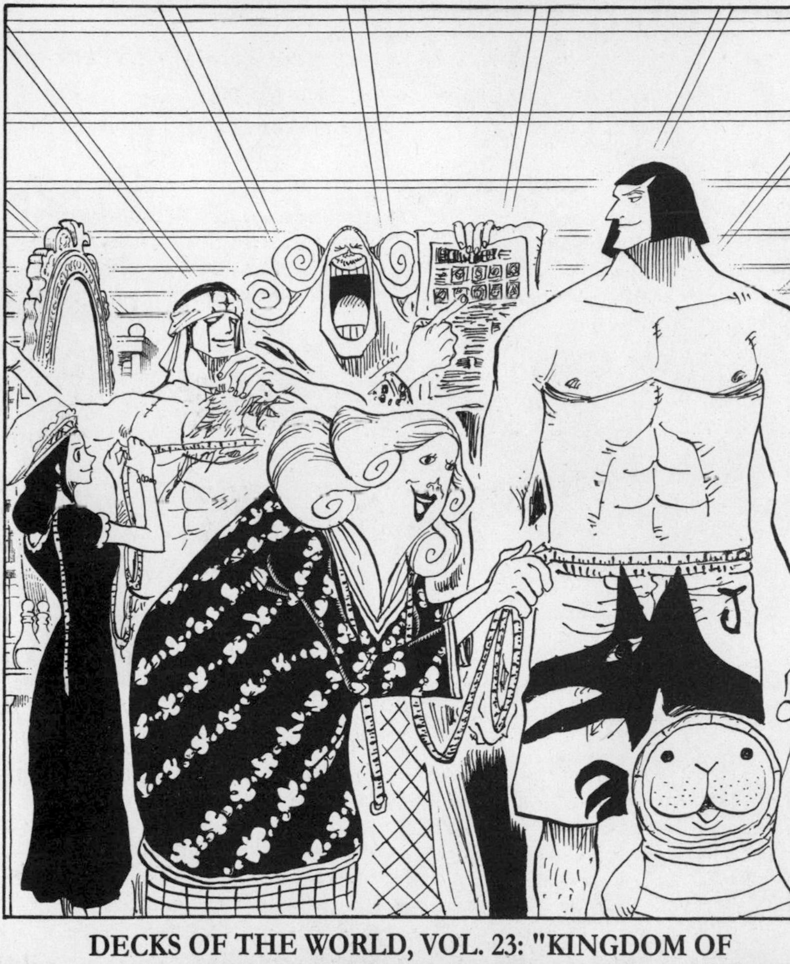

DECKS OF THE WORLD, VOL. 23: "KINGDOM OF ALABASTA—NEW CLOTHES FOR THIS YEAR'S REVERIE"

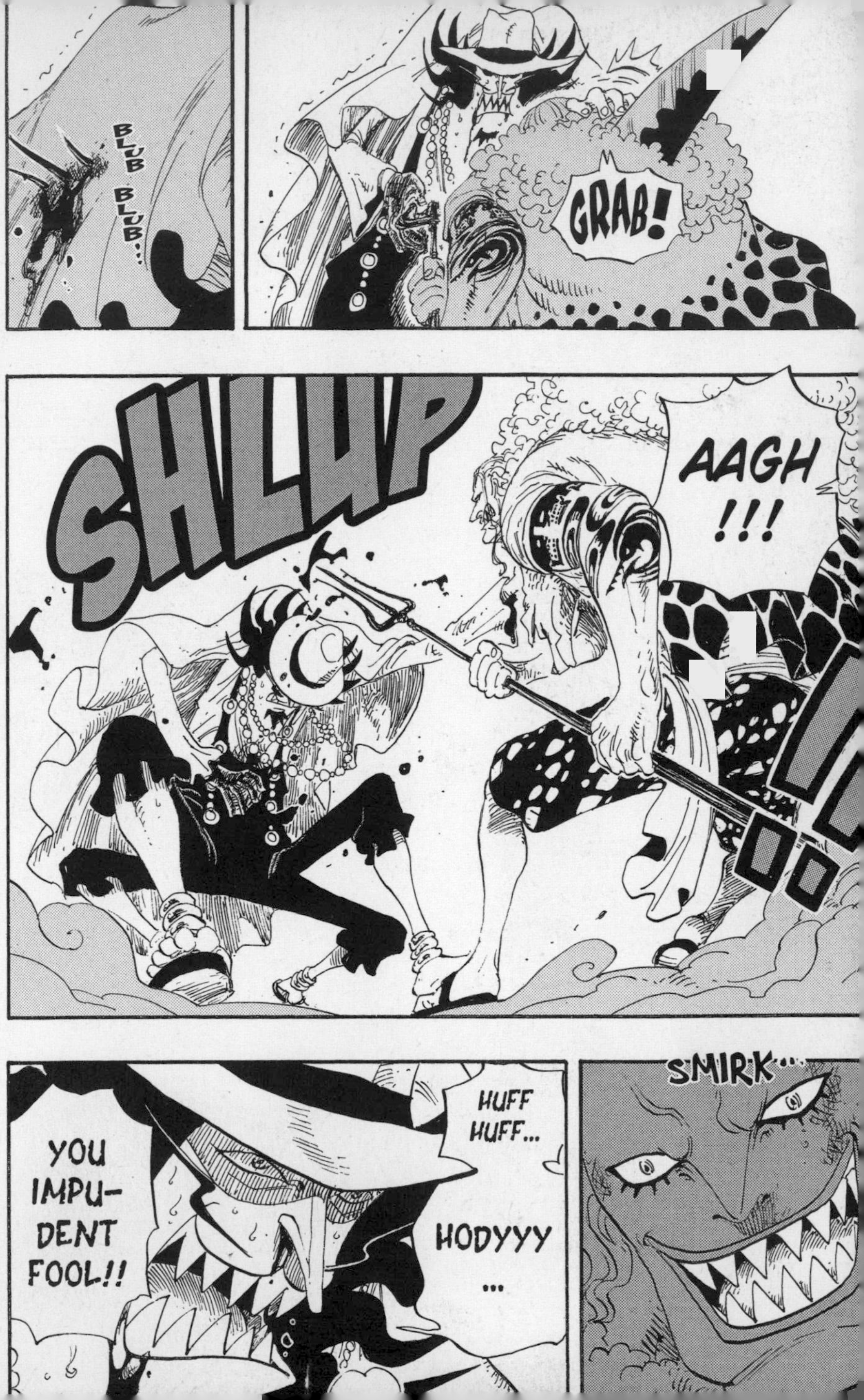
GRAB!
BLUB BLUB...
AAGH!!!
SHLUP
SMIRK...
HUFF HUFF...
HODYYY...
YOU IMPUDENT FOOL!!

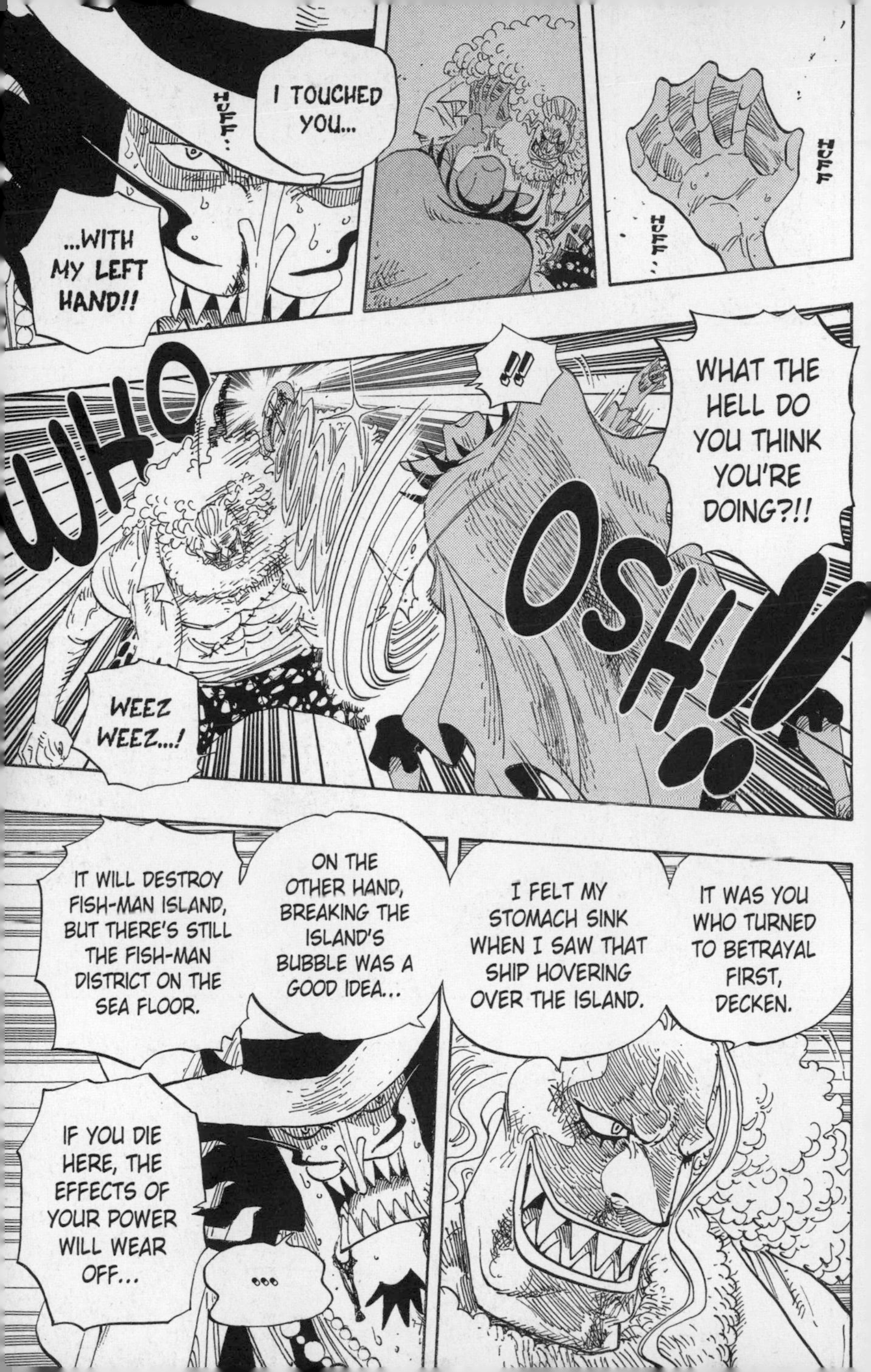
HUFF
HUFF...
I TOUCHED YOU...
HUFF...
...WITH MY LEFT HAND!!
WHAT THE HELL DO YOU THINK YOU'RE DOING?!!
!!
WHOOSH!!
WEEZ WEEZ...!
IT WAS YOU WHO TURNED TO BETRAYAL FIRST, DECKEN.
I FELT MY STOMACH SINK WHEN I SAW THAT SHIP HOVERING OVER THE ISLAND.
ON THE OTHER HAND, BREAKING THE ISLAND'S BUBBLE WAS A GOOD IDEA...
IT WILL DESTROY FISH-MAN ISLAND, BUT THERE'S STILL THE FISH-MAN DISTRICT ON THE SEA FLOOR.
IF YOU DIE HERE, THE EFFECTS OF YOUR POWER WILL WEAR OFF...
...

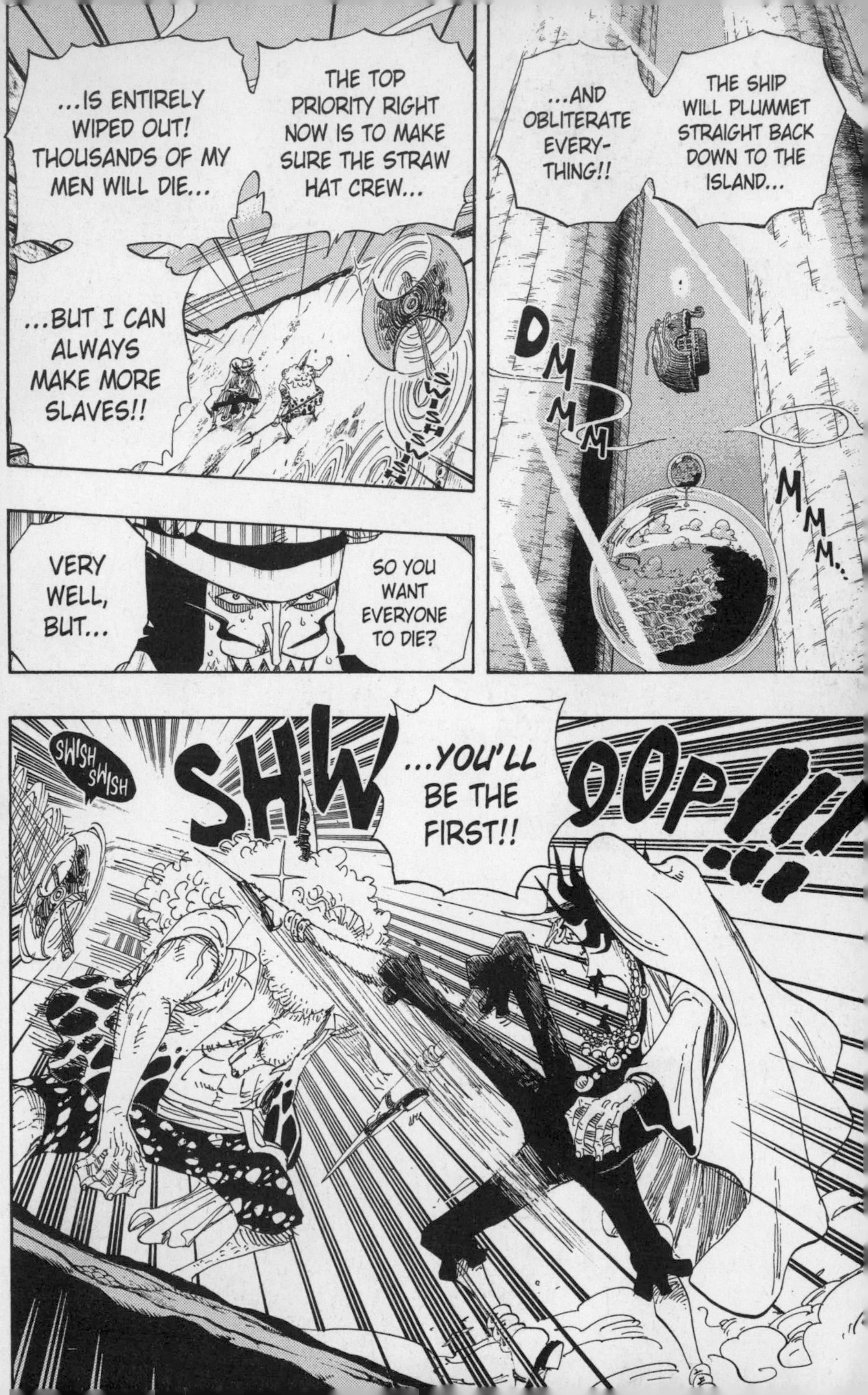

THE SHIP WILL PLUMMET STRAIGHT BACK DOWN TO THE ISLAND...
...AND OBLITERATE EVERY-THING!!
DMMM
MMM...
THE TOP PRIORITY RIGHT NOW IS TO MAKE SURE THE STRAW HAT CREW...
...IS ENTIRELY WIPED OUT! THOUSANDS OF MY MEN WILL DIE...
...BUT I CAN ALWAYS MAKE MORE SLAVES!!
SWISH SWISH
SO YOU WANT EVERYONE TO DIE?
VERY WELL, BUT...
SHWOOP!!!
...YOU'LL BE THE FIRST!!
SWISH SWISH

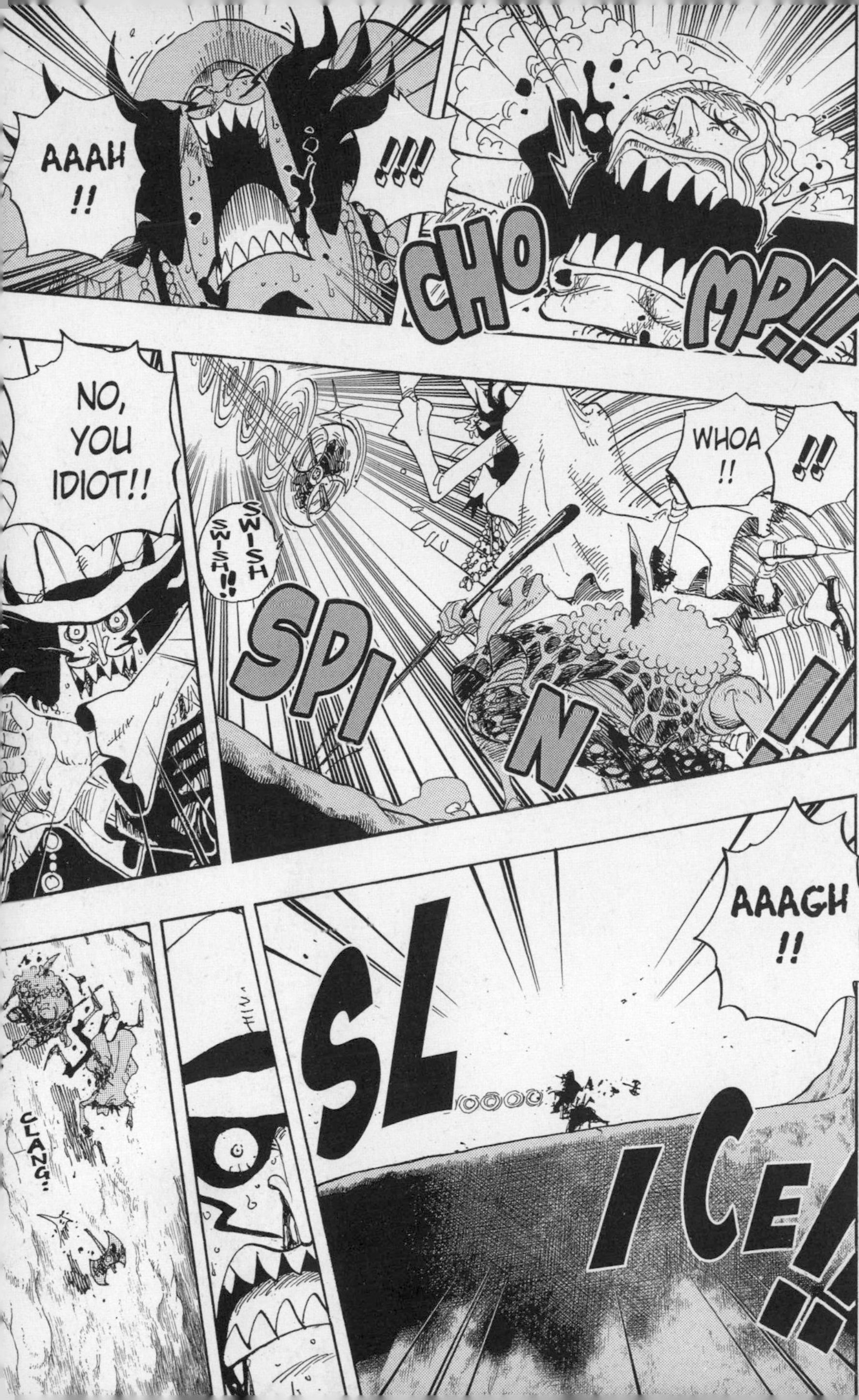
CHOMP!!
!!!
AAAH !!
WHOA !!
!!
SWISH SWISH!!
SPIN!!
NO, YOU IDIOT!!
AAAGH !!
SLICE!!
CLANG!

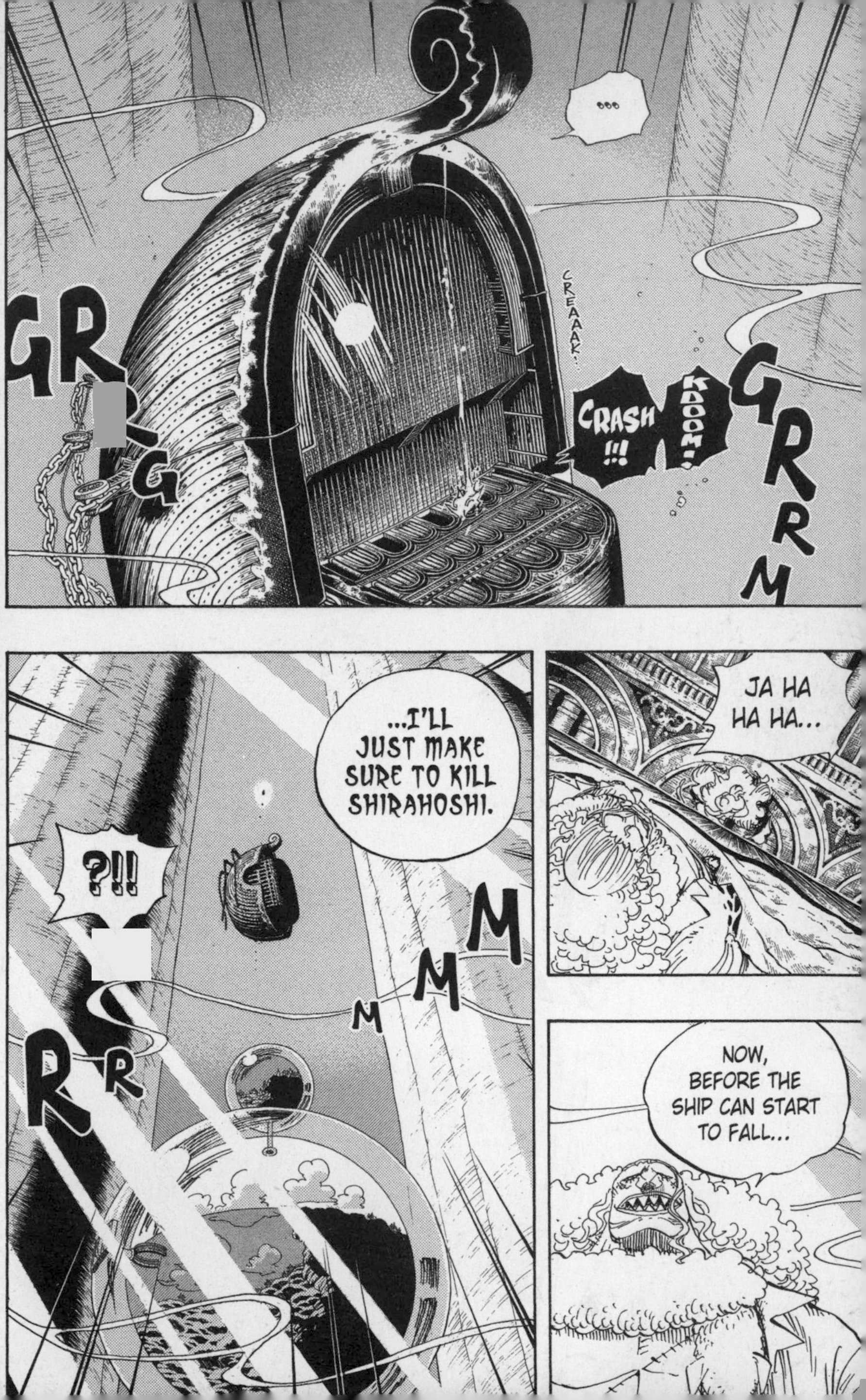
...
CREAAAK...
GRRRM
KDOOM!!
CRASH!!!
GR
G
JA HA HA HA...
NOW, BEFORE THE SHIP CAN START TO FALL...
...I'LL JUST MAKE SURE TO KILL SHIRAHOSHI.
MMM
?!!
RR

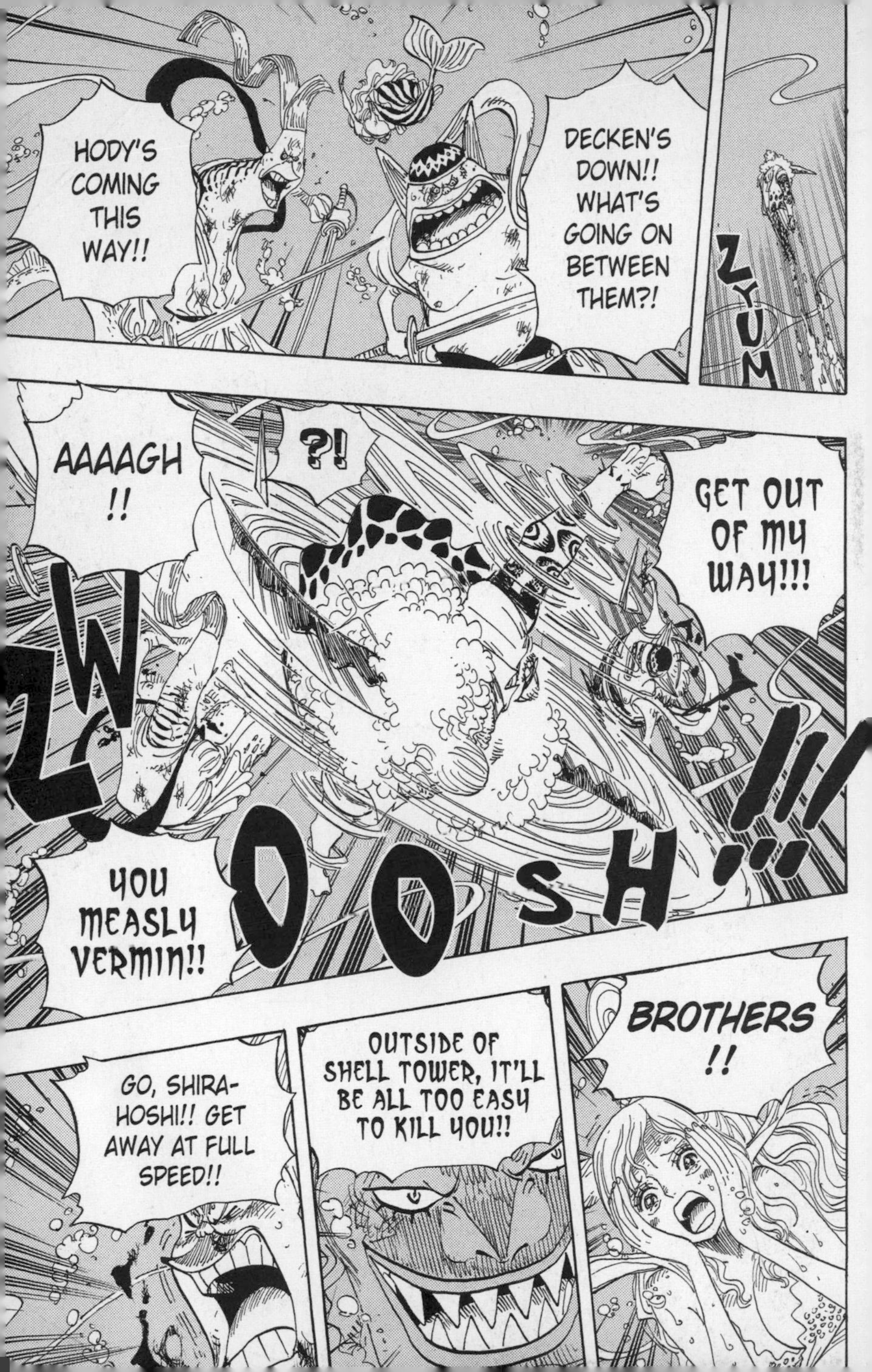
ZYUM
DECKEN'S DOWN!! WHAT'S GOING ON BETWEEN THEM?!
HODY'S COMING THIS WAY!!
GET OUT OF MY WAY!!!
?!
AAAAGH!!
WHOOSH!!!
YOU MEASLY VERMIN!!
BROTHERS!!
OUTSIDE OF SHELL TOWER, IT'LL BE ALL TOO EASY TO KILL YOU!!
GO, SHIRA-HOSHI!! GET AWAY AT FULL SPEED!!

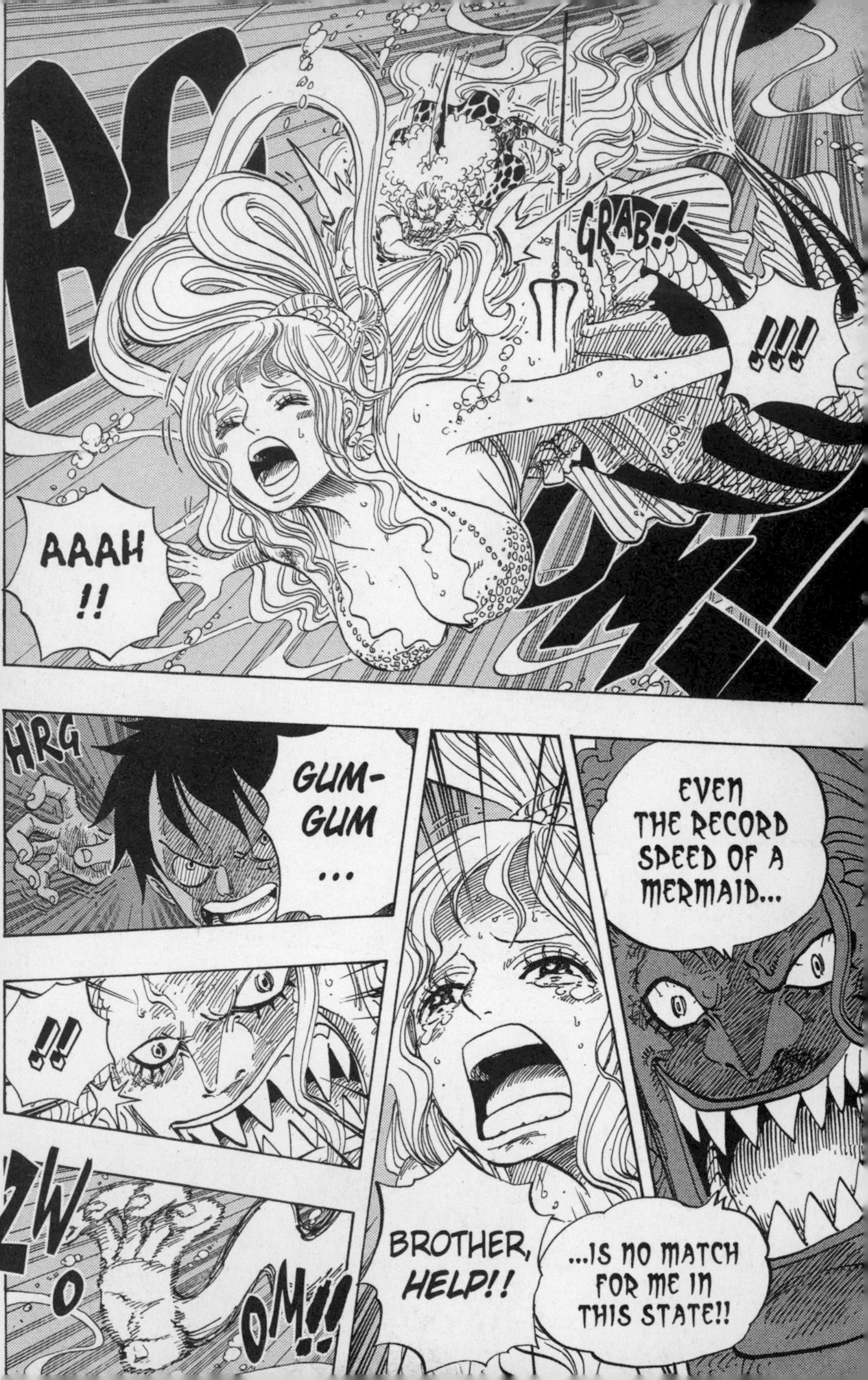
GRAB!!
!!!
AAAH !!
EVEN THE RECORD SPEED OF A MERMAID...
...IS NO MATCH FOR ME IN THIS STATE!!
BROTHER, HELP!!
HRG
GUM-GUM ...
!!
ZWOOM!!

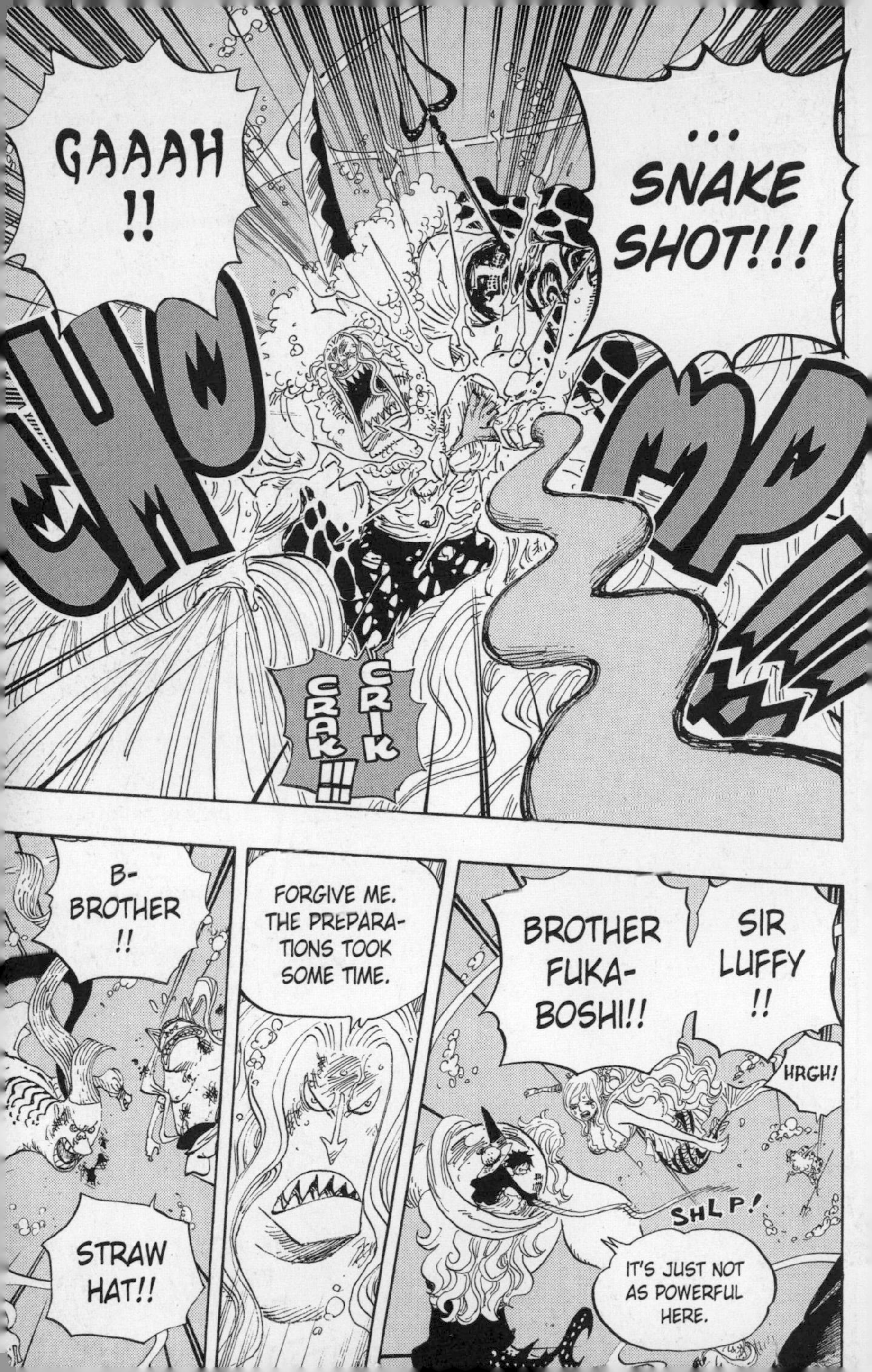
...SNAKE SHOT!!!
GAAAH!!
CHOMP
CRIK CRAK!!!
SIR LUFFY!!
BROTHER FUKA-BOSHI!!
HRGH!
SHLP!
IT'S JUST NOT AS POWERFUL HERE.
FORGIVE ME. THE PREPARA-TIONS TOOK SOME TIME.
B-BROTHER!!
STRAW HAT!!

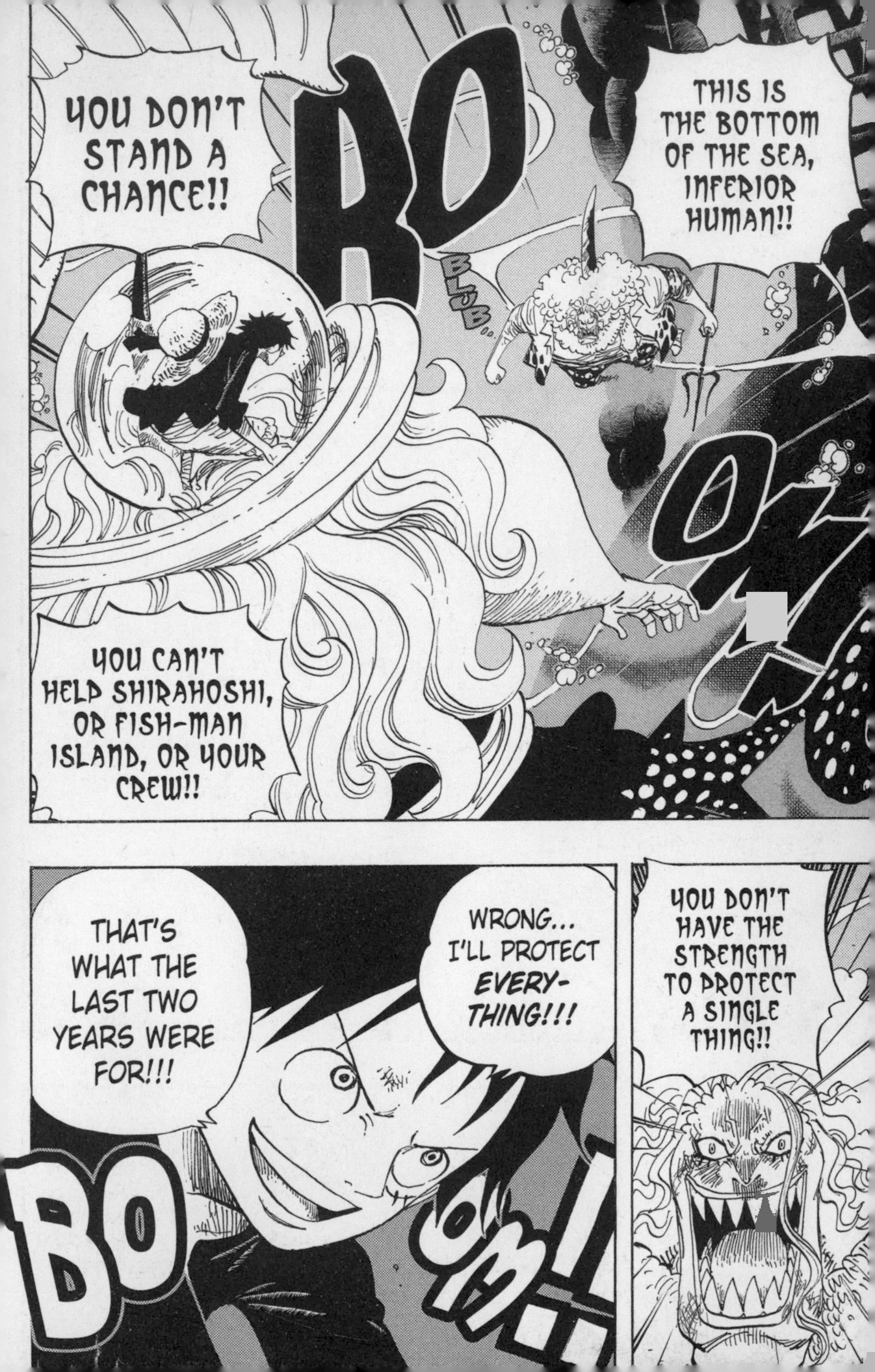
THIS IS THE BOTTOM OF THE SEA, INFERIOR HUMAN!!
YOU DON'T STAND A CHANCE!!
BO
BLUB...
YOU CAN'T HELP SHIRAHOSHI, OR FISH-MAN ISLAND, OR YOUR CREW!!
YOU DON'T HAVE THE STRENGTH TO PROTECT A SINGLE THING!!
WRONG... I'LL PROTECT EVERY-THING!!!
THAT'S WHAT THE LAST TWO YEARS WERE FOR!!!
BO
OM!!

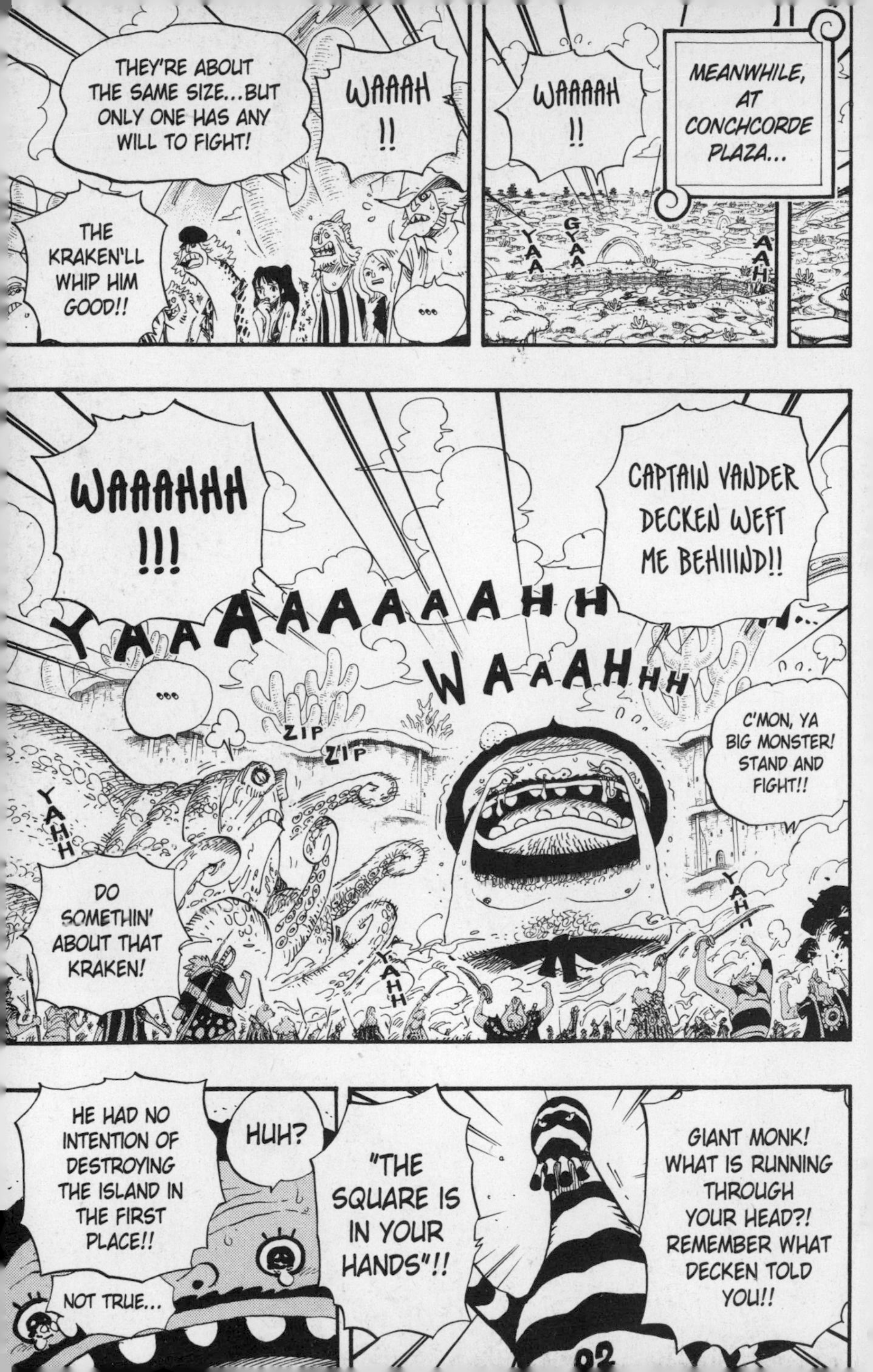
MEANWHILE, AT CONCHCORDE PLAZA...
WAAAAH !!
AAAH
GYAA
YAA
WAAAH !!
THEY'RE ABOUT THE SAME SIZE...BUT ONLY ONE HAS ANY WILL TO FIGHT!
THE KRAKEN'LL WHIP HIM GOOD!!
...
CAPTAIN VANDER DECKEN WEFT ME BEHIIIND!!
WAAAHHH !!!
YAAAAAAAAHH
WAAAHHH
C'MON, YA BIG MONSTER! STAND AND FIGHT!!
YAHH
...
ZIP
ZIP
YAHH
YAHH
DO SOMETHIN' ABOUT THAT KRAKEN!
GIANT MONK! WHAT IS RUNNING THROUGH YOUR HEAD?! REMEMBER WHAT DECKEN TOLD YOU!!
"THE SQUARE IS IN YOUR HANDS"!!
HUH?
HE HAD NO INTENTION OF DESTROYING THE ISLAND IN THE FIRST PLACE!!
NOT TRUE...

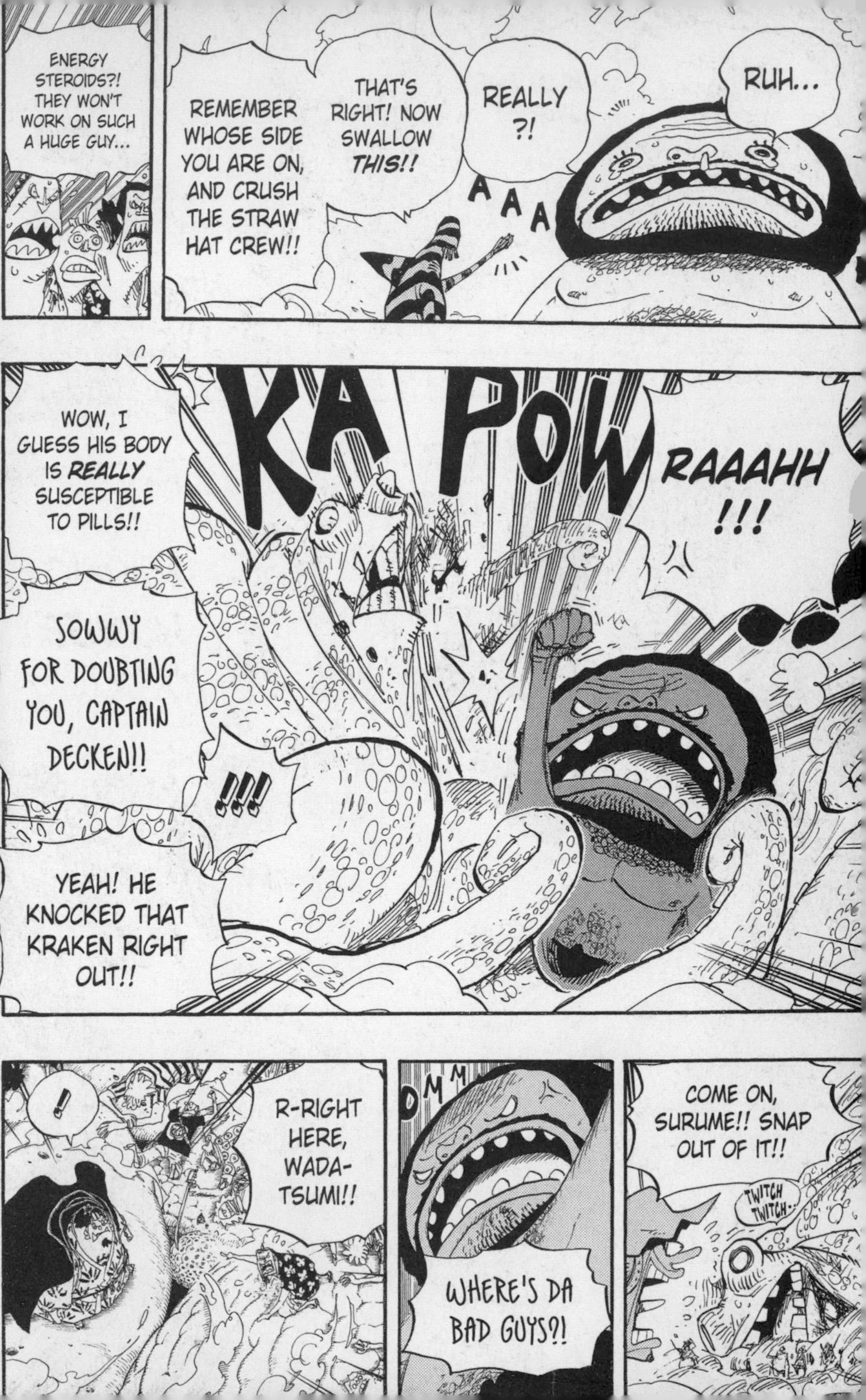
RUH...
REALLY ?!
THAT'S RIGHT! NOW SWALLOW *THIS!!*
AAA
REMEMBER WHOSE SIDE YOU ARE ON, AND CRUSH THE STRAW HAT CREW!!
ENERGY STEROIDS?! THEY WON'T WORK ON SUCH A HUGE GUY...
KA POW
RAAAHH !!!
WOW, I GUESS HIS BODY IS *REALLY* SUSCEPTIBLE TO PILLS!!
!!!
SOWWY FOR DOUBTING YOU, CAPTAIN DECKEN!!
YEAH! HE KNOCKED THAT KRAKEN RIGHT OUT!!
COME ON, SURUME!! SNAP OUT OF IT!!
TWITCH TWITCH...
WHERE'S DA BAD GUYS?!
R-RIGHT HERE, WADA-TSUMI!!
!

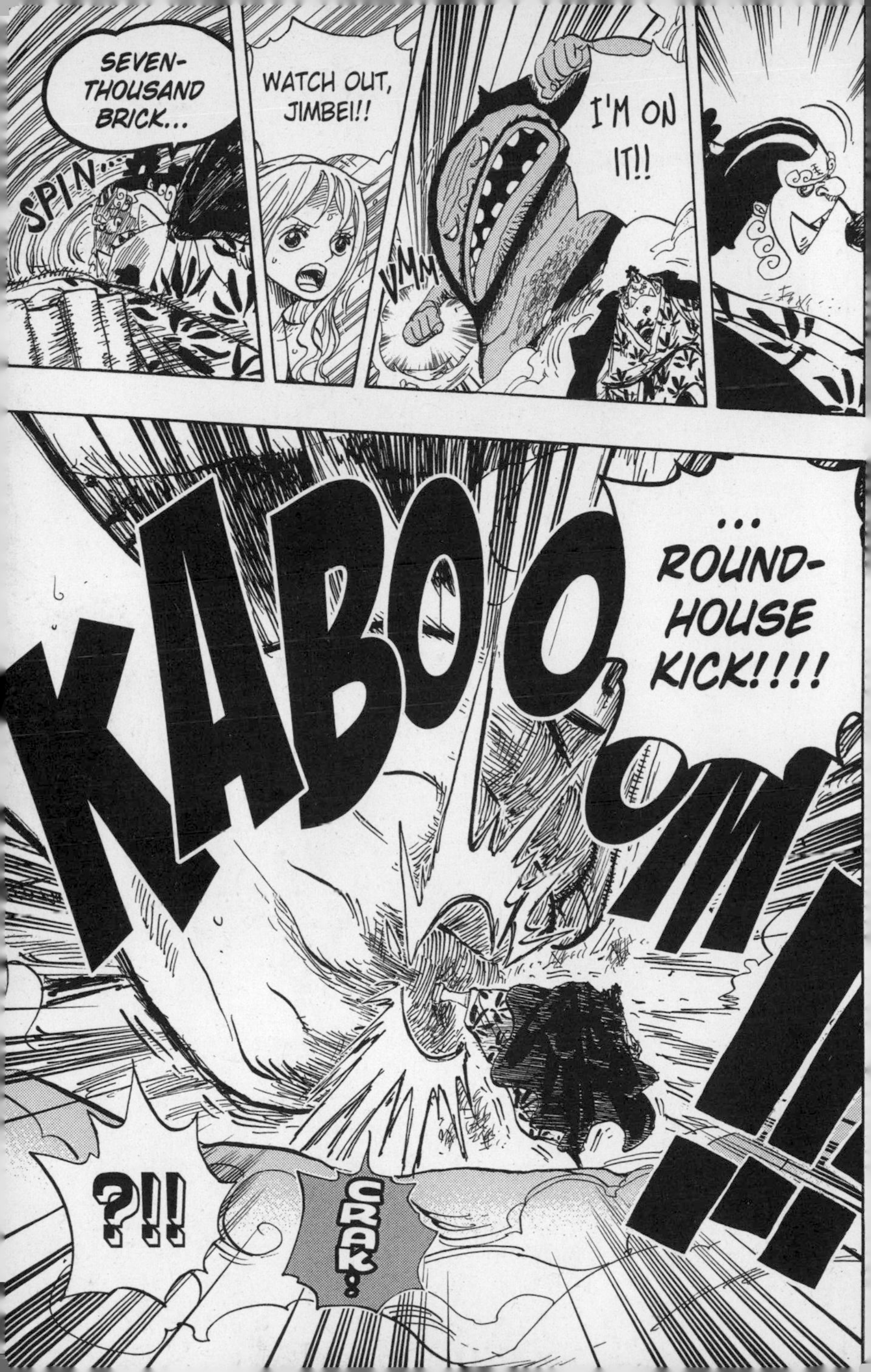
I'M ON IT!!
VMM
WATCH OUT, JIMBEI!!
SEVEN-THOUSAND BRICK...
SPIN
...ROUND-HOUSE KICK!!!!
KABOOM!!!!
CRAK
?!!

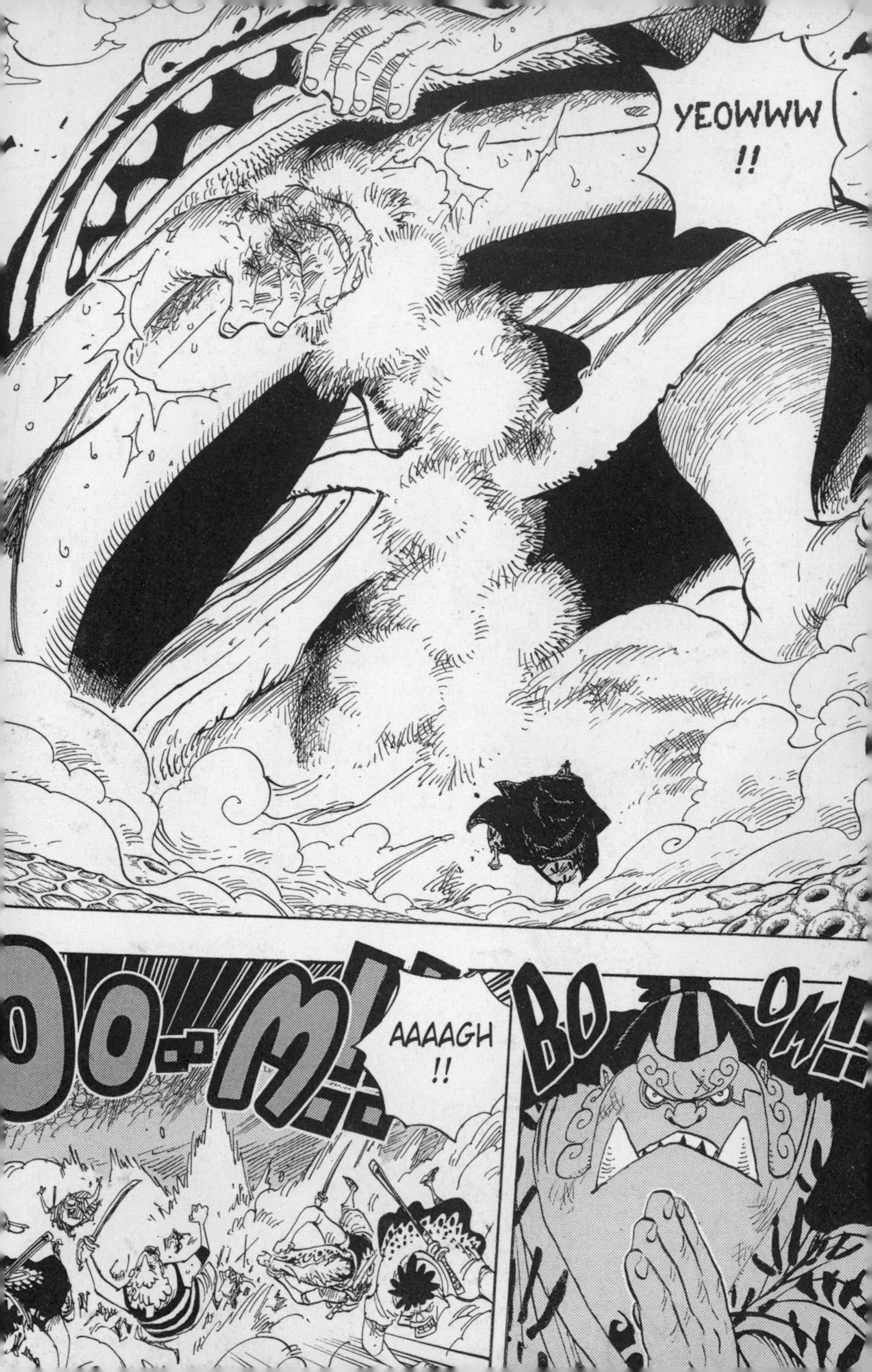
YEOWWW !!
AAAAGH !!

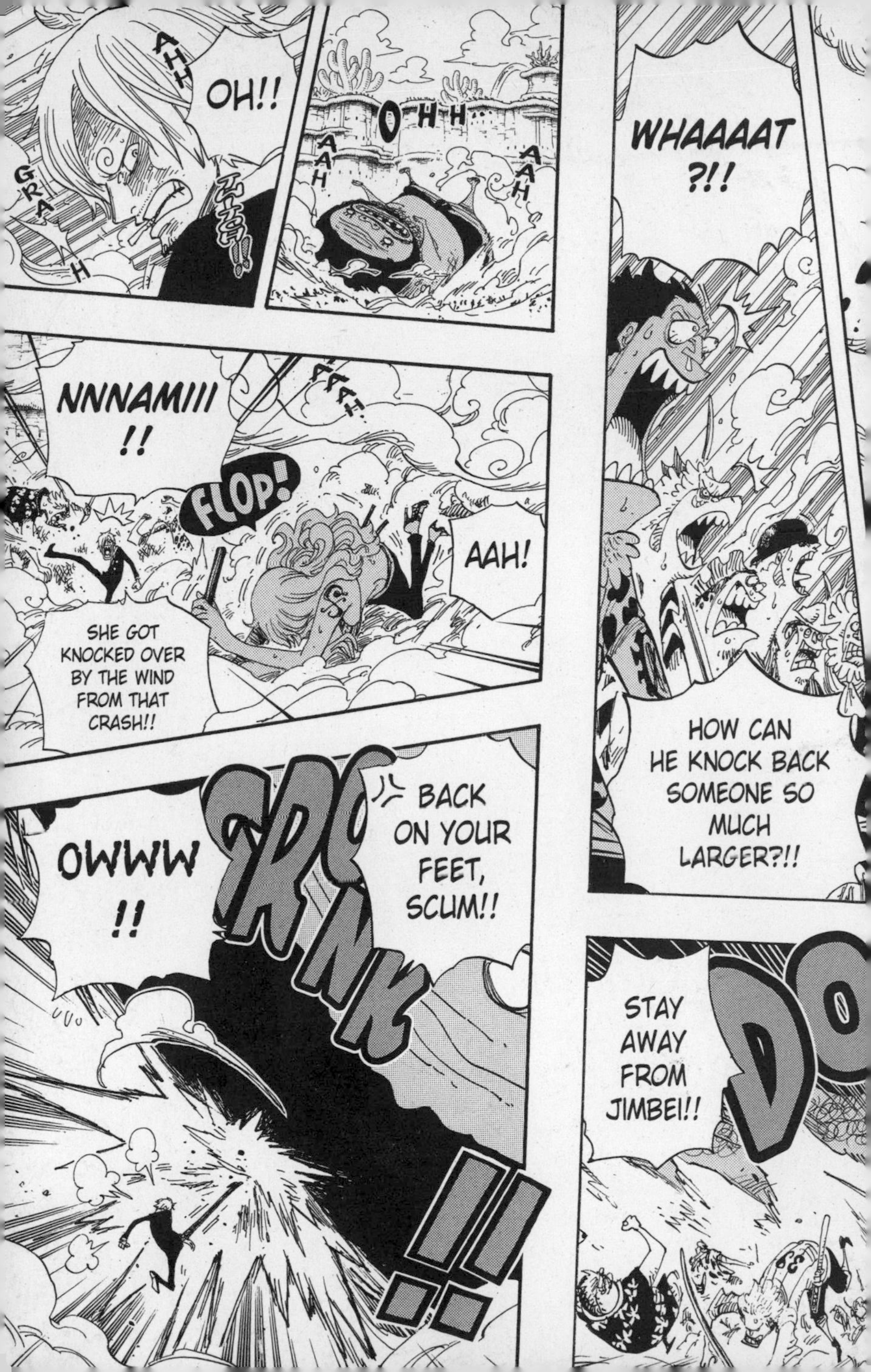
WHAAAAT
?!!
HOW CAN HE KNOCK BACK SOMEONE SO MUCH LARGER?!!
OHH
AAH
AAH
AHH
OH!!
TWITCH!!
GRAAH
NNNAMIII
!!
FLOP!
AAH!
SHE GOT KNOCKED OVER BY THE WIND FROM THAT CRASH!!
BACK ON YOUR FEET, SCUM!!
OWWW
!!
CRINK!!
STAY AWAY FROM JIMBEI!!
DO

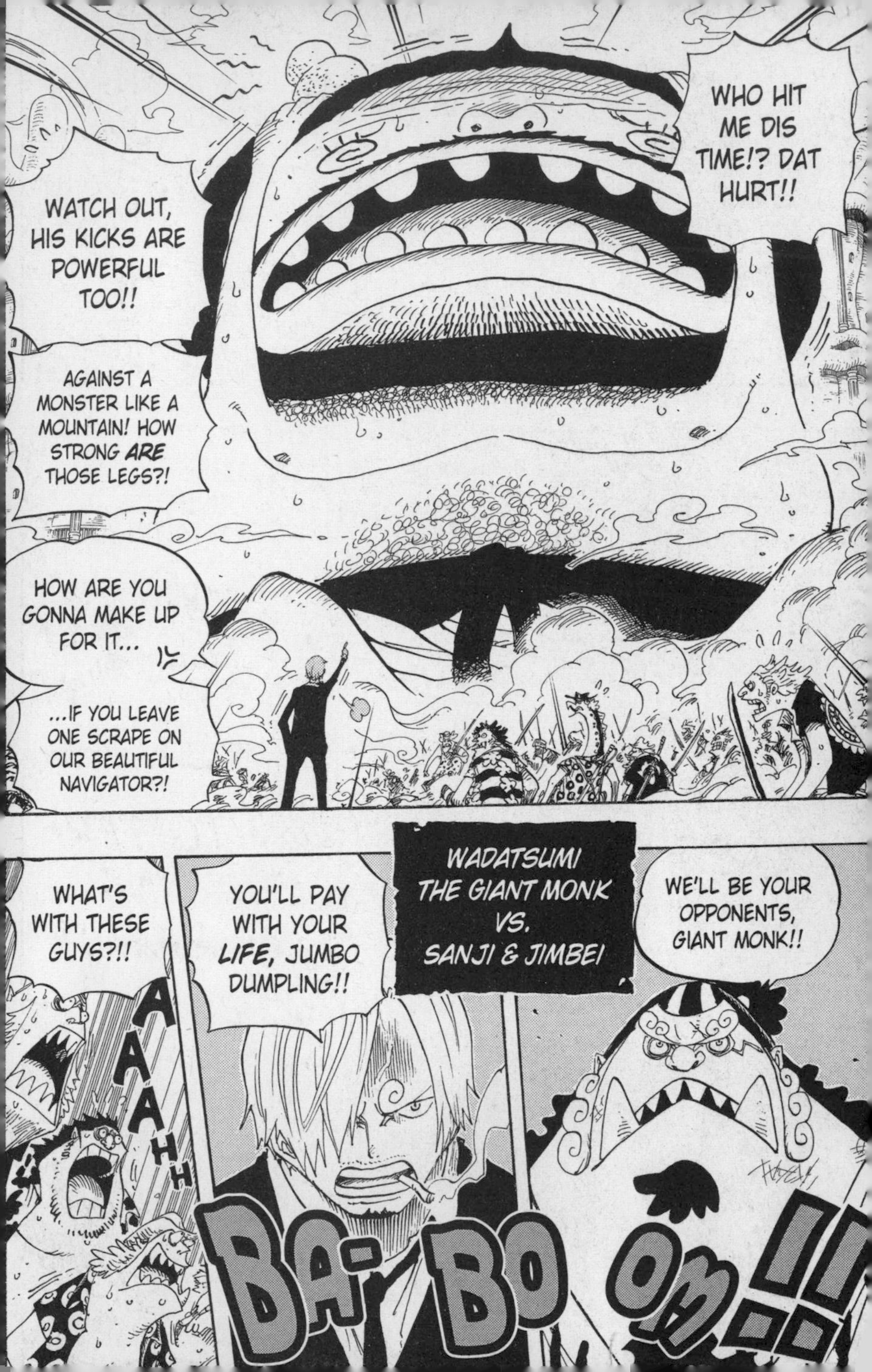
WHO HIT ME DIS TIME!? DAT HURT!!
WATCH OUT, HIS KICKS ARE POWERFUL TOO!!
AGAINST A MONSTER LIKE A MOUNTAIN! HOW STRONG *ARE* THOSE LEGS?!
HOW ARE YOU GONNA MAKE UP FOR IT...
...IF YOU LEAVE ONE SCRAPE ON OUR BEAUTIFUL NAVIGATOR?!
WE'LL BE YOUR OPPONENTS, GIANT MONK!!
WADATSUMI THE GIANT MONK VS. SANJI & JIMBEI
YOU'LL PAY WITH YOUR *LIFE*, JUMBO DUMPLING!!
WHAT'S WITH THESE GUYS?!!
AAAAHH
BA-BOOM!!

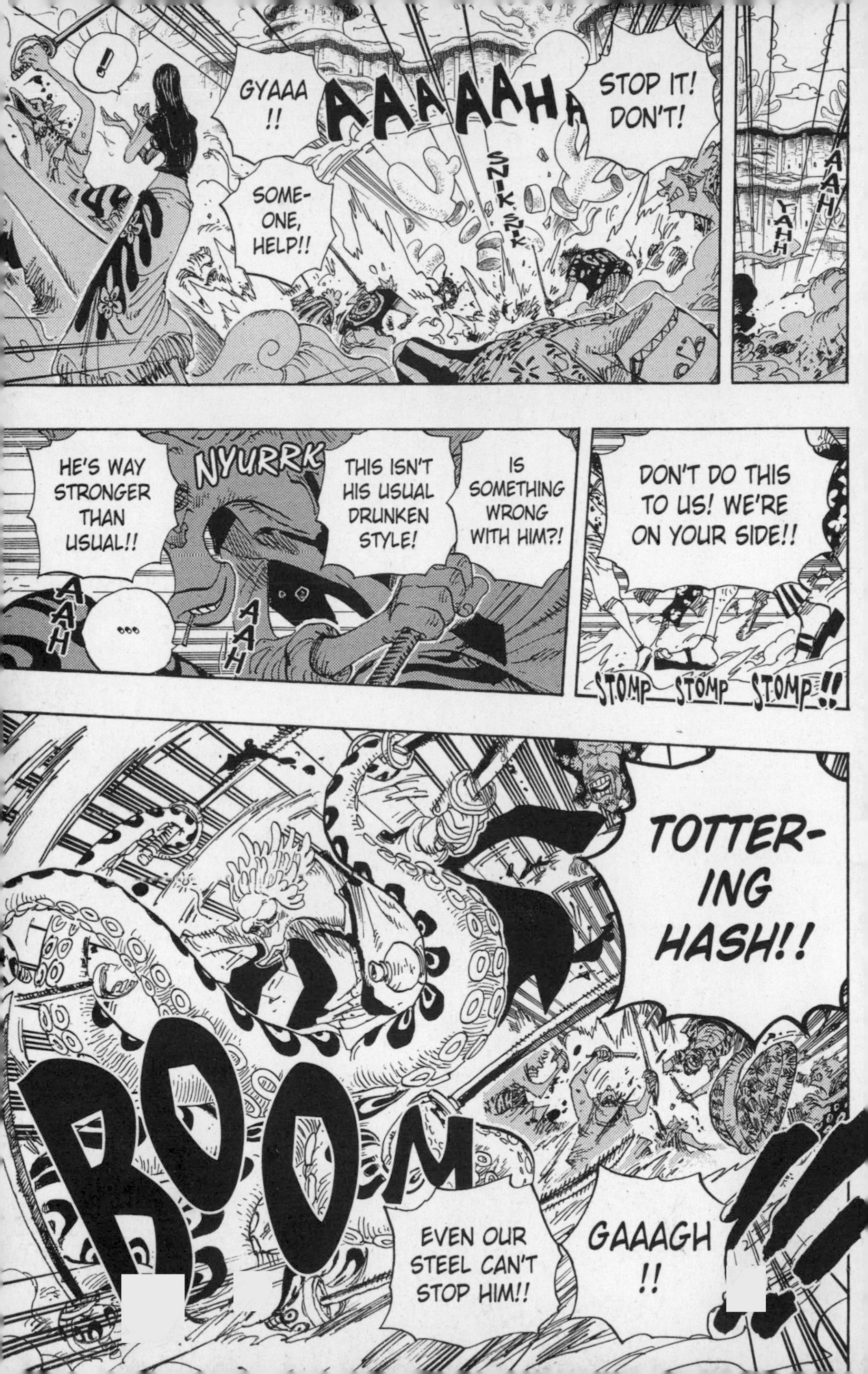
AAAH
YAHH
STOP IT! DON'T!
AAAAAHA
SNIK SNIK
GYAAA !!
SOME-ONE, HELP!!
!
DON'T DO THIS TO US! WE'RE ON YOUR SIDE!!
STOMP STOMP STOMP!!
IS SOMETHING WRONG WITH HIM?!
THIS ISN'T HIS USUAL DRUNKEN STYLE!
NYURRK
HE'S WAY STRONGER THAN USUAL!!
AAH
...
AAH
TOTTER-ING HASH!!
GAAAGH !!
EVEN OUR STEEL CAN'T STOP HIM!!
BOOM!!

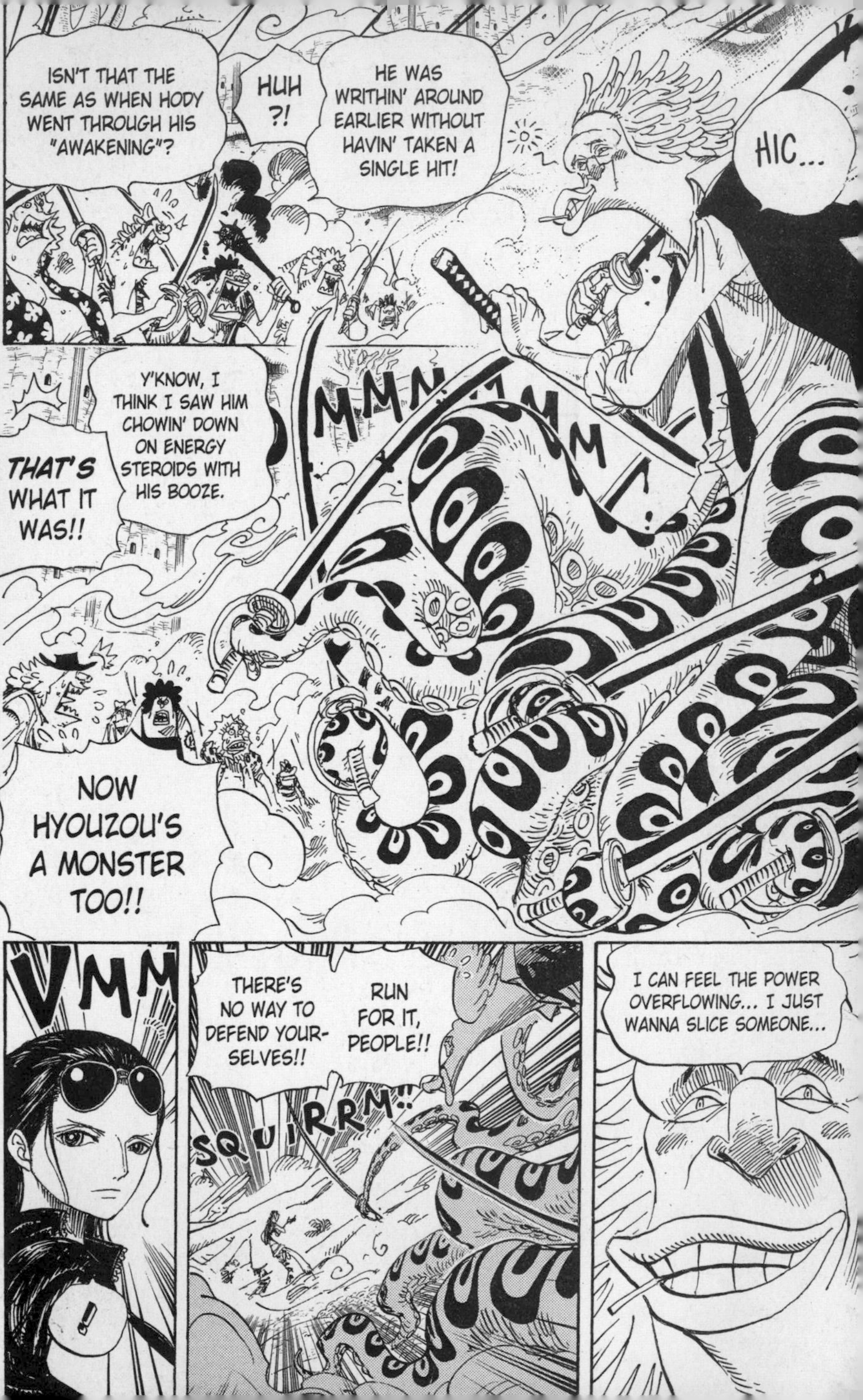
HIC...
HE WAS WRITHIN' AROUND EARLIER WITHOUT HAVIN' TAKEN A SINGLE HIT!
HUH ?!
ISN'T THAT THE SAME AS WHEN HODY WENT THROUGH HIS "AWAKENING"?
MMMMMMM
Y'KNOW, I THINK I SAW HIM CHOWIN' DOWN ON ENERGY STEROIDS WITH HIS BOOZE.
THAT'S WHAT IT WAS!!
NOW HYOUZOU'S A MONSTER TOO!!
I CAN FEEL THE POWER OVERFLOWING... I JUST WANNA SLICE SOMEONE...
RUN FOR IT, PEOPLE!!
THERE'S NO WAY TO DEFEND YOURSELVES!!
SQUIRRRM!!
VMM
!

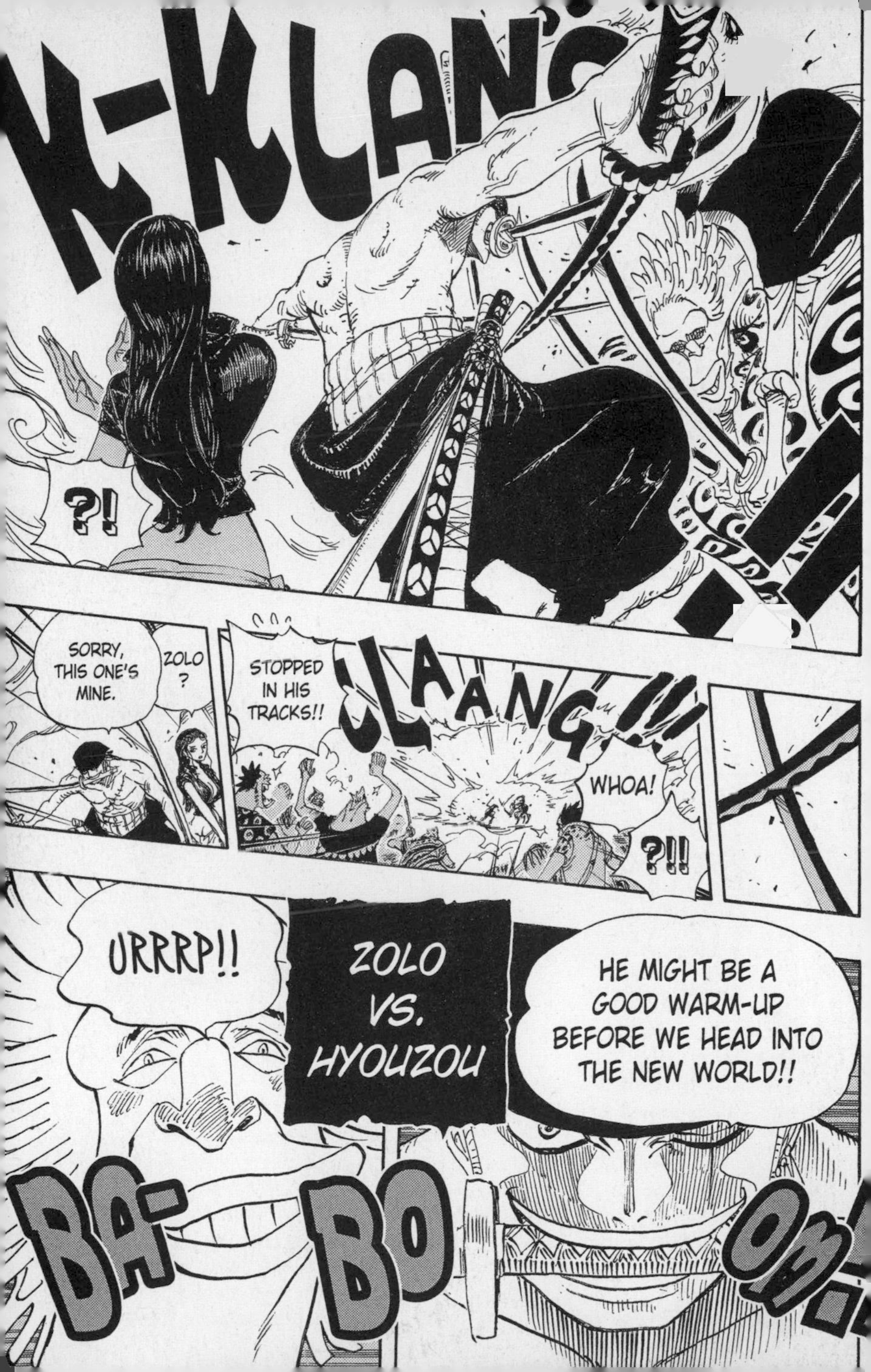
K-KLANG
?!
CLAANG!!!
STOPPED IN HIS TRACKS!!
WHOA!
?!!
ZOLO ?
SORRY, THIS ONE'S MINE.
HE MIGHT BE A GOOD WARM-UP BEFORE WE HEAD INTO THE NEW WORLD!!
ZOLO VS. HYOUZOU
URRRP!!
BA-BO-OM!

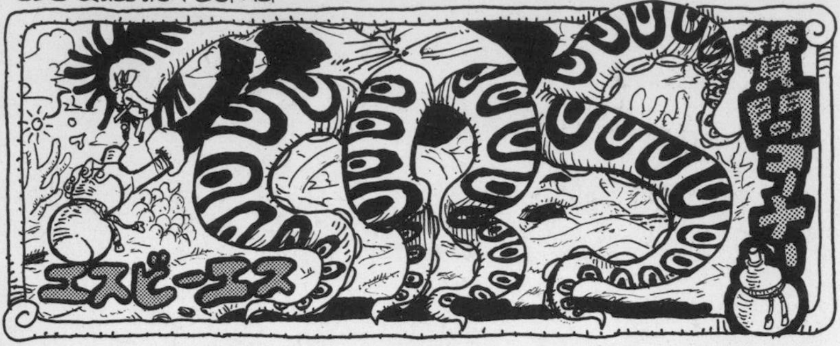
エスピーエス

(Ponio, Aichi)

Q: Greetings! Here's my question! My sister asked me, "Is Ishily, the cute droopy-eyed freckled mermaid at the Mermaid Inlet, a parrotfish mermaid?" Can you answer that for her? She also said, "What are the fish models for the other mermaids?"

--V & UU

A: Yes, that's correct. Ishily the parrotfish, the striped girl who was among the mermaids Caribou kidnapped. As it happens, all those beautiful mermaids at the inlet are dancers at the Mermaid Café. I hear their dances are so gorgeous, they would probably kill Sanji. Here's an introduction to the Mermaid Café's top five dancers.

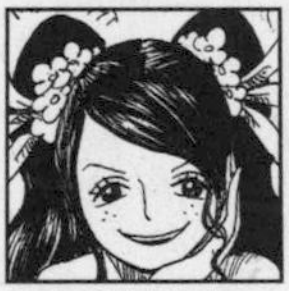
Ishily
(Parrotfish)

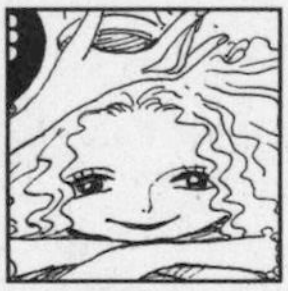
Kairen
(Sole)

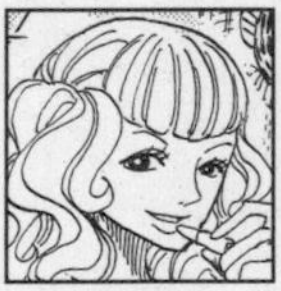
Hiramela
(Flounder)

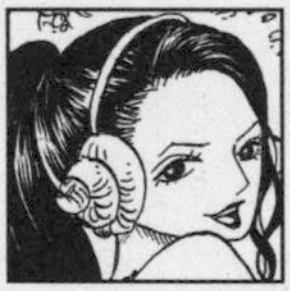
Seira
(Marine Angelfish)

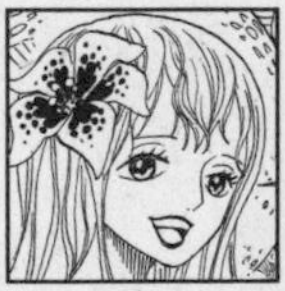
Mello
(Garfish)

Q: Hello! Our whole family loves reading *One Piece*. I've noticed that in the story, you write the "Sun" in "Sun Pirates" in phonetic *kana* rather than Chinese *kanji*. Is there a reason for that? I've always found it curious.

--Makki

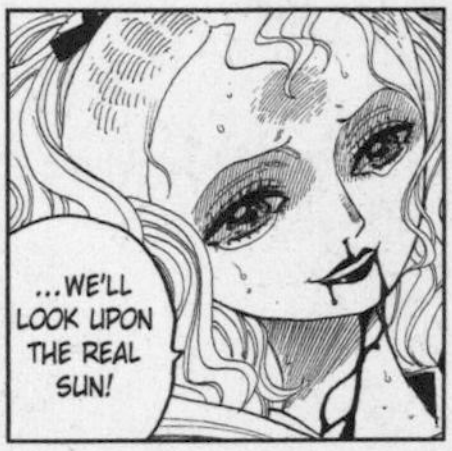
...WE'LL LOOK UPON THE REAL SUN!

A: I see. This actually wasn't an intentional choice on my part; it's just something I always found myself doing. Let's say, for example, I'm writing dialogue for children, or when Luffy's being particularly stupid. In these cases I often use much fewer complex *kanji* and more simple phonetic spellings. That's because those characters may not really grasp the meaning of what they're saying, and the precise definitions of the *kanji* would probably be too complicated for them. Now consider this: the Fish-Men are speaking of a "sun" that exists far above the miles of water over their heads. It's something they rarely ever see, something beyond their knowledge. That's why I choose to write it with simple *kana* rather than more precise *kanji*. It just makes more sense to me.

Chapter 640:
ABOVE FISH-MAN ISLAND

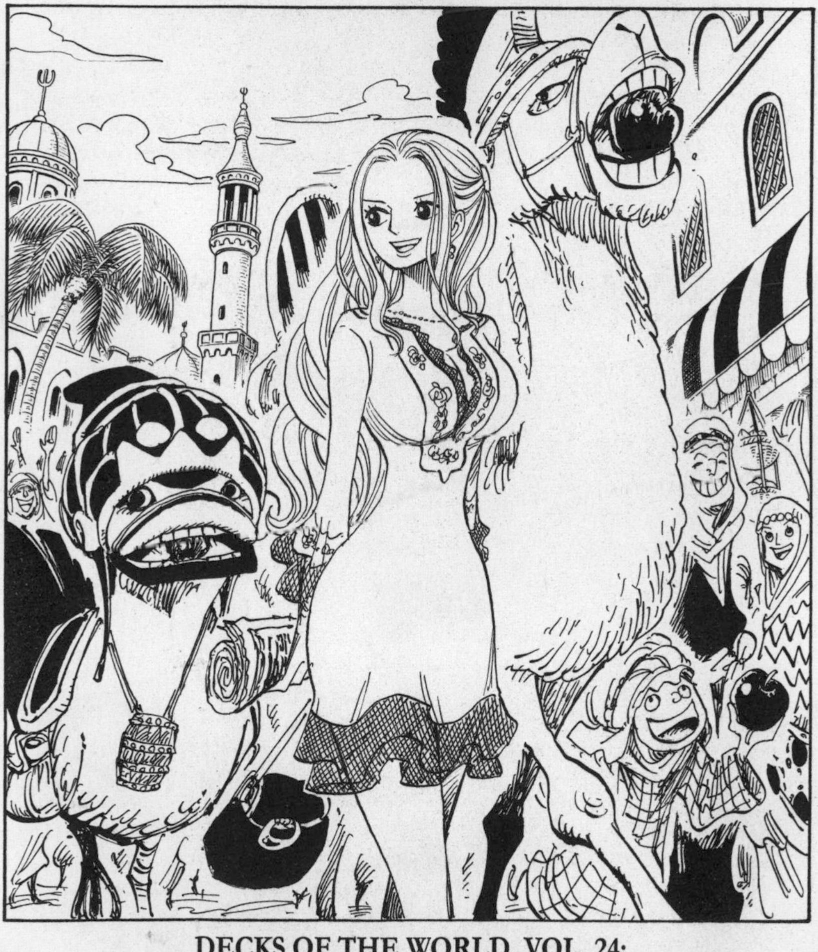

DECKS OF THE WORLD, VOL. 24:
"KINGDOM OF ALABASTA—VIVI, AGE 18"

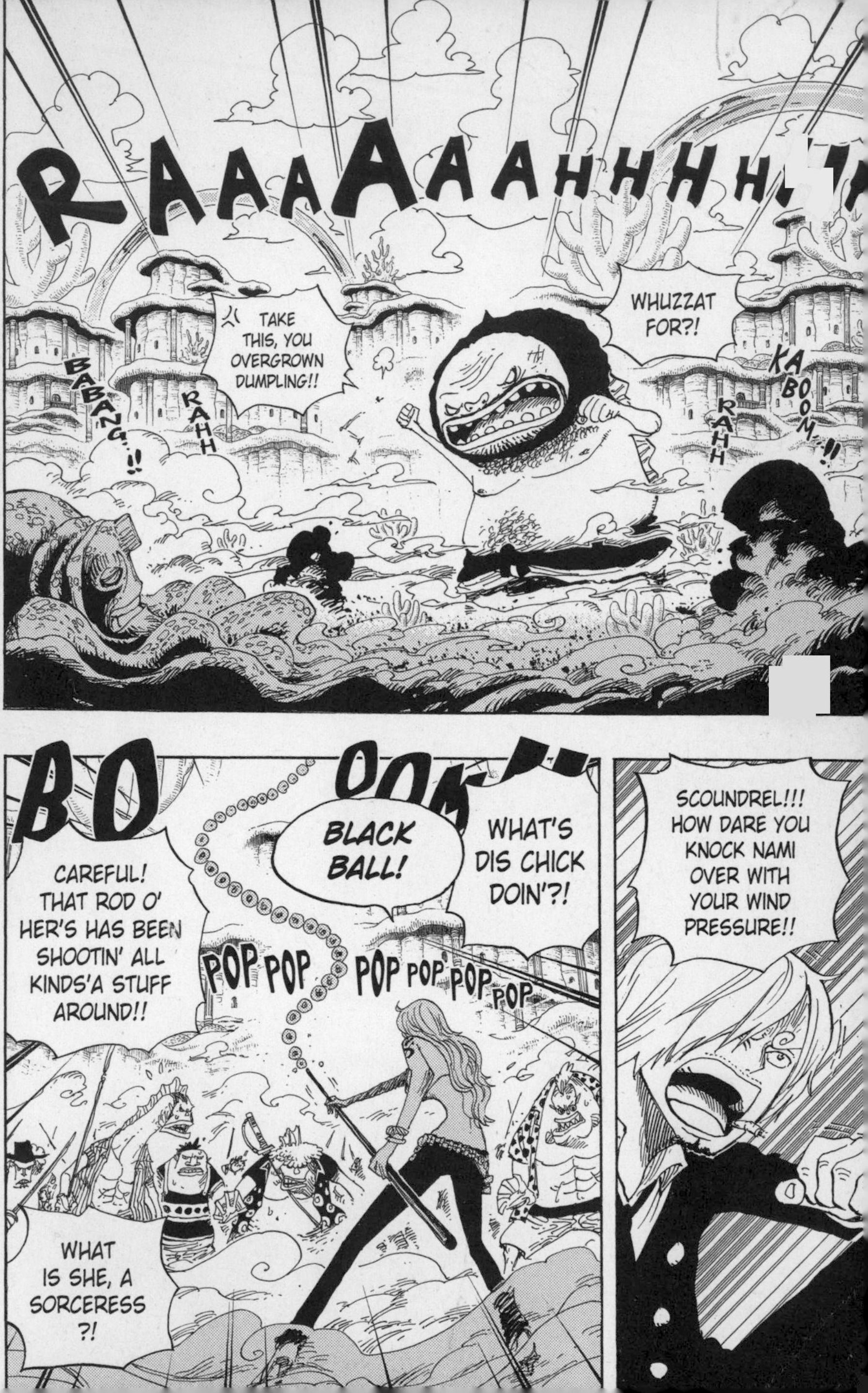
RAAAAAAHHHHH!!
WHUZZAT FOR?!
KABOOM!!
RAHH
TAKE THIS, YOU OVERGROWN DUMPLING!!
RAHH
BABANG!!
SCOUNDREL!!! HOW DARE YOU KNOCK NAMI OVER WITH YOUR WIND PRESSURE!!
BOOOM!!
WHAT'S DIS CHICK DOIN'?!
BLACK BALL!
CAREFUL! THAT ROD O' HER'S HAS BEEN SHOOTIN' ALL KINDS'A STUFF AROUND!!
POP POP POP POP POP POP
WHAT IS SHE, A SORCERESS ?!

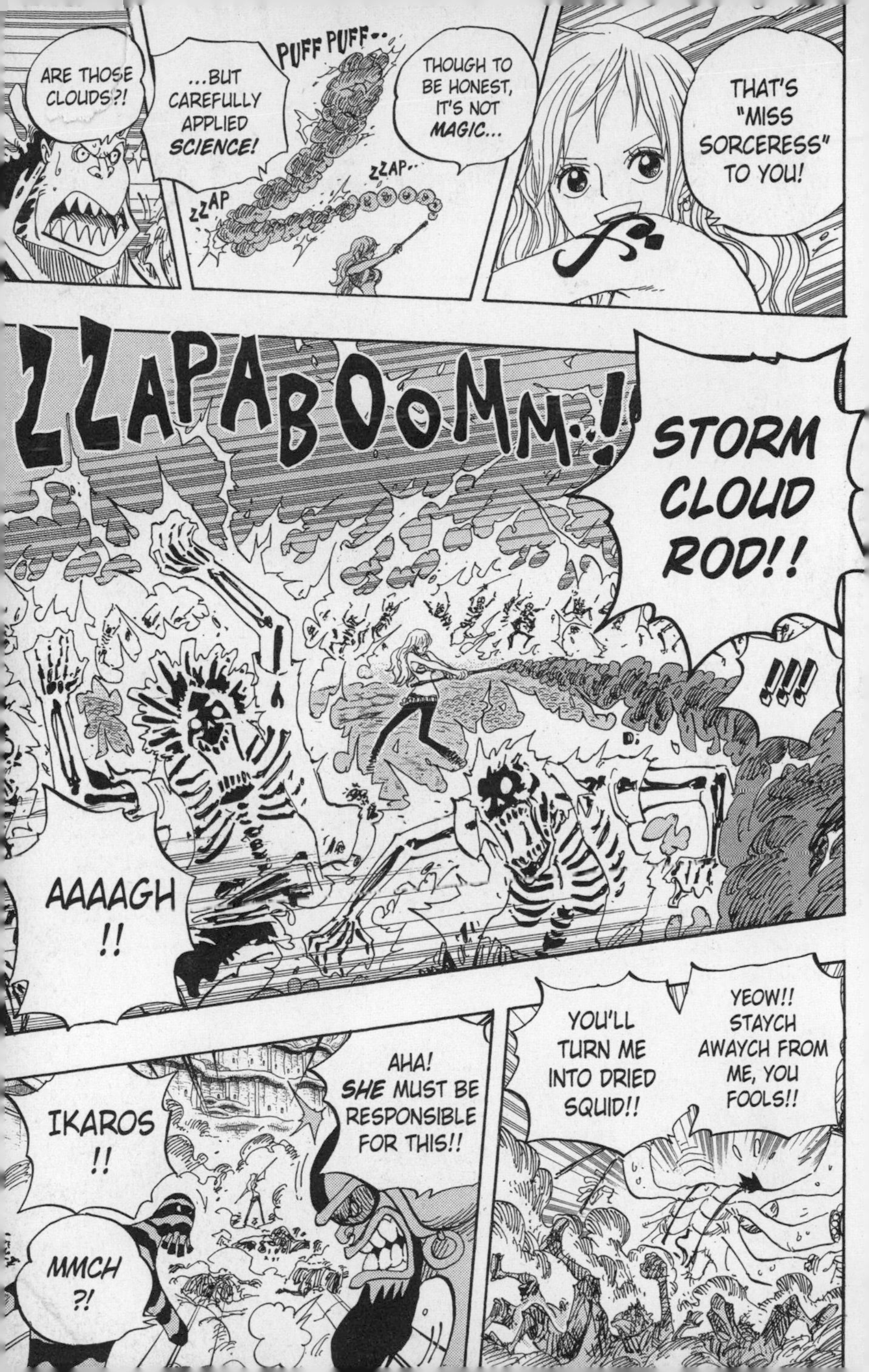
THAT'S "MISS SORCERESS" TO YOU!
THOUGH TO BE HONEST, IT'S NOT MAGIC...
PUFF PUFF...
...BUT CAREFULLY APPLIED SCIENCE!
ZZAP...
ZZAP
ARE THOSE CLOUDS?!
STORM CLOUD ROD!!
ZZAPABOOMM..!
!!!
AAAAGH !!
YEOW!! STAYCH AWAYCH FROM ME, YOU FOOLS!!
YOU'LL TURN ME INTO DRIED SQUID!!
AHA! SHE MUST BE RESPONSIBLE FOR THIS!!
IKAROS !!
MMCH ?!

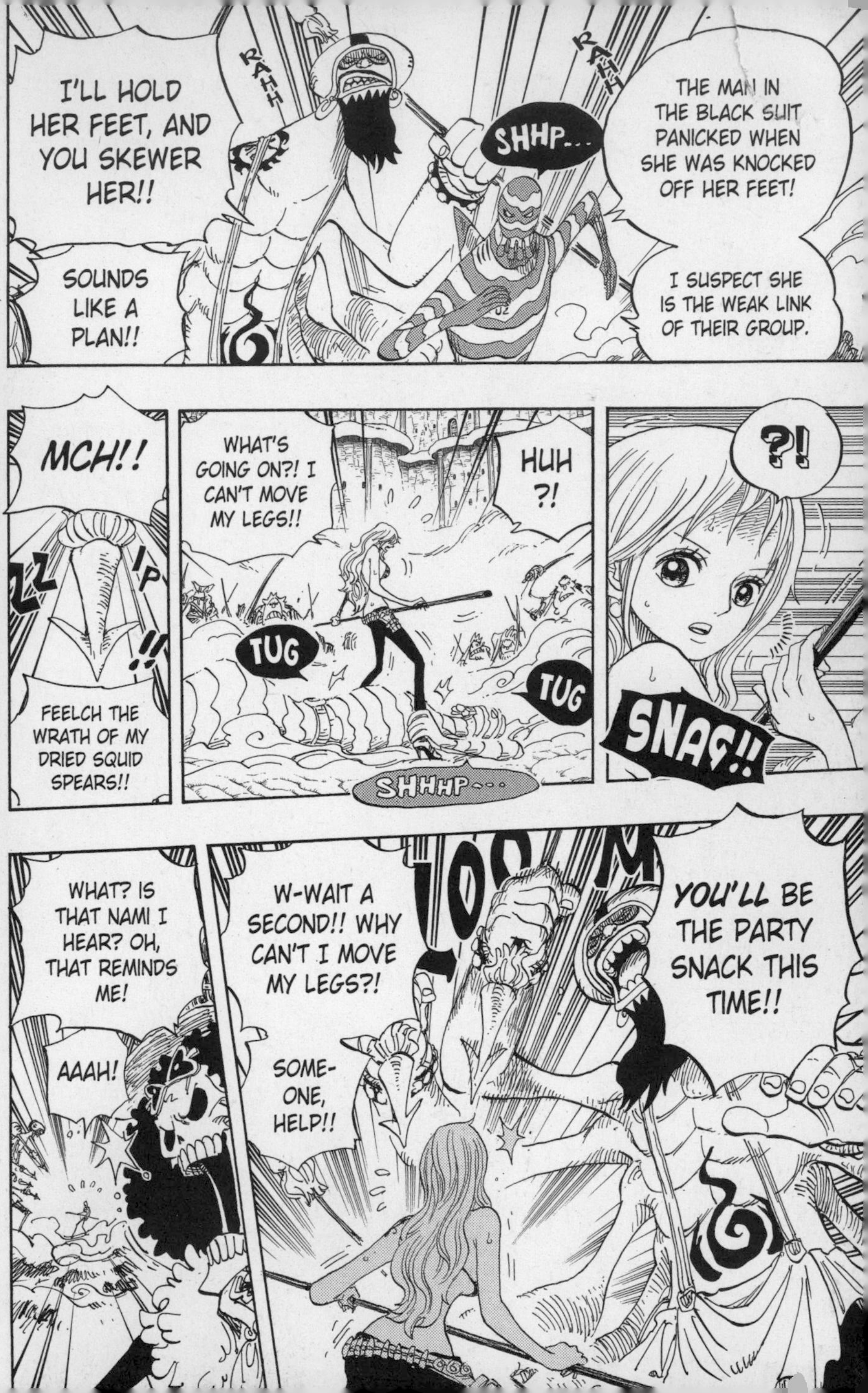
THE MAN IN THE BLACK SUIT PANICKED WHEN SHE WAS KNOCKED OFF HER FEET!
RAHH
SHHP...
RAHH
I'LL HOLD HER FEET, AND YOU SKEWER HER!!
I SUSPECT SHE IS THE WEAK LINK OF THEIR GROUP.
SOUNDS LIKE A PLAN!!
?!
SNAG!!
HUH ?!
WHAT'S GOING ON?! I CAN'T MOVE MY LEGS!!
TUG
TUG
SHHHP...
MCH!!
FEELCH THE WRATH OF MY DRIED SQUID SPEARS!!
YOU'LL BE THE PARTY SNACK THIS TIME!!
W-WAIT A SECOND!! WHY CAN'T I MOVE MY LEGS?!
SOME-ONE, HELP!!
WHAT? IS THAT NAMI I HEAR? OH, THAT REMINDS ME!
AAAH!

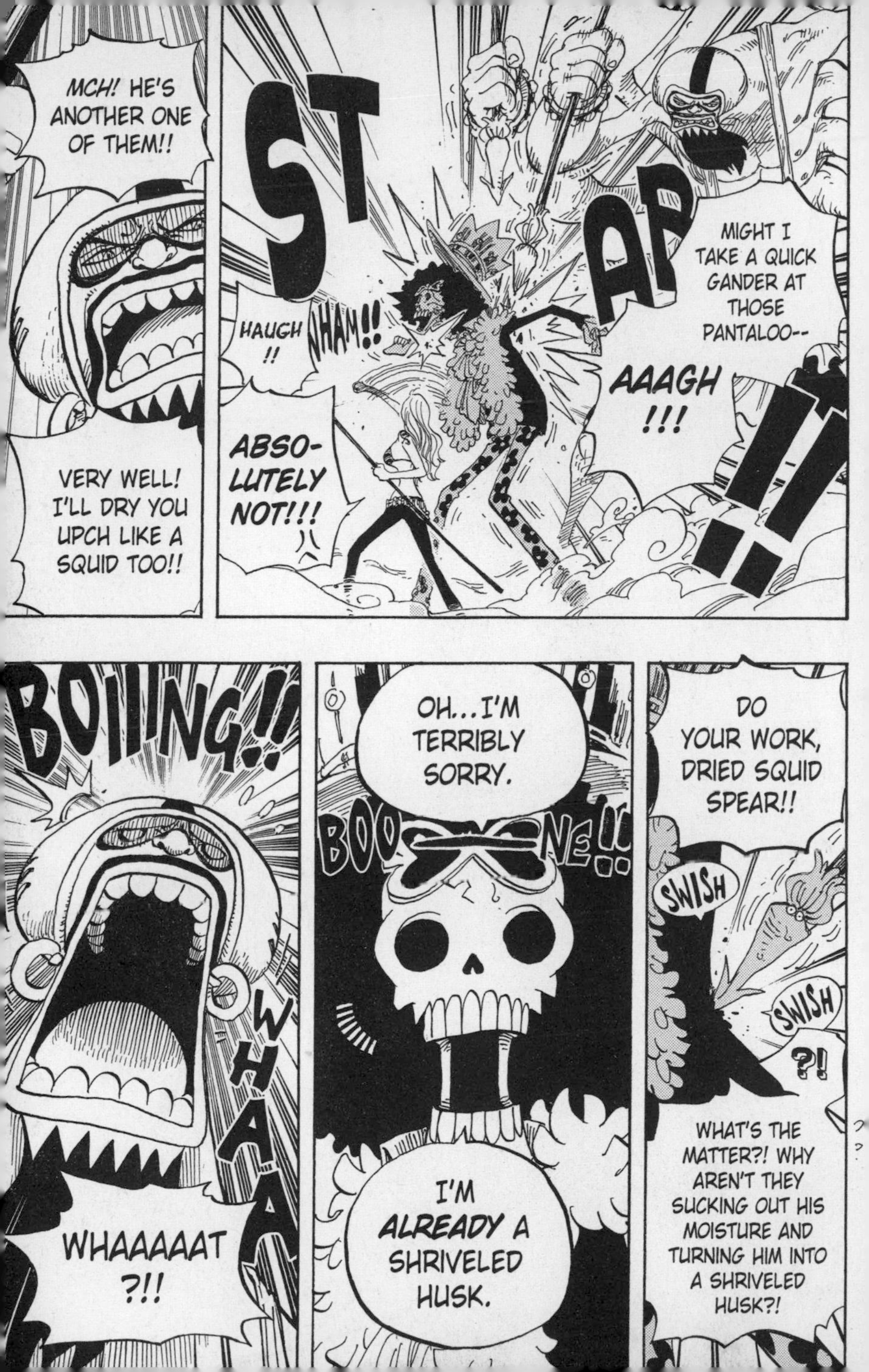
ST
AP
MIGHT I TAKE A QUICK GANDER AT THOSE PANTALOO--
AAAGH !!!
!!
WHAM!!
HAUGH !!
ABSO-LUTELY NOT!!!
MCH! HE'S ANOTHER ONE OF THEM!!
VERY WELL! I'LL DRY YOU UPCH LIKE A SQUID TOO!!
DO YOUR WORK, DRIED SQUID SPEAR!!
SWISH
SWISH
?!
WHAT'S THE MATTER?! WHY AREN'T THEY SUCKING OUT HIS MOISTURE AND TURNING HIM INTO A SHRIVELED HUSK?!
OH...I'M TERRIBLY SORRY.
BOO NE!!
I'M *ALREADY* A SHRIVELED HUSK.
BOIIING!!
WHAAA
WHAAAAAT ?!!

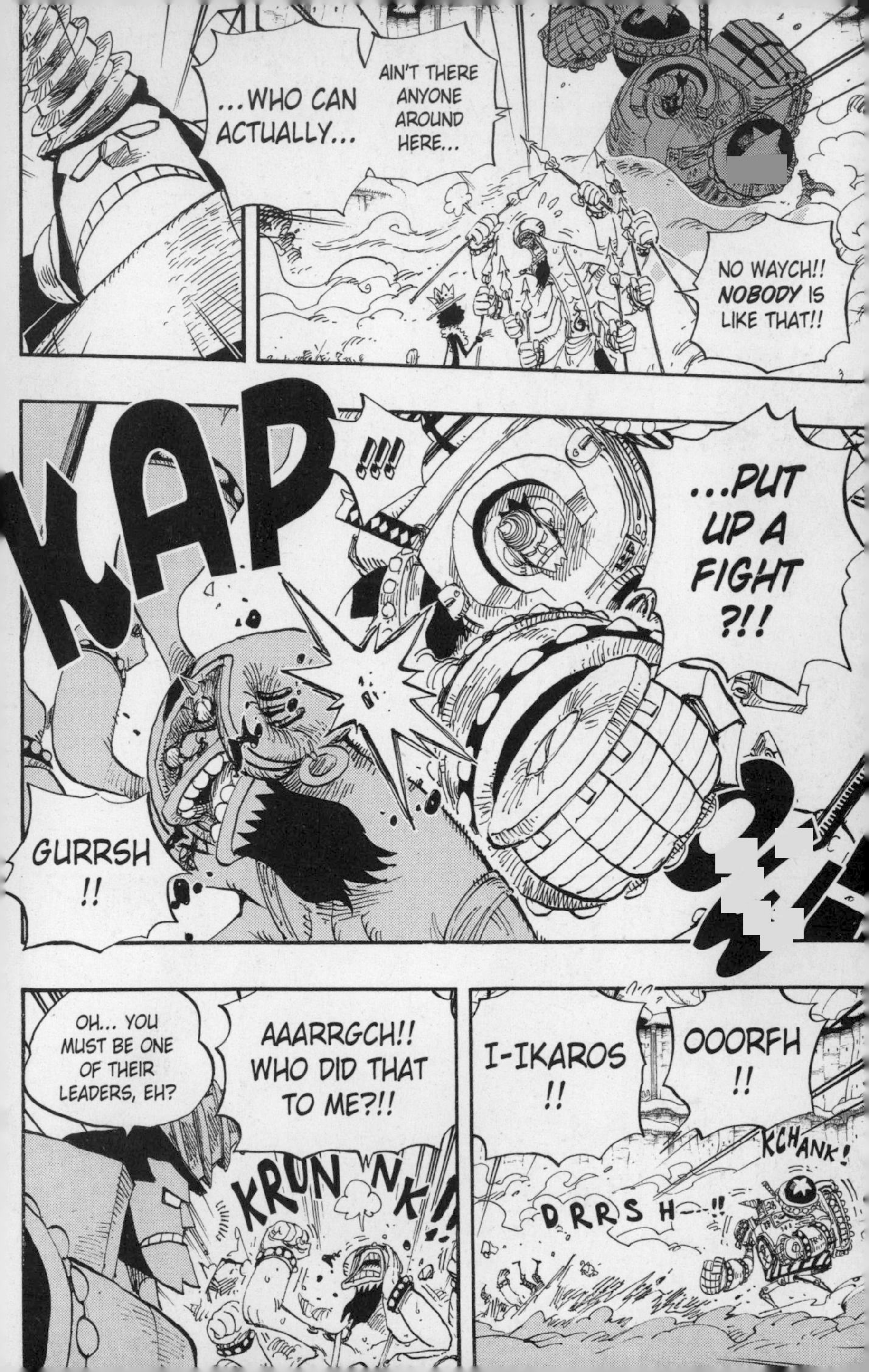
NO WAYCH!! *NOBODY* IS LIKE THAT!!
AIN'T THERE ANYONE AROUND HERE...
...WHO CAN ACTUALLY...
KAP!!!
...PUT UP A FIGHT?!!
GURRSH!!
OOORFH!!
I-IKAROS!!
KCHANK!
DRRSH—!!
AAARRGCH!! WHO DID THAT TO ME?!!
OH... YOU MUST BE ONE OF THEIR LEADERS, EH?
KRUNNK!!

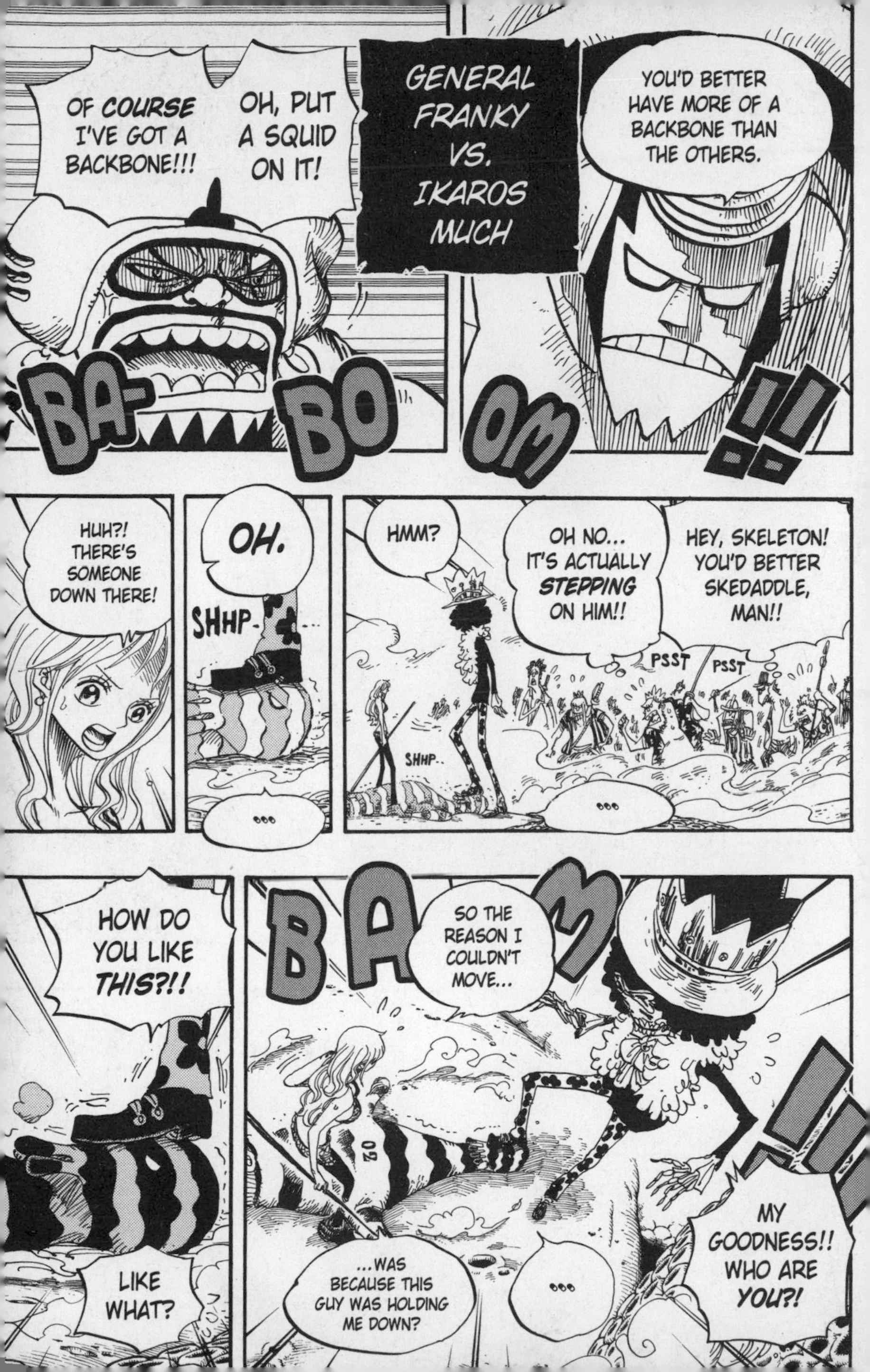
YOU'D BETTER HAVE MORE OF A BACKBONE THAN THE OTHERS.
GENERAL FRANKY VS. IKAROS MUCH
OH, PUT A SQUID ON IT!
OF COURSE I'VE GOT A BACKBONE!!!
BA-BOOM!!
HEY, SKELETON! YOU'D BETTER SKEDADDLE, MAN!!
OH NO... IT'S ACTUALLY STEPPING ON HIM!!
HMM?
PSST
PSST
SHHP..
...
OH.
SHHP-
...
HUH?! THERE'S SOMEONE DOWN THERE!
BAM
SO THE REASON I COULDN'T MOVE...
!!
MY GOODNESS!! WHO ARE YOU?!
...
...WAS BECAUSE THIS GUY WAS HOLDING ME DOWN?
HOW DO YOU LIKE THIS?!!
LIKE WHAT?

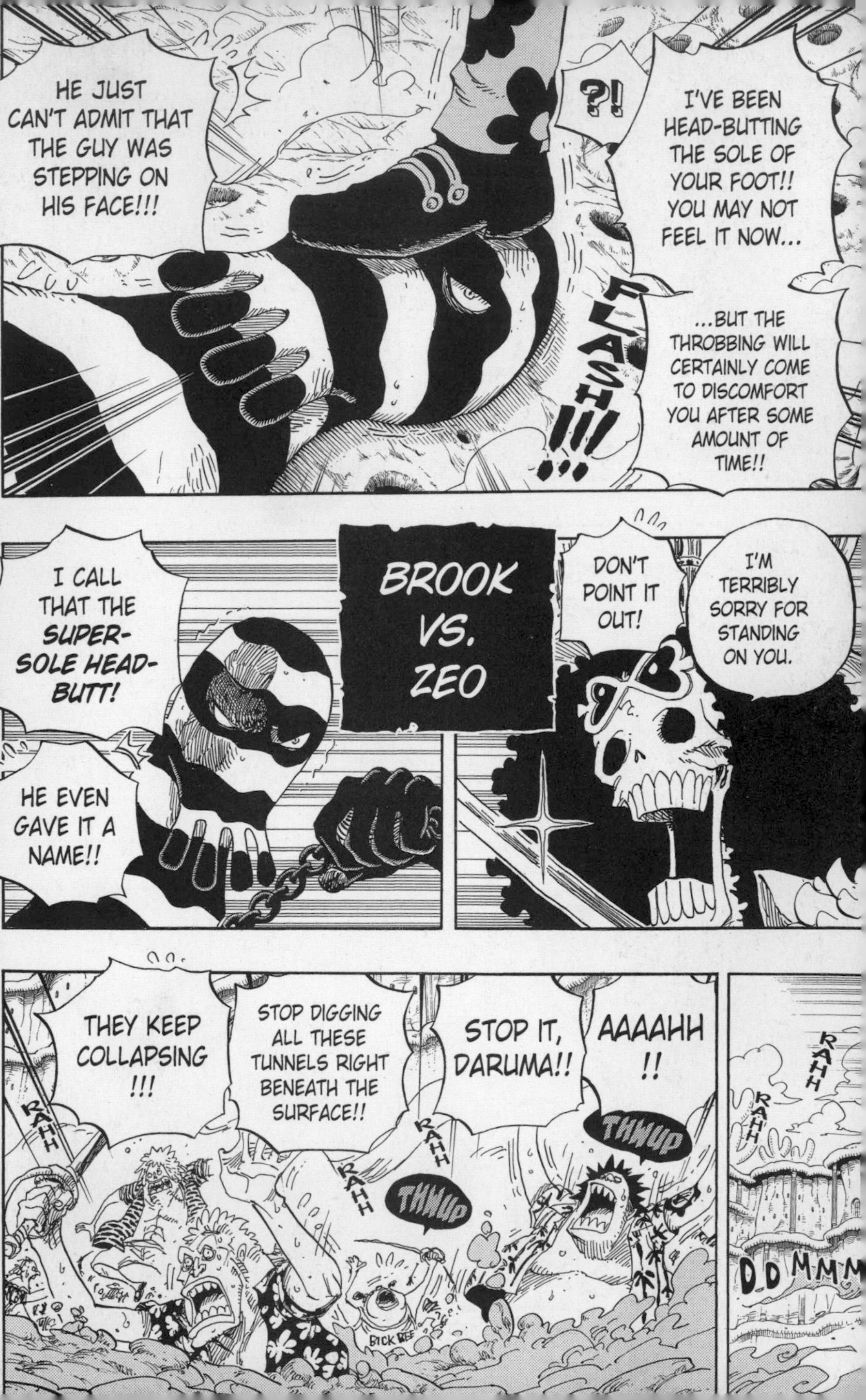
?!
I'VE BEEN HEAD-BUTTING THE SOLE OF YOUR FOOT!! YOU MAY NOT FEEL IT NOW...
...BUT THE THROBBING WILL CERTAINLY COME TO DISCOMFORT YOU AFTER SOME AMOUNT OF TIME!!
FLASH!!!
HE JUST CAN'T ADMIT THAT THE GUY WAS STEPPING ON HIS FACE!!!
I'M TERRIBLY SORRY FOR STANDING ON YOU.
DON'T POINT IT OUT!
BROOK VS. ZEO
I CALL THAT THE **SUPER-SOLE HEAD-BUTT!**
HE EVEN GAVE IT A NAME!!
RAHH
RAHH
D.D MMM
AAAAHH!!
STOP IT, DARUMA!!
STOP DIGGING ALL THESE TUNNELS RIGHT BENEATH THE SURFACE!!
THEY KEEP COLLAPSING!!!
THWUP
RAHH
THWUP
RAHH
RAHH

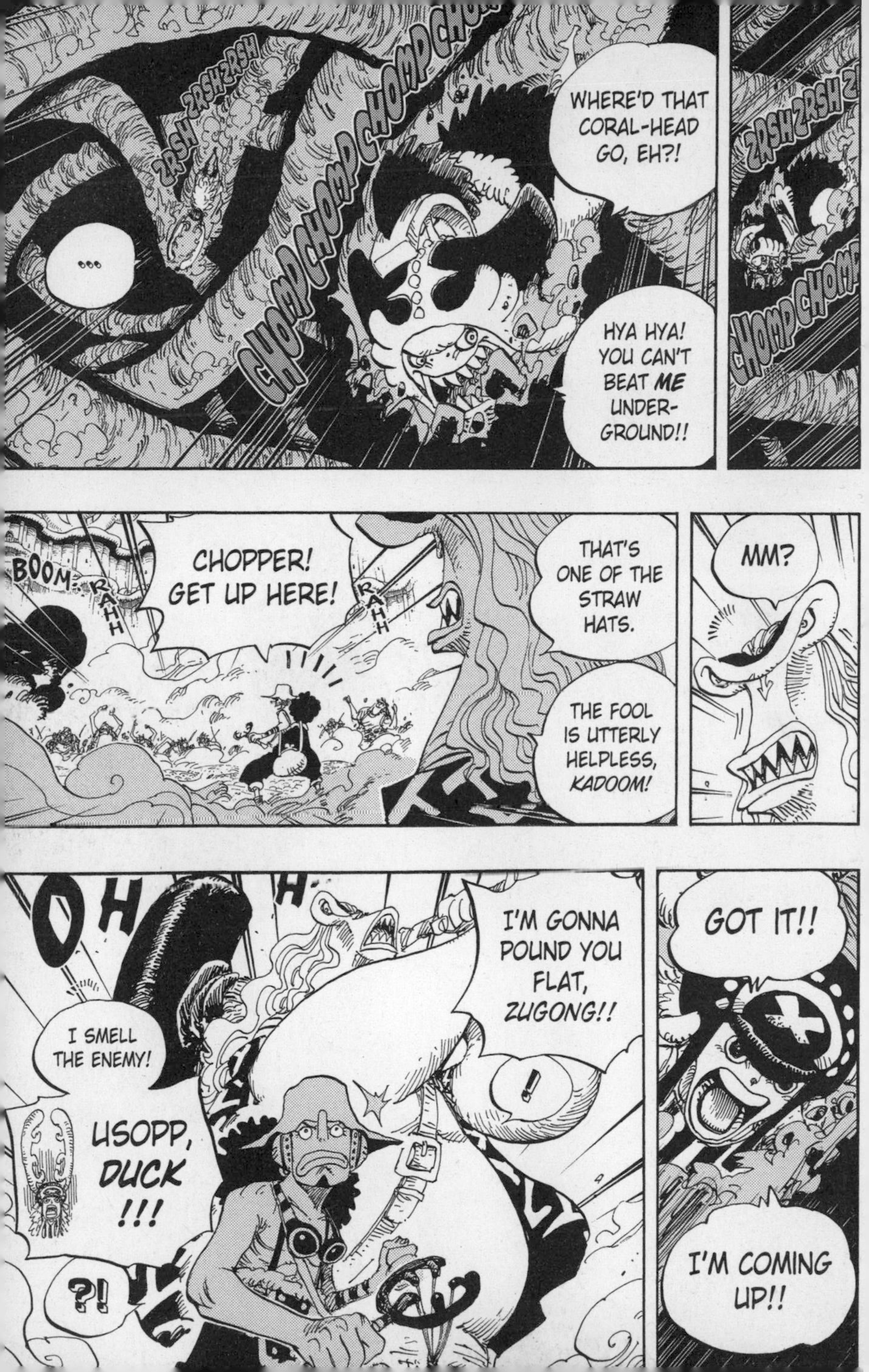
ZRSH ZRSH
CHOMP CHOMP
WHERE'D THAT CORAL-HEAD GO, EH?!
HYA HYA! YOU CAN'T BEAT *ME* UNDERGROUND!!
ZRSH ZRSH ZRSH ZRSH
CHOMP CHOMP CHOMP CHOMP
...
MM?
THAT'S ONE OF THE STRAW HATS.
THE FOOL IS UTTERLY HELPLESS, *KADOOM!*
RAHH
CHOPPER! GET UP HERE!
RAHH
BOOM
GOT IT!!
I'M COMING UP!!
I'M GONNA POUND YOU FLAT, ZUGONG!!
!
OH
I SMELL THE ENEMY!
USOPP, DUCK !!!
?!

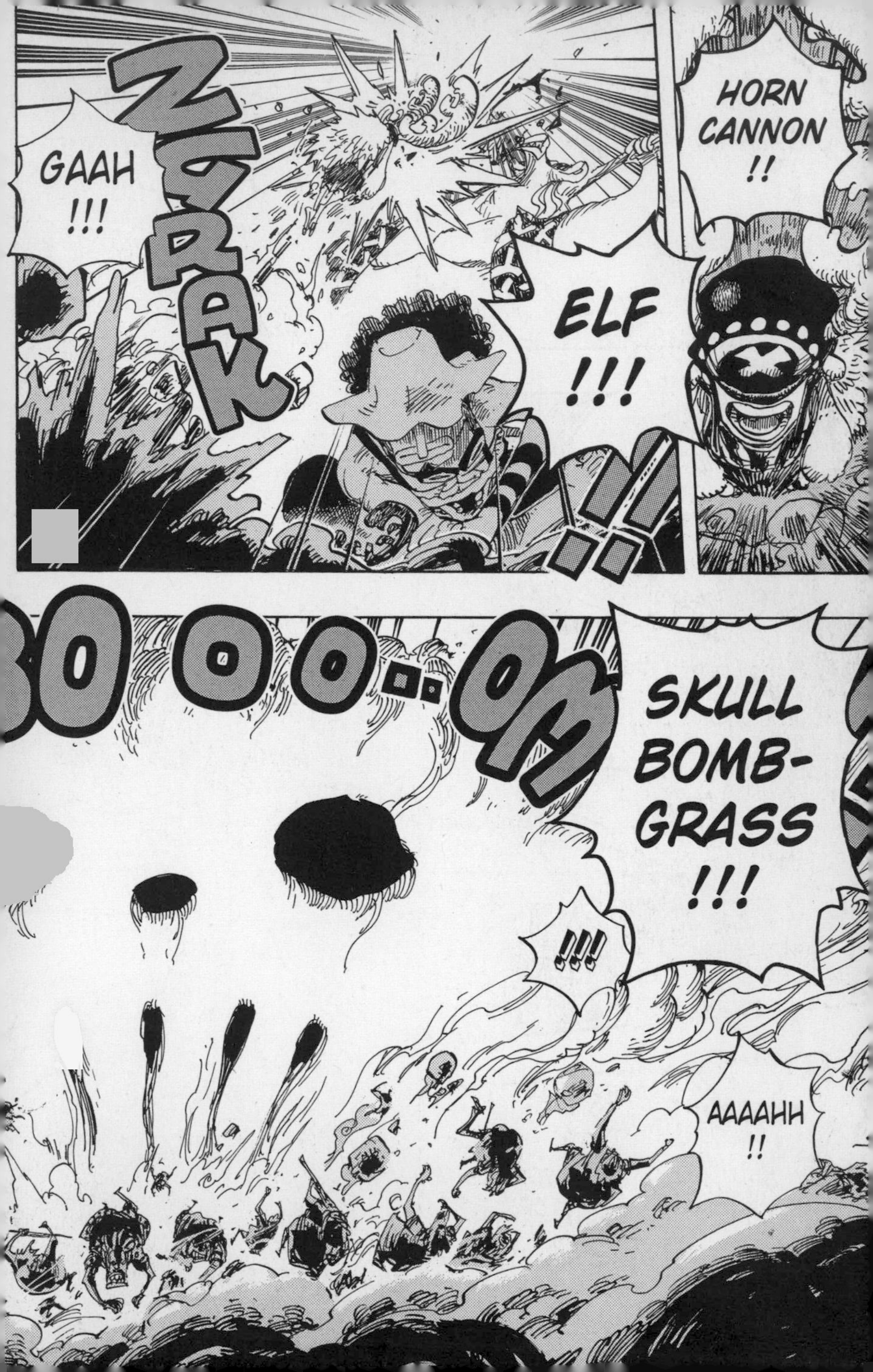
HORN CANNON !!
ELF !!!
!!
GAAH !!!
SKULL BOMB-GRASS !!!
BOOOO..OM
!!!
AAAAH !!

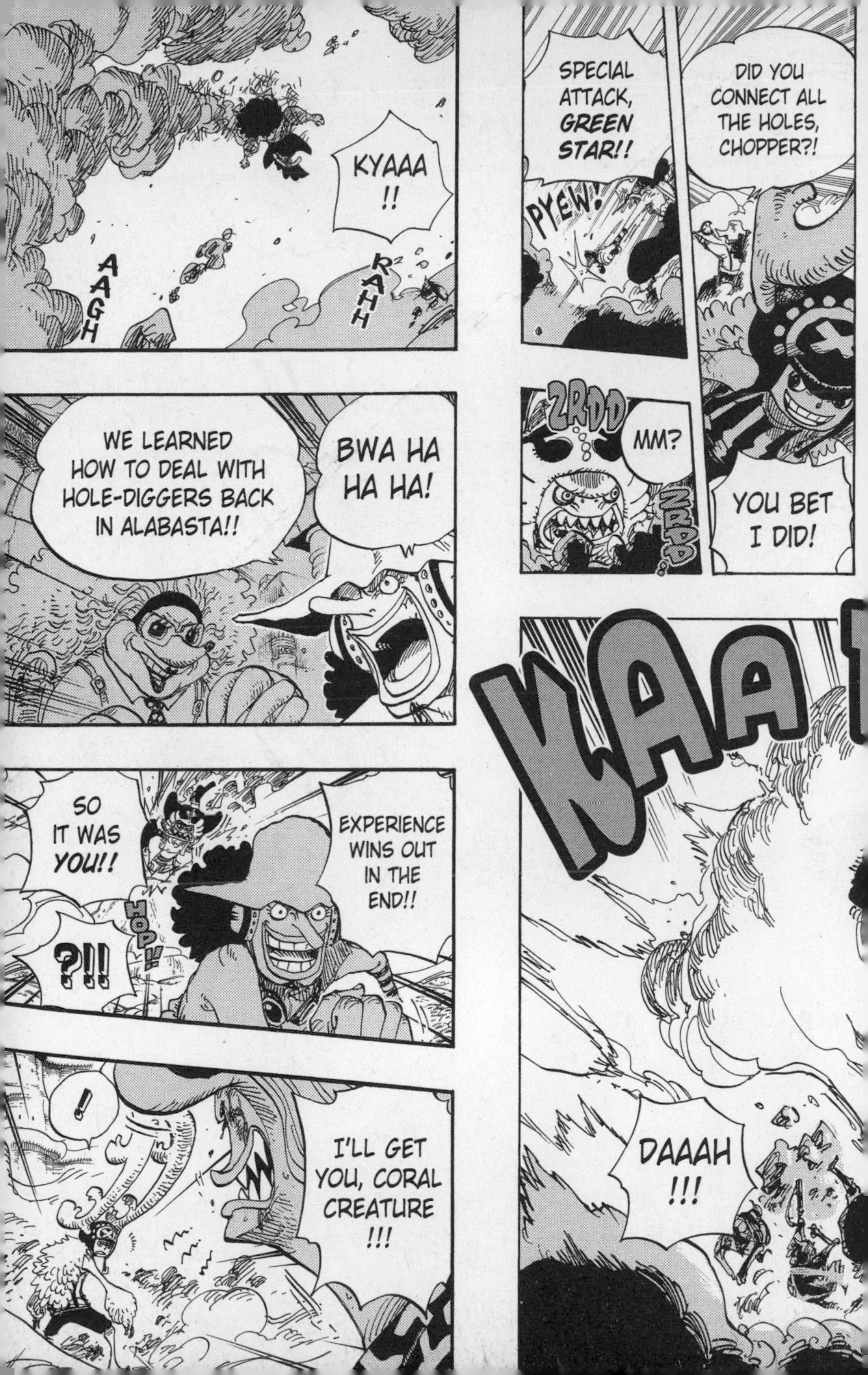
DID YOU CONNECT ALL THE HOLES, CHOPPER?!
YOU BET I DID!
SPECIAL ATTACK, GREEN STAR!!
PYEW
ZRDD
MM?
ZRDD
KAA
DAAAH !!!
KYAAA !!
RAHH
AAGH
BWA HA HA HA!
WE LEARNED HOW TO DEAL WITH HOLE-DIGGERS BACK IN ALABASTA!!
EXPERIENCE WINS OUT IN THE END!!
HOP
SO IT WAS YOU!!
?!!
I'LL GET YOU, CORAL CREATURE !!!
!

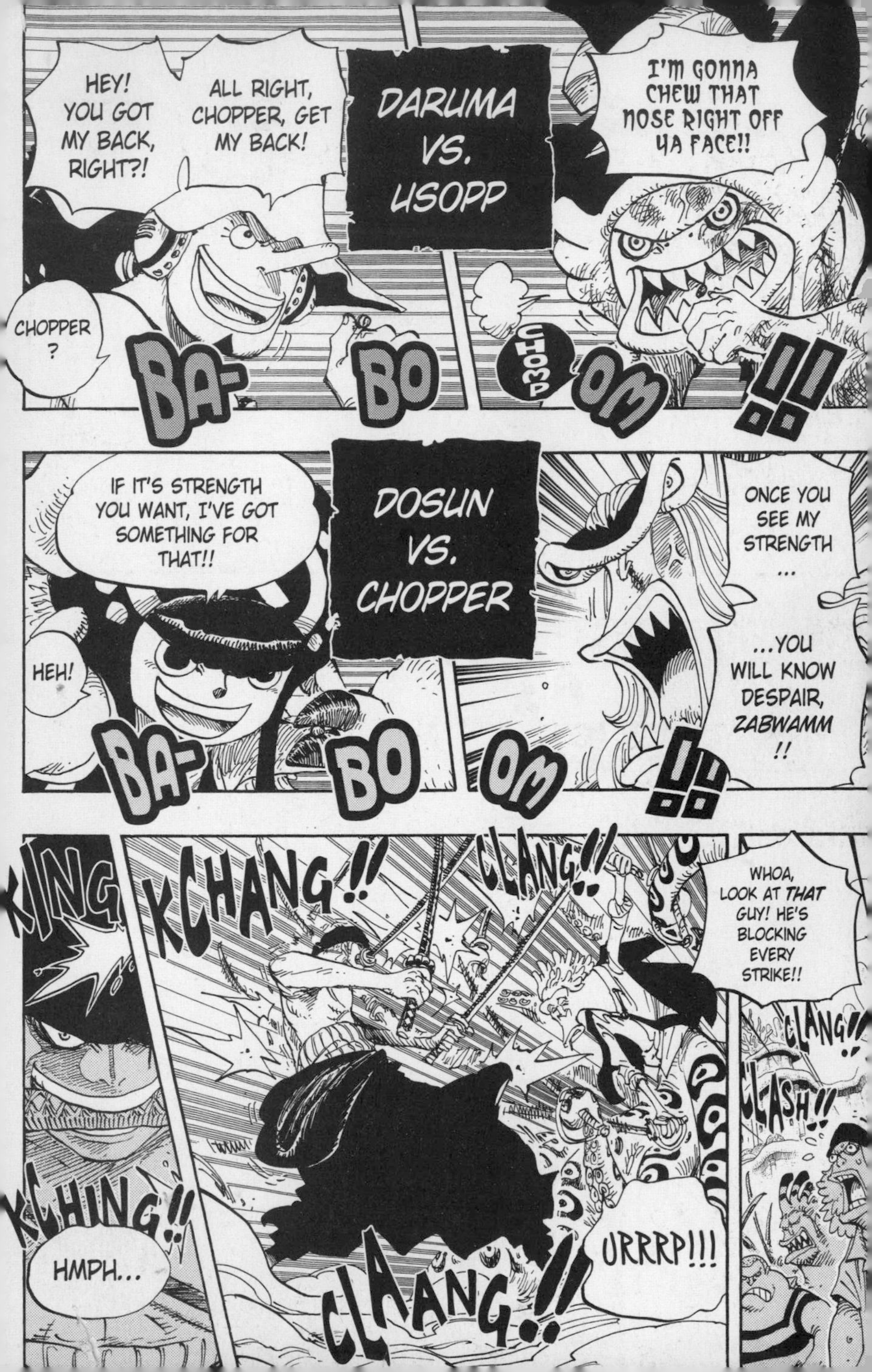
I'M GONNA CHEW THAT NOSE RIGHT OFF YA FACE!!
CHOMP
DARUMA VS. USOPP
ALL RIGHT, CHOPPER, GET MY BACK!
HEY! YOU GOT MY BACK, RIGHT?!
CHOPPER ?
BA-BO-OM!!
ONCE YOU SEE MY STRENGTH ...
...YOU WILL KNOW DESPAIR, ZABWAMM !!
DOSUN VS. CHOPPER
IF IT'S STRENGTH YOU WANT, I'VE GOT SOMETHING FOR THAT!!
HEH!
BA-BO-OM!!
WHOA, LOOK AT *THAT* GUY! HE'S BLOCKING EVERY STRIKE!!
CLANG!!
CLASH!!
CLANG!!
KCHANG!!
URRRP!!!
CLAANG!!
KING
KCHING!!
HMPH...

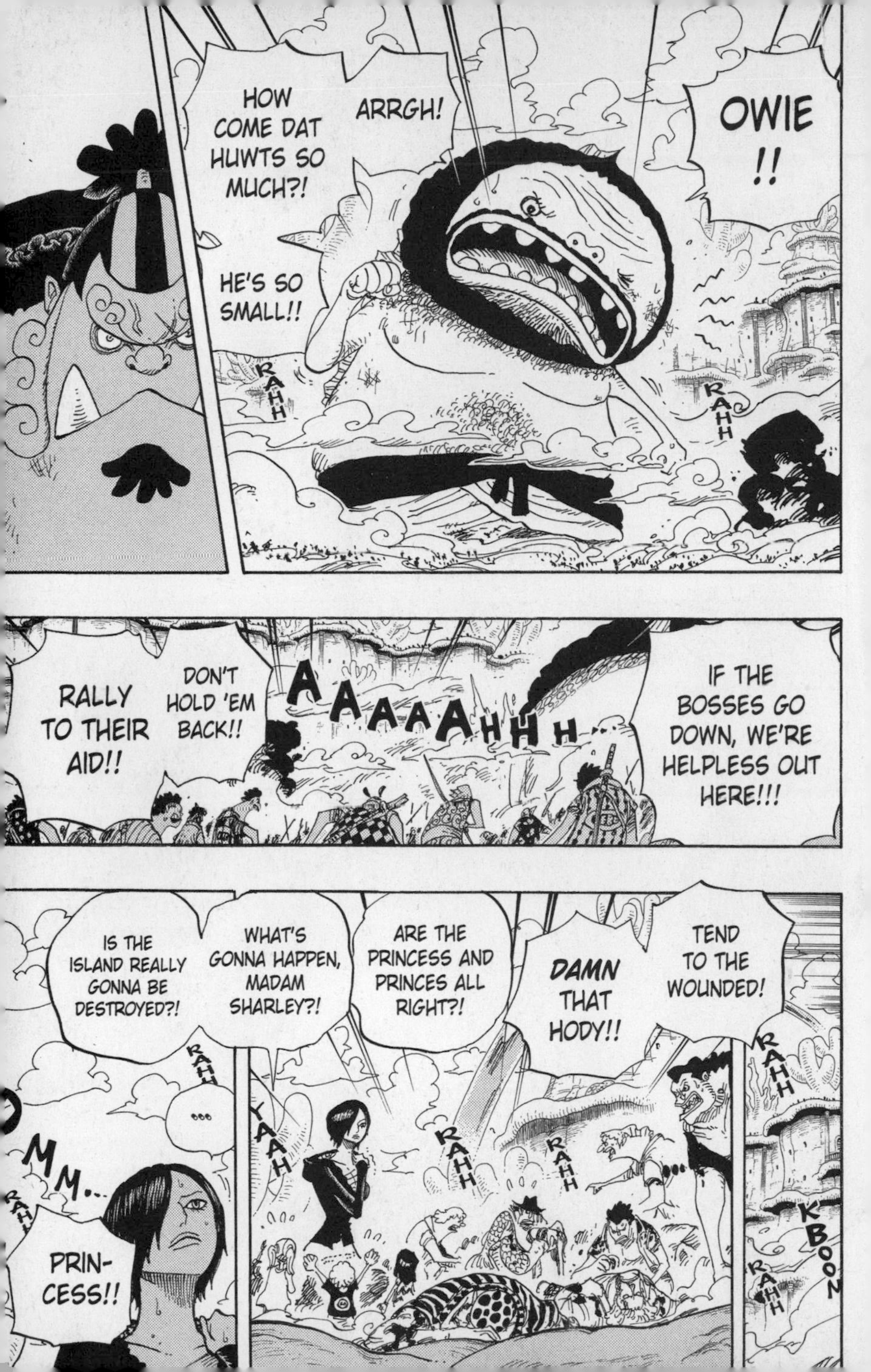
OWIE !!
ARRGH!
HOW COME DAT HUWTS SO MUCH?!
HE'S SO SMALL!!
RAHH
RAHH
IF THE BOSSES GO DOWN, WE'RE HELPLESS OUT HERE!!!
AAAAAHHH
DON'T HOLD 'EM BACK!!
RALLY TO THEIR AID!!
TEND TO THE WOUNDED!
RAHH
KBOON
RAHH
DAMN THAT HODY!!
ARE THE PRINCESS AND PRINCES ALL RIGHT?!
WHAT'S GONNA HAPPEN, MADAM SHARLEY?!
RAHH
RAHH
YAAH
IS THE ISLAND REALLY GONNA BE DESTROYED?!
RAHH
...
MM...
RAHH
PRIN-CESS!!

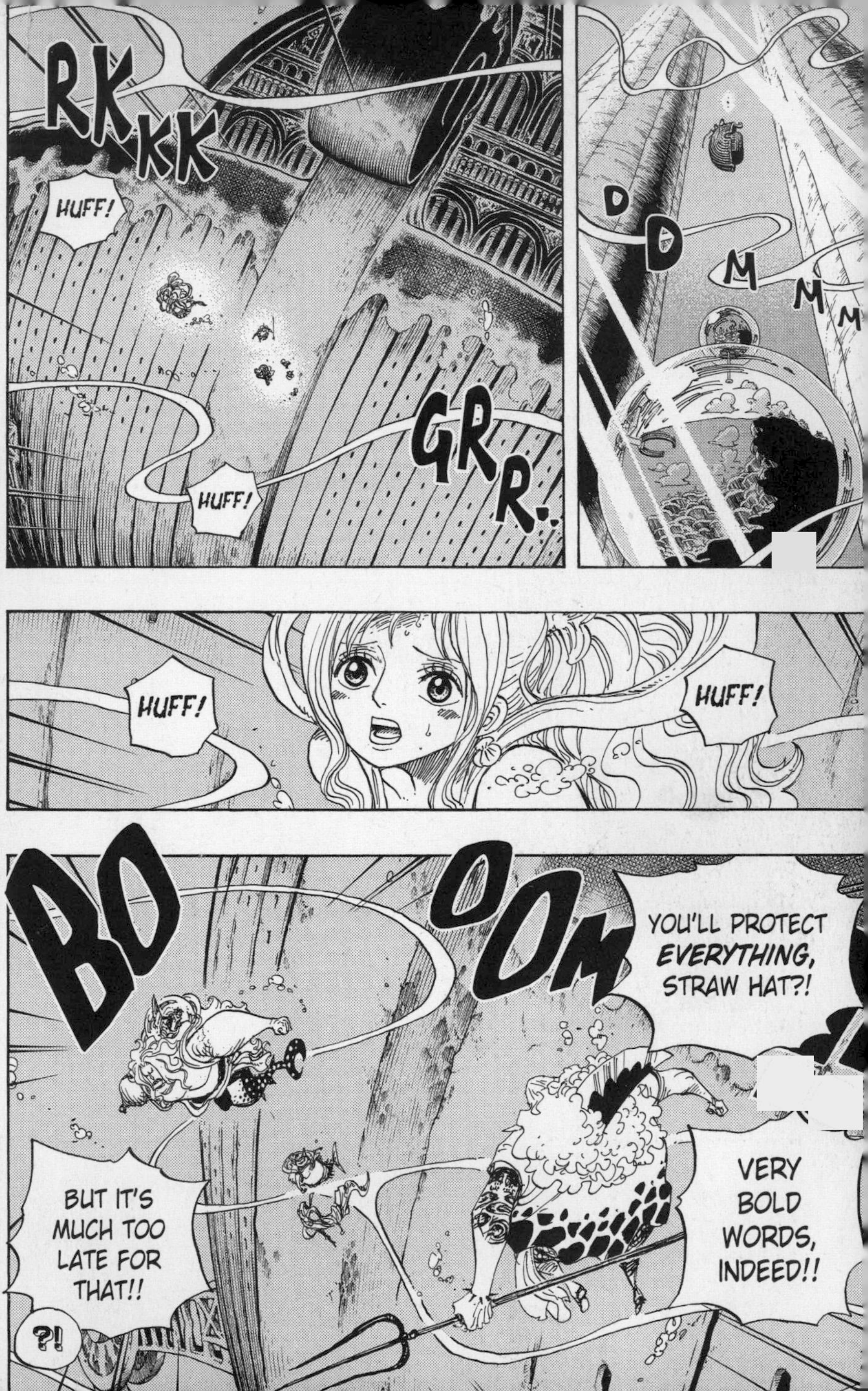
DDMMM
RKKK
HUFF!
GRR..
HUFF!
HUFF!
HUFF!
BOOOM
YOU'LL PROTECT *EVERYTHING,* STRAW HAT?!
VERY BOLD WORDS, INDEED!!
BUT IT'S MUCH TOO LATE FOR THAT!!
?!

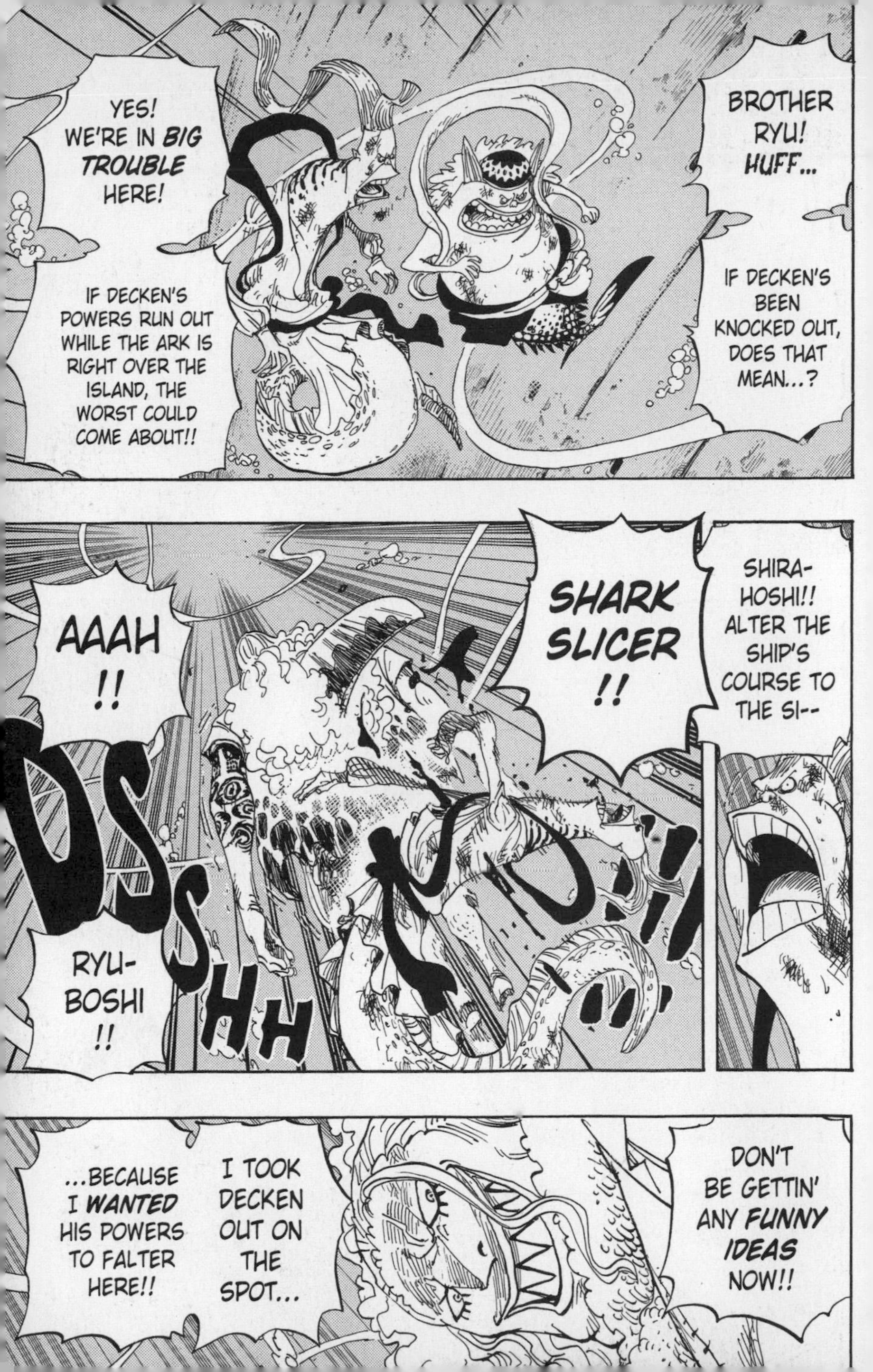
BROTHER RYU! HUFF...
IF DECKEN'S BEEN KNOCKED OUT, DOES THAT MEAN...?
YES! WE'RE IN BIG TROUBLE HERE!
IF DECKEN'S POWERS RUN OUT WHILE THE ARK IS RIGHT OVER THE ISLAND, THE WORST COULD COME ABOUT!!
SHIRA-HOSHI!! ALTER THE SHIP'S COURSE TO THE SI--
SHARK SLICER!!
AAAH!!
DOSSHH
RYU-BOSHI!!
DON'T BE GETTIN' ANY FUNNY IDEAS NOW!!
I TOOK DECKEN OUT ON THE SPOT...
...BECAUSE I WANTED HIS POWERS TO FALTER HERE!!

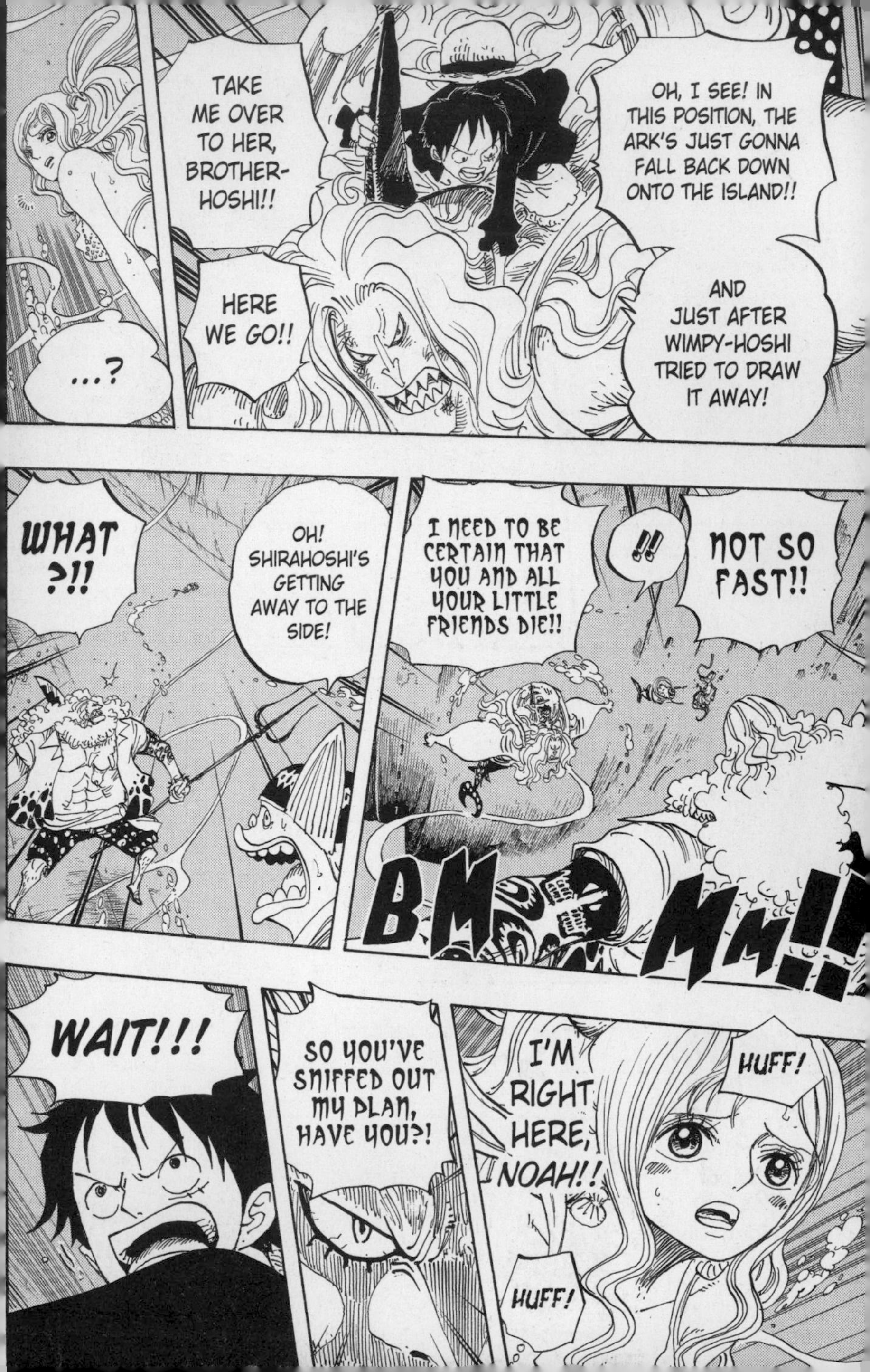
OH, I SEE! IN THIS POSITION, THE ARK'S JUST GONNA FALL BACK DOWN ONTO THE ISLAND!!
AND JUST AFTER WIMPY-HOSHI TRIED TO DRAW IT AWAY!
TAKE ME OVER TO HER, BROTHER-HOSHI!!
HERE WE GO!!
...?
NOT SO FAST!!
!!
I NEED TO BE CERTAIN THAT YOU AND ALL YOUR LITTLE FRIENDS DIE!!
OH! SHIRAHOSHI'S GETTING AWAY TO THE SIDE!
WHAT?!!
HUFF!
I'M RIGHT HERE, NOAH!!
HUFF!
SO YOU'VE SNIFFED OUT MY PLAN, HAVE YOU?!
WAIT!!!

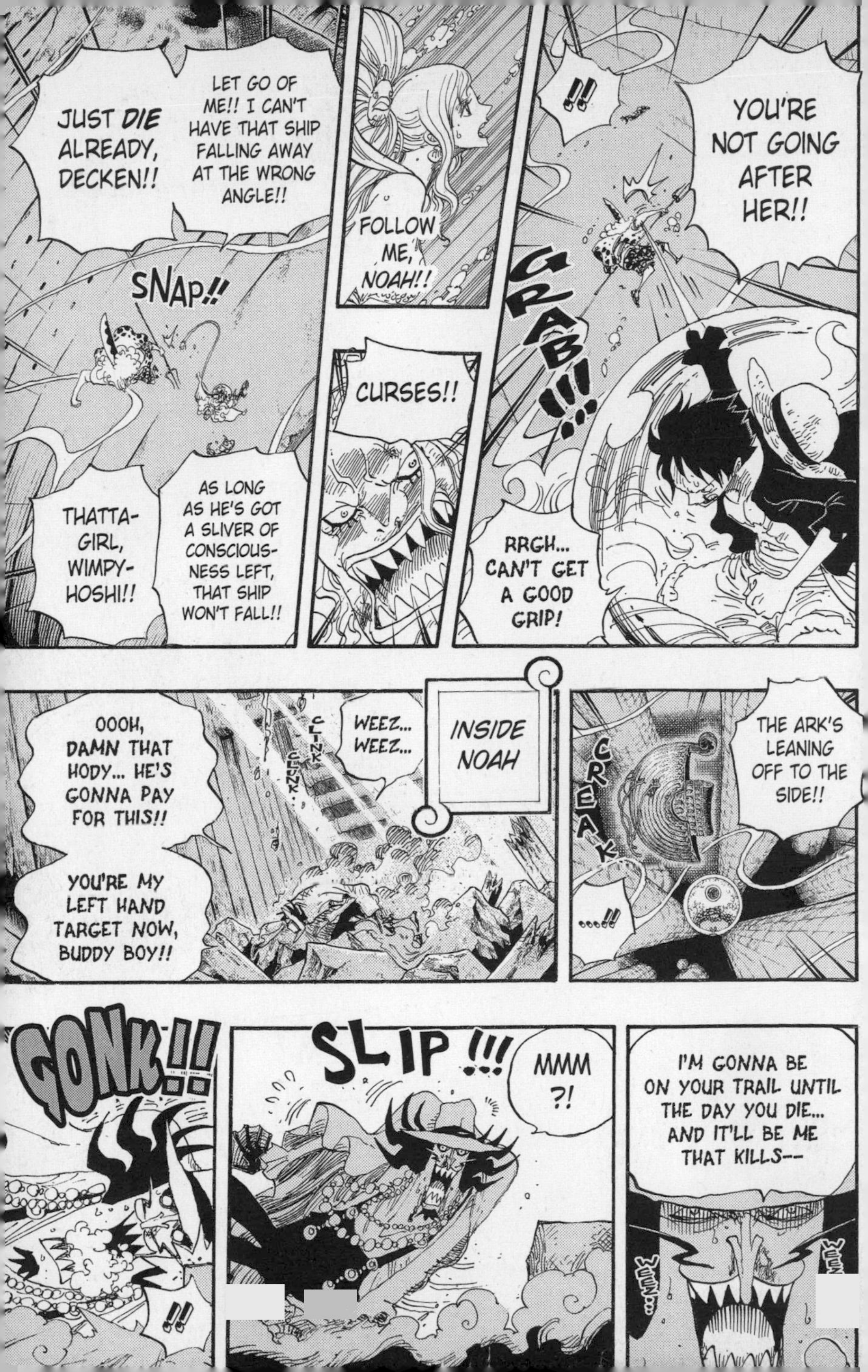
!!
YOU'RE NOT GOING AFTER HER!!
GRAB!!!
RRGH... CAN'T GET A GOOD GRIP!
FOLLOW ME, NOAH!!
CURSES!!
LET GO OF ME!! I CAN'T HAVE THAT SHIP FALLING AWAY AT THE WRONG ANGLE!!
JUST DIE ALREADY, DECKEN!!
SNAP!!
AS LONG AS HE'S GOT A SLIVER OF CONSCIOUSNESS LEFT, THAT SHIP WON'T FALL!!
THATTA-GIRL, WIMPY-HOSHI!!
THE ARK'S LEANING OFF TO THE SIDE!!
CREAK
...!!
INSIDE NOAH
WEEZ... WEEZ...
CLINK
CLINK
OOOH, DAMN THAT HODY... HE'S GONNA PAY FOR THIS!!
YOU'RE MY LEFT HAND TARGET NOW, BUDDY BOY!!
I'M GONNA BE ON YOUR TRAIL UNTIL THE DAY YOU DIE... AND IT'LL BE ME THAT KILLS--
WEEZ...
WEEZ
MMM ?!
SLIP!!!
GONK!!
!!

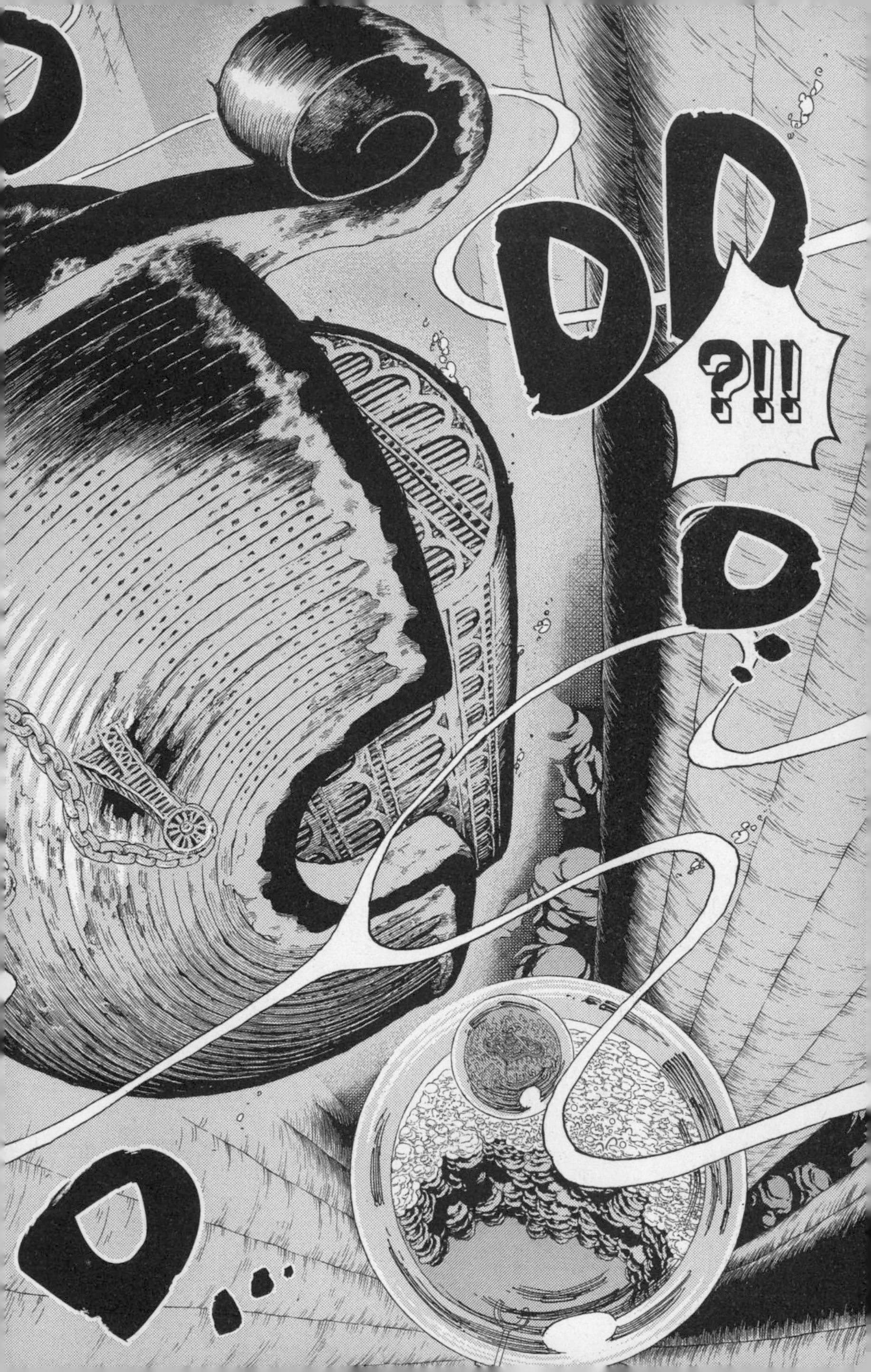
DD
?!!
D.
D...

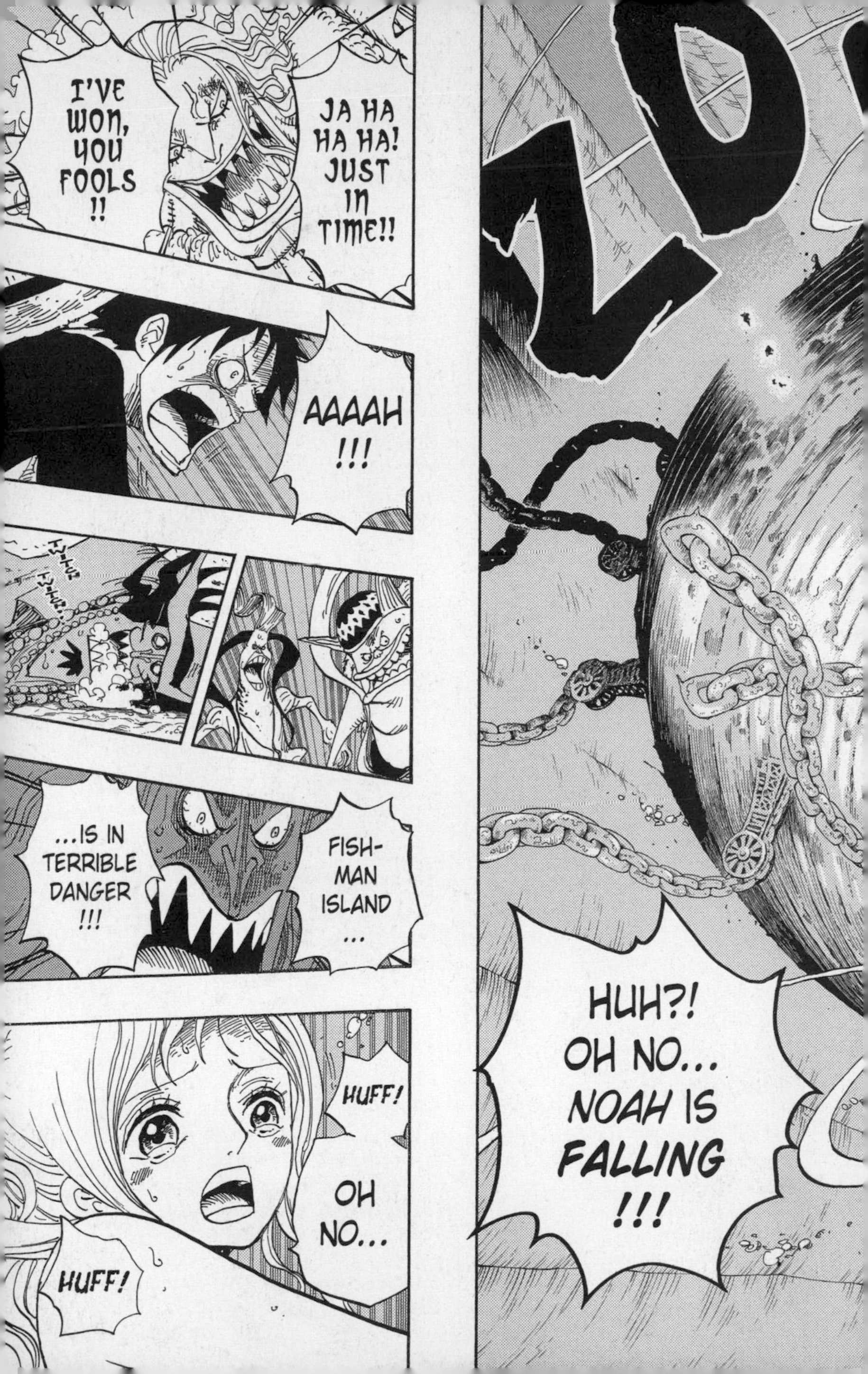
HUH?! OH NO... NOAH IS FALLING!!!
JA HA HA HA! JUST IN TIME!!
I'VE WON, YOU FOOLS!!
AAAAH!!!
FISH-MAN ISLAND...
...IS IN TERRIBLE DANGER!!!
HUFF!
OH NO...
HUFF!

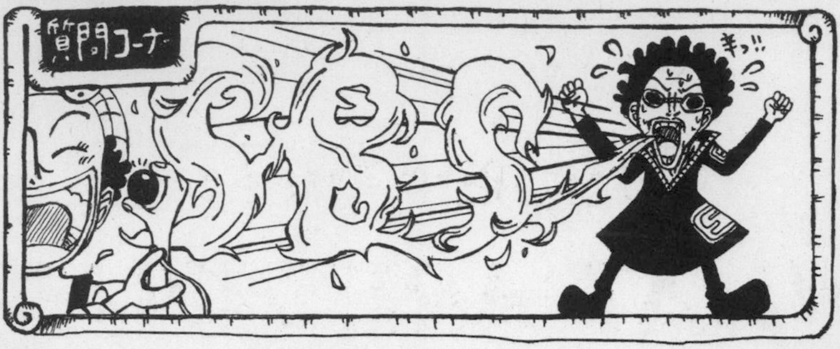
質問コーナー

(Sorako ☆ Sho, Tokyo)

Q: Odacchi!! Canned mackerel is good, huh?!

--Mack Mackerel

A: Yeah, it is! My favorite is canned onion mackerel. It's too good!!

Q: In the Volume 64 scene where the Fish-Man Island kids tell Luffy to fight for them, there's a guy who says "I agree with them." I noticed that his shirt says "Sorega iiyo," which is the same line in Japanese, but written in the Western alphabet! What does it mean?!

--Trafalgar Law♡

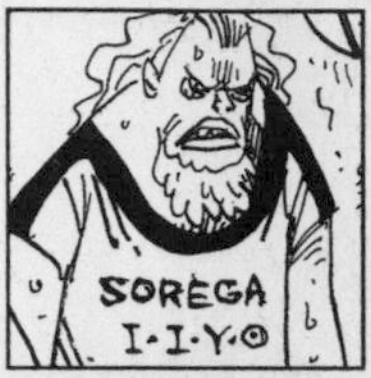
SOREGA
I·I·Y·O

Q: What species is the girl in Chapter 633 wearing the shirt that says "Tega2tsui"? (Two pairs of hands)

--Takaaki T.

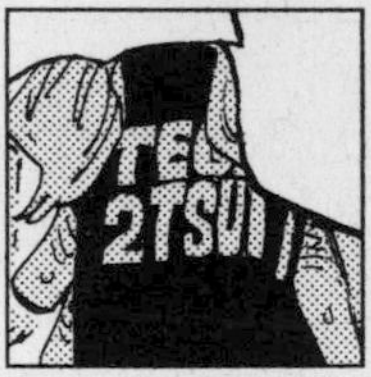

A: Here are two questions. As for the girl, I didn't think of a fish species for her, but I'm betting she'd be some kind of ancient fish. The Fish-Men based on ancient species tend to have many fins. As for the shirts in general, you may notice that I became obsessed with "explanation shirts" in this arc, where I drew characters wearing clothes that repeated one of the original Japanese lines of dialogue from that panel. Look carefully, and you'll see them everywhere. Even in this book!

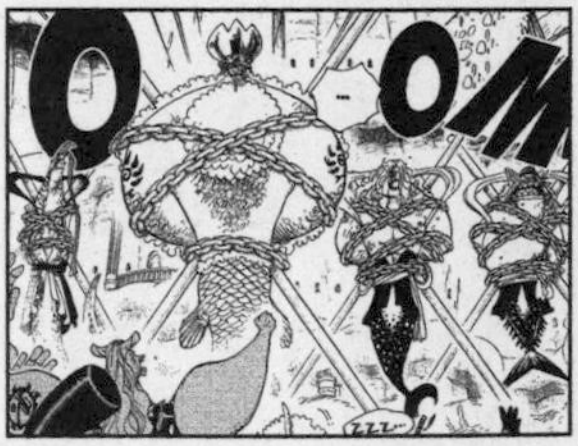

Q: I noticed something wrong with your story, Mr. Oda. When the king and princes were tied up, they seemed to be in pain, right? Isn't that weird? I would have thought their faces would be full of pleasure, like mine is when I get tied up... You're the same way, right?

--Chagero Kiyomizu

A: You towering fool!! What are you saying?! Children read this manga!! Aha! You're Chagero Kiyomizu, the pervert!! I've got your address this time! Hey! Officer! See that guy there? The one who's all tied up and enjoying it! Arrest him at once!
...Huh? What do I have to do with this?! What?! Why are you arresting me too, just because I'm not wearing any pants or underwear?! This is an outrage! *Click clack!* Hey, don't handcuff me! I have a deadline to meet, officer! Officer?! Hey...

Chapter 641:
WHAT ARE YOU?

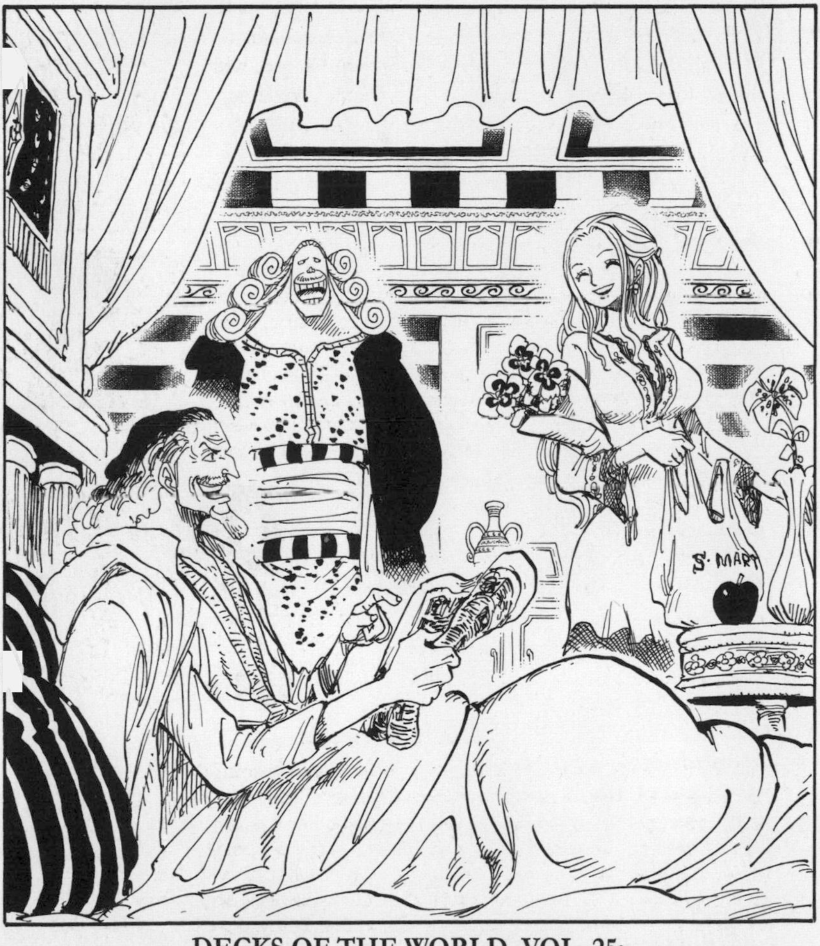
S·MART

DECKS OF THE WORLD, VOL. 25:
"KINGDOM OF ALABASTA—COBRA ON HIS SICKBED"

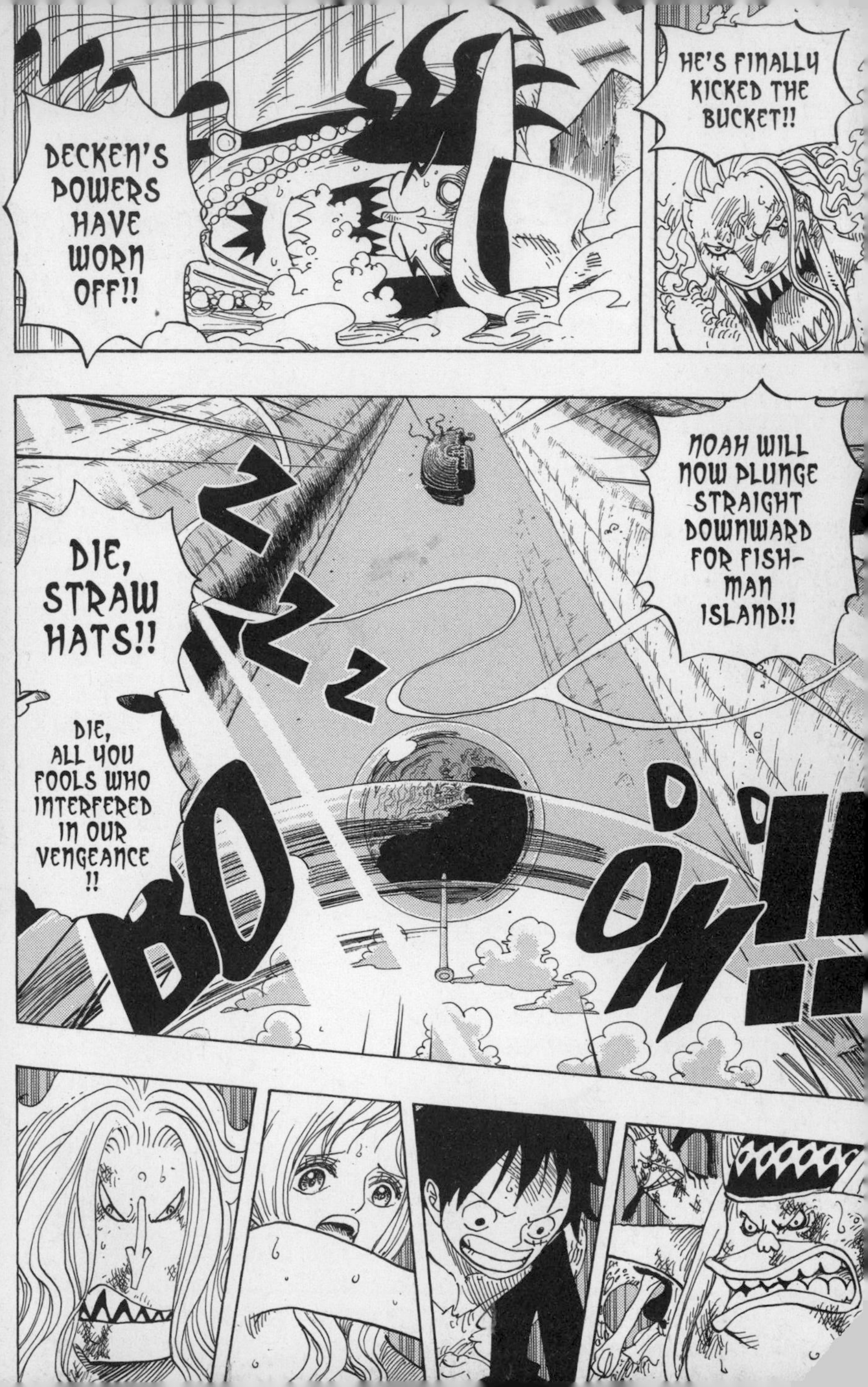
HE'S FINALLY KICKED THE BUCKET!!
DECKEN'S POWERS HAVE WORN OFF!!
NOAH WILL NOW PLUNGE STRAIGHT DOWNWARD FOR FISH-MAN ISLAND!!
DIE, STRAW HATS!!
DIE, ALL YOU FOOLS WHO INTERFERED IN OUR VENGEANCE!!
ZZZ
BOOOM!!

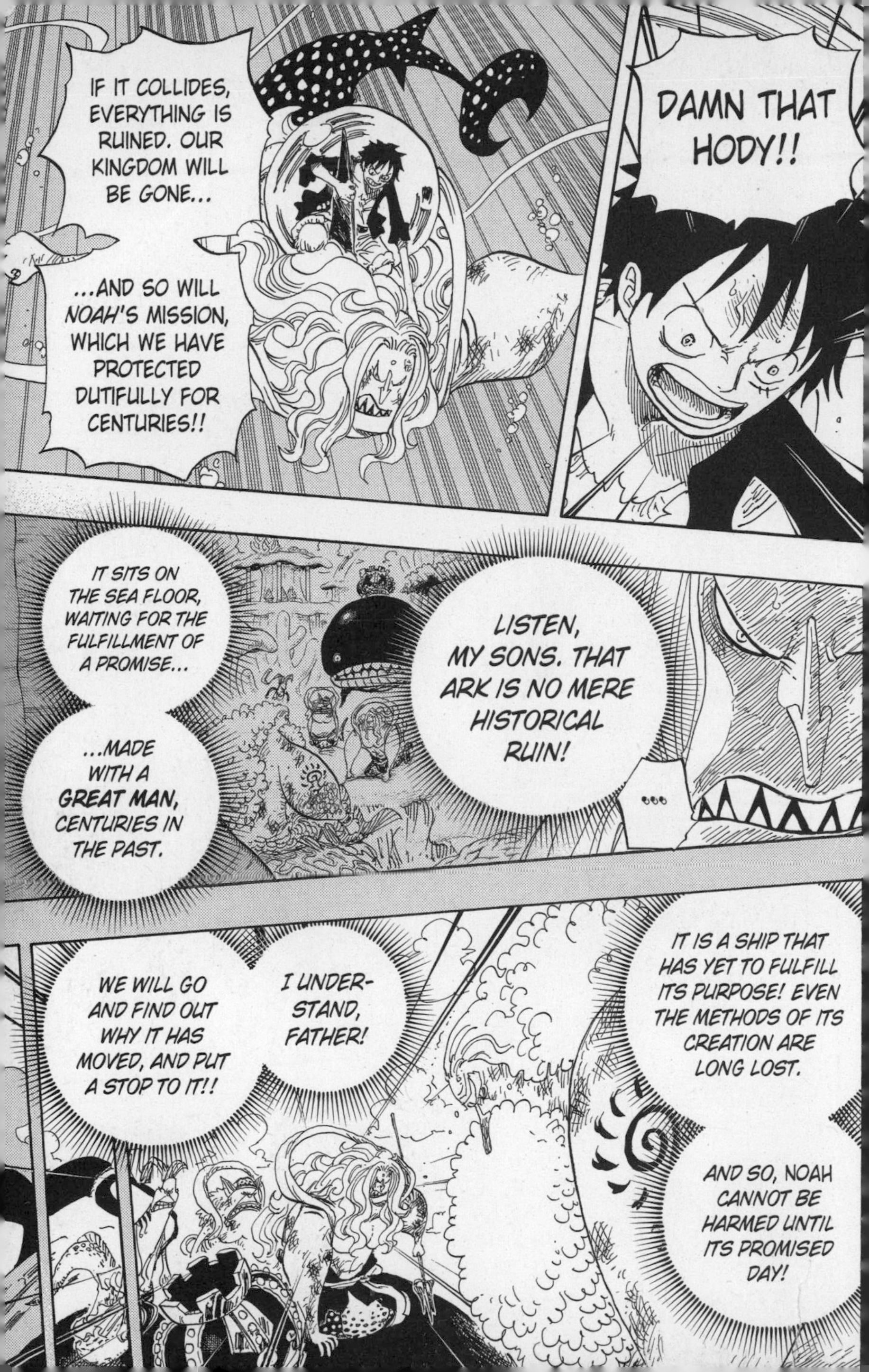
DAMN THAT HODY!!
IF IT COLLIDES, EVERYTHING IS RUINED. OUR KINGDOM WILL BE GONE...
...AND SO WILL NOAH'S MISSION, WHICH WE HAVE PROTECTED DUTIFULLY FOR CENTURIES!!
...
LISTEN, MY SONS. THAT ARK IS NO MERE HISTORICAL RUIN!
IT SITS ON THE SEA FLOOR, WAITING FOR THE FULFILLMENT OF A PROMISE...
...MADE WITH A GREAT MAN, CENTURIES IN THE PAST.
IT IS A SHIP THAT HAS YET TO FULFILL ITS PURPOSE! EVEN THE METHODS OF ITS CREATION ARE LONG LOST.
AND SO, NOAH CANNOT BE HARMED UNTIL ITS PROMISED DAY!
I UNDER-STAND, FATHER!
WE WILL GO AND FIND OUT WHY IT HAS MOVED, AND PUT A STOP TO IT!!

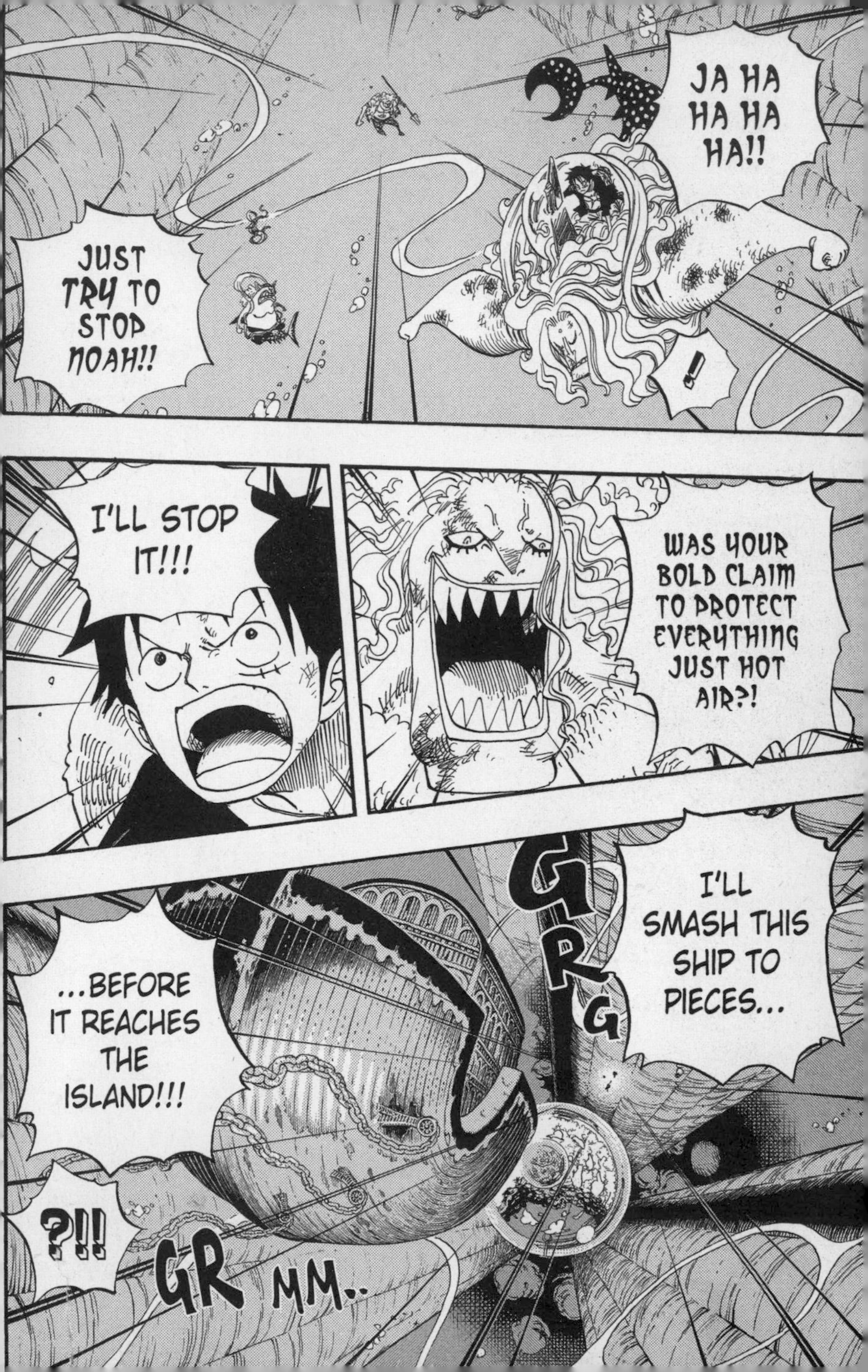
JA HA HA HA HA!!
JUST TRY TO STOP NOAH!!
!
WAS YOUR BOLD CLAIM TO PROTECT EVERYTHING JUST HOT AIR?!
I'LL STOP IT!!!
I'LL SMASH THIS SHIP TO PIECES...
GRG
...BEFORE IT REACHES THE ISLAND!!!
?!!
GR MM..

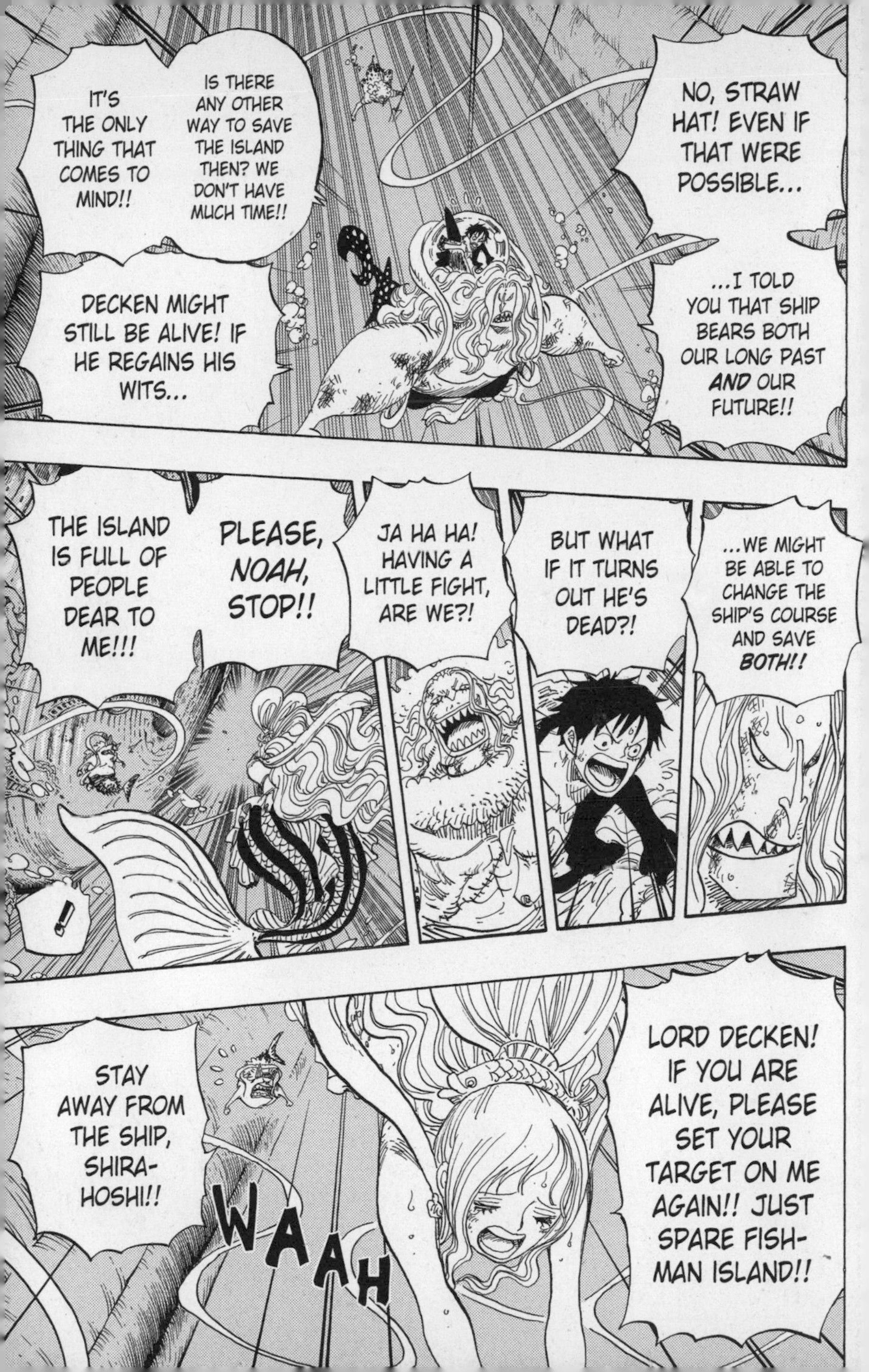
NO, STRAW HAT! EVEN IF THAT WERE POSSIBLE...
...I TOLD YOU THAT SHIP BEARS BOTH OUR LONG PAST *AND* OUR FUTURE!!
IS THERE ANY OTHER WAY TO SAVE THE ISLAND THEN? WE DON'T HAVE MUCH TIME!!
IT'S THE ONLY THING THAT COMES TO MIND!!
DECKEN MIGHT STILL BE ALIVE! IF HE REGAINS HIS WITS...
...WE MIGHT BE ABLE TO CHANGE THE SHIP'S COURSE AND SAVE *BOTH!!*
BUT WHAT IF IT TURNS OUT HE'S DEAD?!
JA HA HA! HAVING A LITTLE FIGHT, ARE WE?!
PLEASE, *NOAH,* STOP!!
THE ISLAND IS FULL OF PEOPLE DEAR TO ME!!!
!
LORD DECKEN! IF YOU ARE ALIVE, PLEASE SET YOUR TARGET ON ME AGAIN!! JUST SPARE FISH-MAN ISLAND!!
WAAH
STAY AWAY FROM THE SHIP, SHIRAHOSHI!!

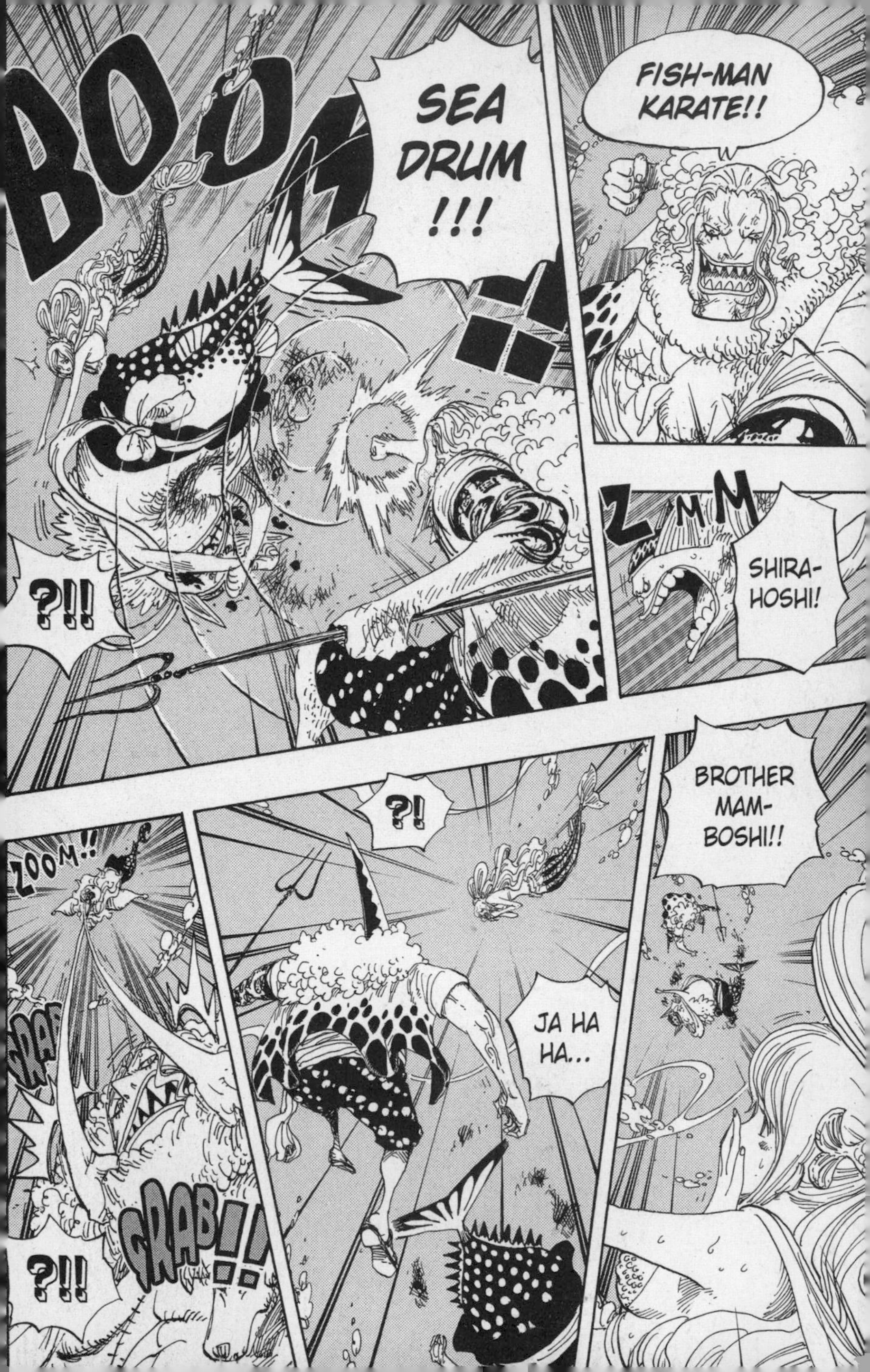
FISH-MAN KARATE!!
ZMM
SHIRA-HOSHI!
SEA DRUM!!!
BOOM
?!!
BROTHER MAM-BOSHI!!
?!
JA HA HA...
ZOOM!!
GRAB!!
?!!

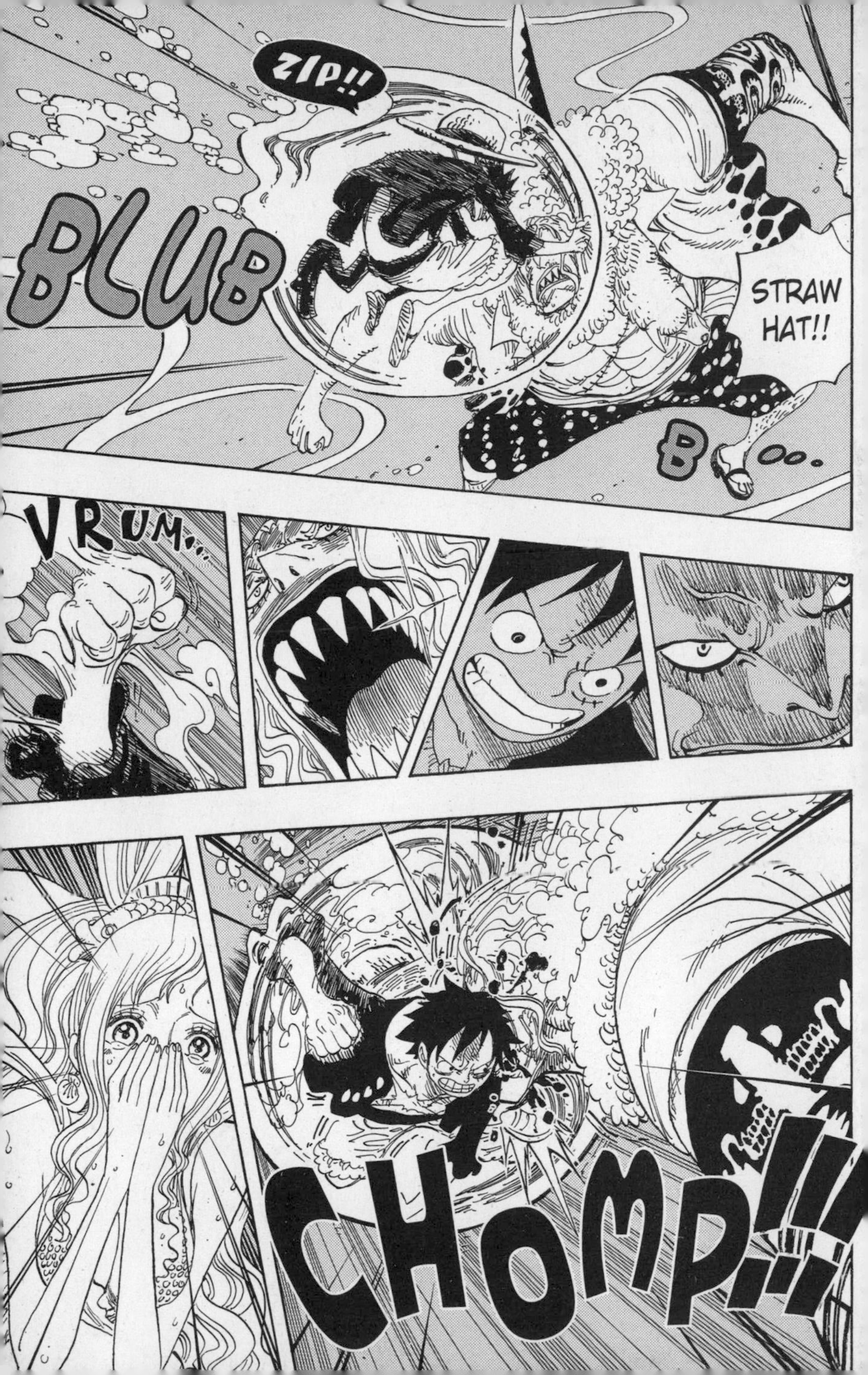
ZIP!!
STRAW HAT!!
BLUB
B ooo..
VRUM...
CHOMP!!!

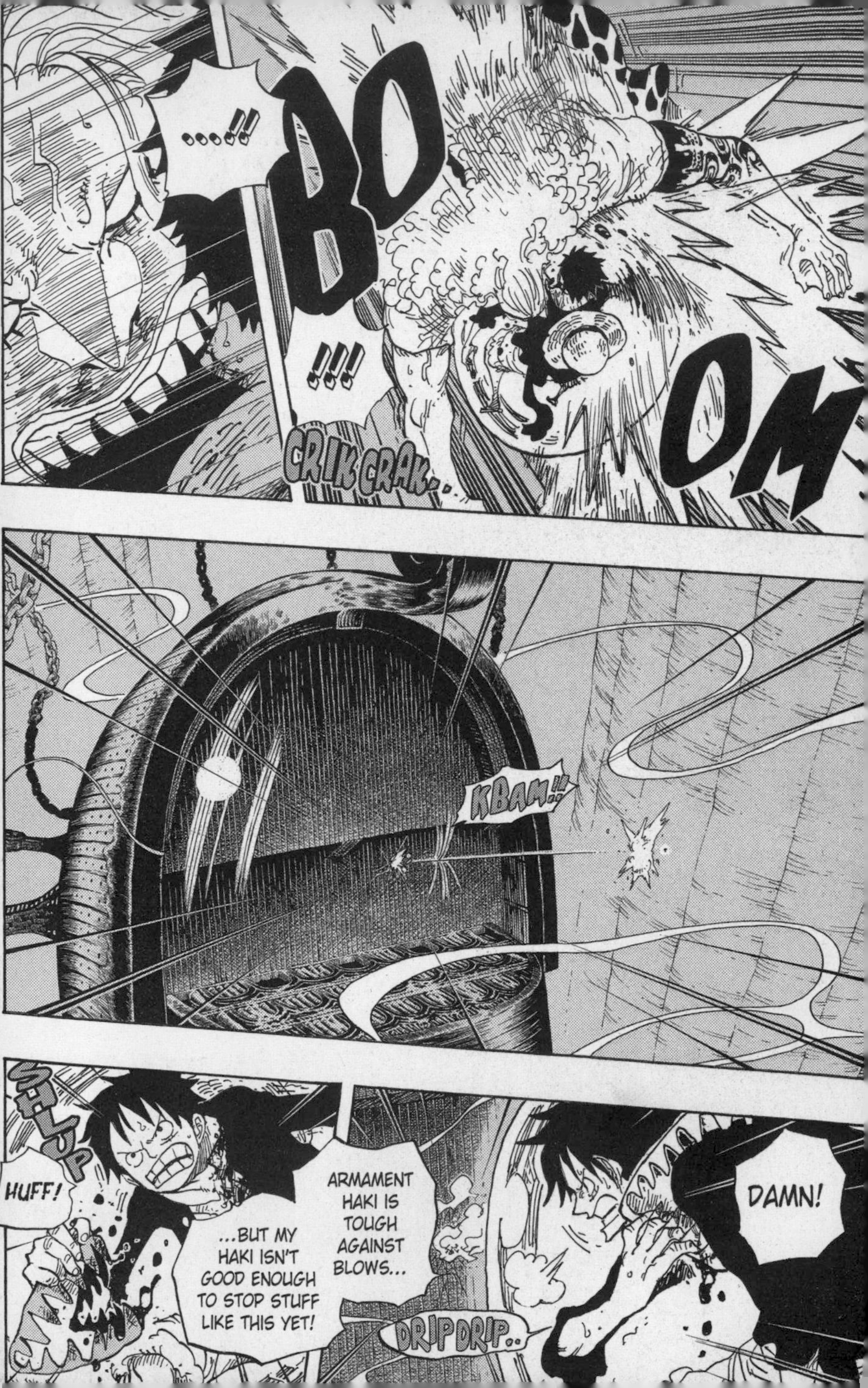
BOOM
....!!
!!!
CRIK CRAK..
KBAM!!
DAMN!
DRIPDRIP..
ARMAMENT HAKI IS TOUGH AGAINST BLOWS...
...BUT MY HAKI ISN'T GOOD ENOUGH TO STOP STUFF LIKE THIS YET!
HUFF!
SHLUP

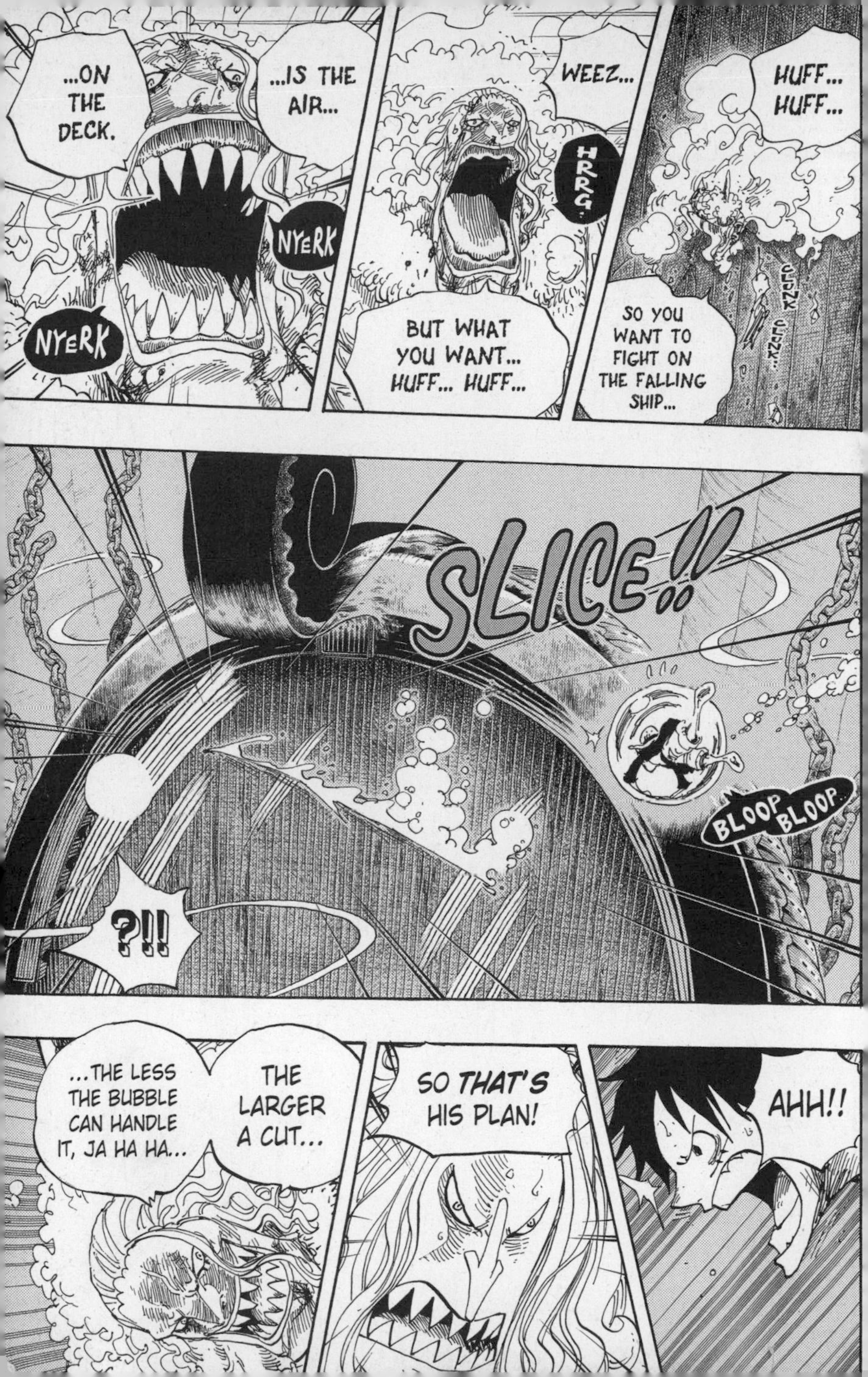
HUFF... HUFF...
SO YOU WANT TO FIGHT ON THE FALLING SHIP...
CLUNK CLUNK...
WEEZ...
HRRG
BUT WHAT YOU WANT... HUFF... HUFF...
...IS THE AIR...
...ON THE DECK.
NYERK
NYERK
SLICE!!
BLOOP BLOOP...
?!!
AHH!!
SO THAT'S HIS PLAN!
THE LARGER A CUT...
...THE LESS THE BUBBLE CAN HANDLE IT, JA HA HA...

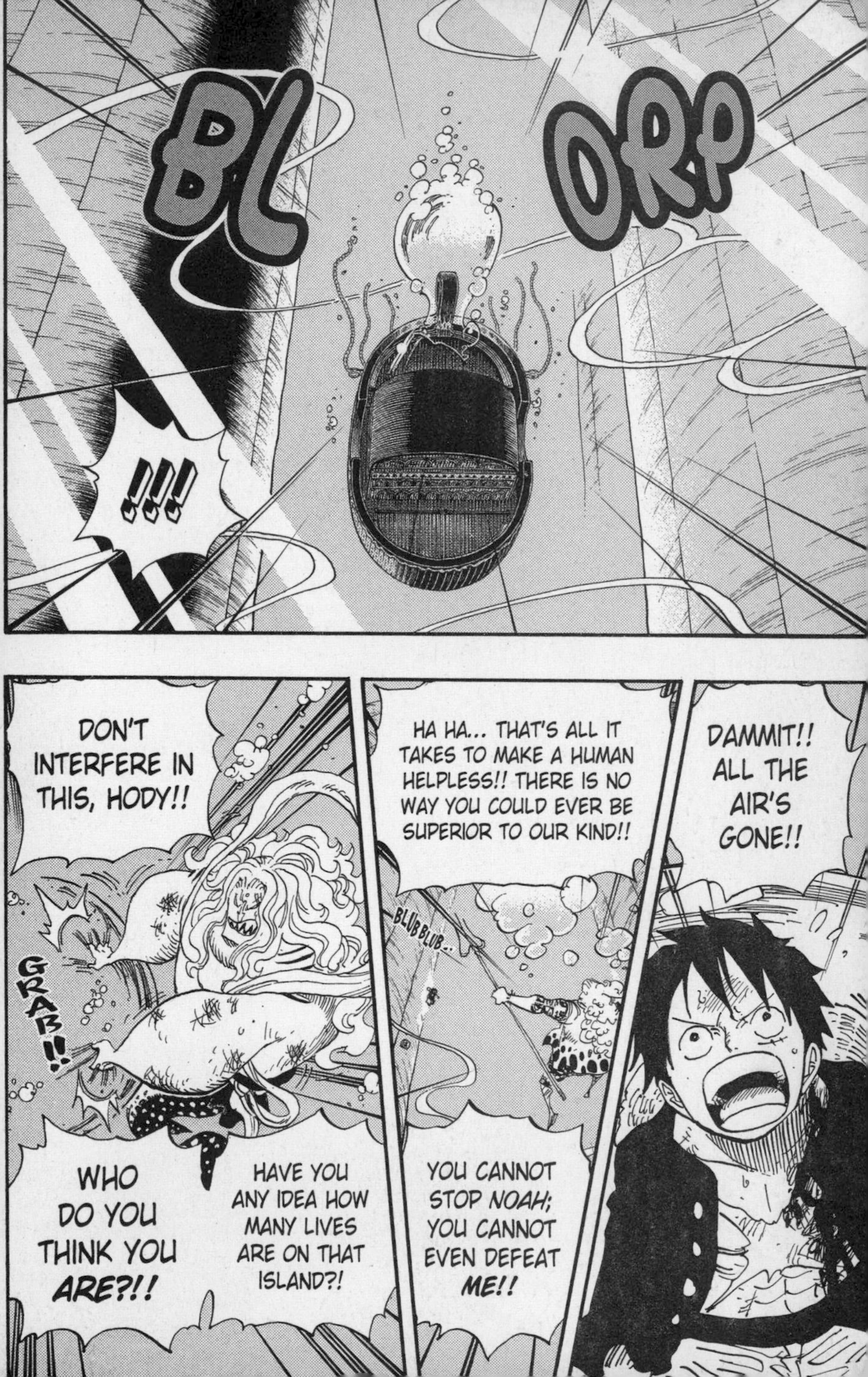

BLORP
!!!
DAMMIT!! ALL THE AIR'S GONE!!
HA HA... THAT'S ALL IT TAKES TO MAKE A HUMAN HELPLESS!! THERE IS NO WAY YOU COULD EVER BE SUPERIOR TO OUR KIND!!
BLUB BLUB...
YOU CANNOT STOP *NOAH*; YOU CANNOT EVEN DEFEAT ***ME!!***
DON'T INTERFERE IN THIS, HODY!!
GRAB!!
HAVE YOU ANY IDEA HOW MANY LIVES ARE ON THAT ISLAND?!
WHO DO YOU THINK YOU ***ARE?!!***

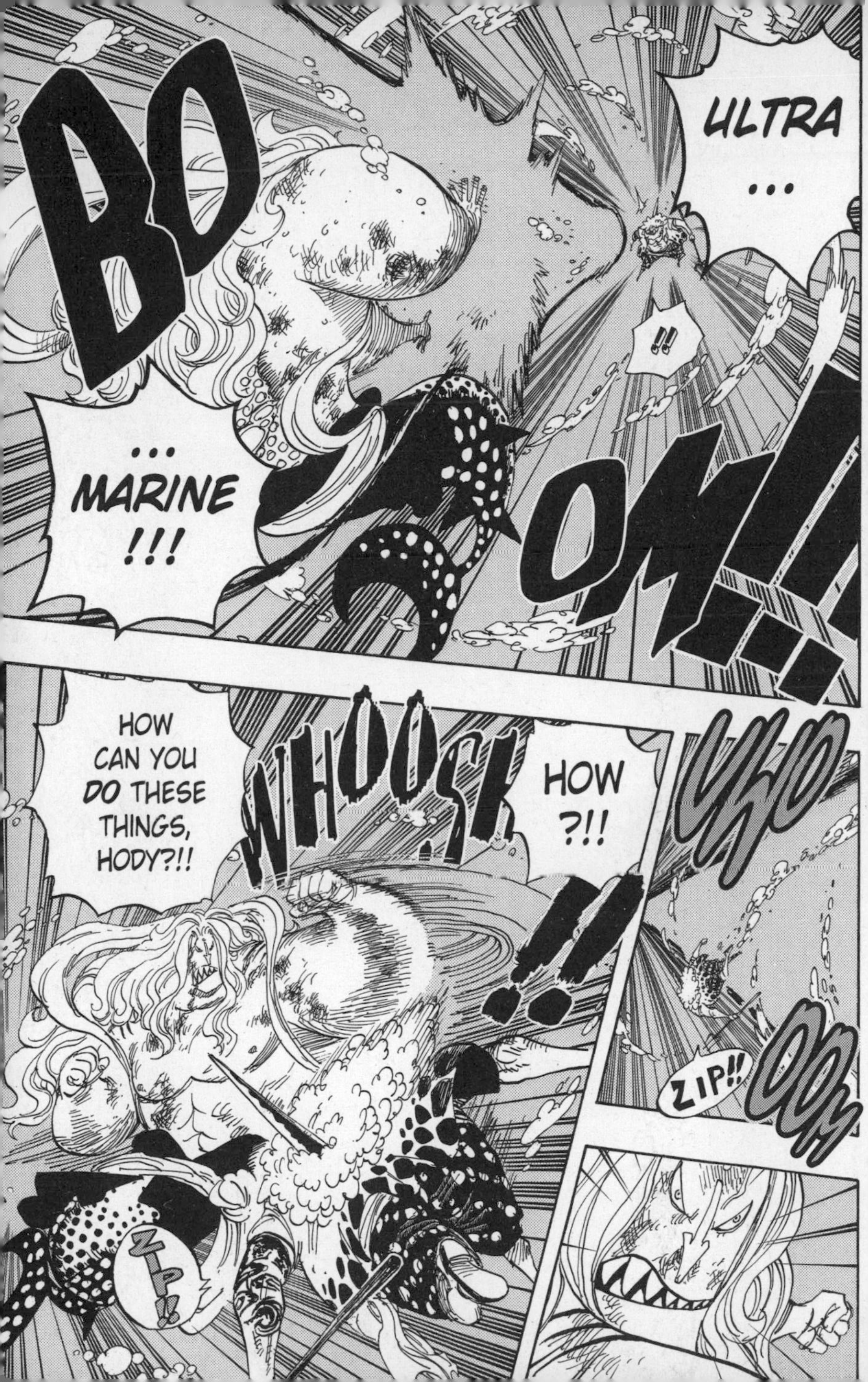
ULTRA ...
!!
BO
OM!!
... MARINE !!!
ZIP!!
HOW ?!!
WHOOSH!!
HOW CAN YOU DO THESE THINGS, HODY?!!

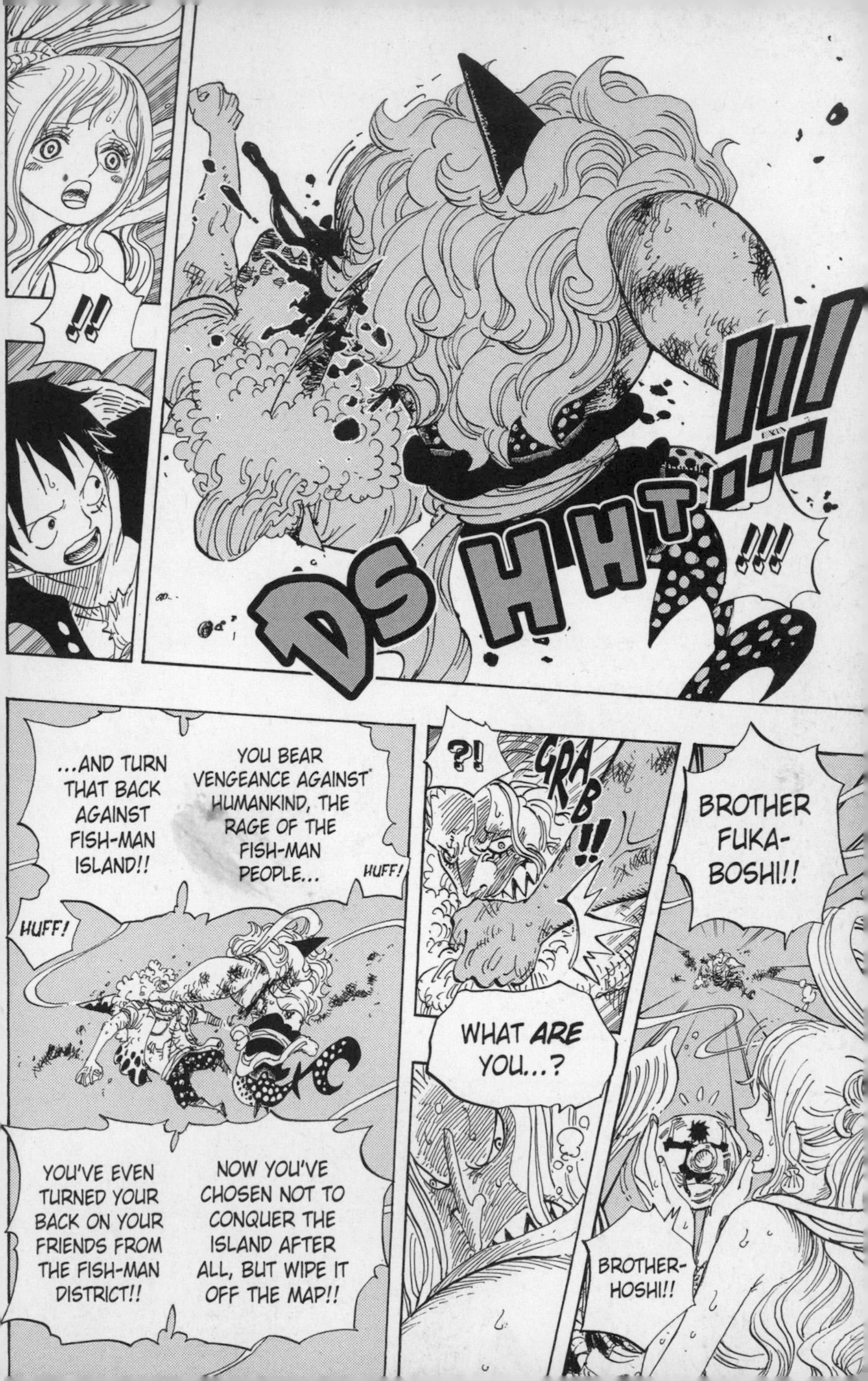
DSHHT!!!
!!
BROTHER FUKA-BOSHI!!
BROTHER-HOSHI!!
?!
GRAB!!
WHAT ARE YOU...?
YOU BEAR VENGEANCE AGAINST HUMANKIND, THE RAGE OF THE FISH-MAN PEOPLE...
...AND TURN THAT BACK AGAINST FISH-MAN ISLAND!!
HUFF!
HUFF!
NOW YOU'VE CHOSEN NOT TO CONQUER THE ISLAND AFTER ALL, BUT WIPE IT OFF THE MAP!!
YOU'VE EVEN TURNED YOUR BACK ON YOUR FRIENDS FROM THE FISH-MAN DISTRICT!!

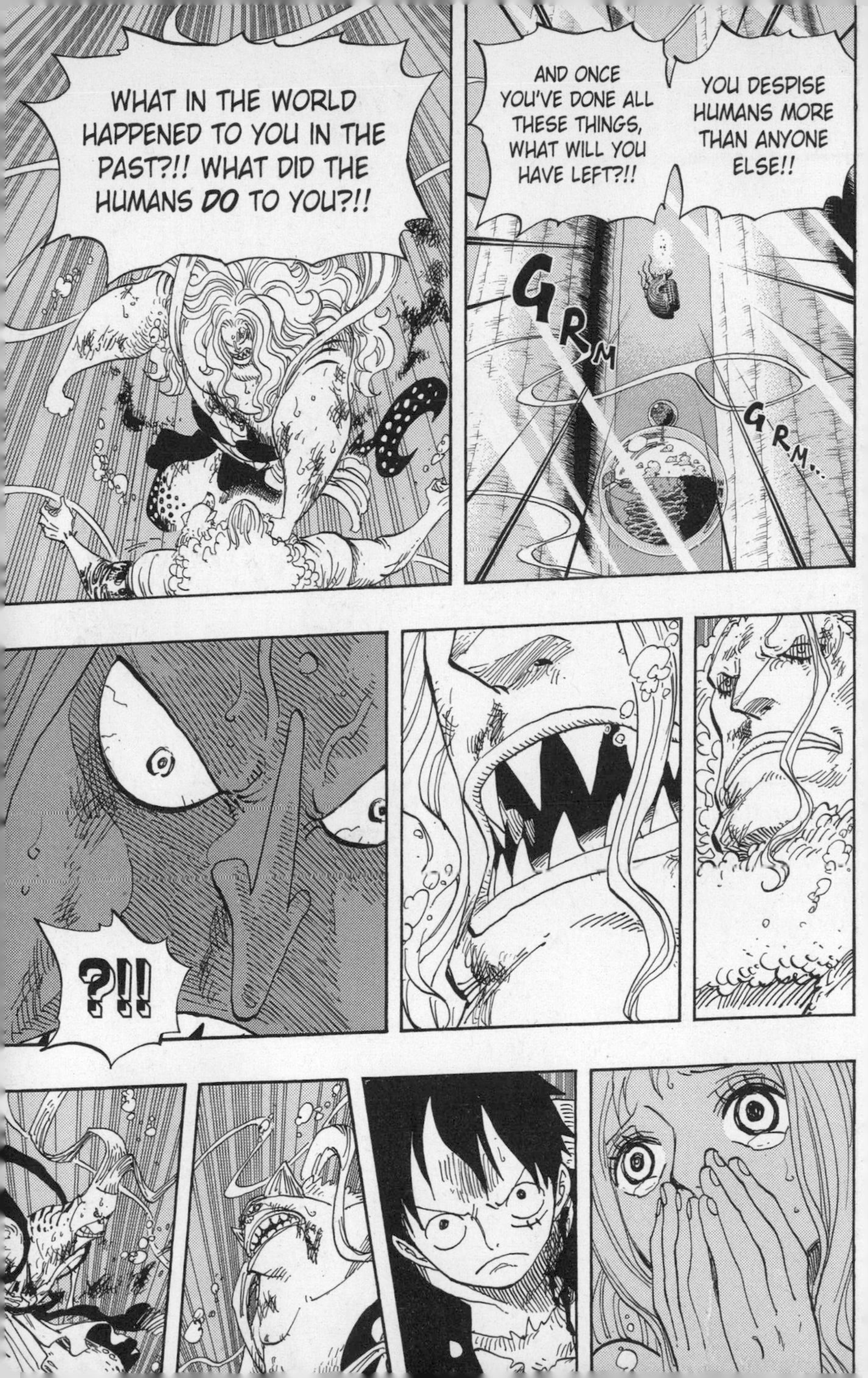
YOU DESPISE HUMANS MORE THAN ANYONE ELSE!!
AND ONCE YOU'VE DONE ALL THESE THINGS, WHAT WILL YOU HAVE LEFT?!!
GRM
GRM...
WHAT IN THE WORLD HAPPENED TO YOU IN THE PAST?!! WHAT DID THE HUMANS *DO* TO YOU?!!
?!!

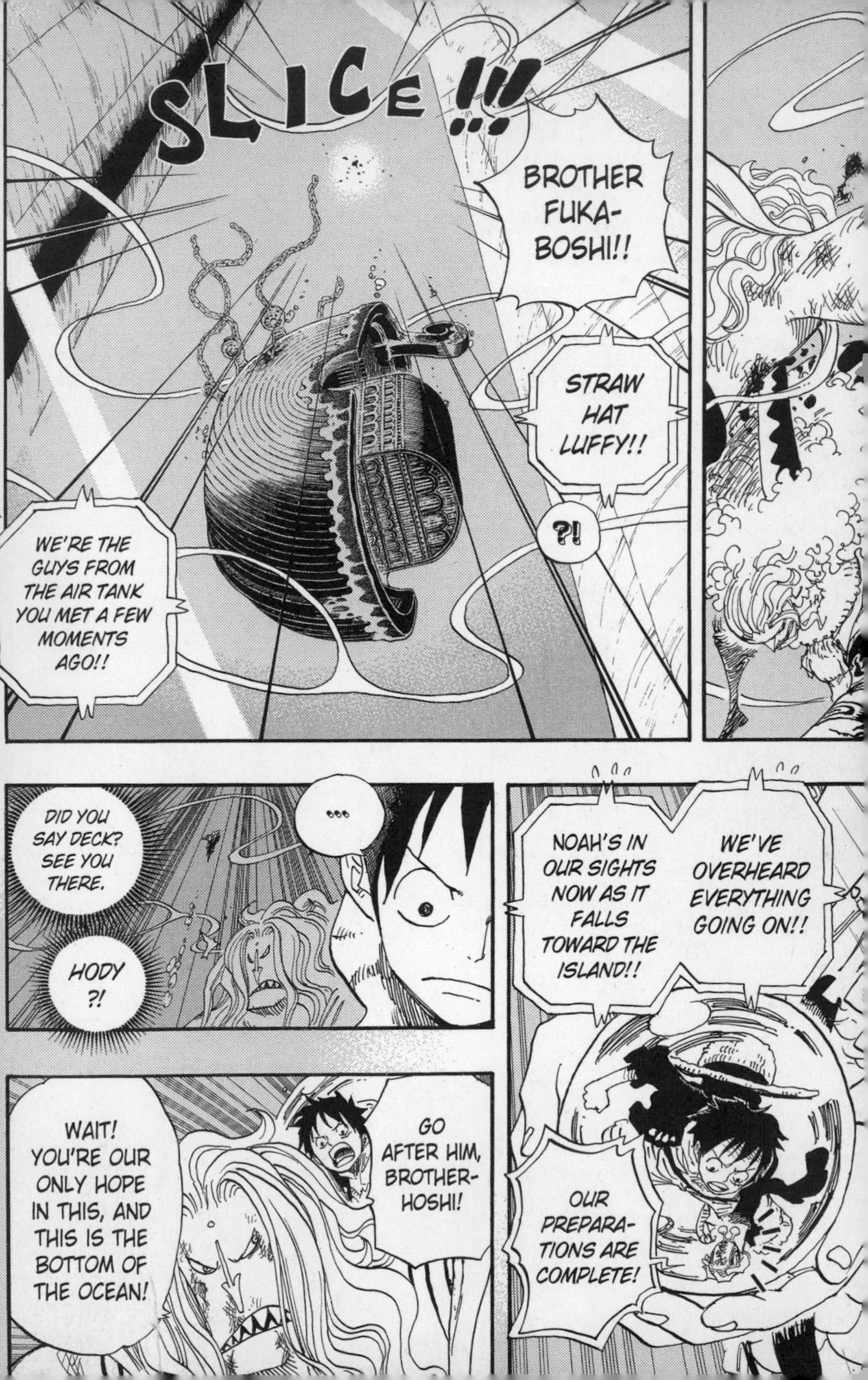
SLICE!!!
BROTHER FUKA-BOSHI!!
STRAW HAT LUFFY!!
?!
WE'RE THE GUYS FROM THE AIR TANK YOU MET A FEW MOMENTS AGO!!
WE'VE OVERHEARD EVERYTHING GOING ON!!
NOAH'S IN OUR SIGHTS NOW AS IT FALLS TOWARD THE ISLAND!!
OUR PREPARA-TIONS ARE COMPLETE!
...
DID YOU SAY DECK? SEE YOU THERE.
HODY ?!
GO AFTER HIM, BROTHER-HOSHI!
WAIT! YOU'RE OUR ONLY HOPE IN THIS, AND THIS IS THE BOTTOM OF THE OCEAN!

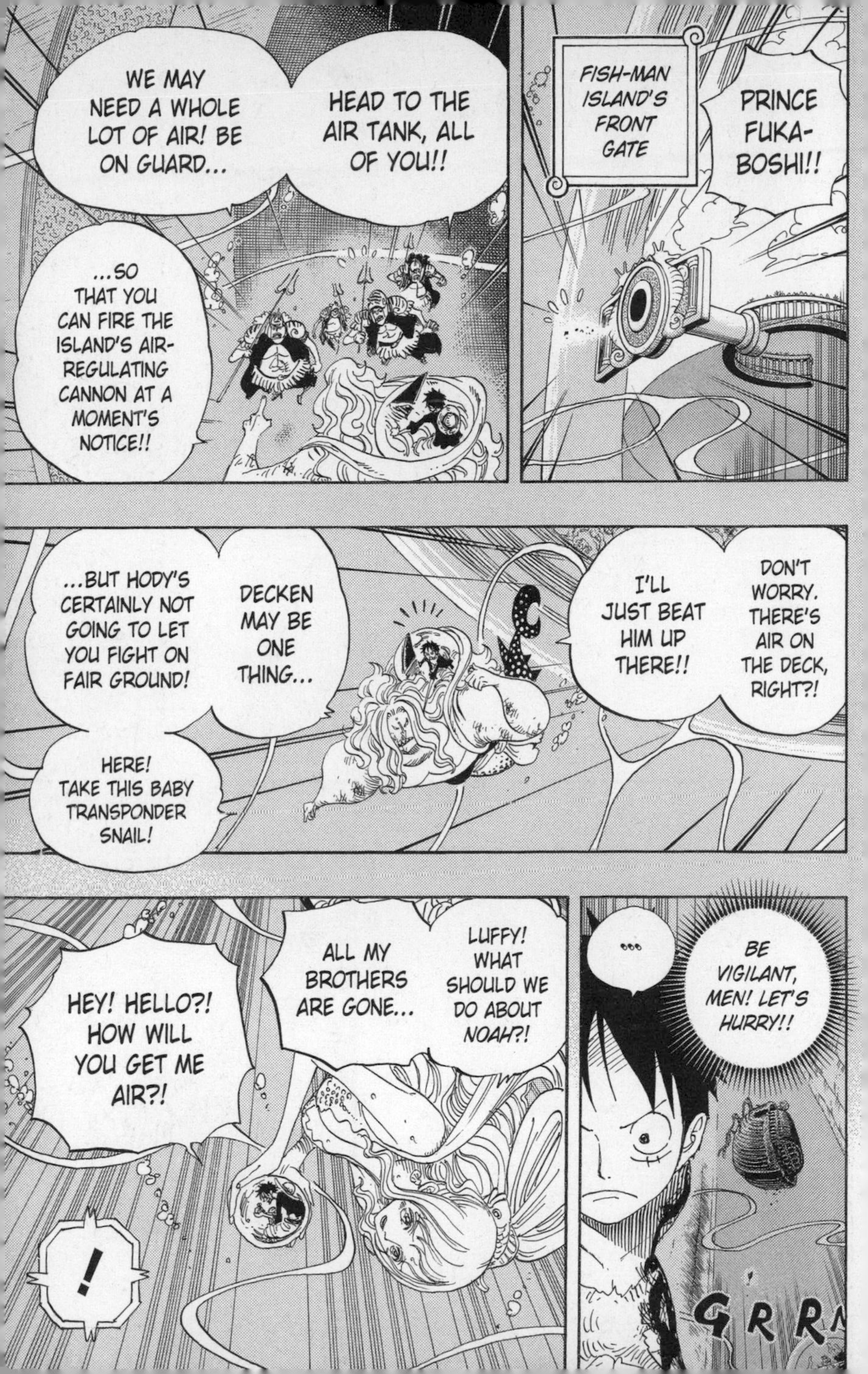
FISH-MAN ISLAND'S FRONT GATE
PRINCE FUKA-BOSHI!!
HEAD TO THE AIR TANK, ALL OF YOU!!
WE MAY NEED A WHOLE LOT OF AIR! BE ON GUARD...
...SO THAT YOU CAN FIRE THE ISLAND'S AIR-REGULATING CANNON AT A MOMENT'S NOTICE!!
DON'T WORRY. THERE'S AIR ON THE DECK, RIGHT?!
I'LL JUST BEAT HIM UP THERE!!
DECKEN MAY BE ONE THING...
...BUT HODY'S CERTAINLY NOT GOING TO LET YOU FIGHT ON FAIR GROUND!
HERE! TAKE THIS BABY TRANSPONDER SNAIL!
...
BE VIGILANT, MEN! LET'S HURRY!!
GRR
LUFFY! WHAT SHOULD WE DO ABOUT NOAH?!
ALL MY BROTHERS ARE GONE...
HEY! HELLO?! HOW WILL YOU GET ME AIR?!
!

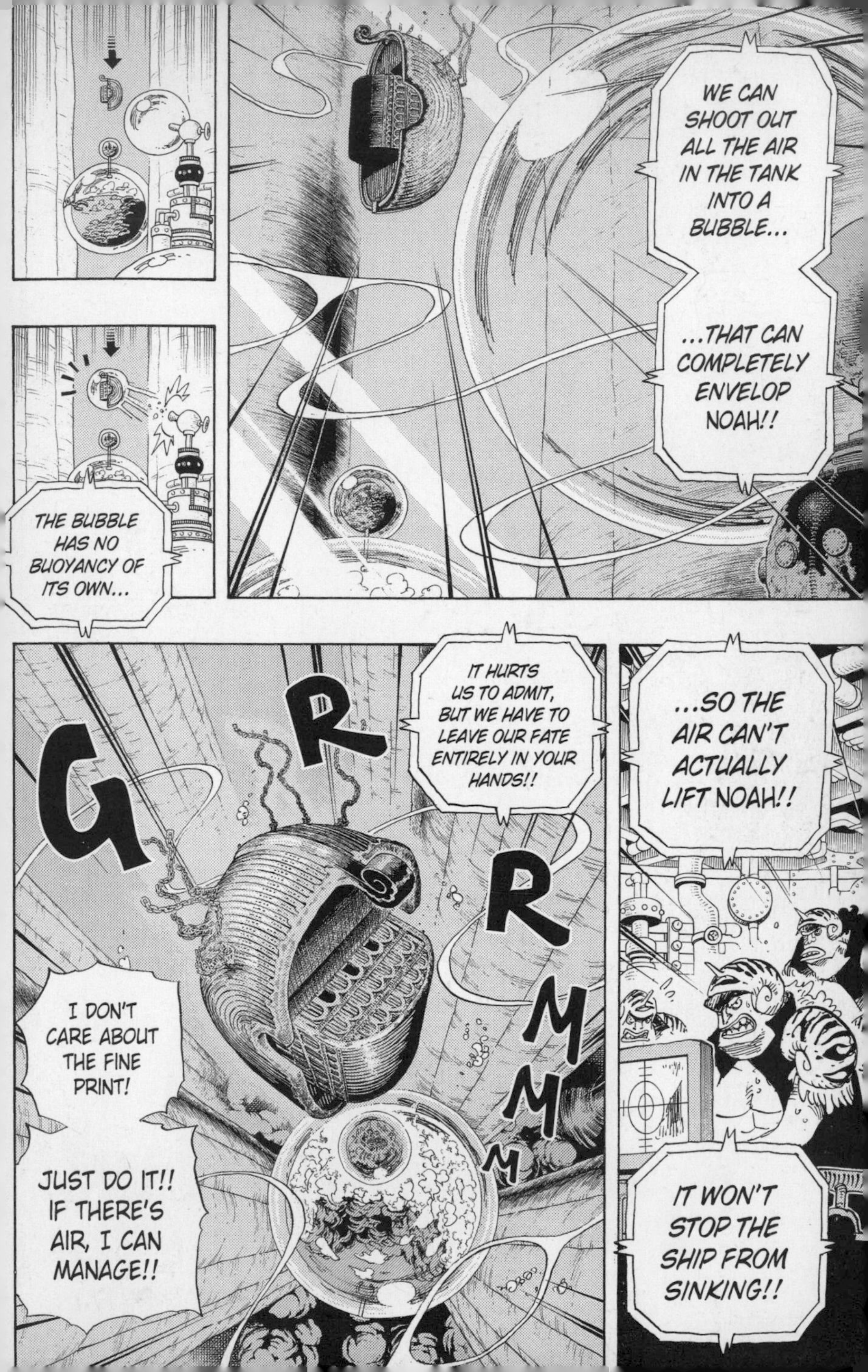
WE CAN SHOOT OUT ALL THE AIR IN THE TANK INTO A BUBBLE...
...THAT CAN COMPLETELY ENVELOP NOAH!!
THE BUBBLE HAS NO BUOYANCY OF ITS OWN...
...SO THE AIR CAN'T ACTUALLY LIFT NOAH!!
IT WON'T STOP THE SHIP FROM SINKING!!
IT HURTS US TO ADMIT, BUT WE HAVE TO LEAVE OUR FATE ENTIRELY IN YOUR HANDS!!
GRRRMMMM
I DON'T CARE ABOUT THE FINE PRINT!
JUST DO IT!! IF THERE'S AIR, I CAN MANAGE!!

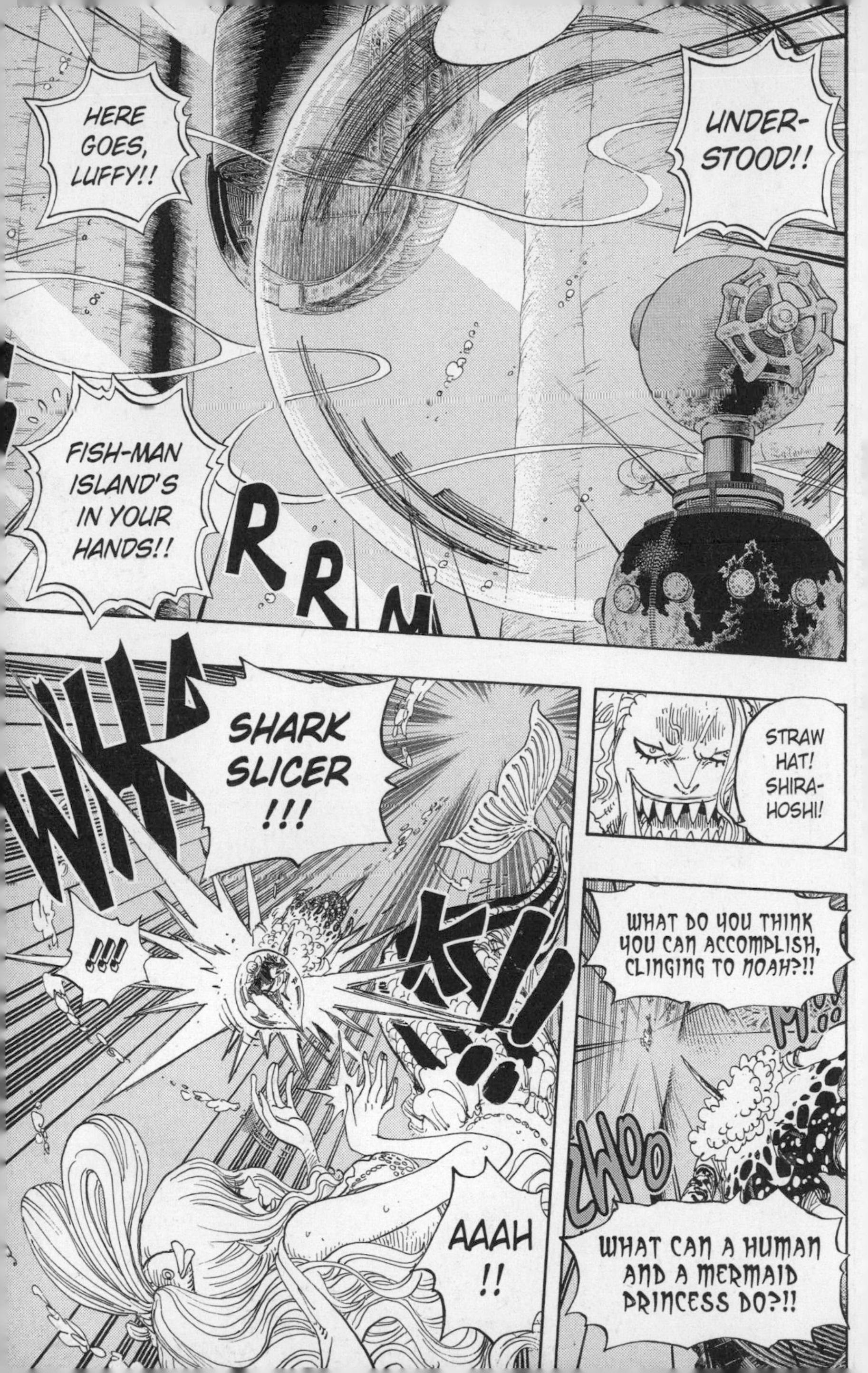
UNDER-STOOD!!
HERE GOES, LUFFY!!
FISH-MAN ISLAND'S IN YOUR HANDS!!
RRM
STRAW HAT! SHIRA-HOSHI!
WHAT DO YOU THINK YOU CAN ACCOMPLISH, CLINGING TO NOAH?!!
WHAT CAN A HUMAN AND A MERMAID PRINCESS DO?!!
ZHOO
SHARK SLICER !!!
!!!
AAAH !!

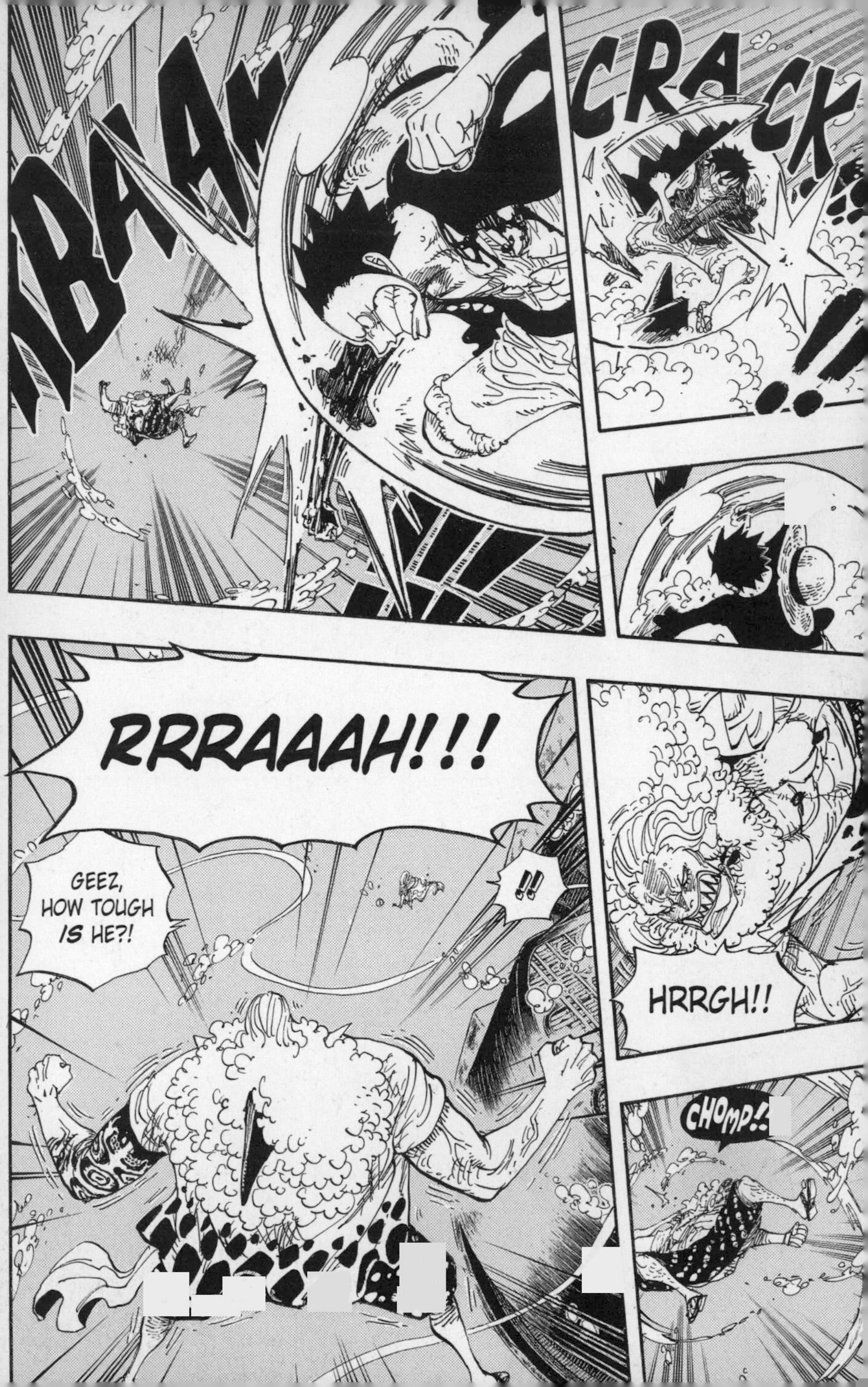
CRACK!!
BAAN
HRRGH!!
CHOMP!!
RRRAAAH!!!
!!
GEEZ, HOW TOUGH IS HE?!

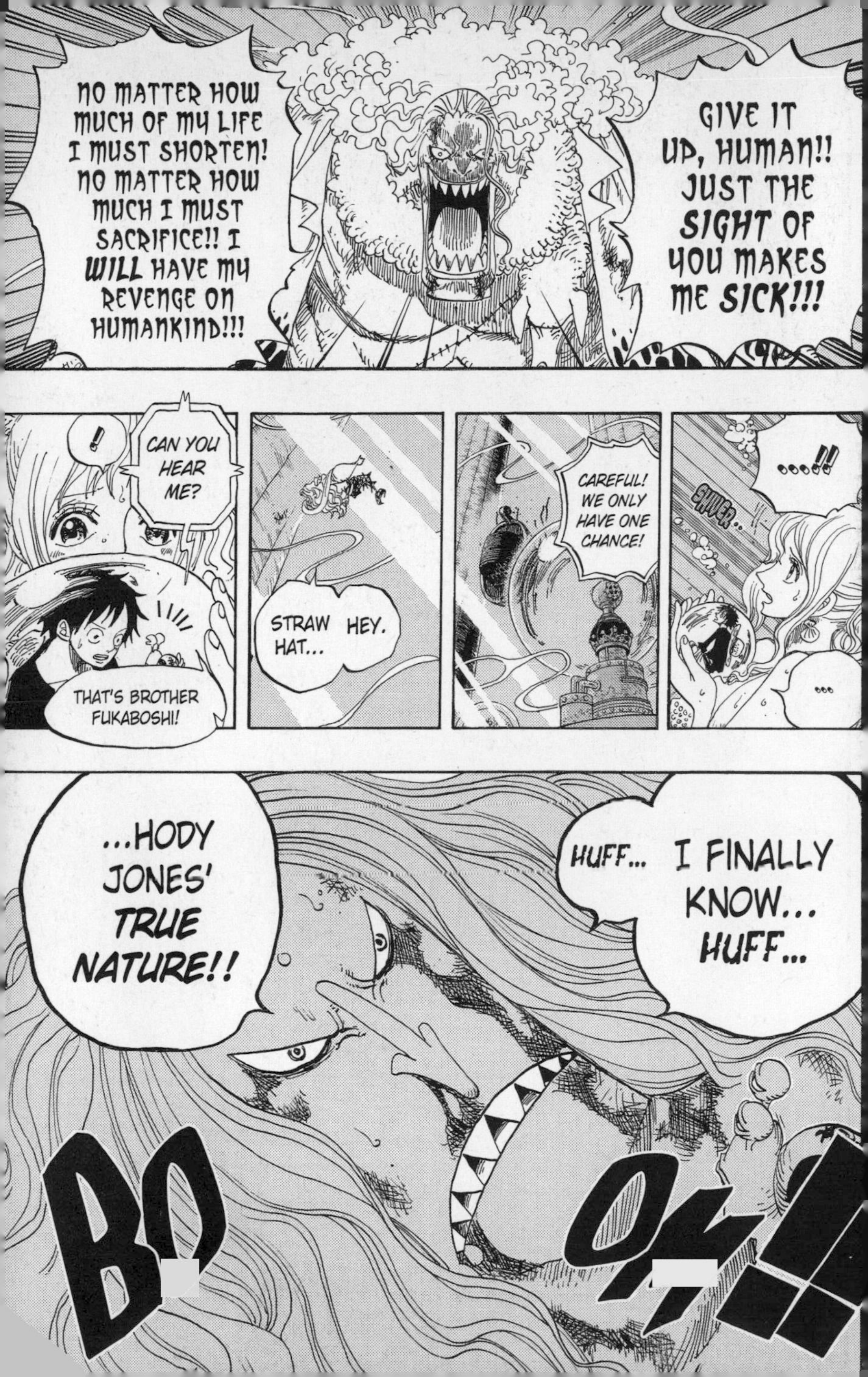
GIVE IT UP, HUMAN!! JUST THE SIGHT OF YOU MAKES ME SICK!!!
NO MATTER HOW MUCH OF MY LIFE I MUST SHORTEN! NO MATTER HOW MUCH I MUST SACRIFICE!! I WILL HAVE MY REVENGE ON HUMANKIND!!!
...!!
SHIVER...
...
CAREFUL! WE ONLY HAVE ONE CHANCE!
HEY.
STRAW HAT...
CAN YOU HEAR ME?
!
THAT'S BROTHER FUKABOSHI!
HUFF... I FINALLY KNOW... HUFF...
...HODY JONES' TRUE NATURE!!
BO
OH!!

LOST ALL FACE

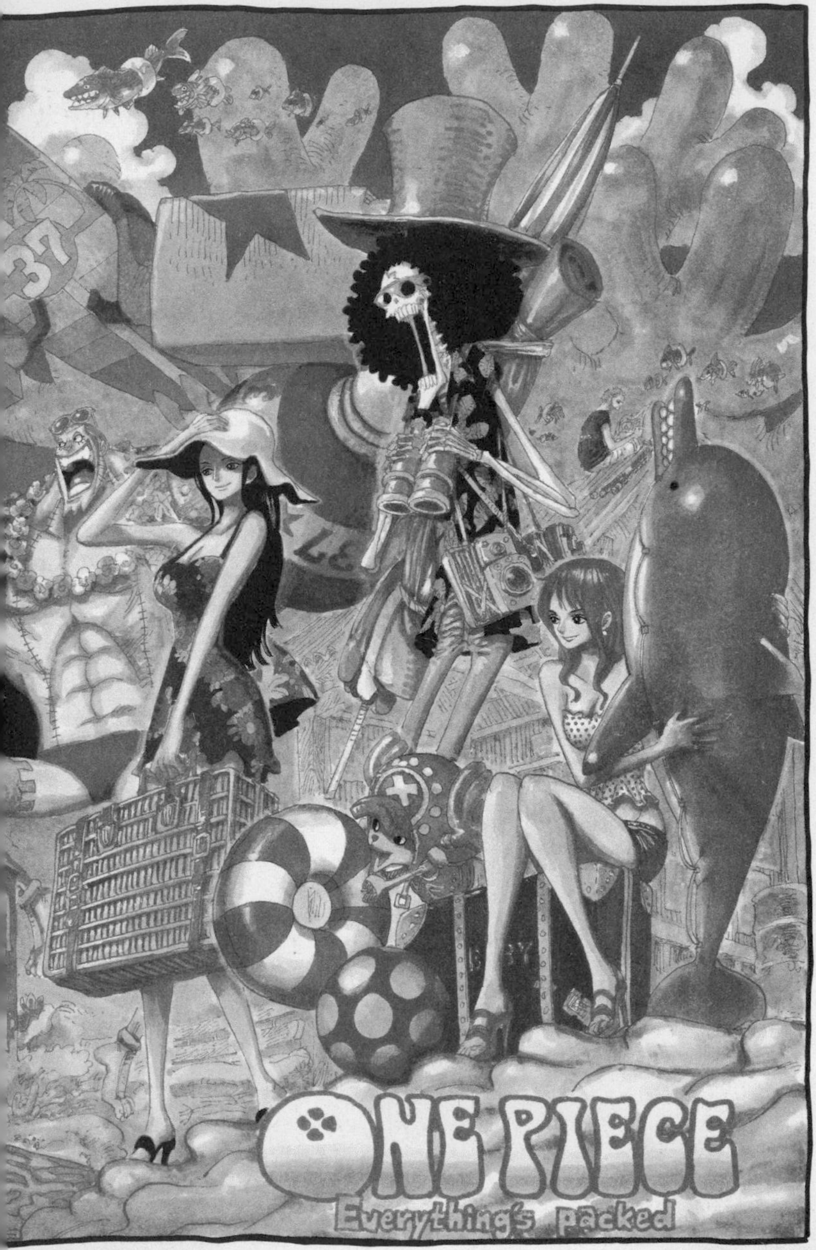
ONE PIECE
Everything's packed

Chapter 642:

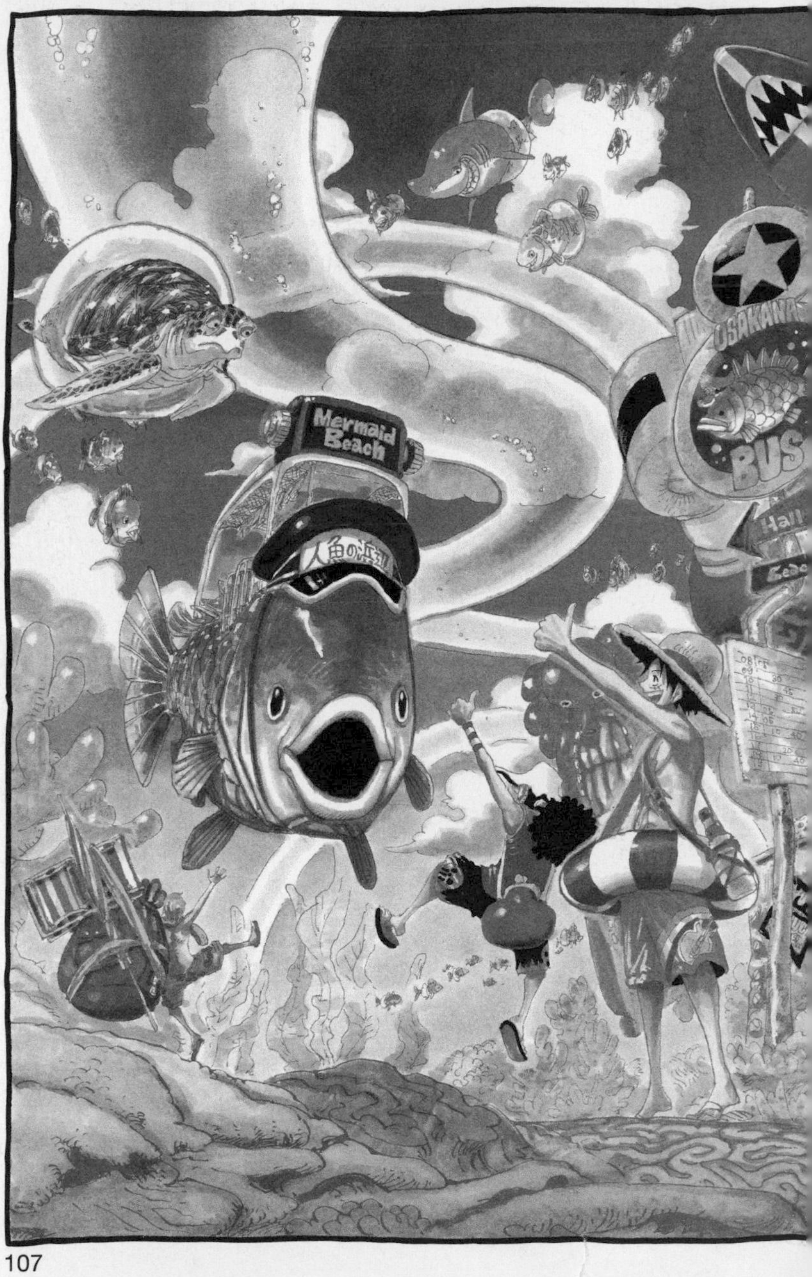

Mermaid Beach
人魚の浜辺
OSAKANA
BUS

ONE PIECE
vol.65

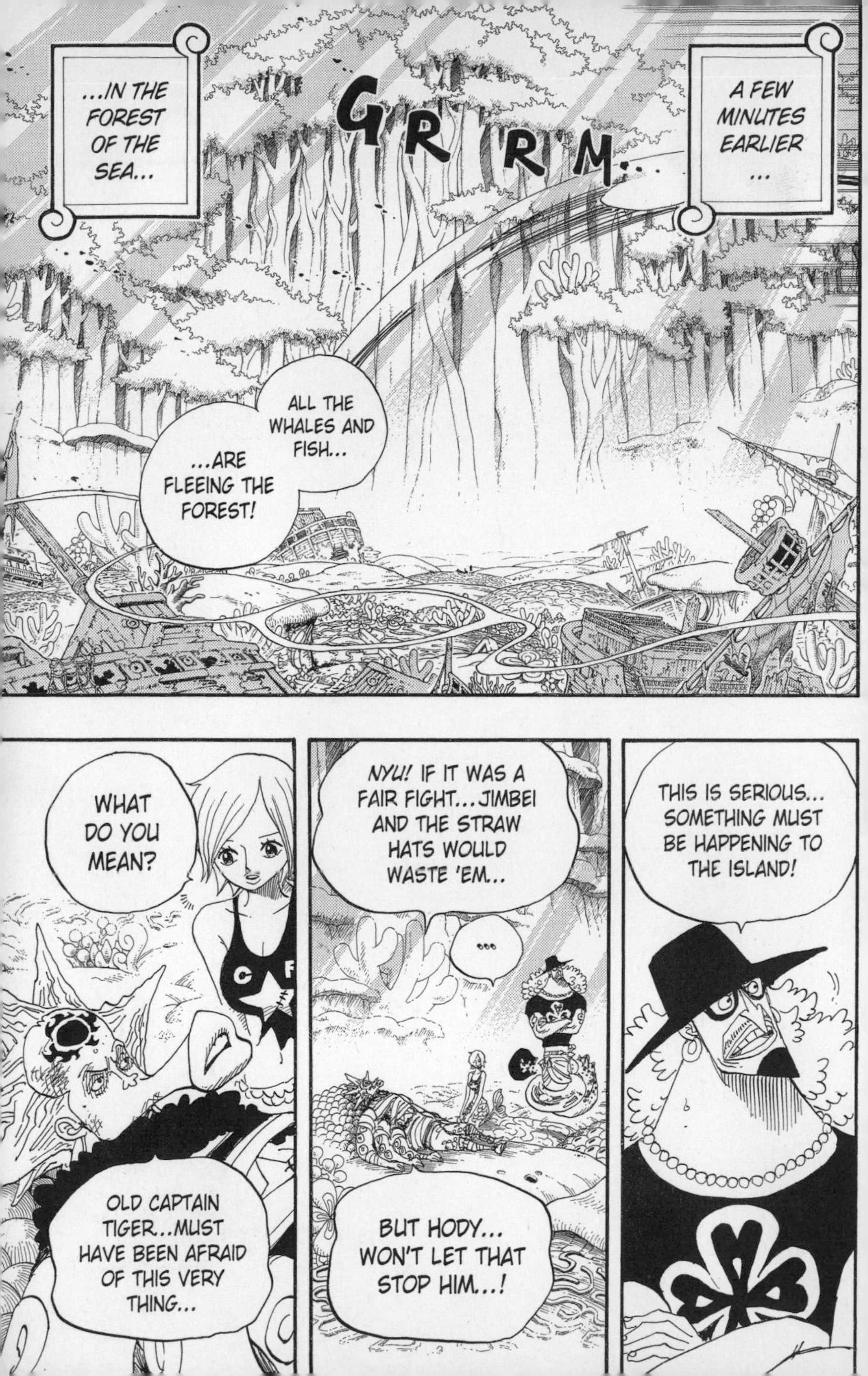
A FEW MINUTES EARLIER...
...IN THE FOREST OF THE SEA...
GRRRM...
ALL THE WHALES AND FISH...
...ARE FLEEING THE FOREST!
THIS IS SERIOUS... SOMETHING MUST BE HAPPENING TO THE ISLAND!
NYU! IF IT WAS A FAIR FIGHT... JIMBEI AND THE STRAW HATS WOULD WASTE 'EM...
...
BUT HODY... WON'T LET THAT STOP HIM...!
WHAT DO YOU MEAN?
OLD CAPTAIN TIGER... MUST HAVE BEEN AFRAID OF THIS VERY THING...

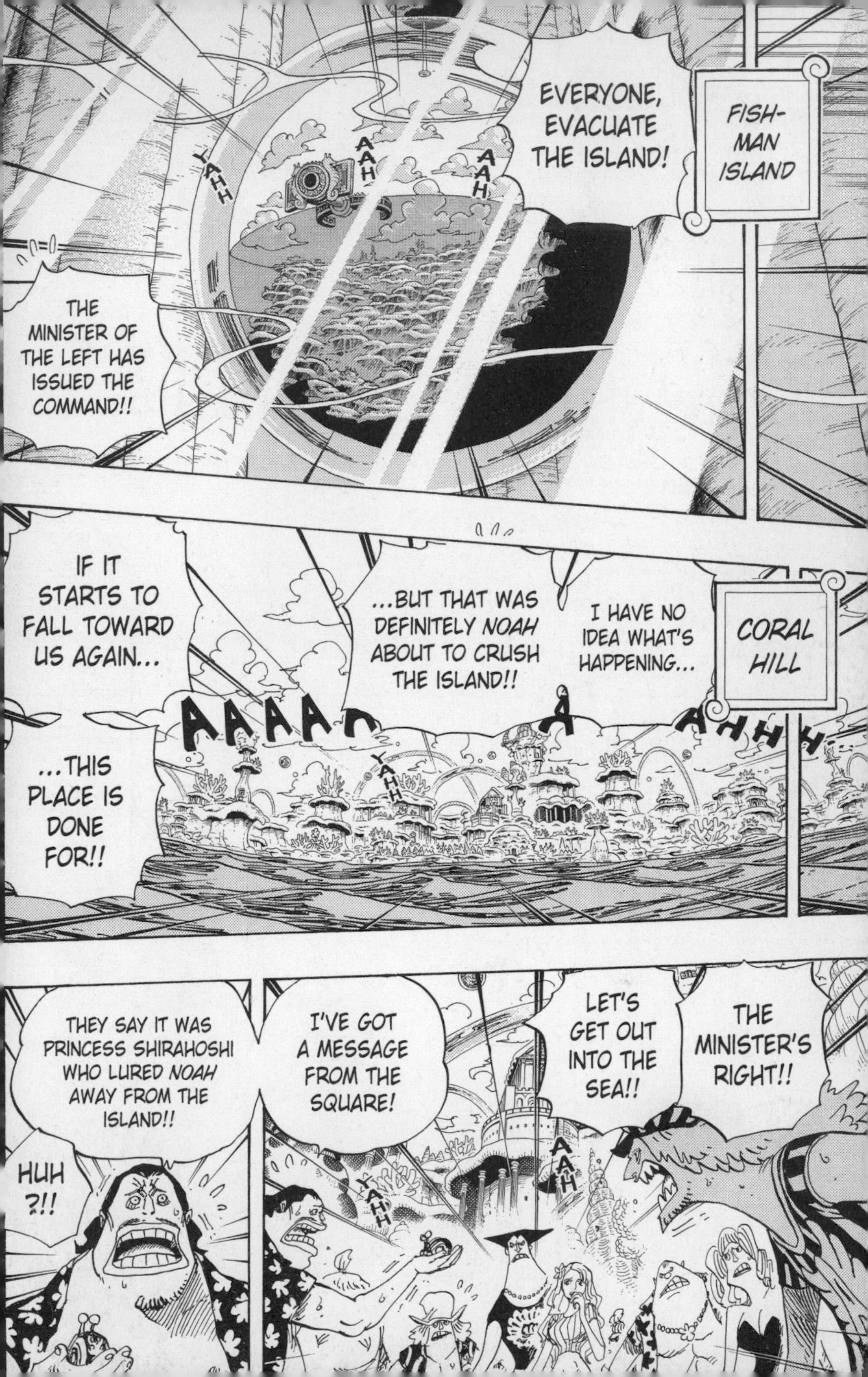
FISH-MAN ISLAND
EVERYONE, EVACUATE THE ISLAND!
AAH
AAH
YAHH
THE MINISTER OF THE LEFT HAS ISSUED THE COMMAND!!
CORAL HILL
I HAVE NO IDEA WHAT'S HAPPENING...
...BUT THAT WAS DEFINITELY *NOAH* ABOUT TO CRUSH THE ISLAND!!
IF IT STARTS TO FALL TOWARD US AGAIN...
AHHHH
YAHH
...THIS PLACE IS DONE FOR!!
THE MINISTER'S RIGHT!!
LET'S GET OUT INTO THE SEA!!
AAH
YAHH
I'VE GOT A MESSAGE FROM THE SQUARE!
THEY SAY IT WAS PRINCESS SHIRAHOSHI WHO LURED *NOAH* AWAY FROM THE ISLAND!!
HUH ?!!

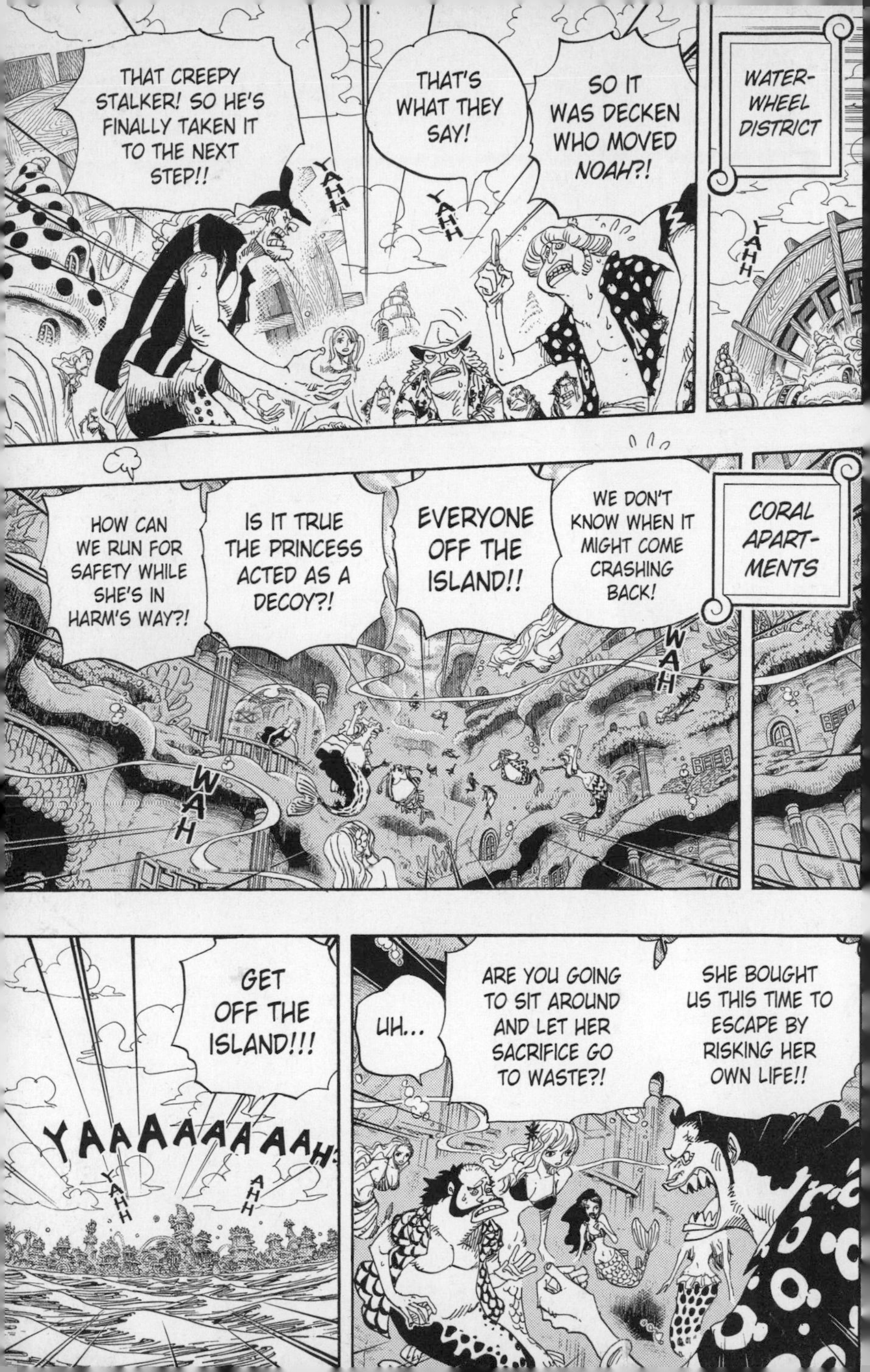
WATER-WHEEL DISTRICT
YAHH
SO IT WAS DECKEN WHO MOVED NOAH?!
THAT'S WHAT THEY SAY!
YAHH
THAT CREEPY STALKER! SO HE'S FINALLY TAKEN IT TO THE NEXT STEP!!
YAHH
CORAL APARTMENTS
WE DON'T KNOW WHEN IT MIGHT COME CRASHING BACK!
EVERYONE OFF THE ISLAND!!
IS IT TRUE THE PRINCESS ACTED AS A DECOY?!
HOW CAN WE RUN FOR SAFETY WHILE SHE'S IN HARM'S WAY?!
WAH
WAH
SHE BOUGHT US THIS TIME TO ESCAPE BY RISKING HER OWN LIFE!!
ARE YOU GOING TO SIT AROUND AND LET HER SACRIFICE GO TO WASTE?!
UH...
GET OFF THE ISLAND!!!
YAAAAAAAAAH!
YAHH
AHH

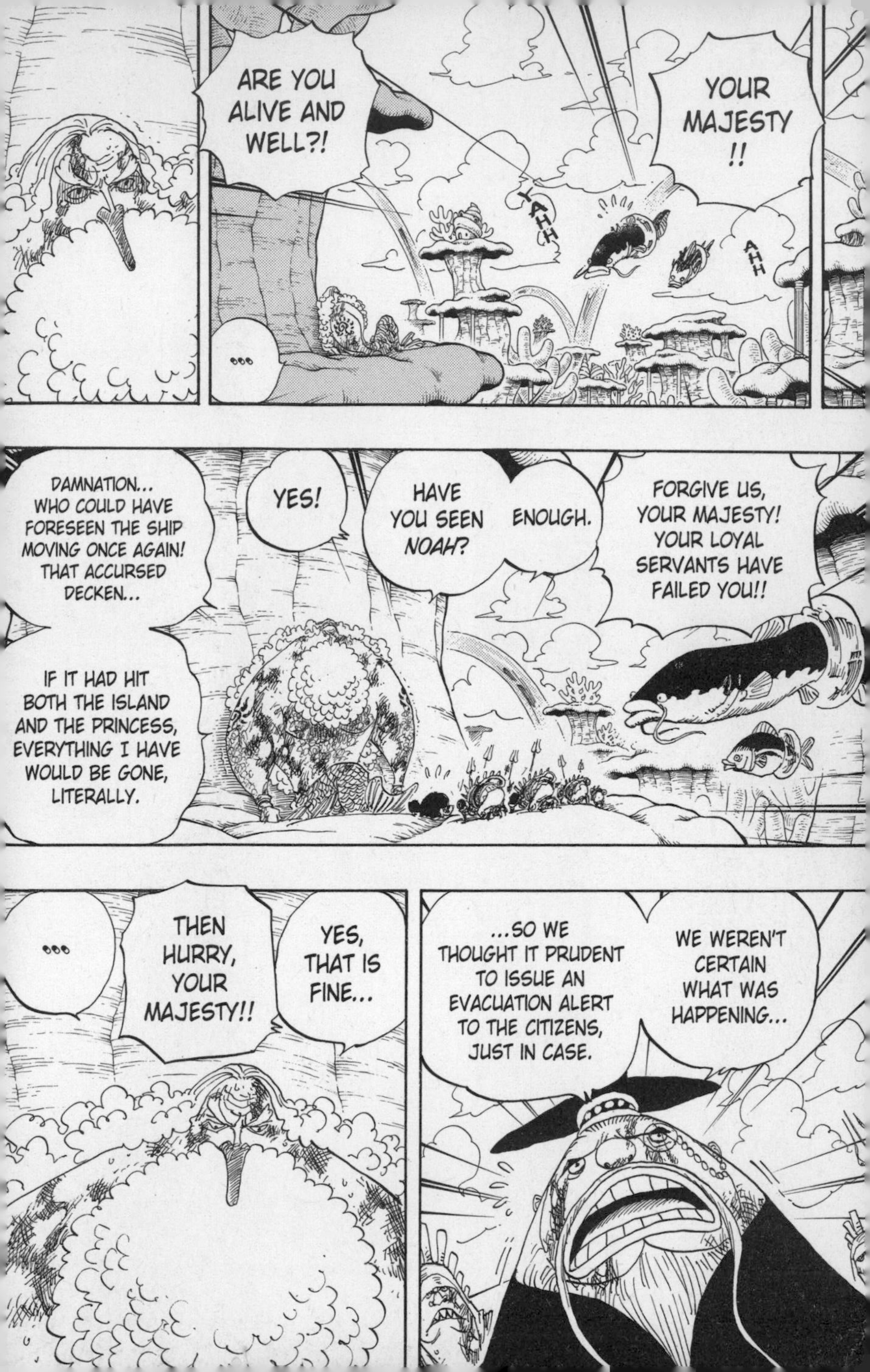
YOUR MAJESTY !!
AHH
YAHH
ARE YOU ALIVE AND WELL?!
...
FORGIVE US, YOUR MAJESTY! YOUR LOYAL SERVANTS HAVE FAILED YOU!!
ENOUGH.
HAVE YOU SEEN *NOAH*?
YES!
DAMNATION... WHO COULD HAVE FORESEEN THE SHIP MOVING ONCE AGAIN! THAT ACCURSED DECKEN...
IF IT HAD HIT BOTH THE ISLAND AND THE PRINCESS, EVERYTHING I HAVE WOULD BE GONE, LITERALLY.
WE WEREN'T CERTAIN WHAT WAS HAPPENING...
...SO WE THOUGHT IT PRUDENT TO ISSUE AN EVACUATION ALERT TO THE CITIZENS, JUST IN CASE.
YES, THAT IS FINE...
THEN HURRY, YOUR MAJESTY!!
...

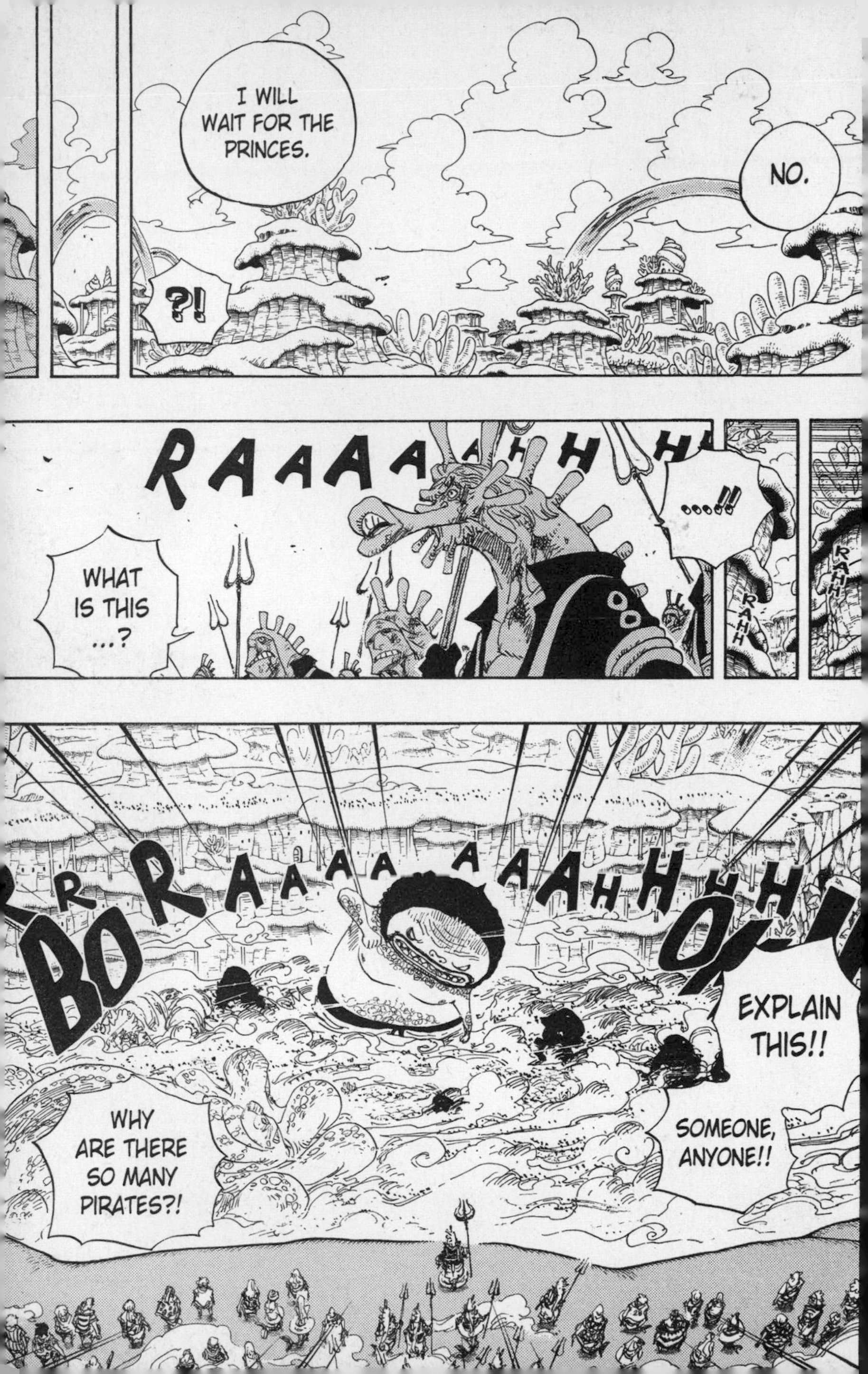
NO.
I WILL WAIT FOR THE PRINCES.
?!
RAHH
RAHH
RAAAAAHHH
....!!
WHAT IS THIS ...?
RRAAAAAAAHHHH
BO
O
EXPLAIN THIS!!
SOMEONE, ANYONE!!
WHY ARE THERE SO MANY PIRATES?!

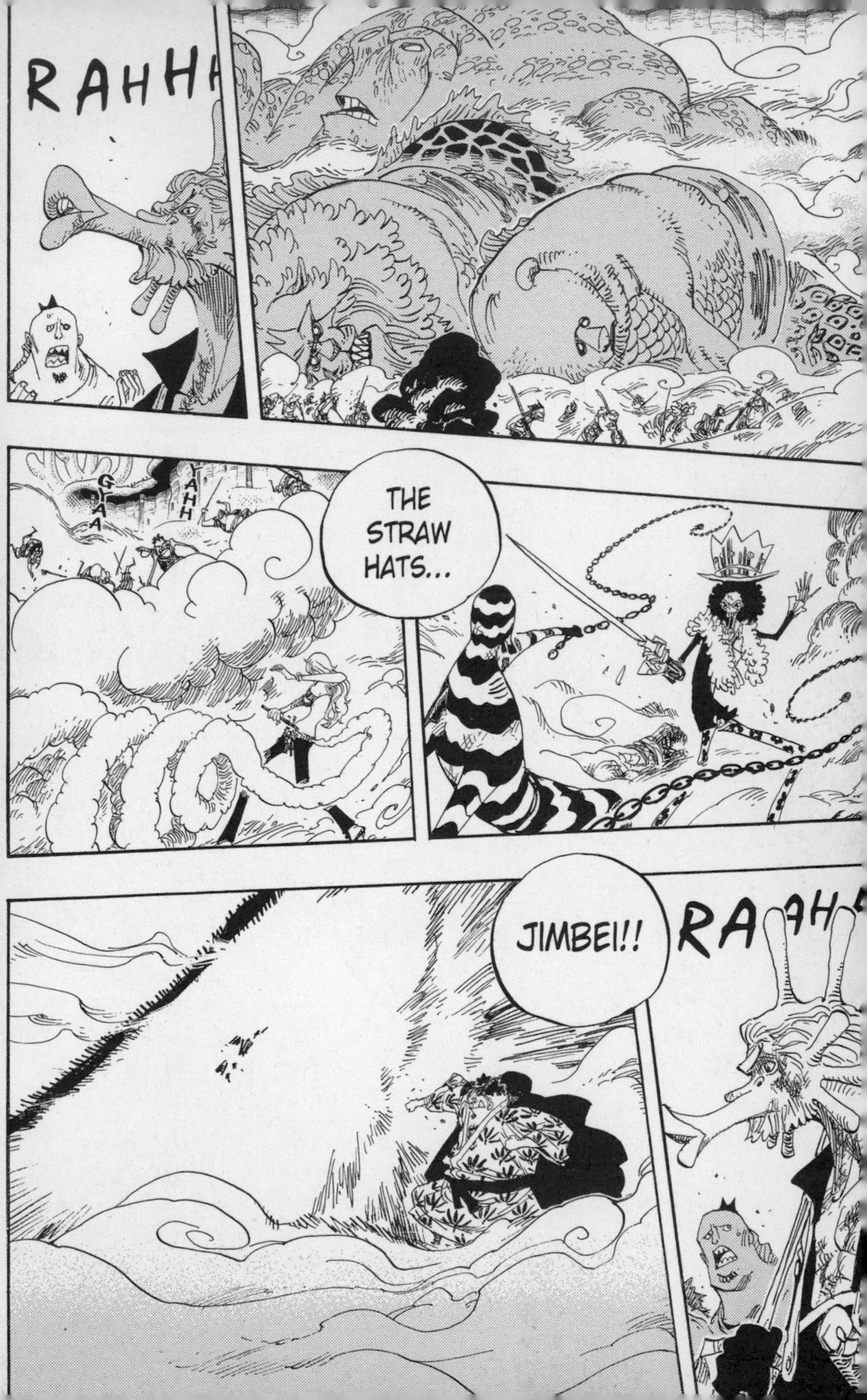
RAHHH
THE STRAW HATS...
RA AH
JIMBEI!!

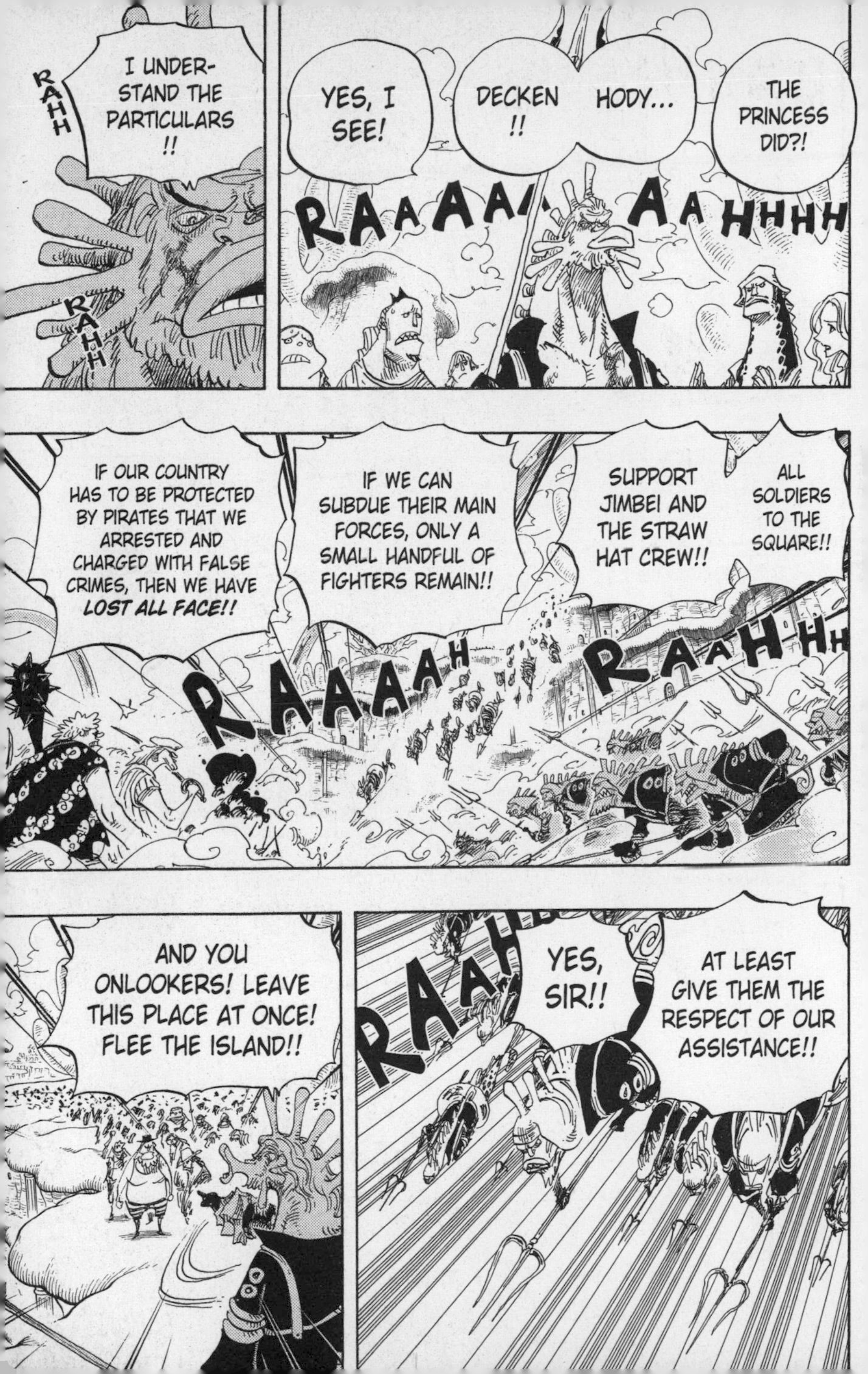
THE PRINCESS DID?!
HODY...
DECKEN !!
YES, I SEE!
RAAAA AAHHHH
I UNDER-STAND THE PARTICULARS !!
RAHH
RAHH
ALL SOLDIERS TO THE SQUARE!!
SUPPORT JIMBEI AND THE STRAW HAT CREW!!
IF WE CAN SUBDUE THEIR MAIN FORCES, ONLY A SMALL HANDFUL OF FIGHTERS REMAIN!!
IF OUR COUNTRY HAS TO BE PROTECTED BY PIRATES THAT WE ARRESTED AND CHARGED WITH FALSE CRIMES, THEN WE HAVE *LOST ALL FACE!!*
RAAHHH
RAAAAH
AT LEAST GIVE THEM THE RESPECT OF OUR ASSISTANCE!!
YES, SIR!!
RAAH
AND YOU ONLOOKERS! LEAVE THIS PLACE AT ONCE! FLEE THE ISLAND!!

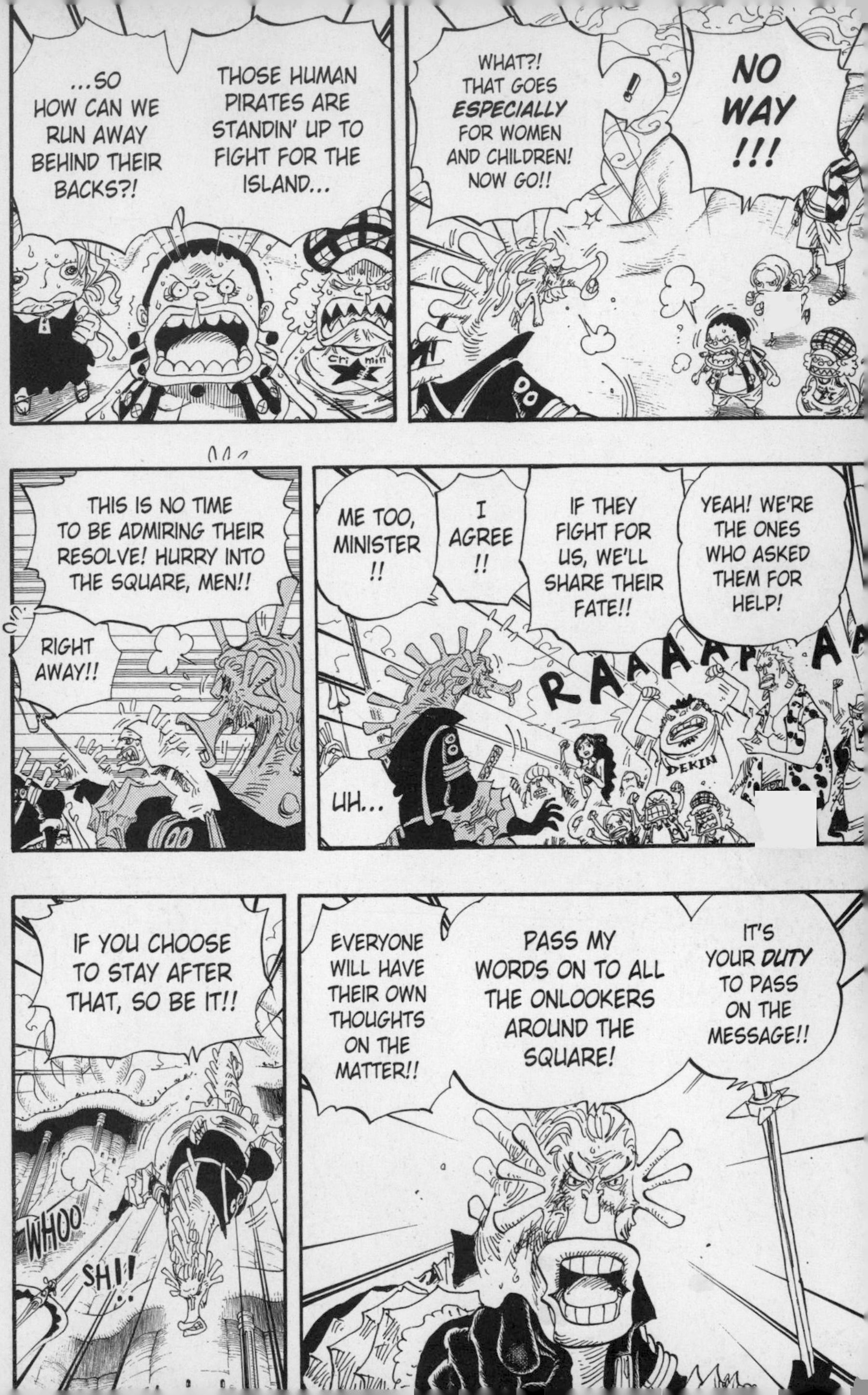
NO WAY !!!
WHAT?! THAT GOES ESPECIALLY FOR WOMEN AND CHILDREN! NOW GO!!
THOSE HUMAN PIRATES ARE STANDIN' UP TO FIGHT FOR THE ISLAND...
...SO HOW CAN WE RUN AWAY BEHIND THEIR BACKS?!
YEAH! WE'RE THE ONES WHO ASKED THEM FOR HELP!
IF THEY FIGHT FOR US, WE'LL SHARE THEIR FATE!!
I AGREE !!
ME TOO, MINISTER !!
RAAAAAA
DEKIN
UH...
THIS IS NO TIME TO BE ADMIRING THEIR RESOLVE! HURRY INTO THE SQUARE, MEN!!
RIGHT AWAY!!
IT'S YOUR DUTY TO PASS ON THE MESSAGE!!
PASS MY WORDS ON TO ALL THE ONLOOKERS AROUND THE SQUARE!
EVERYONE WILL HAVE THEIR OWN THOUGHTS ON THE MATTER!!
IF YOU CHOOSE TO STAY AFTER THAT, SO BE IT!!
WHOO
SH!!

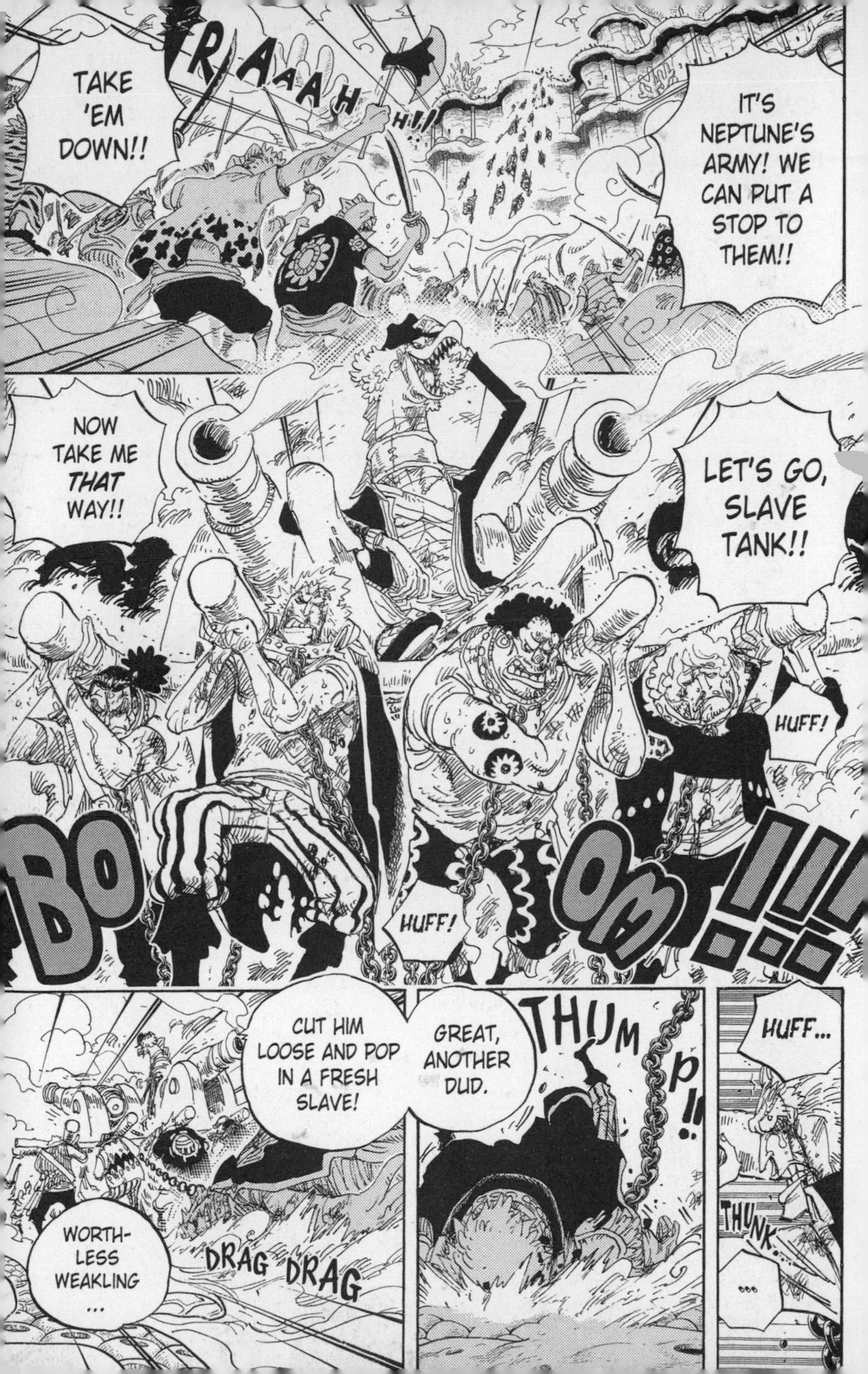
IT'S NEPTUNE'S ARMY! WE CAN PUT A STOP TO THEM!!
RAAAHH!!
TAKE 'EM DOWN!!
LET'S GO, SLAVE TANK!!
NOW TAKE ME THAT WAY!!
HUFF!
BOOM!!!
HUFF!
HUFF...
THUNK...
...
THUMP!!
GREAT, ANOTHER DUD.
CUT HIM LOOSE AND POP IN A FRESH SLAVE!
DRAG DRAG
WORTH-LESS WEAKLING ...

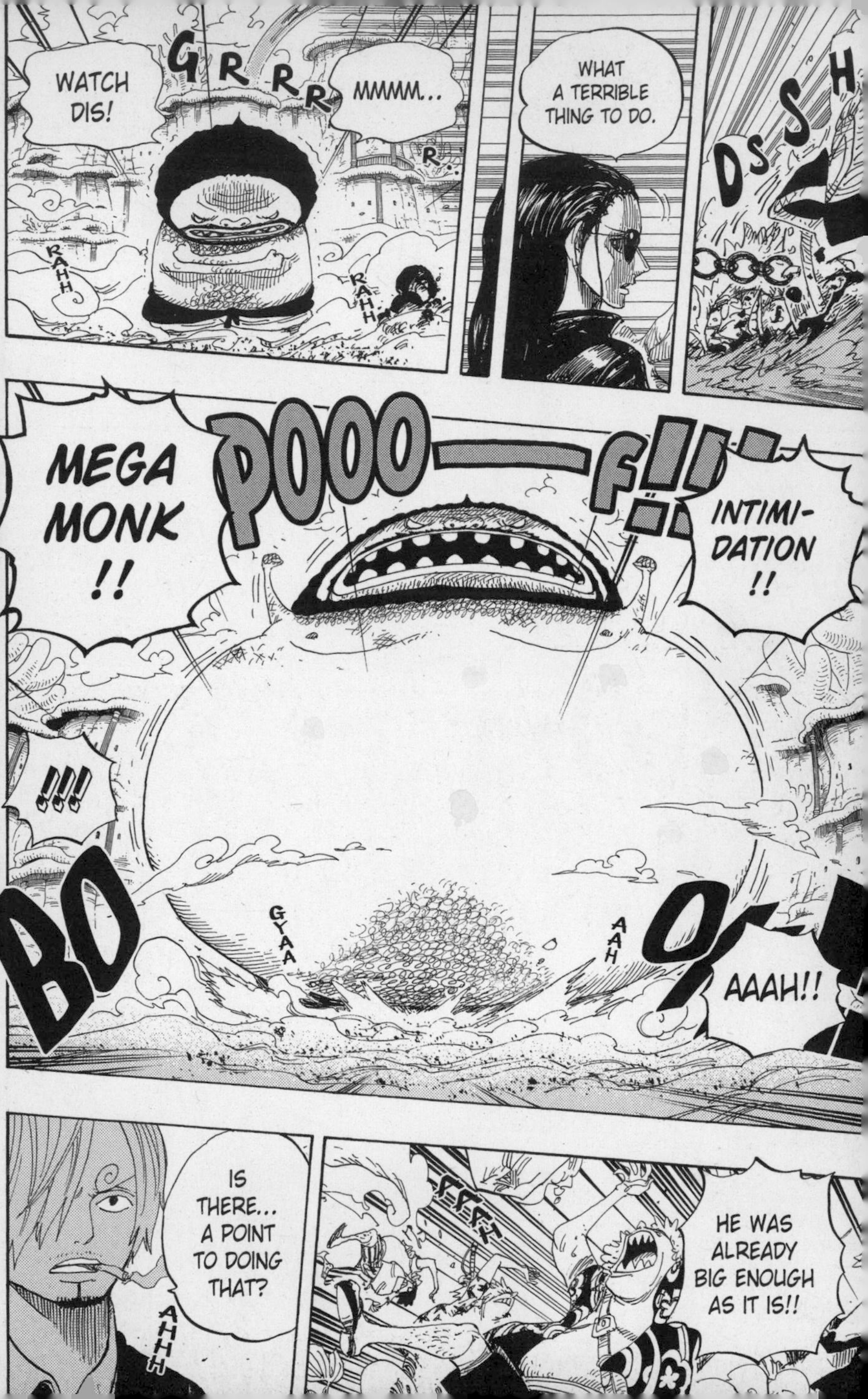
DSSH
WHAT A TERRIBLE THING TO DO.
MMMM...
GRRRR
WATCH DIS!
RAHH
RAHH
INTIMIDATION!!
POOO—F!!
MEGA MONK!!
!!!
AAAH!!
AAH
GYAA
HE WAS ALREADY BIG ENOUGH AS IT IS!!
FFFH
IS THERE... A POINT TO DOING THAT?
AHHH

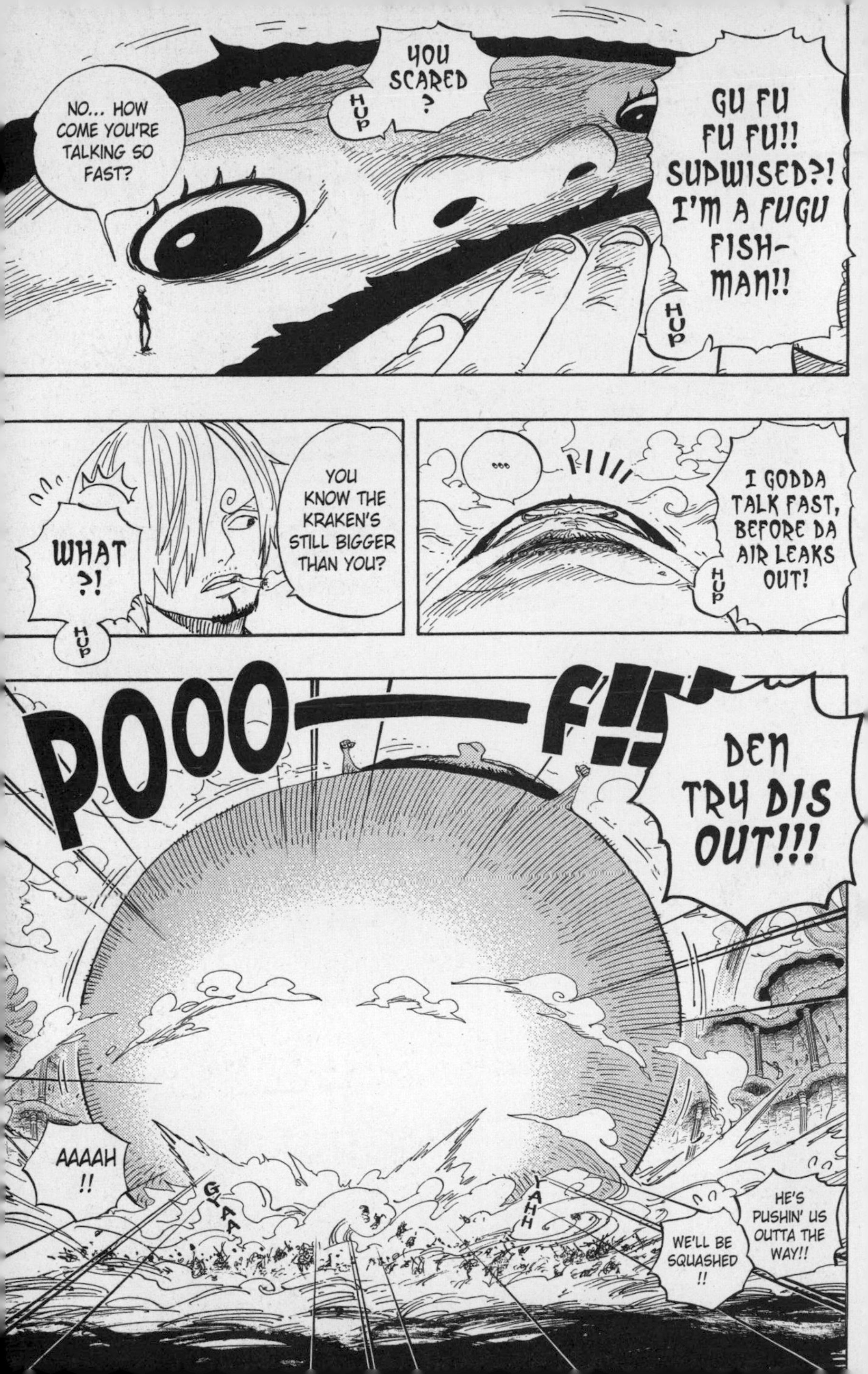
GU FU FU FU!! SUPWISED?! I'M A FUGU FISH-MAN!!
HUP
YOU SCARED ?
HUP
NO... HOW COME YOU'RE TALKING SO FAST?
I GODDA TALK FAST, BEFORE DA AIR LEAKS OUT!
HUP
...
YOU KNOW THE KRAKEN'S STILL BIGGER THAN YOU?
WHAT ?!
HUP
DEN TRY DIS OUT!!!
POOO—F!!
HE'S PUSHIN' US OUTTA THE WAY!!
WE'LL BE SQUASHED !!
YAHH
GYAA
AAAAH !!

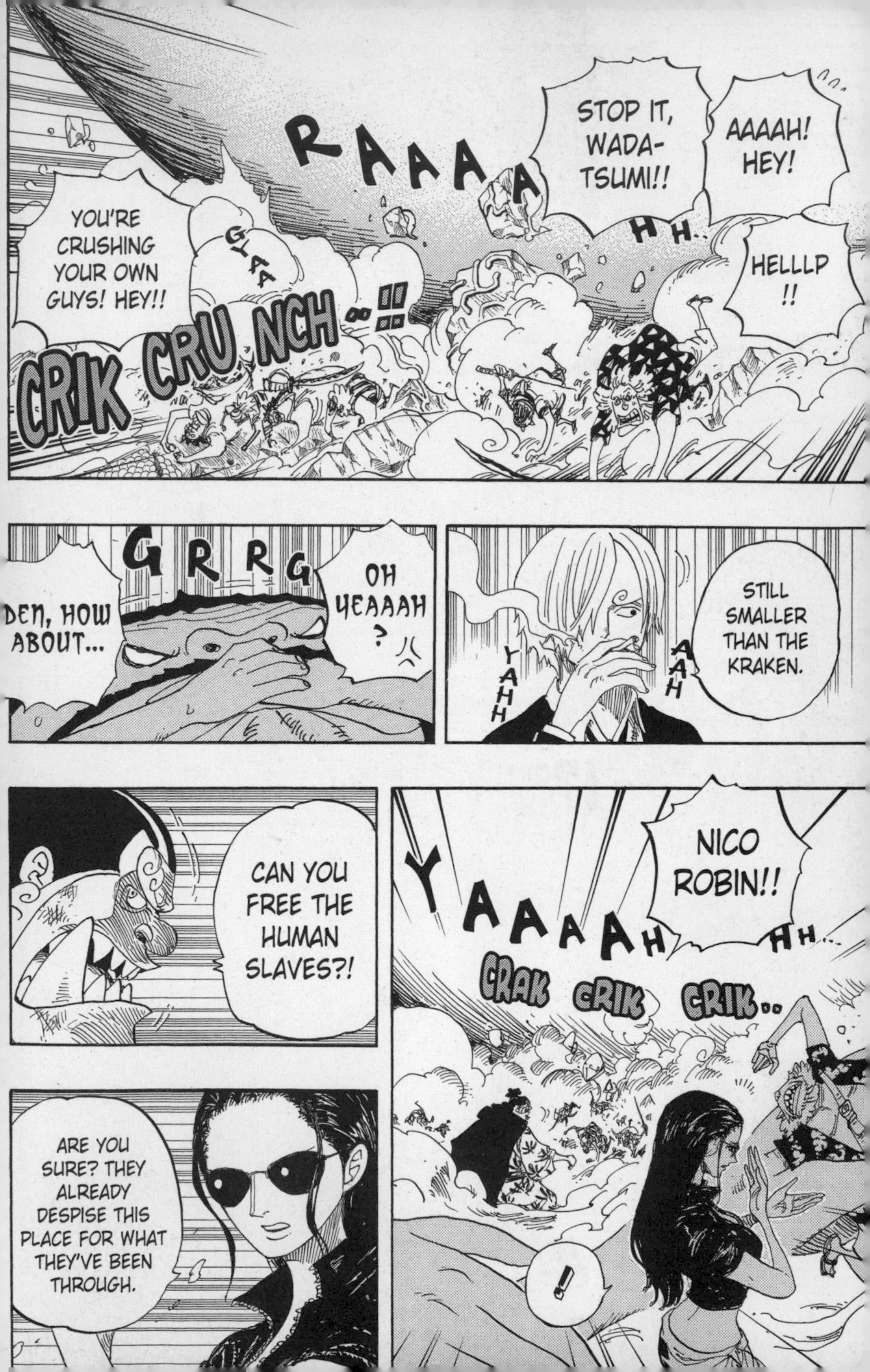
AAAAH! HEY!
STOP IT, WADA-TSUMI!!
RAAAAHH..
HELLLP !!
YOU'RE CRUSHING YOUR OWN GUYS! HEY!!
GYAA
CRIK CRUNCH..!!
STILL SMALLER THAN THE KRAKEN.
AAH
YAHH
OH YEAAAH ?
GRRG
DEN, HOW ABOUT...
NICO ROBIN!!
YAAAAHH HH...
CRAK CRIK CRIK..
!
CAN YOU FREE THE HUMAN SLAVES?!
ARE YOU SURE? THEY ALREADY DESPISE THIS PLACE FOR WHAT THEY'VE BEEN THROUGH.

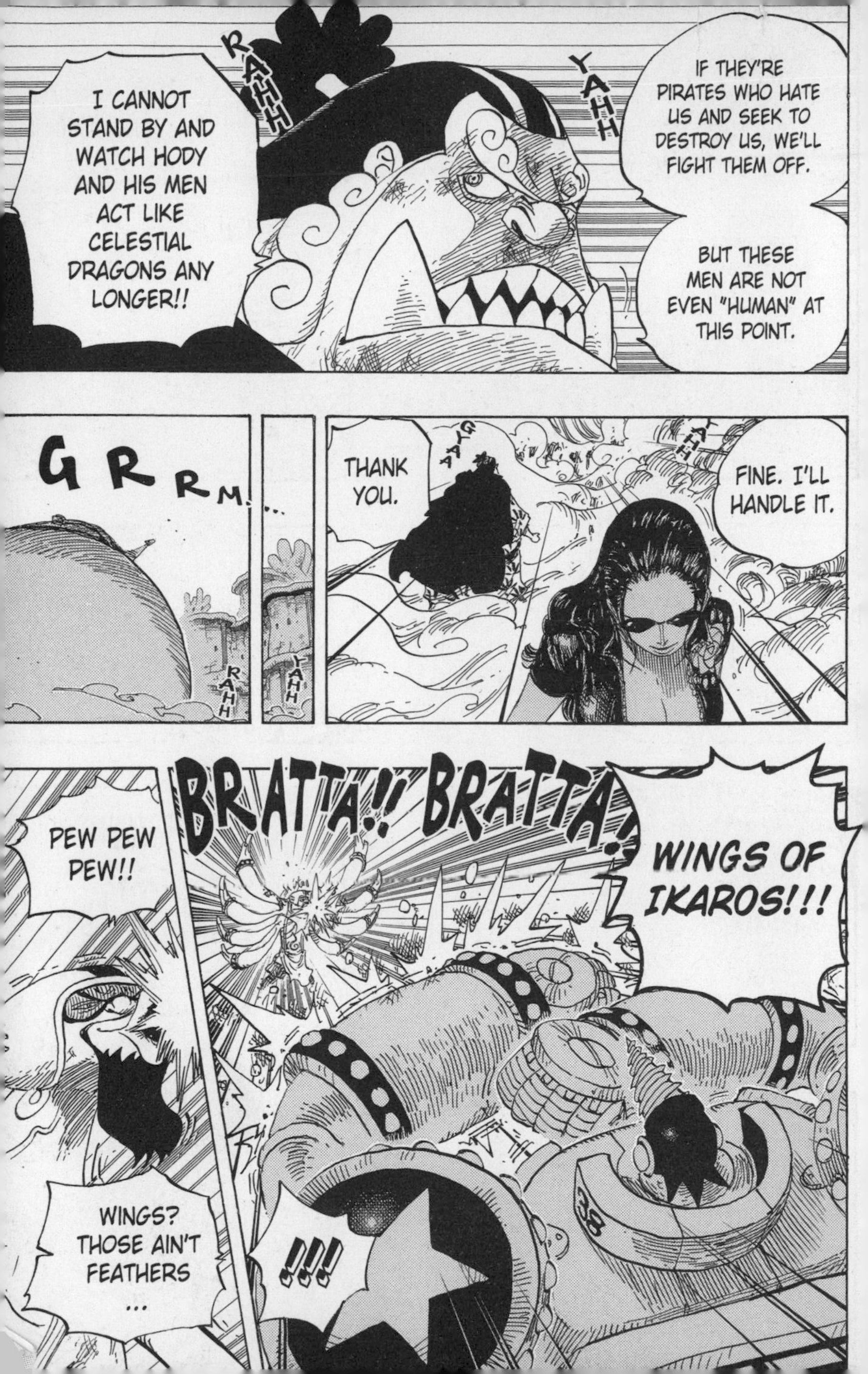
YAHH
IF THEY'RE PIRATES WHO HATE US AND SEEK TO DESTROY US, WE'LL FIGHT THEM OFF.
BUT THESE MEN ARE NOT EVEN "HUMAN" AT THIS POINT.
RAHHH
I CANNOT STAND BY AND WATCH HODY AND HIS MEN ACT LIKE CELESTIAL DRAGONS ANY LONGER!!
YAHH
FINE. I'LL HANDLE IT.
GYAA
THANK YOU.
YAHH
GRRRM...
RAHH
BRATTA!! BRATTA!!
WINGS OF IKAROS!!!
PEW PEW PEW!!
!!!
WINGS? THOSE AIN'T FEATHERS ...

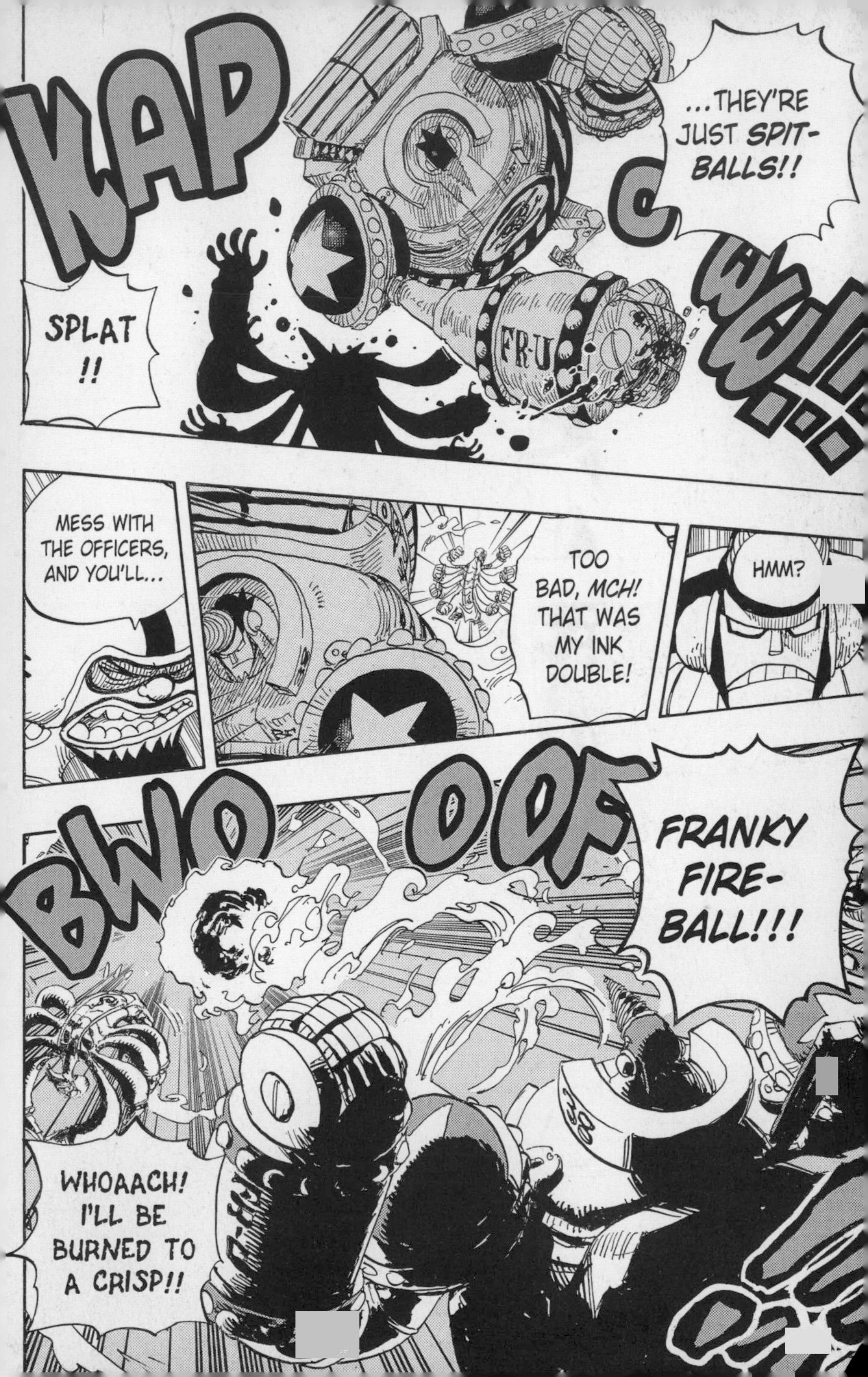
...THEY'RE JUST SPIT-BALLS!!
KAP
SPLAT !!
HMM?
TOO BAD, MCH! THAT WAS MY INK DOUBLE!
MESS WITH THE OFFICERS, AND YOU'LL...
FRANKY FIRE-BALL!!!
BWOOOF
WHOAACH! I'LL BE BURNED TO A CRISP!!

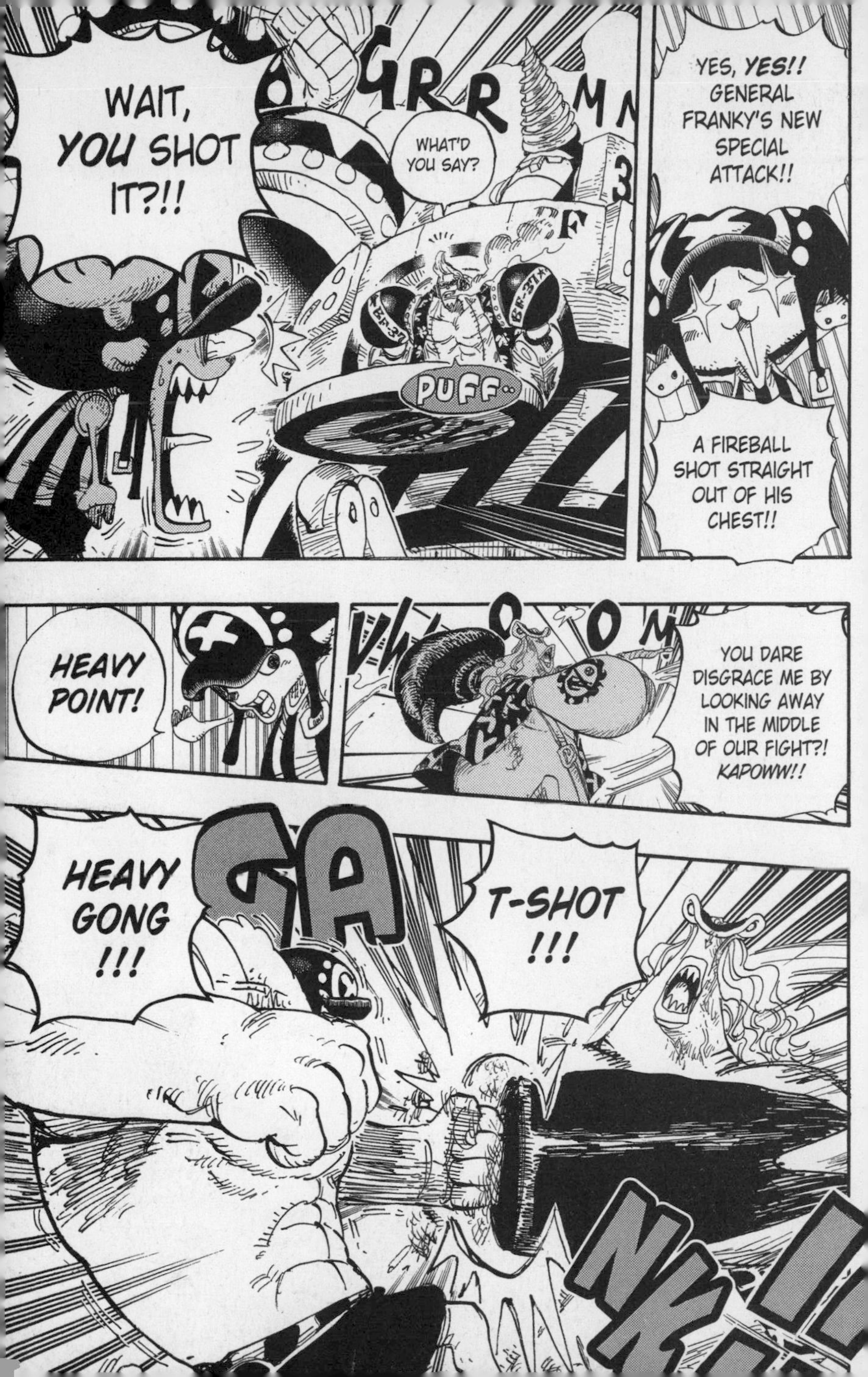
YES, YES!! GENERAL FRANKY'S NEW SPECIAL ATTACK!!
A FIREBALL SHOT STRAIGHT OUT OF HIS CHEST!!
GRRRM
WHAT'D YOU SAY?
WAIT, YOU SHOT IT?!!
PUFF..
VWOOOM
YOU DARE DISGRACE ME BY LOOKING AWAY IN THE MIDDLE OF OUR FIGHT?! KAPOWW!!
HEAVY POINT!
T-SHOT !!!
GA
HEAVY GONG !!!

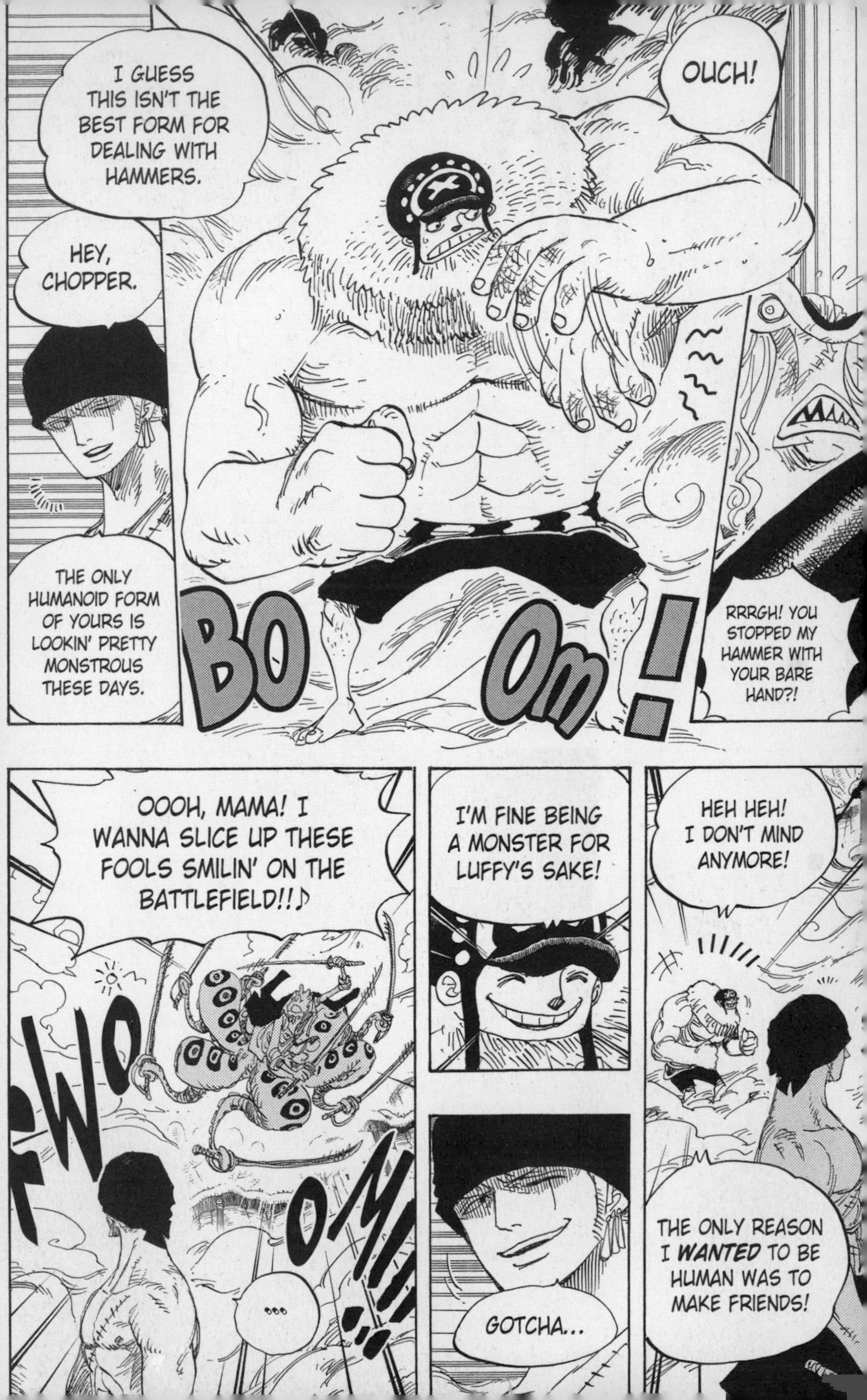
RRRGH! YOU STOPPED MY HAMMER WITH YOUR BARE HAND?!
OUCH!
BOOM!
I GUESS THIS ISN'T THE BEST FORM FOR DEALING WITH HAMMERS.
HEY, CHOPPER.
THE ONLY HUMANOID FORM OF YOURS IS LOOKIN' PRETTY MONSTROUS THESE DAYS.
HEH HEH! I DON'T MIND ANYMORE!
THE ONLY REASON I *WANTED* TO BE HUMAN WAS TO MAKE FRIENDS!
I'M FINE BEING A MONSTER FOR LUFFY'S SAKE!
GOTCHA...
OOOH, MAMA! I WANNA SLICE UP THESE FOOLS SMILIN' ON THE BATTLEFIELD!!♪
...
FWOOM!!

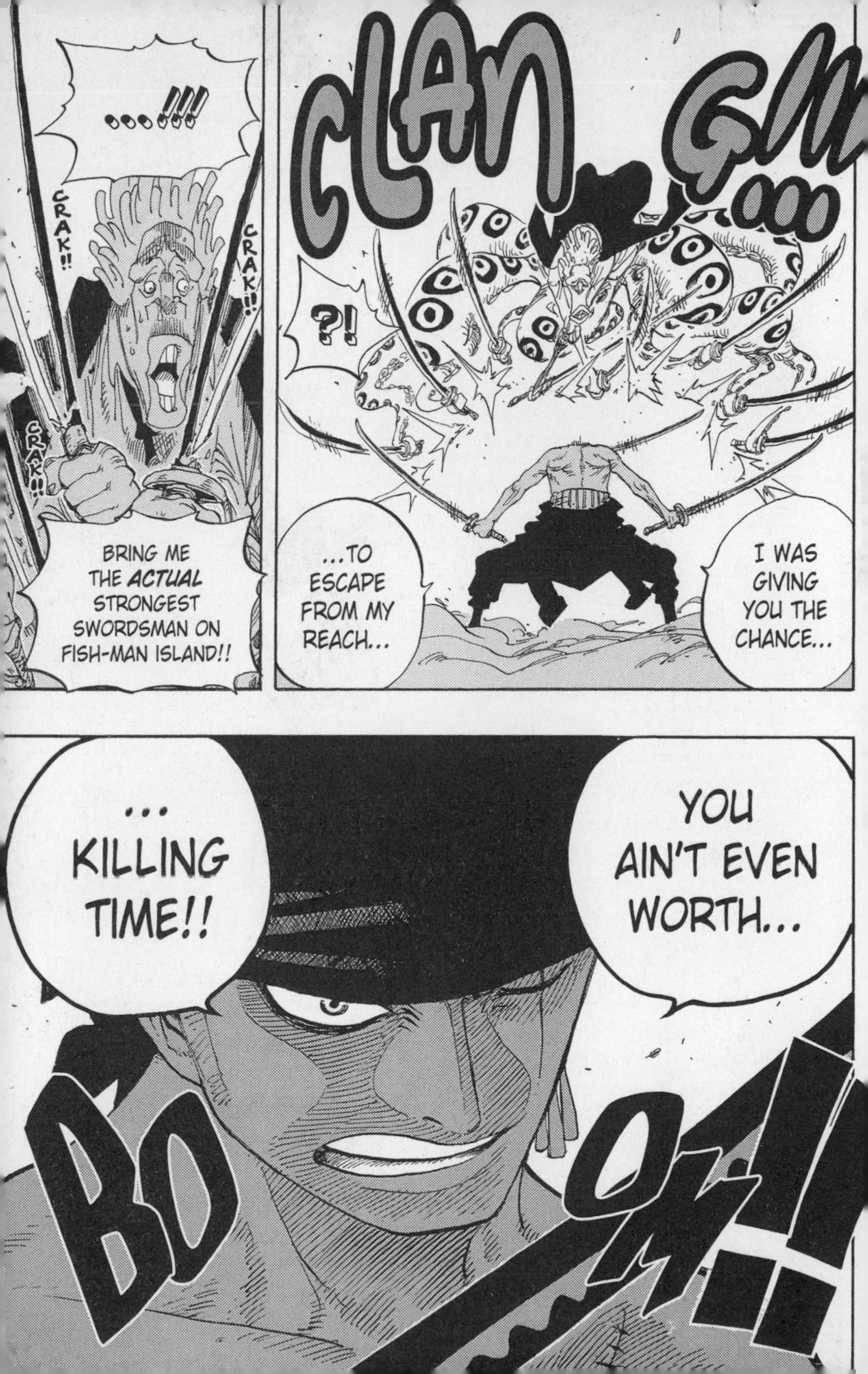
CLAN GIN...
?!
I WAS GIVING YOU THE CHANCE...
...TO ESCAPE FROM MY REACH...
...!!!
CRAK!!
CRAK!!
CRAK!!
BRING ME THE *ACTUAL* STRONGEST SWORDSMAN ON FISH-MAN ISLAND!!
YOU AIN'T EVEN WORTH...
... KILLING TIME!!
BOOM!!

SBS Question Corner

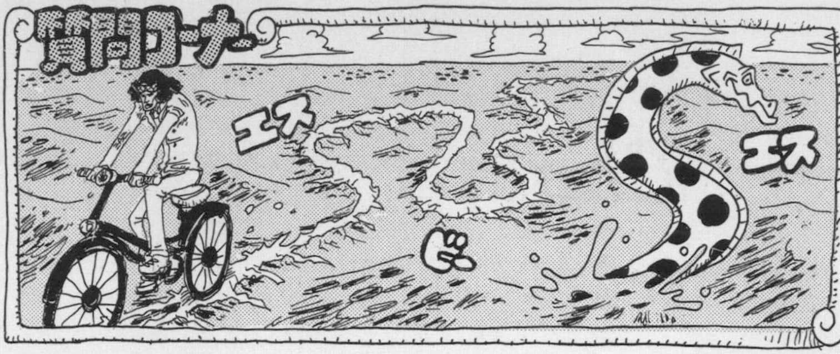
質問コーナー
エス
エス
ピ

(Ponio, Aichi)

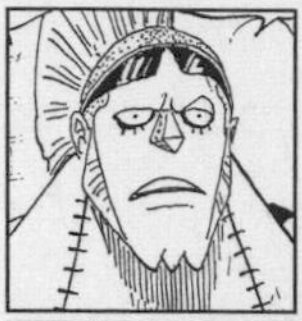

Q: Out of all the characters in *One Piece,* who's your rival? It's Franky, right? I just thought I'd ask.

--Toku

A: Who says?! Would you not put words into my mouth? You're acting like I'm some kind of pervert. Let's see, if anyone's going to be my rival, it'd be...Nami. I had my measurements taken for a suit, and my chest was 39 inches. Huh? My waist? Somewhere between 20 and 39 inches. Basically, I'm saying that I have centerfold proportions. Next letter!

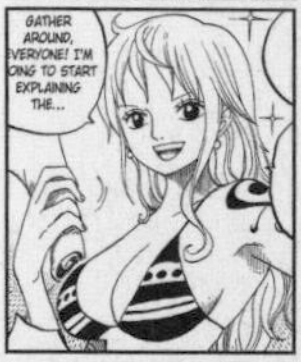
GATHER AROUND, EVERYONE! I'M
TO START EXPLAINING THE...

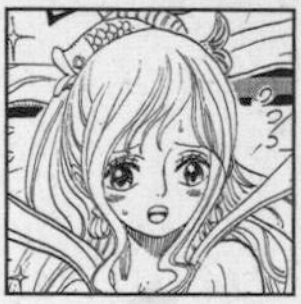

Q: Can Princess Shirahoshi's birthday be April 4th? Can it? Please! (cry)

--Dokkoi

A: Sure.

Q: So Luffy's Supreme King Haki can knock out fifty thousand. How many can Shanks knock out with his?

--Captain Nobuo

A: If they were in the exact same situation as Luffy's, Shanks and Rayleigh could probably manage up to a hundred thousand. You really can't compare "how many" in different situations. Defeating someone with haki is a phenomenon that occurs only when the user is overwhelmingly more powerful than the opponent. Basically, it's showing how many of Luffy's opponents weren't even worth fighting. If Luffy were facing a hundred thousand pirates of a certain strength, he might not be able to knock out a single one with haki. By the way, by training and practicing one's Haki of the Supreme King, you can pick a few out of a crowd and spare them from its effects.

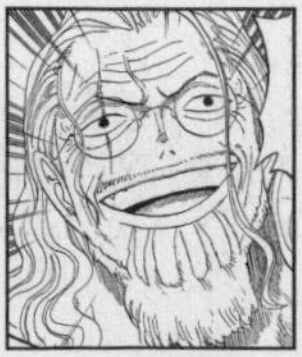

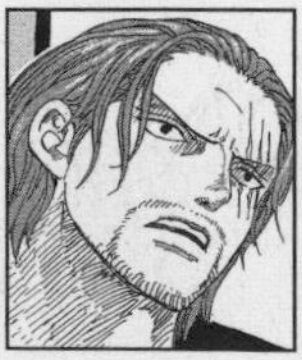

Chapter 643: PHANTOM

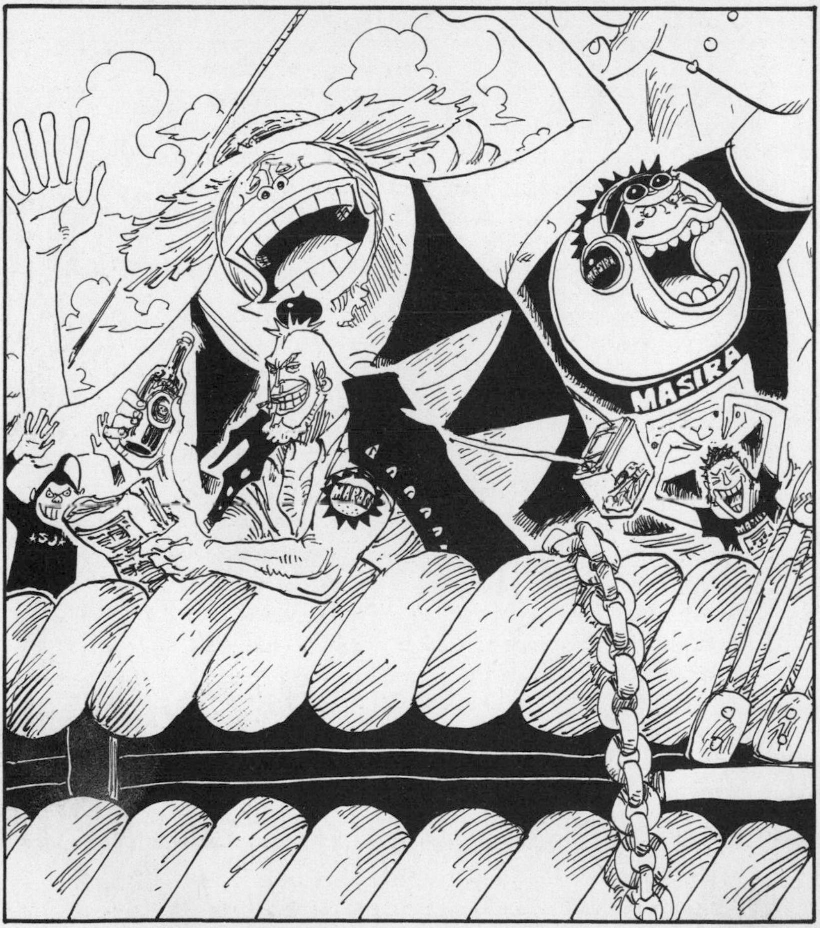
MASIRA

DECKS OF THE WORLD, VOL. 26: "THE MONKEY MOUNTAIN ALLIANCE SEEKS NAKROWA, ISLAND OF DREAMS"

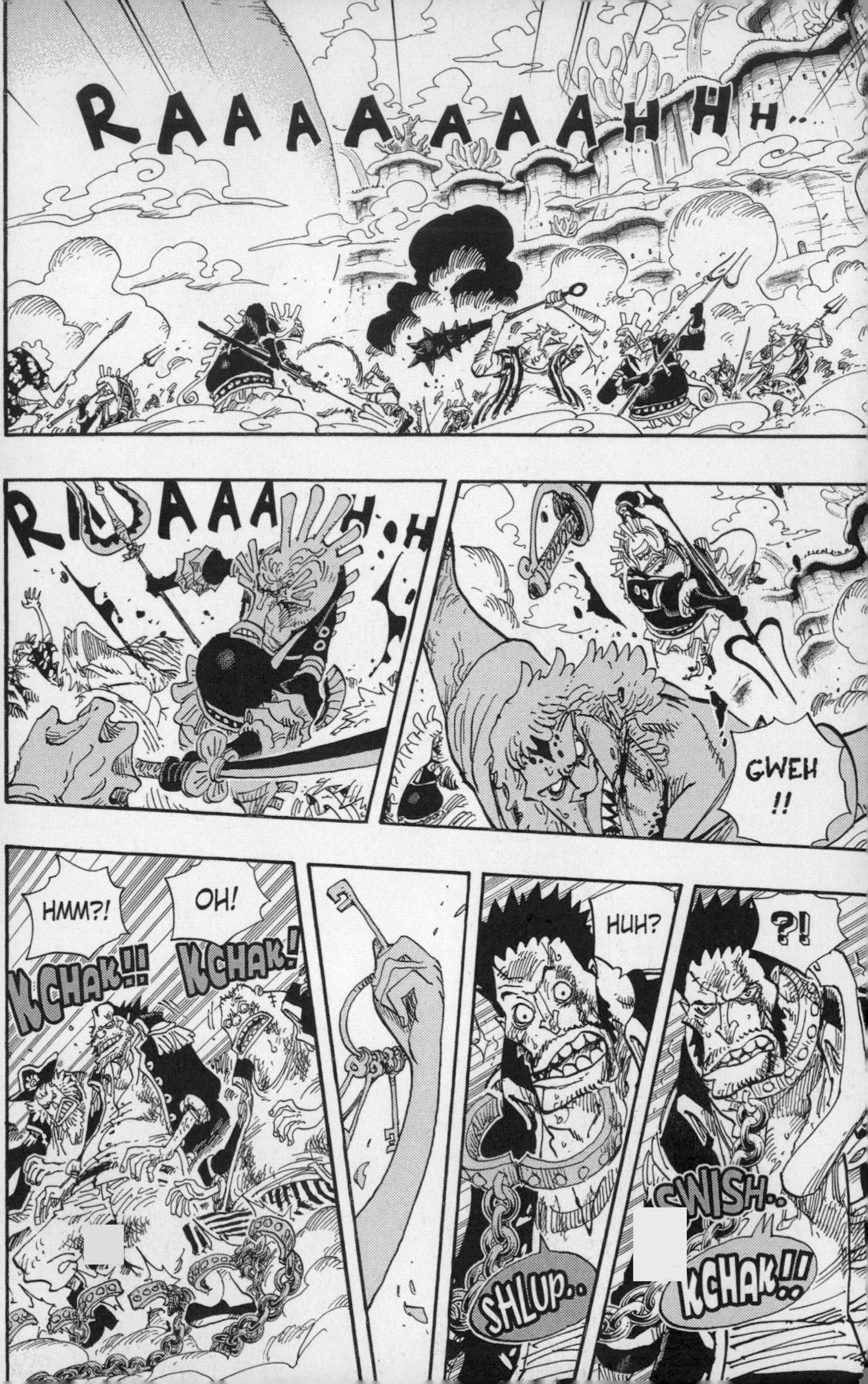
RAAAAAAAHHH..
GWEH!!
?!
SWISH..
KCHAK!!..
HUH?
SHLUP..
OH!
KCHAK!
HMM?!
KCHAK!!

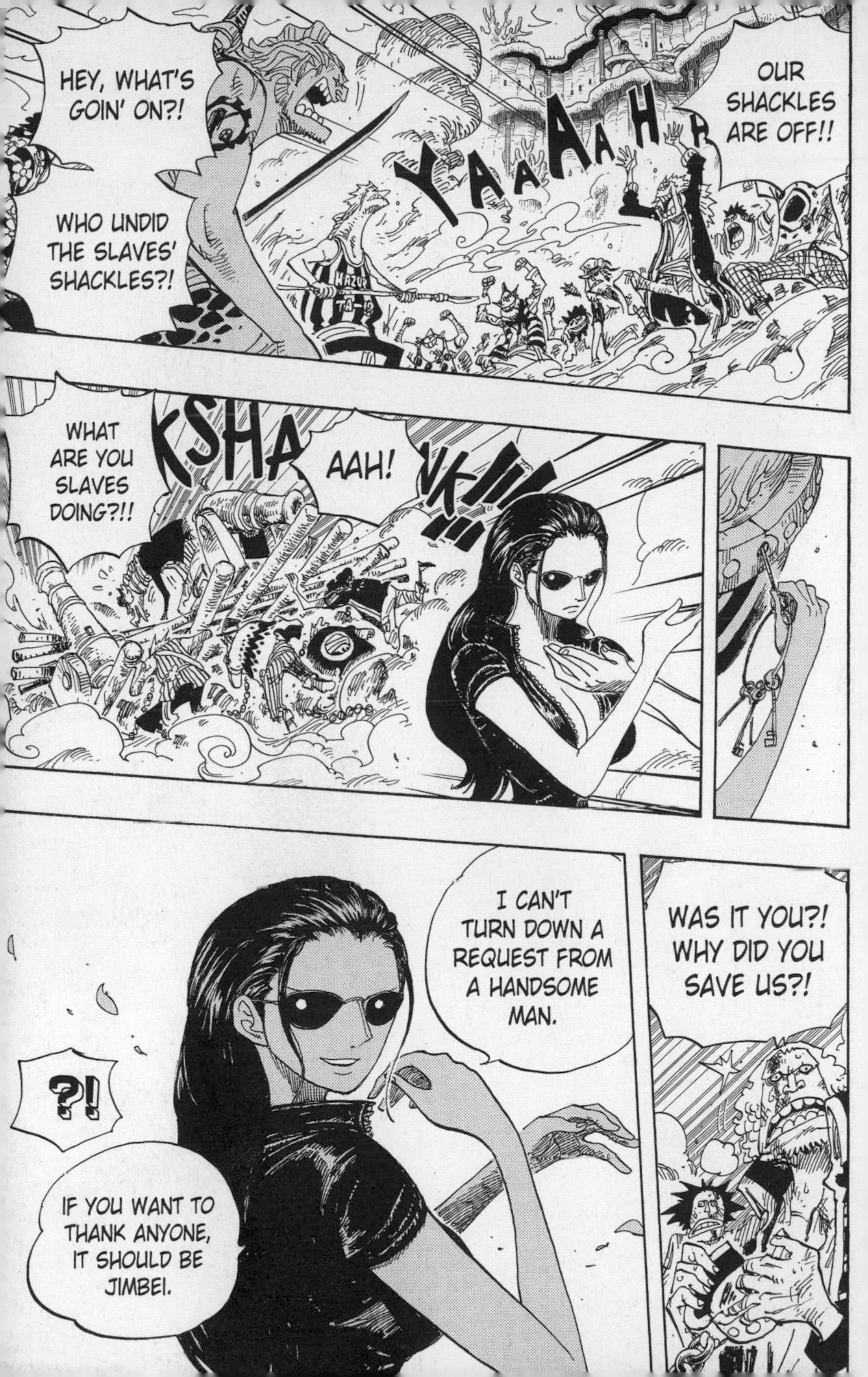
OUR SHACKLES ARE OFF!!
YAAAAHH
HEY, WHAT'S GOIN' ON?!
WHO UNDID THE SLAVES' SHACKLES?!
KSHANK!!!
AAH!
WHAT ARE YOU SLAVES DOING?!!
WAS IT YOU?! WHY DID YOU SAVE US?!
I CAN'T TURN DOWN A REQUEST FROM A HANDSOME MAN.
?!
IF YOU WANT TO THANK ANYONE, IT SHOULD BE JIMBEI.

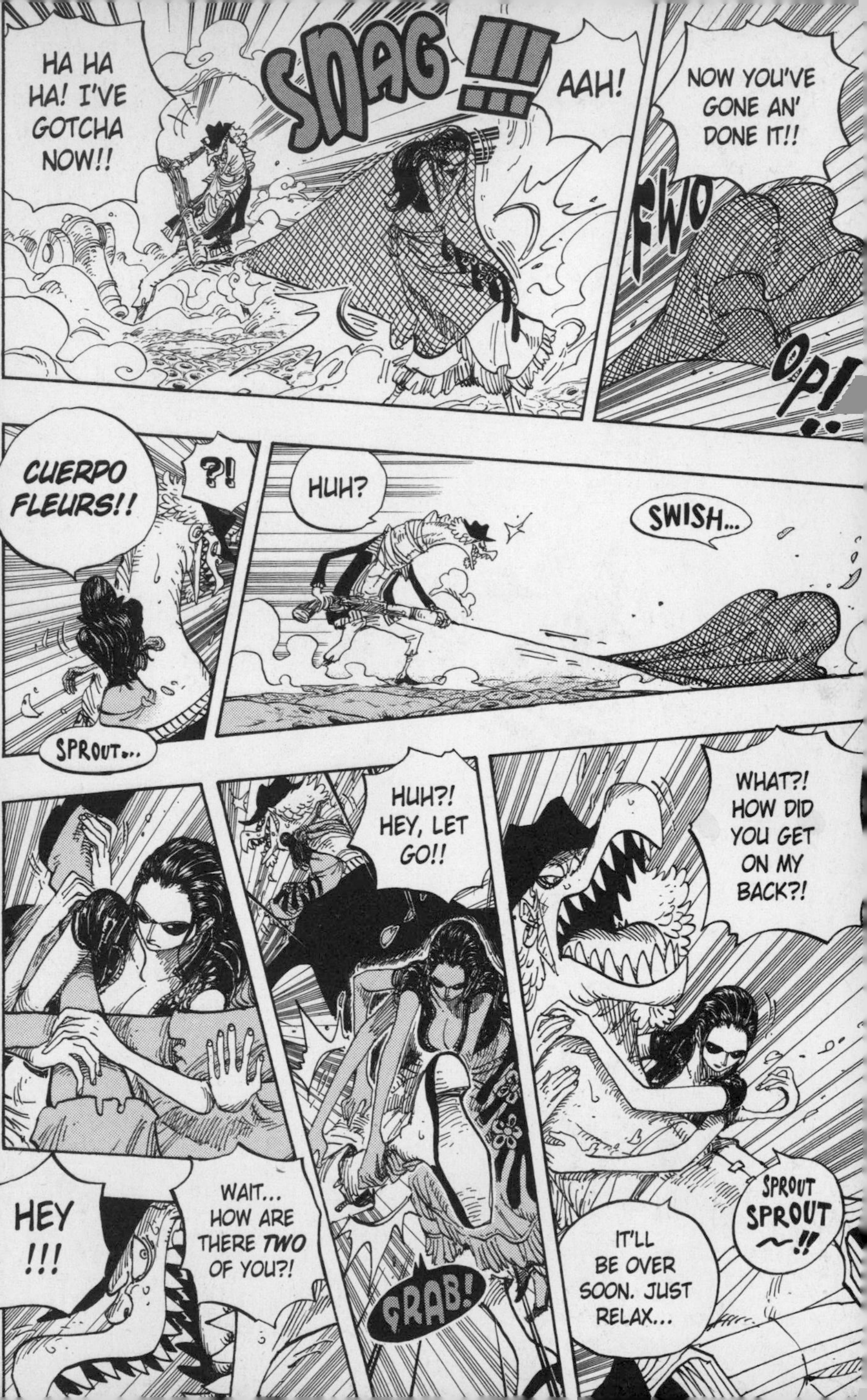

NOW YOU'VE GONE AN' DONE IT!!
FWOOP!!
AAH!
SNAG!!!
HA HA HA! I'VE GOTCHA NOW!!
SWISH...
HUH?
?!
CUERPO FLEURS!!
SPROUT...
WHAT?! HOW DID YOU GET ON MY BACK?!
SPROUT SPROUT~!!
IT'LL BE OVER SOON. JUST RELAX...
HUH?! HEY, LET GO!!
GRAB!
WAIT... HOW ARE THERE *TWO* OF YOU?!
HEY!!!

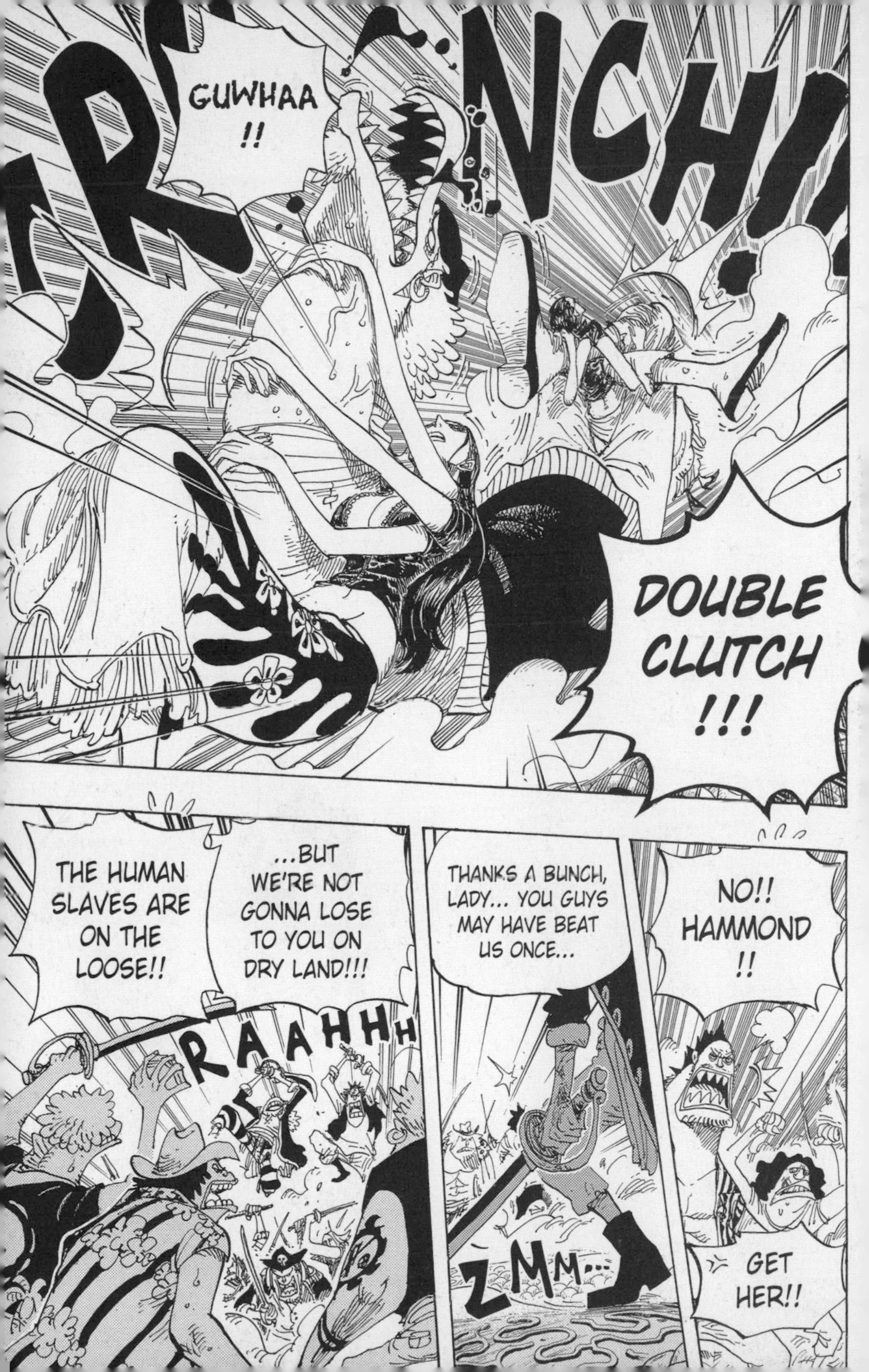
DOUBLE CLUTCH !!!
GUWHAA !!
NO!! HAMMOND !!
GET HER!!
THANKS A BUNCH, LADY... YOU GUYS MAY HAVE BEAT US ONCE...
ZMM...
...BUT WE'RE NOT GONNA LOSE TO YOU ON DRY LAND!!!
THE HUMAN SLAVES ARE ON THE LOOSE!!
RAAHHH

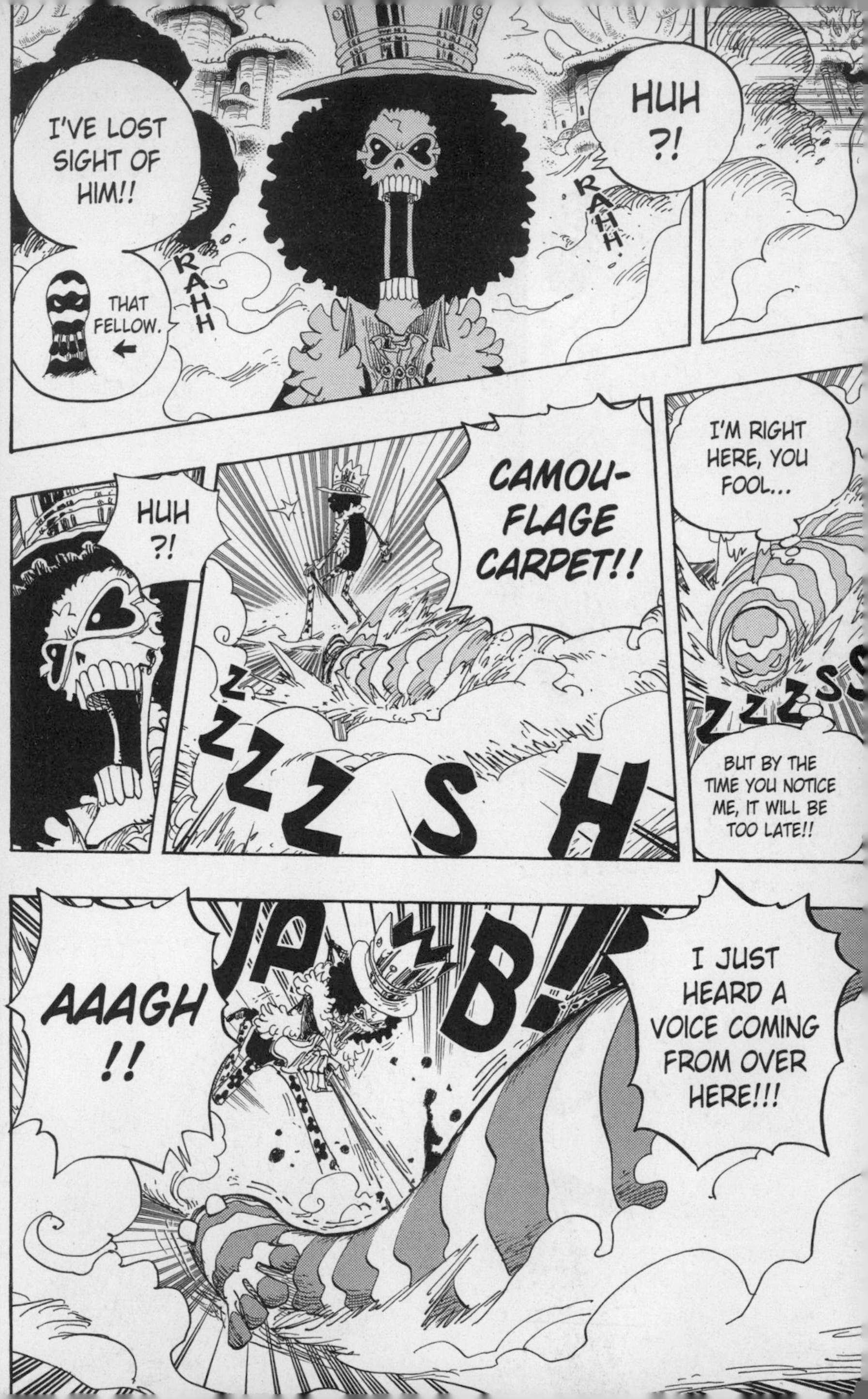
HUH ?!
RAHH
I'VE LOST SIGHT OF HIM!!
RAHH
THAT FELLOW.
I'M RIGHT HERE, YOU FOOL...
ZZZSS
BUT BY THE TIME YOU NOTICE ME, IT WILL BE TOO LATE!!
CAMOUFLAGE CARPET!!
ZZZSH
HUH ?!
I JUST HEARD A VOICE COMING FROM OVER HERE!!!
AAAGH !!

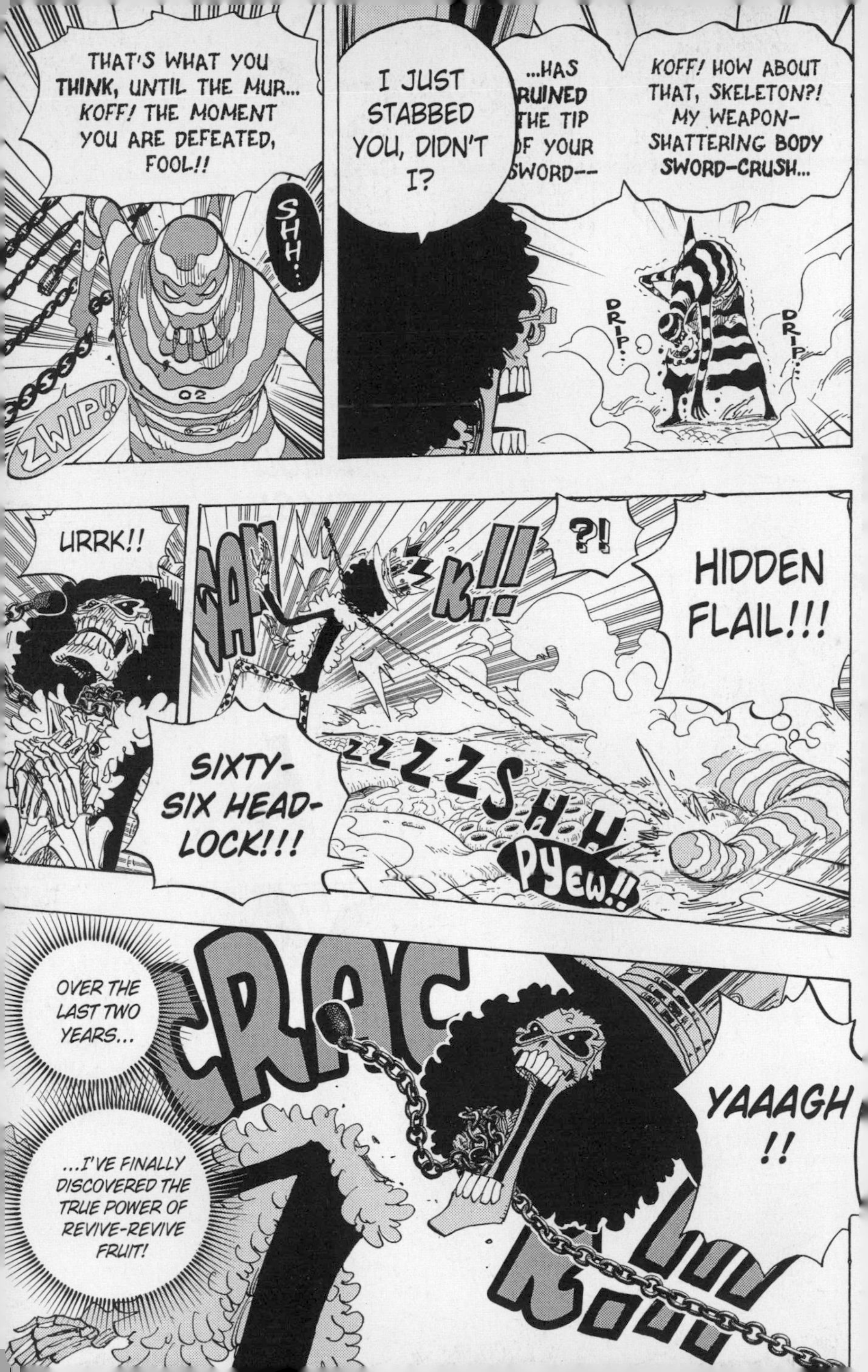

KOFF! HOW ABOUT THAT, SKELETON?! MY WEAPON-SHATTERING BODY SWORD-CRUSH...
...HAS RUINED THE TIP OF YOUR SWORD--
I JUST STABBED YOU, DIDN'T I?
DRIP...
DRIP...
THAT'S WHAT YOU THINK, UNTIL THE MUR... KOFF! THE MOMENT YOU ARE DEFEATED, FOOL!!
SHH...
ZWIP!!
?!
HIDDEN FLAIL!!!
SIXTY-SIX HEAD-LOCK!!!
ZZZZSHH
PYEW!!
URRK!!
YAAAGH!!
OVER THE LAST TWO YEARS...
...I'VE FINALLY DISCOVERED THE TRUE POWER OF REVIVE-REVIVE FRUIT!

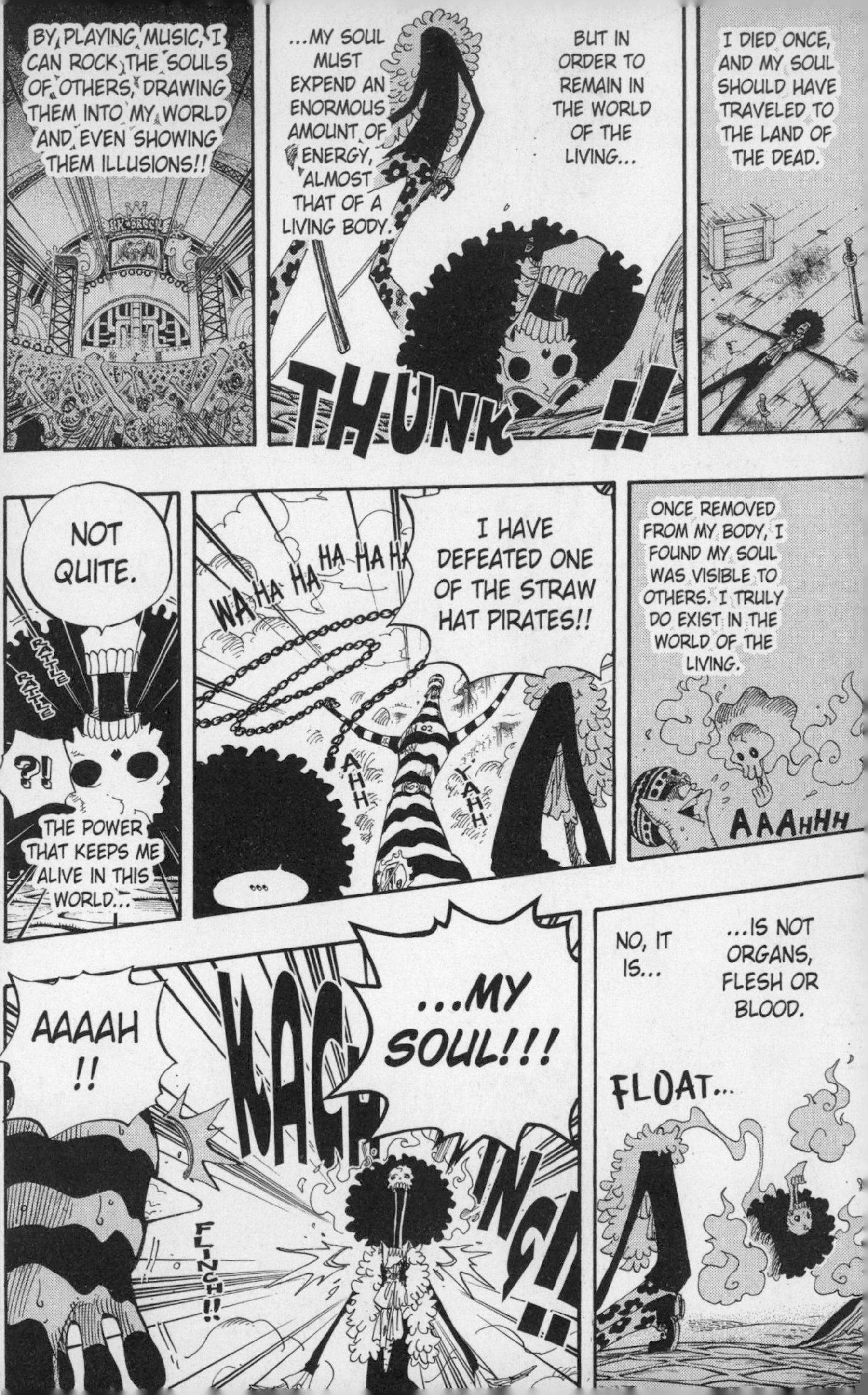

I DIED ONCE, AND MY SOUL SHOULD HAVE TRAVELED TO THE LAND OF THE DEAD.
BUT IN ORDER TO REMAIN IN THE WORLD OF THE LIVING...
...MY SOUL MUST EXPEND AN ENORMOUS AMOUNT OF ENERGY, ALMOST THAT OF A LIVING BODY.
THUNK!!
BY PLAYING MUSIC, I CAN ROCK THE SOULS OF OTHERS, DRAWING THEM INTO MY WORLD AND EVEN SHOWING THEM ILLUSIONS!!
ONCE REMOVED FROM MY BODY, I FOUND MY SOUL WAS VISIBLE TO OTHERS. I TRULY DO EXIST IN THE WORLD OF THE LIVING.
AAAHHH
I HAVE DEFEATED ONE OF THE STRAW HAT PIRATES!!
WA HA HA HA HA HA
AHH
YAHH
...
NOT QUITE.
?!
THE POWER THAT KEEPS ME ALIVE IN THIS WORLD...
NO, IT IS...
...IS NOT ORGANS, FLESH OR BLOOD.
FLOAT...
...MY SOUL!!!
KAC
ING!!
AAAAH !!
FLINCH!!

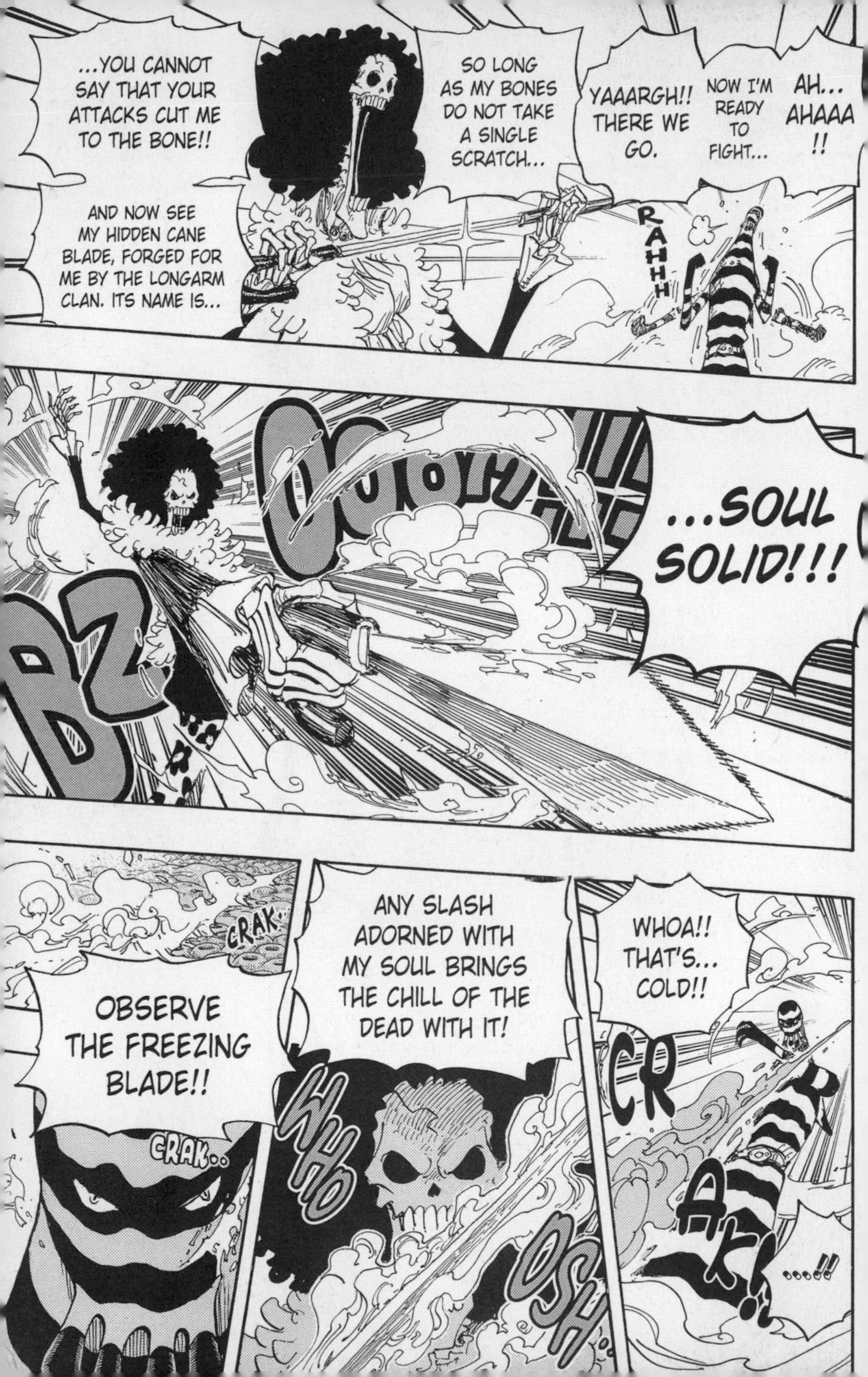
AH... AHAAA!!
NOW I'M READY TO FIGHT...
YAAARGH!! THERE WE GO.
RAHHH
SO LONG AS MY BONES DO NOT TAKE A SINGLE SCRATCH...
...YOU CANNOT SAY THAT YOUR ATTACKS CUT ME TO THE BONE!!
AND NOW SEE MY HIDDEN CANE BLADE, FORGED FOR ME BY THE LONGARM CLAN. ITS NAME IS...
...SOUL SOLID!!!
WHOA!! THAT'S... COLD!!
CR
ANY SLASH ADORNED WITH MY SOUL BRINGS THE CHILL OF THE DEAD WITH IT!
WHO
OSH
CRAK..
OBSERVE THE FREEZING BLADE!!
CRAK..

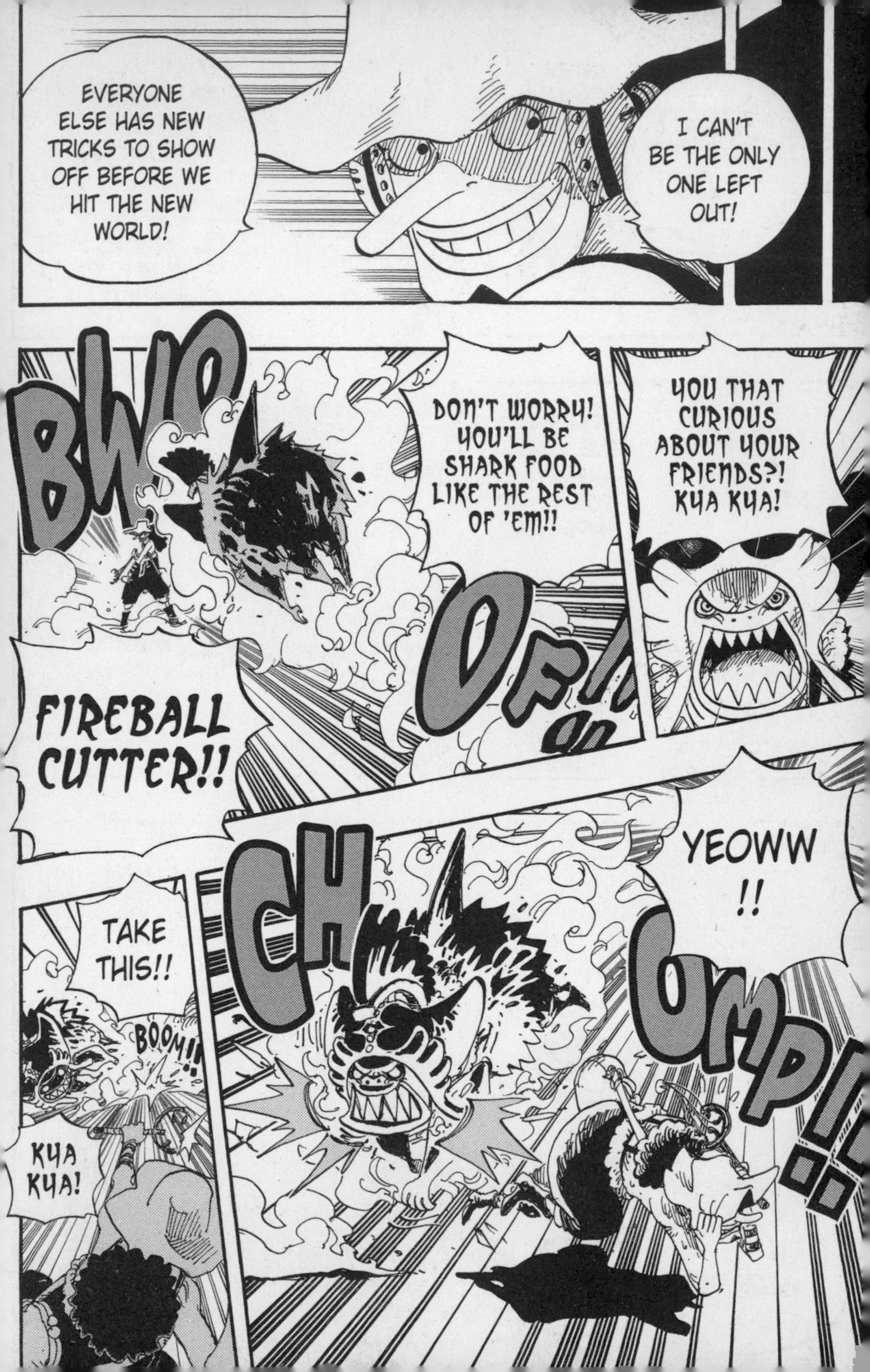
I CAN'T BE THE ONLY ONE LEFT OUT!
EVERYONE ELSE HAS NEW TRICKS TO SHOW OFF BEFORE WE HIT THE NEW WORLD!
YOU THAT CURIOUS ABOUT YOUR FRIENDS?! KYA KYA!
DON'T WORRY! YOU'LL BE SHARK FOOD LIKE THE REST OF 'EM!!
BWO
OF
FIREBALL CUTTER!!
YEOWW!!
CH
OMP!!
TAKE THIS!!
BOOM!!
KYA KYA!

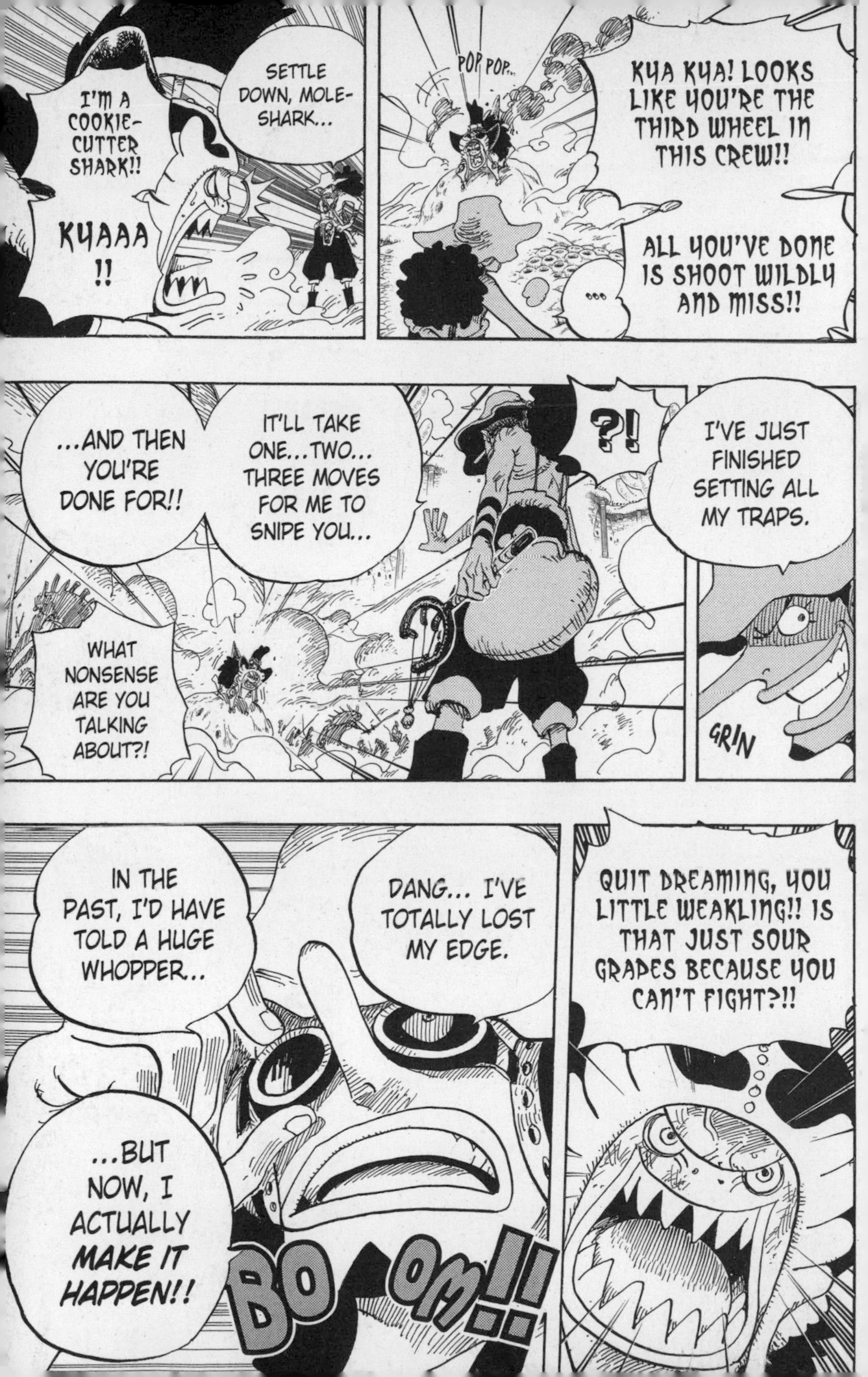

POP POP...
KYA KYA! LOOKS LIKE YOU'RE THE THIRD WHEEL IN THIS CREW!!
ALL YOU'VE DONE IS SHOOT WILDLY AND MISS!!
...
SETTLE DOWN, MOLE-SHARK...
I'M A COOKIE-CUTTER SHARK!!
KYAAA !!
I'VE JUST FINISHED SETTING ALL MY TRAPS.
GRIN
?!
IT'LL TAKE ONE...TWO... THREE MOVES FOR ME TO SNIPE YOU...
...AND THEN YOU'RE DONE FOR!!
WHAT NONSENSE ARE YOU TALKING ABOUT?!
QUIT DREAMING, YOU LITTLE WEAKLING!! IS THAT JUST SOUR GRAPES BECAUSE YOU CAN'T FIGHT?!!
DANG... I'VE TOTALLY LOST MY EDGE.
IN THE PAST, I'D HAVE TOLD A HUGE WHOPPER...
...BUT NOW, I ACTUALLY *MAKE IT HAPPEN!!*
BO OM!!

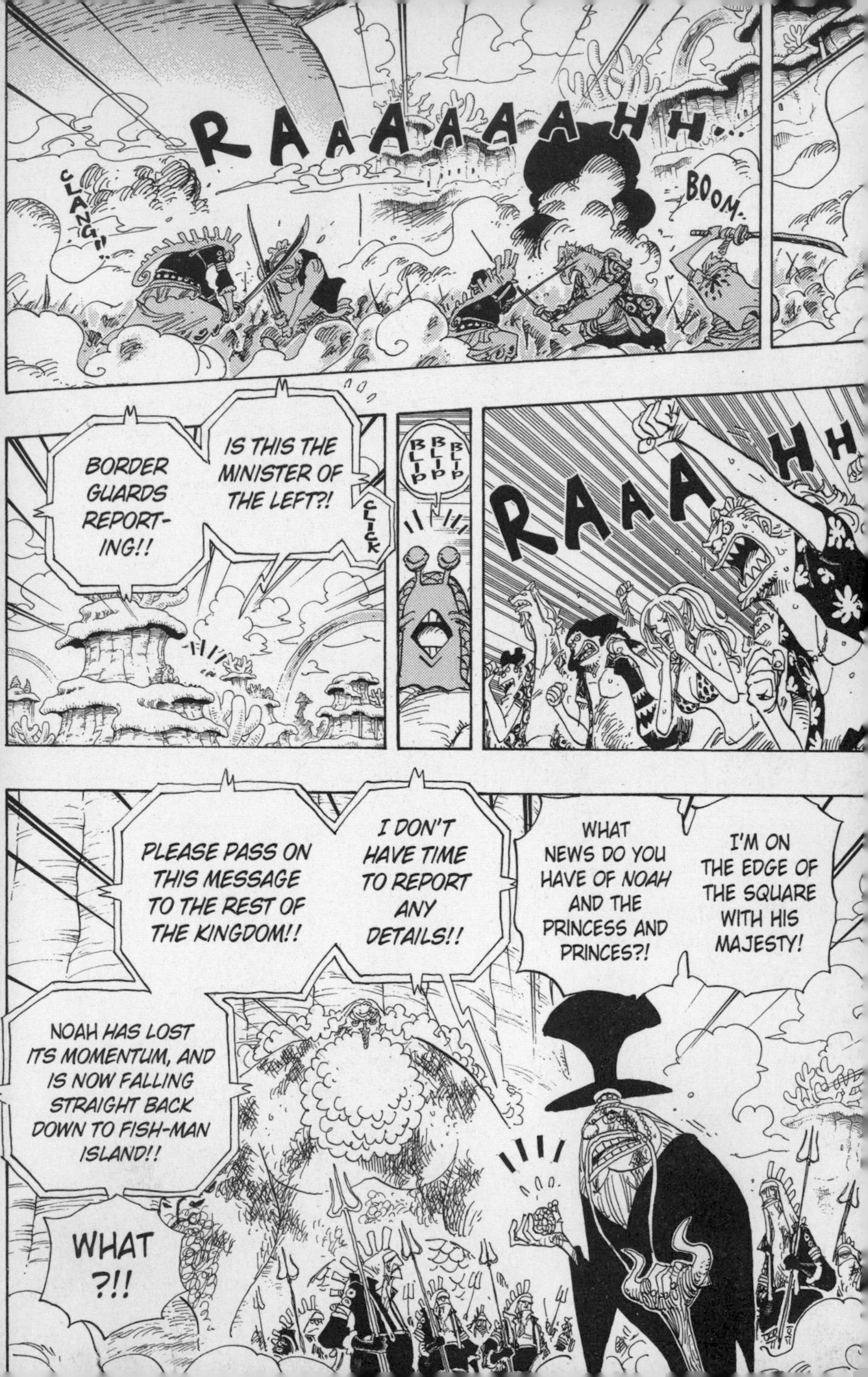
BOOM
RAAAAAAHH...
CLANG!!
RAAAHH
BLIP BLIP BLIP
CLICK
IS THIS THE MINISTER OF THE LEFT?!
BORDER GUARDS REPORTING!!
I'M ON THE EDGE OF THE SQUARE WITH HIS MAJESTY!
WHAT NEWS DO YOU HAVE OF NOAH AND THE PRINCESS AND PRINCES?!
I DON'T HAVE TIME TO REPORT ANY DETAILS!!
PLEASE PASS ON THIS MESSAGE TO THE REST OF THE KINGDOM!!
NOAH HAS LOST ITS MOMENTUM, AND IS NOW FALLING STRAIGHT BACK DOWN TO FISH-MAN ISLAND!!
WHAT?!!

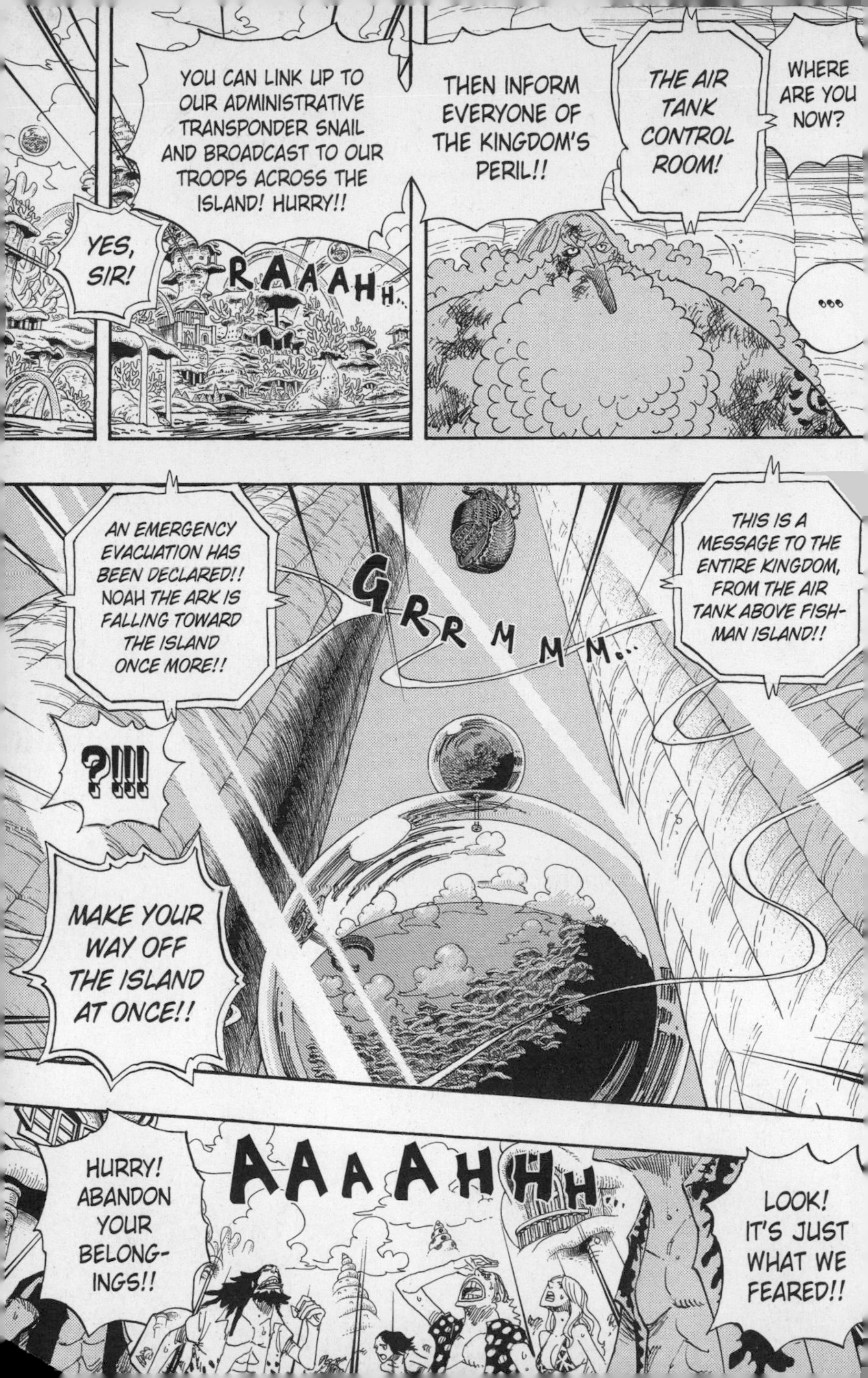
WHERE ARE YOU NOW?
THE AIR TANK CONTROL ROOM!
...
THEN INFORM EVERYONE OF THE KINGDOM'S PERIL!!
YOU CAN LINK UP TO OUR ADMINISTRATIVE TRANSPONDER SNAIL AND BROADCAST TO OUR TROOPS ACROSS THE ISLAND! HURRY!!
YES, SIR!
RAAAHH...
THIS IS A MESSAGE TO THE ENTIRE KINGDOM, FROM THE AIR TANK ABOVE FISH-MAN ISLAND!!
GRRMMMM...
AN EMERGENCY EVACUATION HAS BEEN DECLARED!! NOAH THE ARK IS FALLING TOWARD THE ISLAND ONCE MORE!!
?!!!
MAKE YOUR WAY OFF THE ISLAND AT ONCE!!
LOOK! IT'S JUST WHAT WE FEARED!!
AAAAHHH
HURRY! ABANDON YOUR BELONG-INGS!!

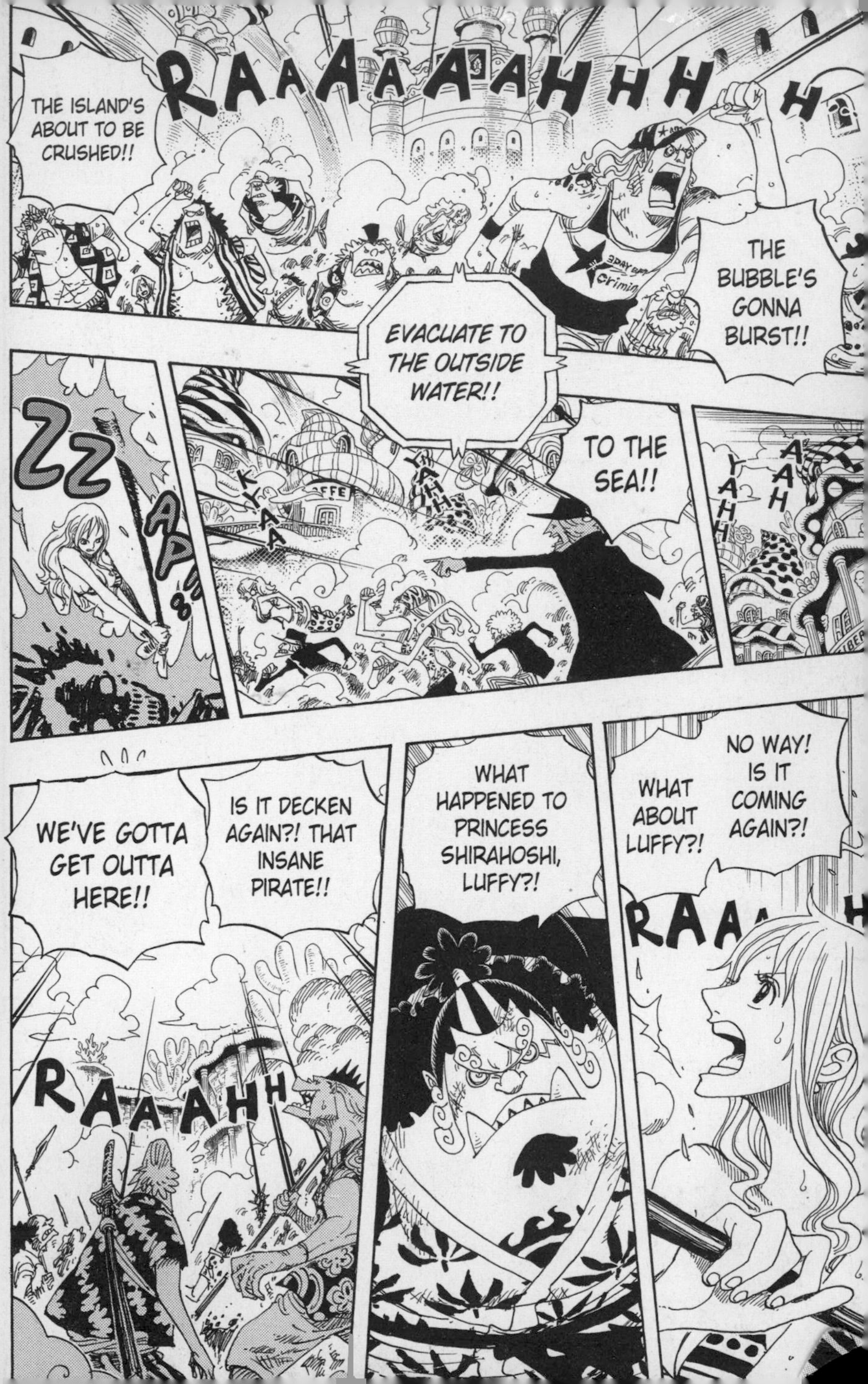
RAAAAAAHHHH H
THE BUBBLE'S GONNA BURST!!
THE ISLAND'S ABOUT TO BE CRUSHED!!
EVACUATE TO THE OUTSIDE WATER!!
YAHHH
AAH
TO THE SEA!!
YAHHH
KYAA
ZZAP
NO WAY! IS IT COMING AGAIN?!
WHAT ABOUT LUFFY?!
RAAA H
WHAT HAPPENED TO PRINCESS SHIRAHOSHI, LUFFY?!
IS IT DECKEN AGAIN?! THAT INSANE PIRATE!!
WE'VE GOTTA GET OUTTA HERE!!
RAAAHH

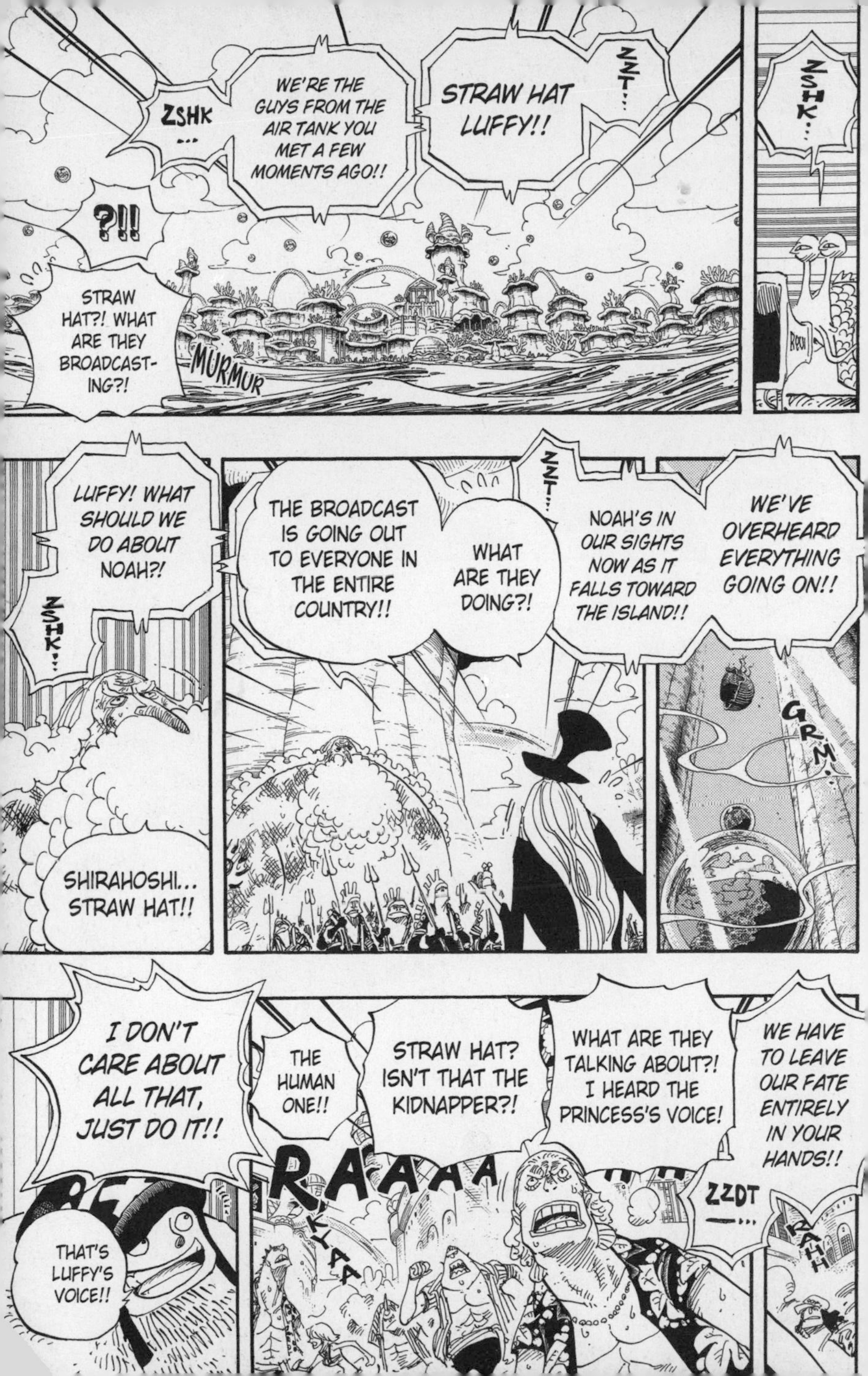
ZSHK...
ZZT...
STRAW HAT LUFFY!!
WE'RE THE GUYS FROM THE AIR TANK YOU MET A FEW MOMENTS AGO!!
ZSHK...
?!!
STRAW HAT?! WHAT ARE THEY BROADCASTING?!
MURMUR
WE'VE OVERHEARD EVERYTHING GOING ON!!
GRM
ZZT...
NOAH'S IN OUR SIGHTS NOW AS IT FALLS TOWARD THE ISLAND!!
WHAT ARE THEY DOING?!
THE BROADCAST IS GOING OUT TO EVERYONE IN THE ENTIRE COUNTRY!!
LUFFY! WHAT SHOULD WE DO ABOUT NOAH?!
ZSHK...
SHIRAHOSHI... STRAW HAT!!
WE HAVE TO LEAVE OUR FATE ENTIRELY IN YOUR HANDS!!
RAHH
WHAT ARE THEY TALKING ABOUT?! I HEARD THE PRINCESS'S VOICE!
ZZDT—...
STRAW HAT? ISN'T THAT THE KIDNAPPER?!
THE HUMAN ONE!!
RAAAA
KYAA
I DON'T CARE ABOUT ALL THAT, JUST DO IT!!
THAT'S LUFFY'S VOICE!!

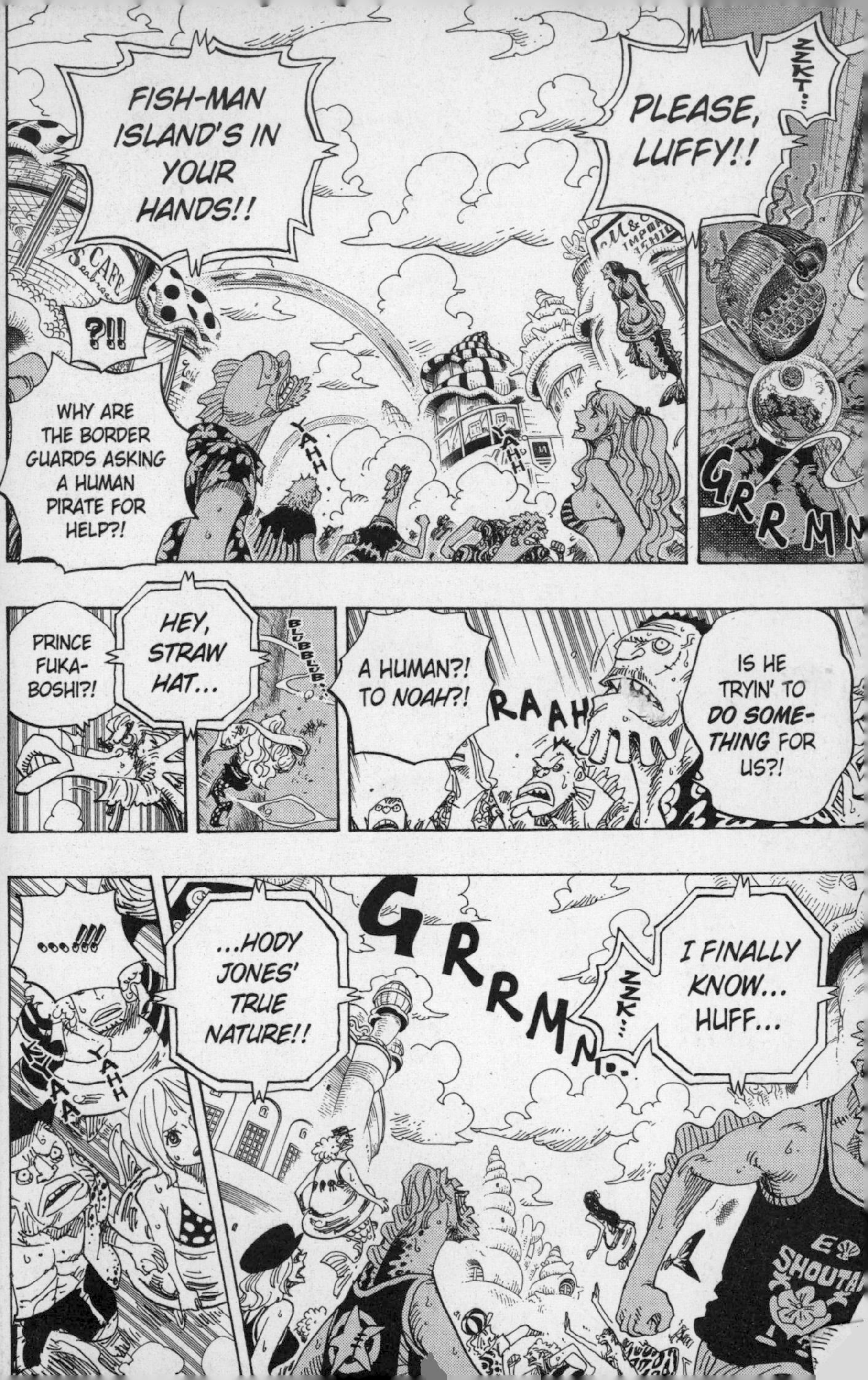
ZZKT...
GRRMN
PLEASE, LUFFY!!
FISH-MAN ISLAND'S IN YOUR HANDS!!
?!!
WHY ARE THE BORDER GUARDS ASKING A HUMAN PIRATE FOR HELP?!
YAHH
YAHH
IS HE TRYIN' TO DO SOME-THING FOR US?!
RAAH
A HUMAN?! TO NOAH?!
BLUBBLUB
HEY, STRAW HAT...
PRINCE FUKA-BOSHI?!
I FINALLY KNOW... HUFF...
ZZK...
GRRRMN..
...HODY JONES' TRUE NATURE!!
...!!!
YAHH

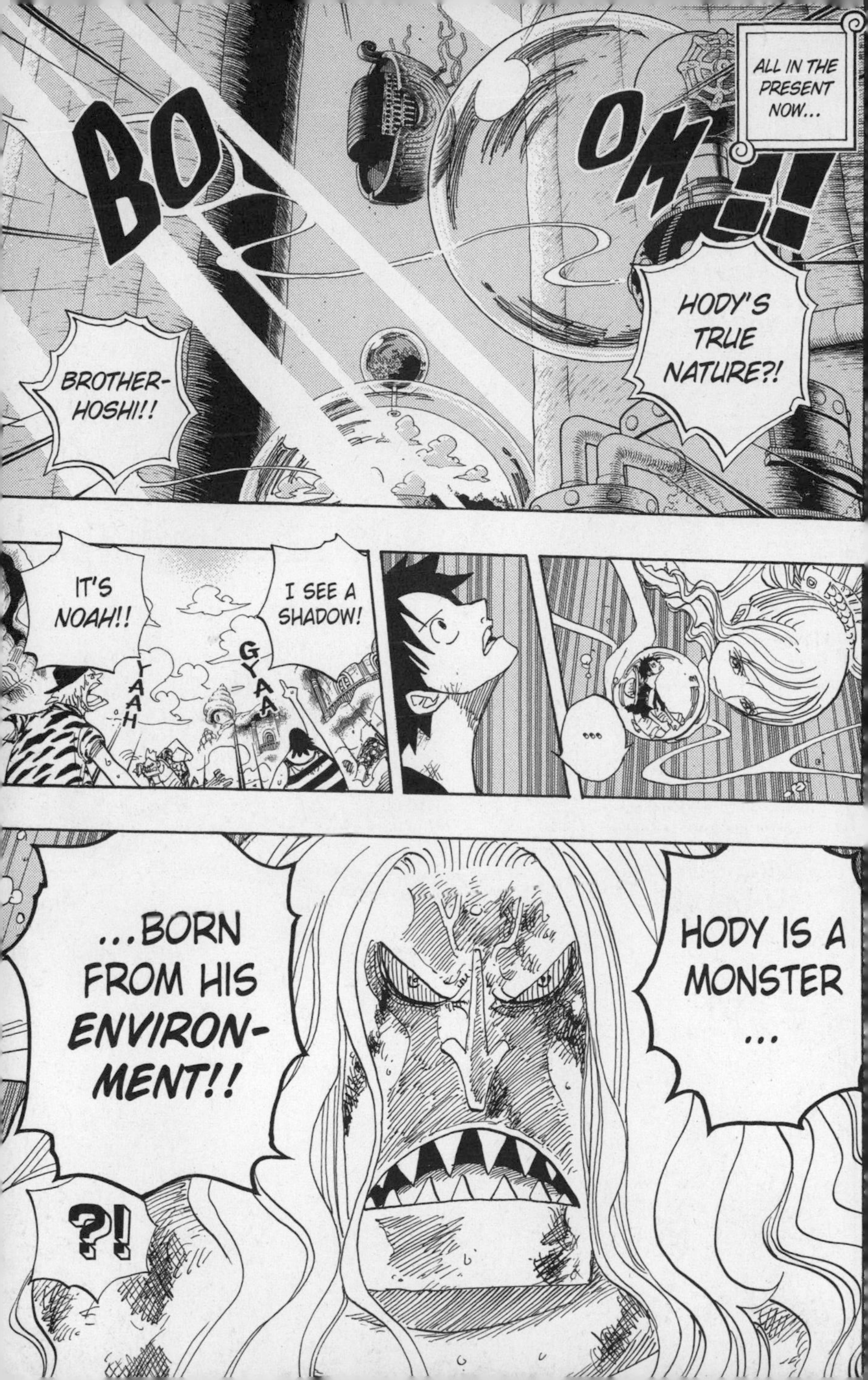
ALL IN THE PRESENT NOW...
BOOM!!
HODY'S TRUE NATURE?!
BROTHER-HOSHI!!
...
I SEE A SHADOW!
GYAA
IT'S NOAH!!
YAAH
HODY IS A MONSTER ...
...BORN FROM HIS ENVIRON-MENT!!
?!

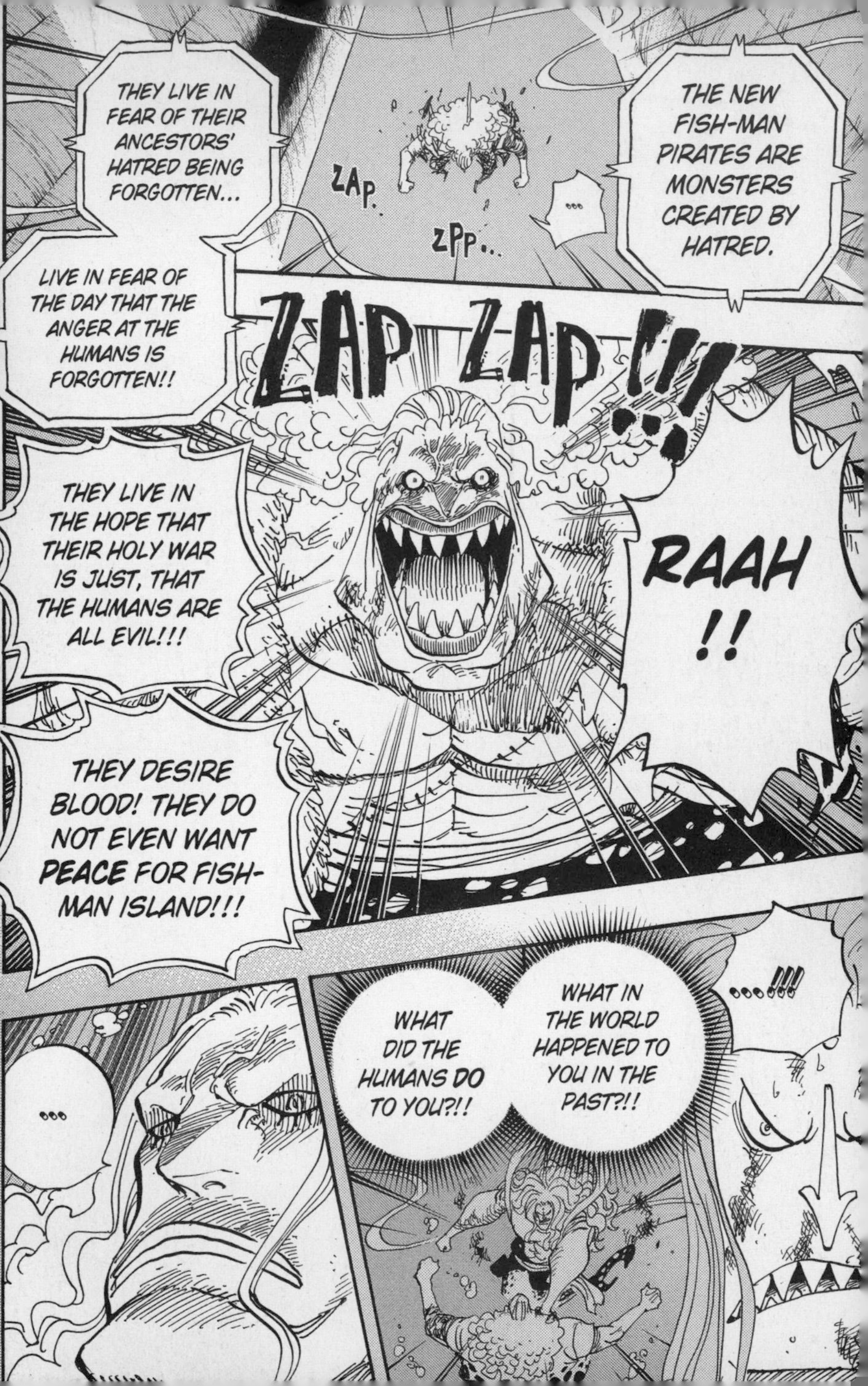

THE NEW FISH-MAN PIRATES ARE MONSTERS CREATED BY HATRED.
...
ZAP.
ZPP...
THEY LIVE IN FEAR OF THEIR ANCESTORS' HATRED BEING FORGOTTEN...
LIVE IN FEAR OF THE DAY THAT THE ANGER AT THE HUMANS IS FORGOTTEN!!
RAAH!!
ZAP ZAP!!!
THEY LIVE IN THE HOPE THAT THEIR HOLY WAR IS JUST, THAT THE HUMANS ARE ALL EVIL!!!
THEY DESIRE BLOOD! THEY DO NOT EVEN WANT **PEACE** FOR FISH-MAN ISLAND!!!
...!!!
WHAT IN THE WORLD HAPPENED TO YOU IN THE PAST?!!
WHAT DID THE HUMANS DO TO YOU?!!
...

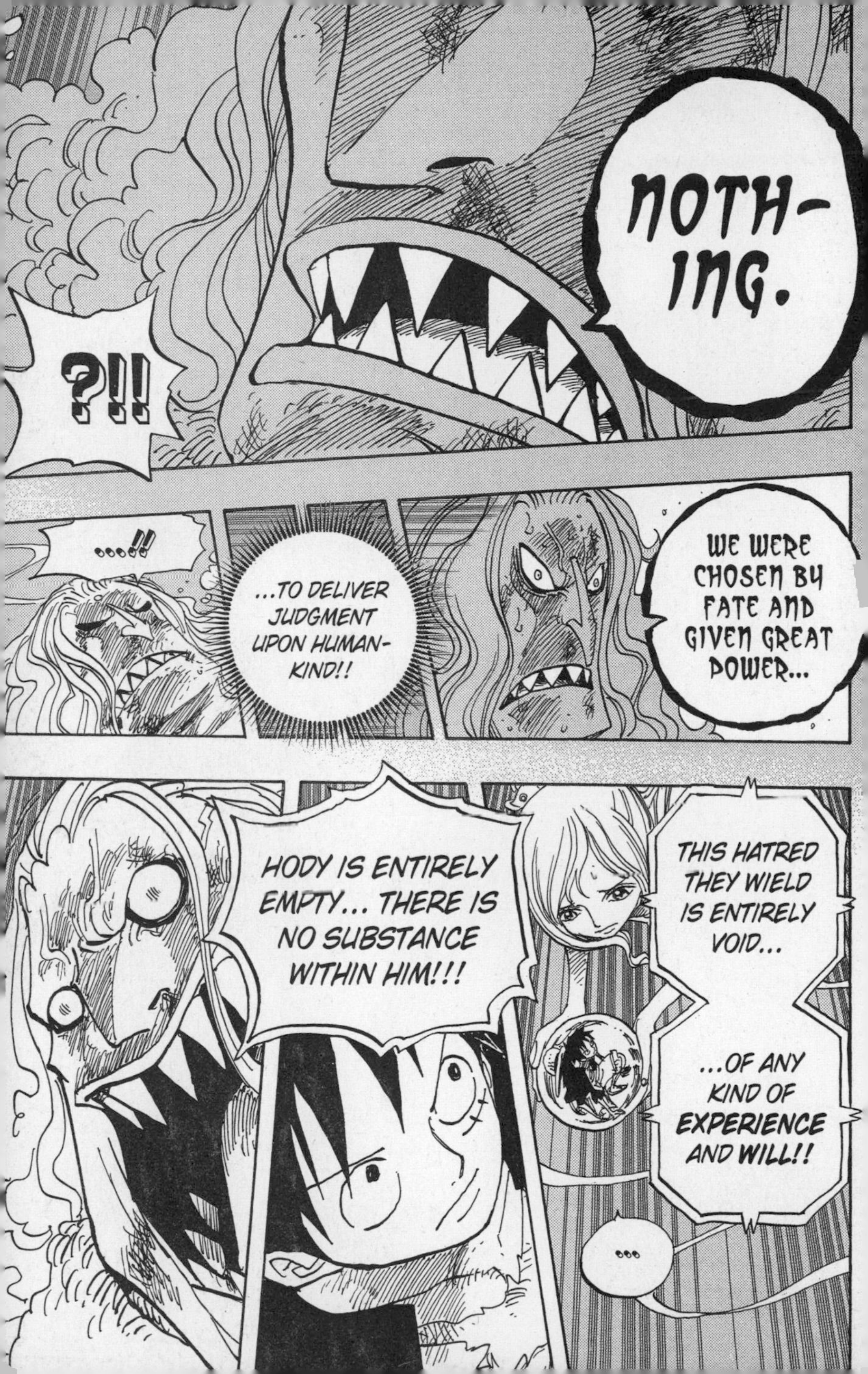
NOTH-ING.
?!!
WE WERE CHOSEN BY FATE AND GIVEN GREAT POWER...
...TO DELIVER JUDGMENT UPON HUMAN-KIND!!
....!!
THIS HATRED THEY WIELD IS ENTIRELY VOID...
...OF ANY KIND OF EXPERIENCE AND WILL!!
...
HODY IS ENTIRELY EMPTY... THERE IS NO SUBSTANCE WITHIN HIM!!!

SBS Question Corner

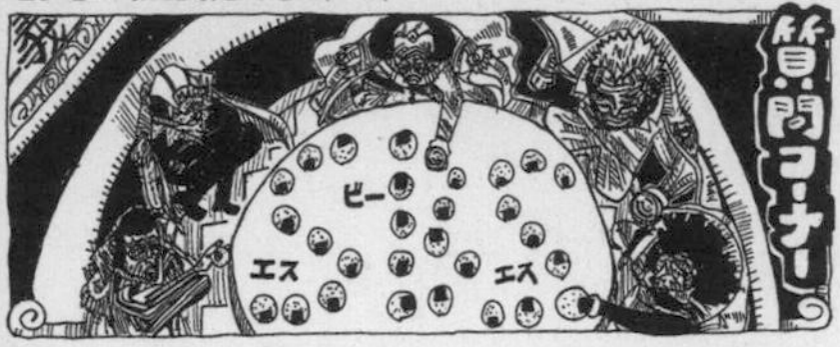
質問コーナー
ビー
エス
エス

(Satomo, Yamanashi)

Q: Dear Odacchi♡, draw these navy officers as children: Sengoku, Garp, Akainu, Kizaru, and Aokiji. Please!♡♡♡♡

--Emukichi

A: Oh, you're trying the seduction angle?♡ Let's see, you didn't specify an age, so...I'll just assume you're a 22-year-old beauty in a bikini... In that case, sure!♡ Oh, and this is the end of the SBS. See you next volume!!

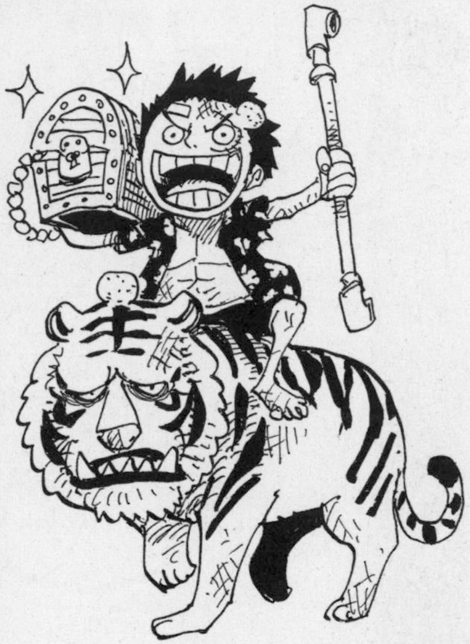

Garp

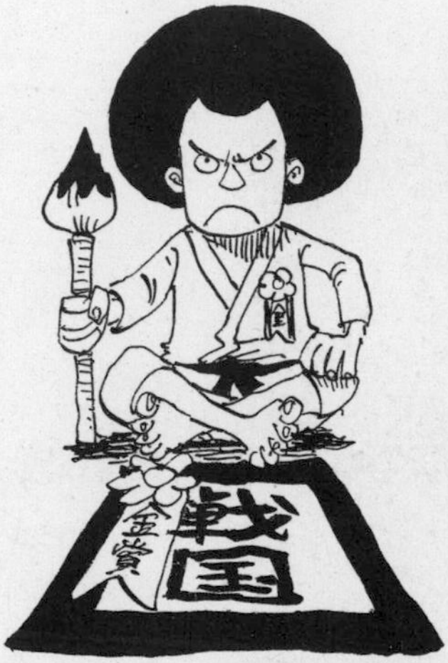
戦国

Sengoku

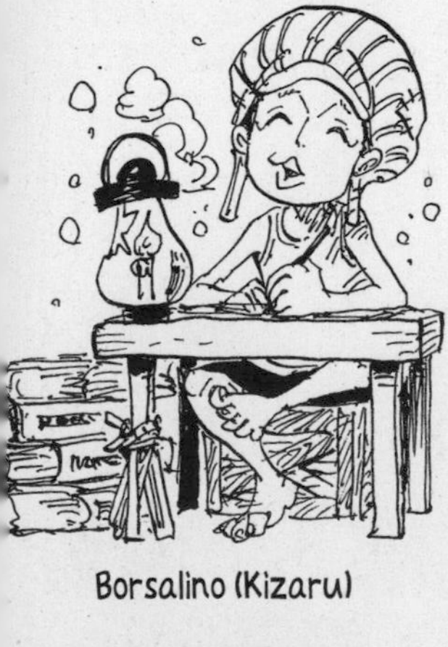

Borsalino (Kizaru)

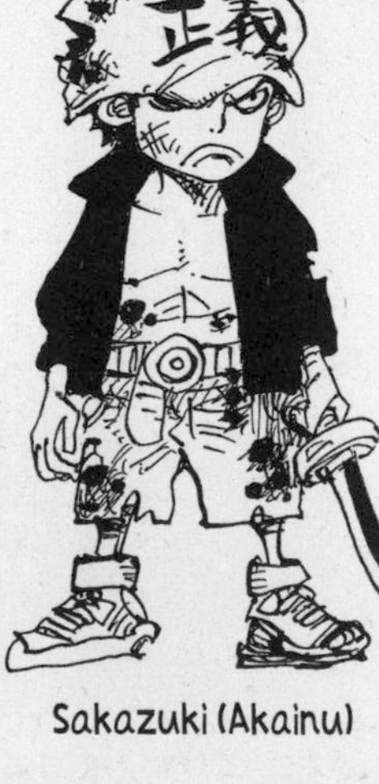
正義

Sakazuki (Akainu)

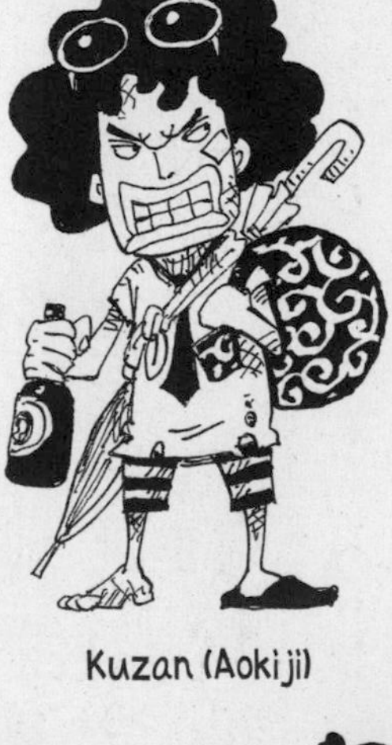

Kuzan (Aokiji)

Chapter 644:
TO NOTHING

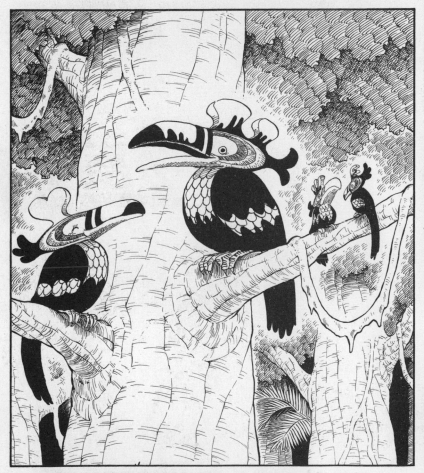

DECKS OF THE WORLD, VOL. 27: "JAYA—SOUTHBIRD LOVES NORTHBIRD, PLUS WESTBIRD AND EASTBIRD"

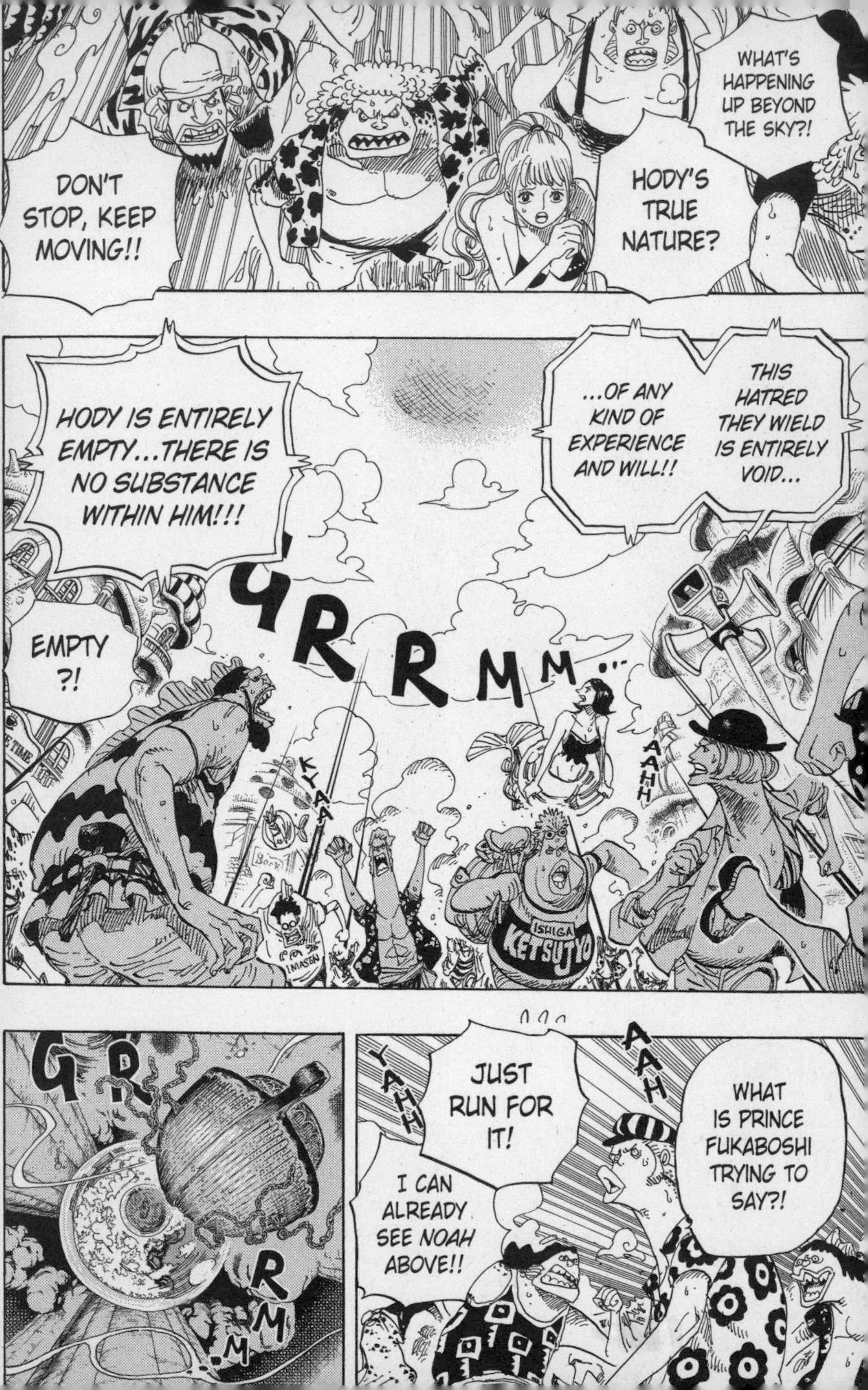
WHAT'S HAPPENING UP BEYOND THE SKY?!
HODY'S TRUE NATURE?
DON'T STOP, KEEP MOVING!!
THIS HATRED THEY WIELD IS ENTIRELY VOID...
...OF ANY KIND OF EXPERIENCE AND WILL!!
HODY IS ENTIRELY EMPTY...THERE IS NO SUBSTANCE WITHIN HIM!!!
GRRMM...
AAHH
KYAA
EMPTY ?!
ISHIGA KETSUYO
IMASEN
AAAH
WHAT IS PRINCE FUKABOSHI TRYING TO SAY?!
JUST RUN FOR IT!
YAHH
I CAN ALREADY SEE NOAH ABOVE!!
GRRMM

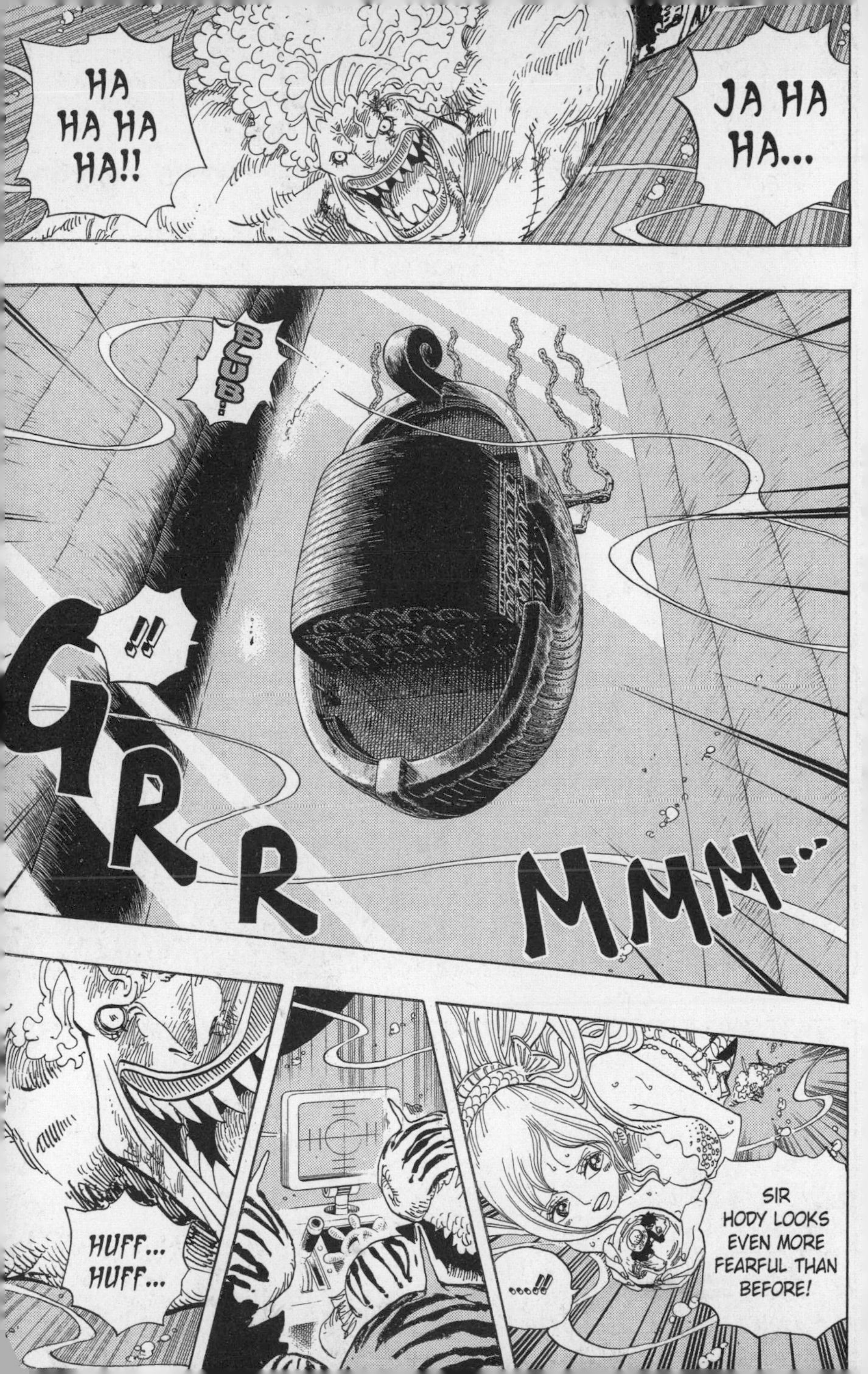
JA HA HA...
HA HA HA HA!!
BLUB..
!!
GRRRMMM...
SIR HODY LOOKS EVEN MORE FEARFUL THAN BEFORE!
...!!
HUFF... HUFF...

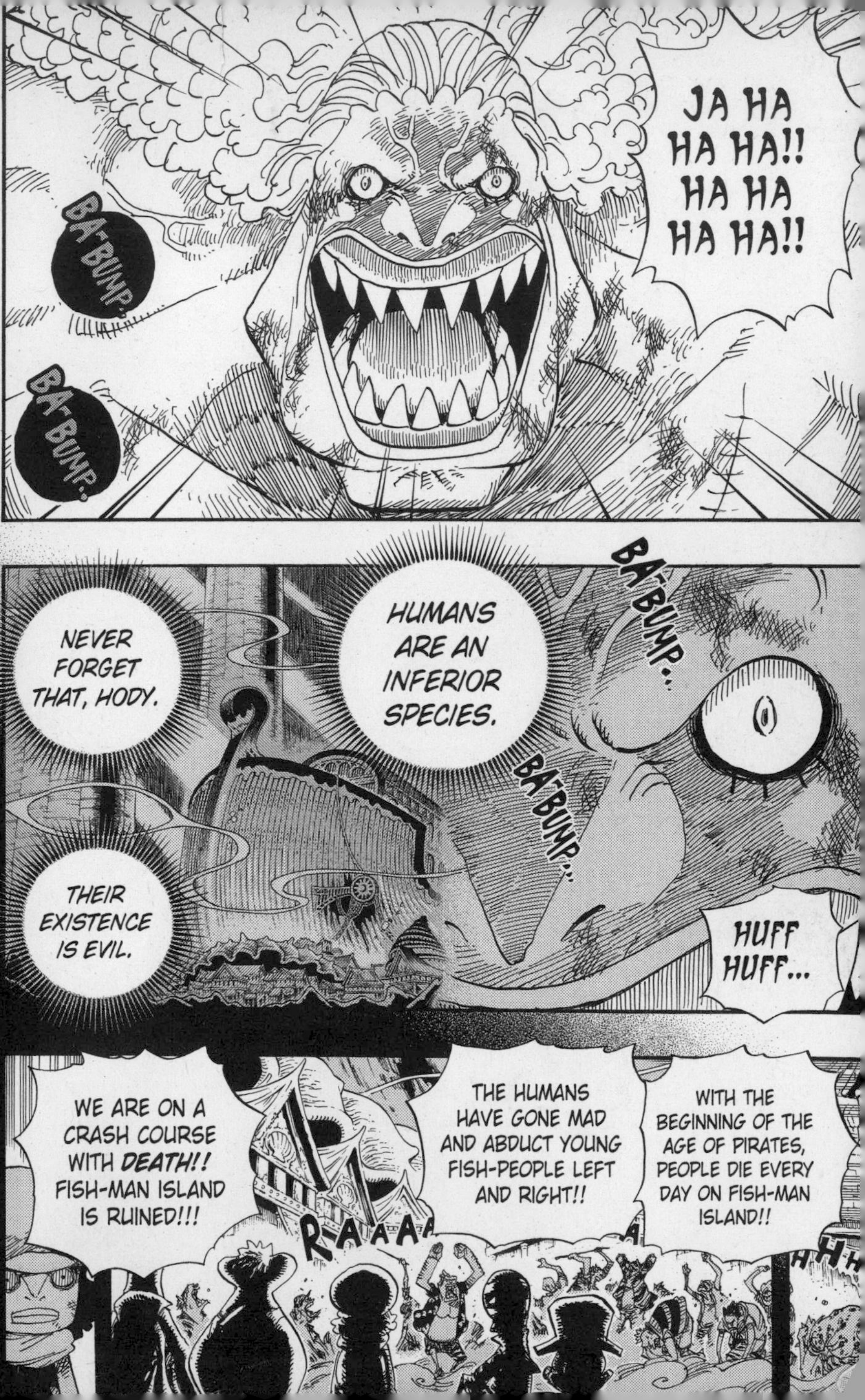
JA HA HA HA!! HA HA HA HA!!
BA-BUMP..
BA-BUMP..
BA-BUMP..
HUMANS ARE AN INFERIOR SPECIES.
NEVER FORGET THAT, HODY.
BA-BUMP..
HUFF HUFF...
THEIR EXISTENCE IS EVIL.
WITH THE BEGINNING OF THE AGE OF PIRATES, PEOPLE DIE EVERY DAY ON FISH-MAN ISLAND!!
THE HUMANS HAVE GONE MAD AND ABDUCT YOUNG FISH-PEOPLE LEFT AND RIGHT!!
WE ARE ON A CRASH COURSE WITH ***DEATH!!*** FISH-MAN ISLAND IS RUINED!!!
R-A-A-A

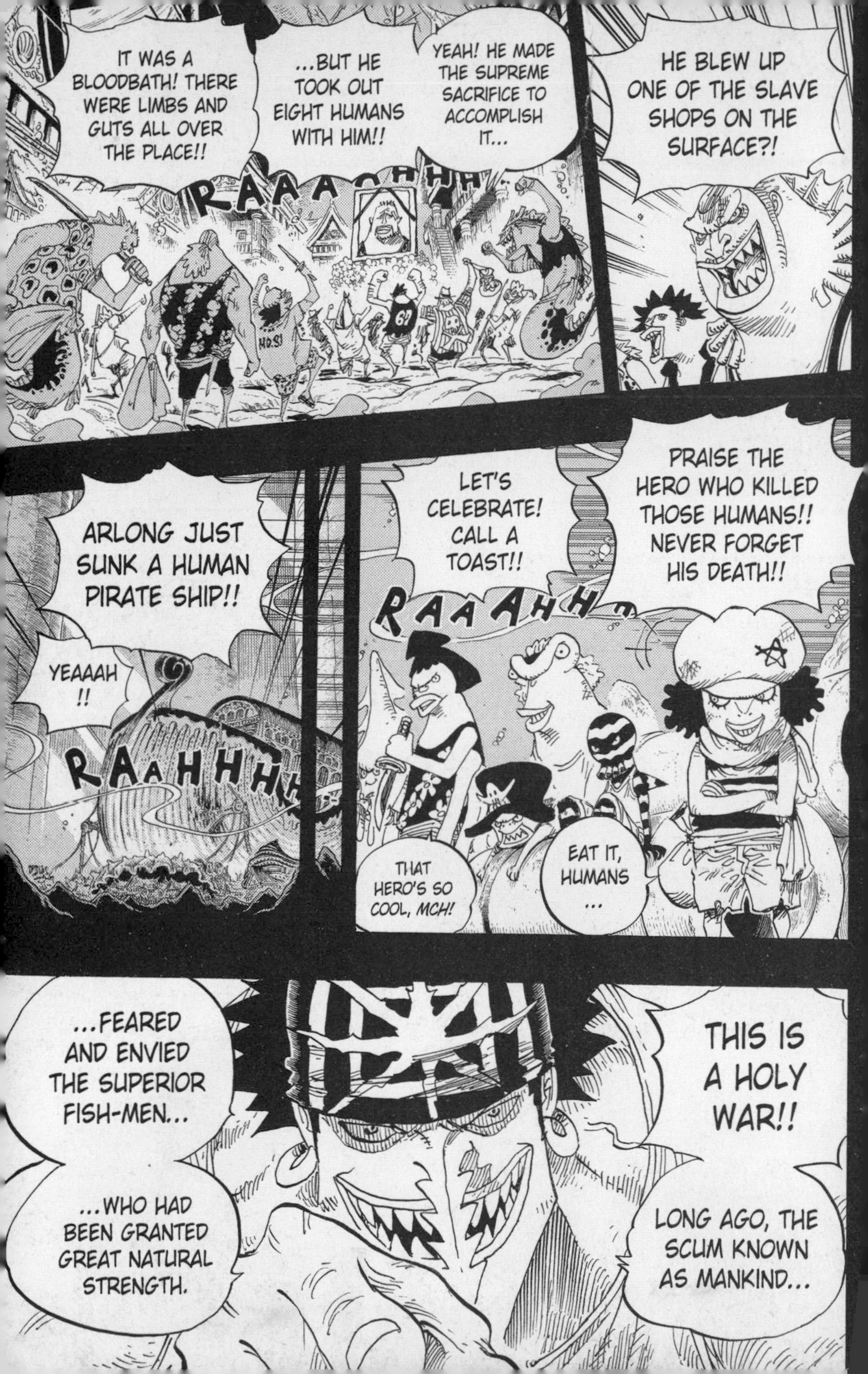
HE BLEW UP ONE OF THE SLAVE SHOPS ON THE SURFACE?!
YEAH! HE MADE THE SUPREME SACRIFICE TO ACCOMPLISH IT...
...BUT HE TOOK OUT EIGHT HUMANS WITH HIM!!
IT WAS A BLOODBATH! THERE WERE LIMBS AND GUTS ALL OVER THE PLACE!!
RAAAAHHHH
PRAISE THE HERO WHO KILLED THOSE HUMANS!! NEVER FORGET HIS DEATH!!
LET'S CELEBRATE! CALL A TOAST!!
RAAAAHHH
EAT IT, HUMANS ...
THAT HERO'S SO COOL, MCH!
ARLONG JUST SUNK A HUMAN PIRATE SHIP!!
YEAAAH !!
RAAHHHH
THIS IS A HOLY WAR!!
LONG AGO, THE SCUM KNOWN AS MANKIND...
...FEARED AND ENVIED THE SUPERIOR FISH-MEN...
...WHO HAD BEEN GRANTED GREAT NATURAL STRENGTH.

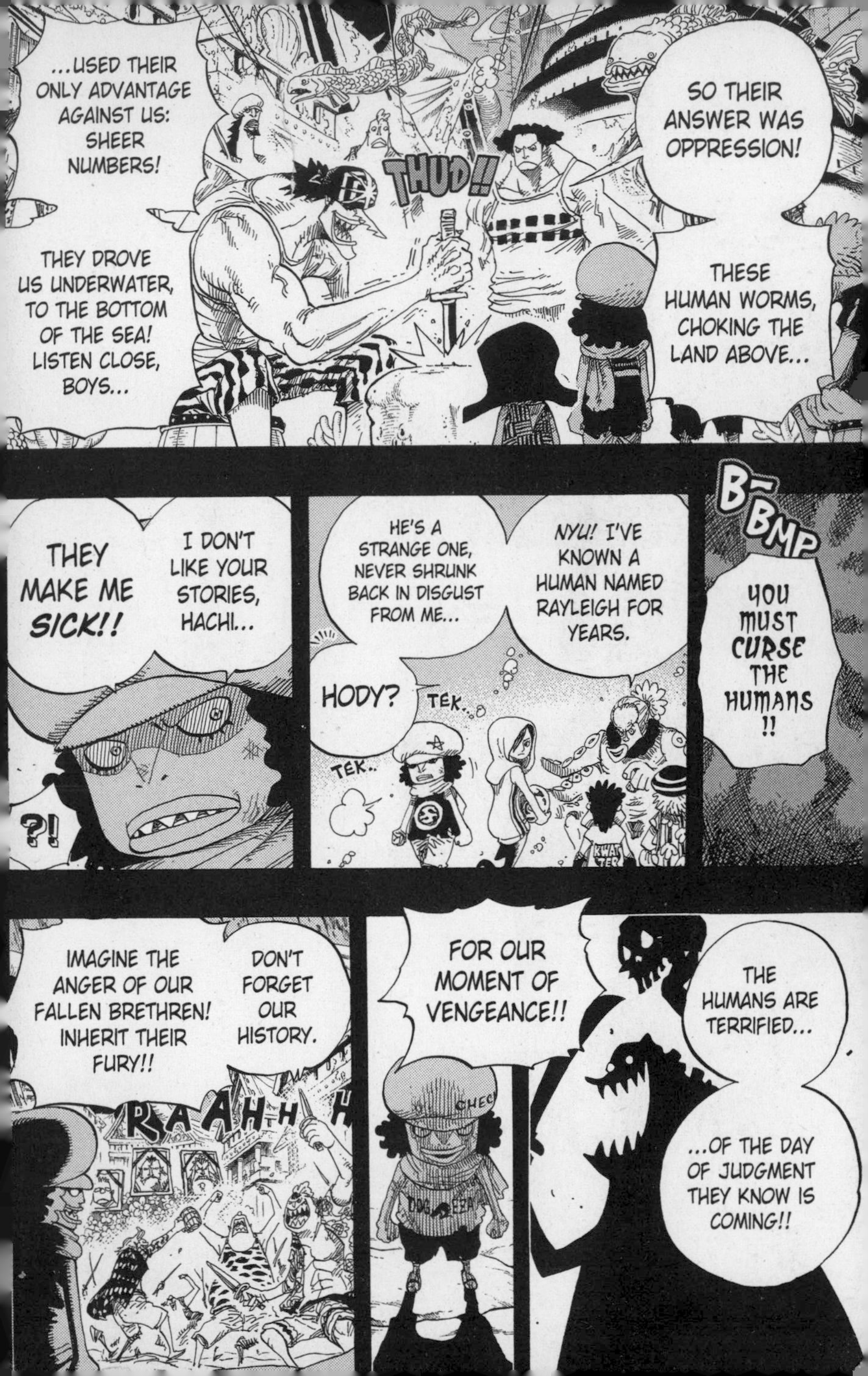
SO THEIR ANSWER WAS OPPRESSION!
THESE HUMAN WORMS, CHOKING THE LAND ABOVE...
...USED THEIR ONLY ADVANTAGE AGAINST US: SHEER NUMBERS!
THUD!!
THEY DROVE US UNDERWATER, TO THE BOTTOM OF THE SEA! LISTEN CLOSE, BOYS...
B-BMP
YOU MUST CURSE THE HUMANS!!
NYU! I'VE KNOWN A HUMAN NAMED RAYLEIGH FOR YEARS.
HE'S A STRANGE ONE, NEVER SHRUNK BACK IN DISGUST FROM ME...
HODY?
TEK..
TEK..
I DON'T LIKE YOUR STORIES, HACHI...
THEY MAKE ME SICK!!
?!
THE HUMANS ARE TERRIFIED...
...OF THE DAY OF JUDGMENT THEY KNOW IS COMING!!
FOR OUR MOMENT OF VENGEANCE!!
DON'T FORGET OUR HISTORY.
IMAGINE THE ANGER OF OUR FALLEN BRETHREN! INHERIT THEIR FURY!!
RAAHHH

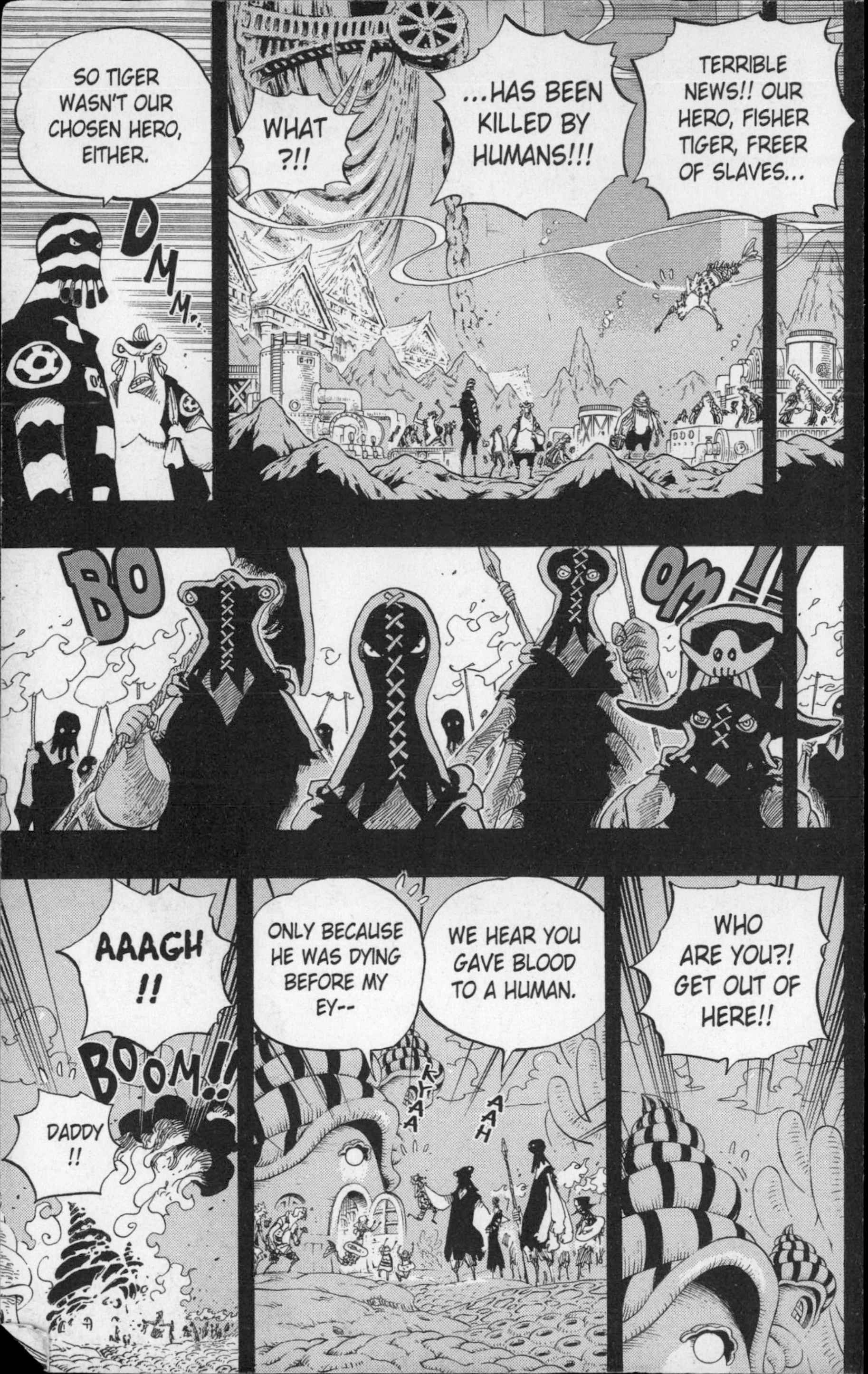
TERRIBLE NEWS!! OUR HERO, FISHER TIGER, FREER OF SLAVES...
...HAS BEEN KILLED BY HUMANS!!!
WHAT ?!!
SO TIGER WASN'T OUR CHOSEN HERO, EITHER.
DMM..
BO
OM!!
WHO ARE YOU?! GET OUT OF HERE!!
WE HEAR YOU GAVE BLOOD TO A HUMAN.
ONLY BECAUSE HE WAS DYING BEFORE MY EY--
KYAA
AAH
AAAGH !!
BOOM!!
DADDY !!

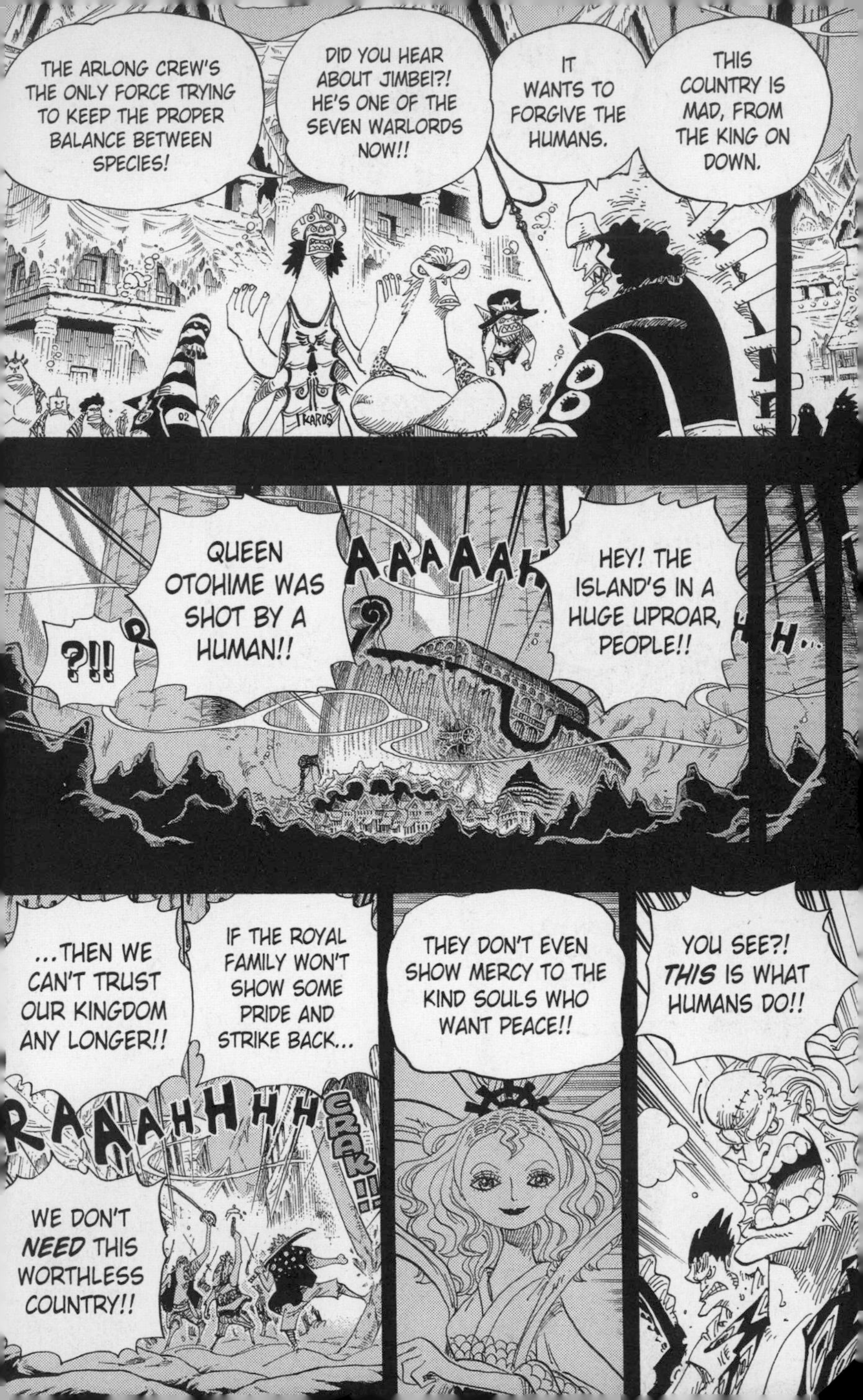
THIS COUNTRY IS MAD, FROM THE KING ON DOWN.
IT WANTS TO FORGIVE THE HUMANS.
DID YOU HEAR ABOUT JIMBEI?! HE'S ONE OF THE SEVEN WARLORDS NOW!!
THE ARLONG CREW'S THE ONLY FORCE TRYING TO KEEP THE PROPER BALANCE BETWEEN SPECIES!
H...
HEY! THE ISLAND'S IN A HUGE UPROAR, PEOPLE!!
AAAAAH
QUEEN OTOHIME WAS SHOT BY A HUMAN!!
R
?!!
YOU SEE?! *THIS* IS WHAT HUMANS DO!!
THEY DON'T EVEN SHOW MERCY TO THE KIND SOULS WHO WANT PEACE!!
IF THE ROYAL FAMILY WON'T SHOW SOME PRIDE AND STRIKE BACK...
...THEN WE CAN'T TRUST OUR KINGDOM ANY LONGER!!
CRAK!!
RAAAHHHH
WE DON'T *NEED* THIS WORTHLESS COUNTRY!!

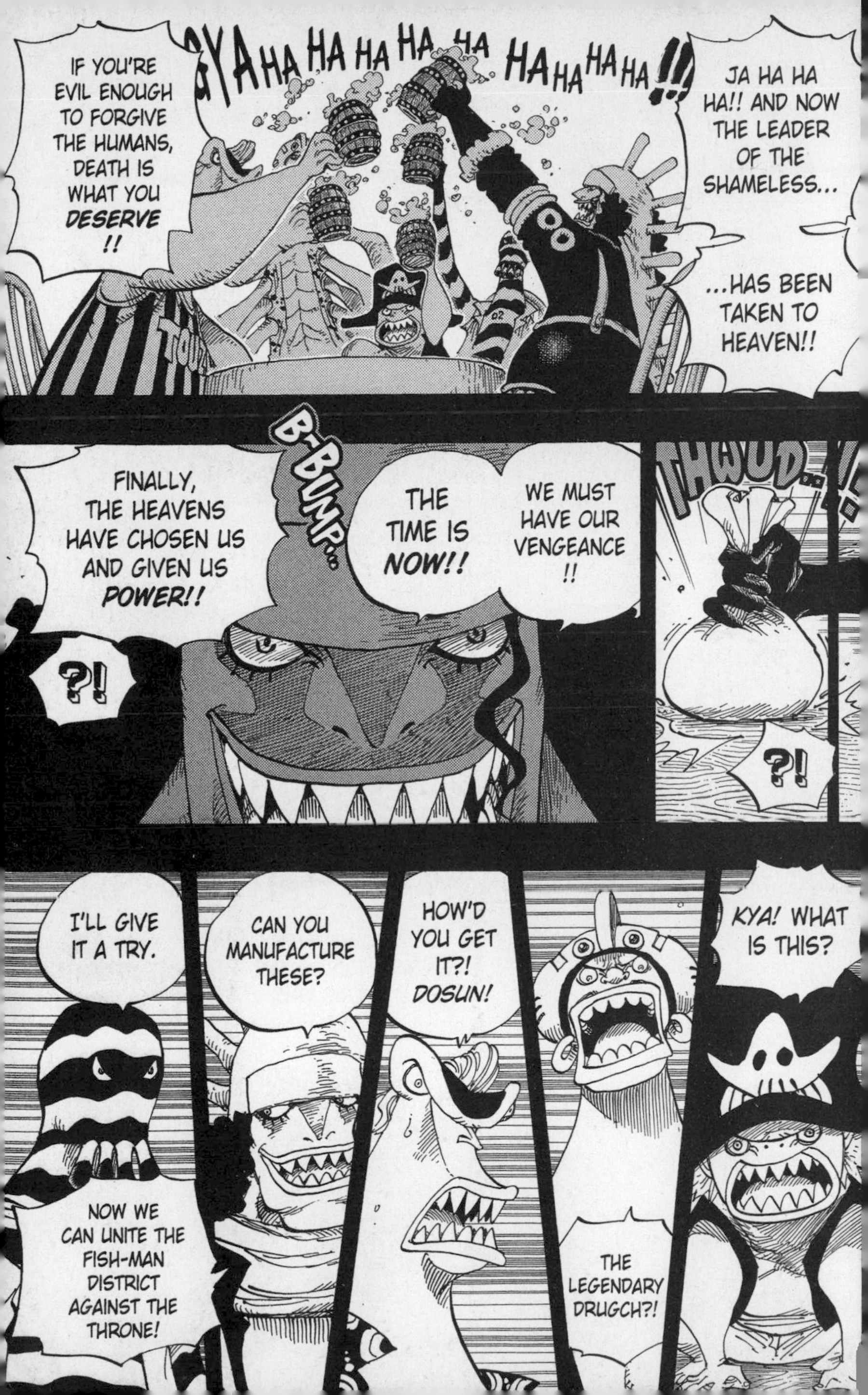
GYAHAHAHAHA HA HA HAHAHAHAHA!!
JA HA HA HA!! AND NOW THE LEADER OF THE SHAMELESS...
...HAS BEEN TAKEN TO HEAVEN!!
IF YOU'RE EVIL ENOUGH TO FORGIVE THE HUMANS, DEATH IS WHAT YOU *DESERVE* !!
THWUD...
?!
WE MUST HAVE OUR VENGEANCE !!
THE TIME IS *NOW!!*
B-BUMP...
FINALLY, THE HEAVENS HAVE CHOSEN US AND GIVEN US *POWER!!*
?!
KYA! WHAT IS THIS?
THE LEGENDARY DRUGCH?!
HOW'D YOU GET IT?! *DOSUN!*
CAN YOU MANUFACTURE THESE?
I'LL GIVE IT A TRY.
NOW WE CAN UNITE THE FISH-MAN DISTRICT AGAINST THE THRONE!

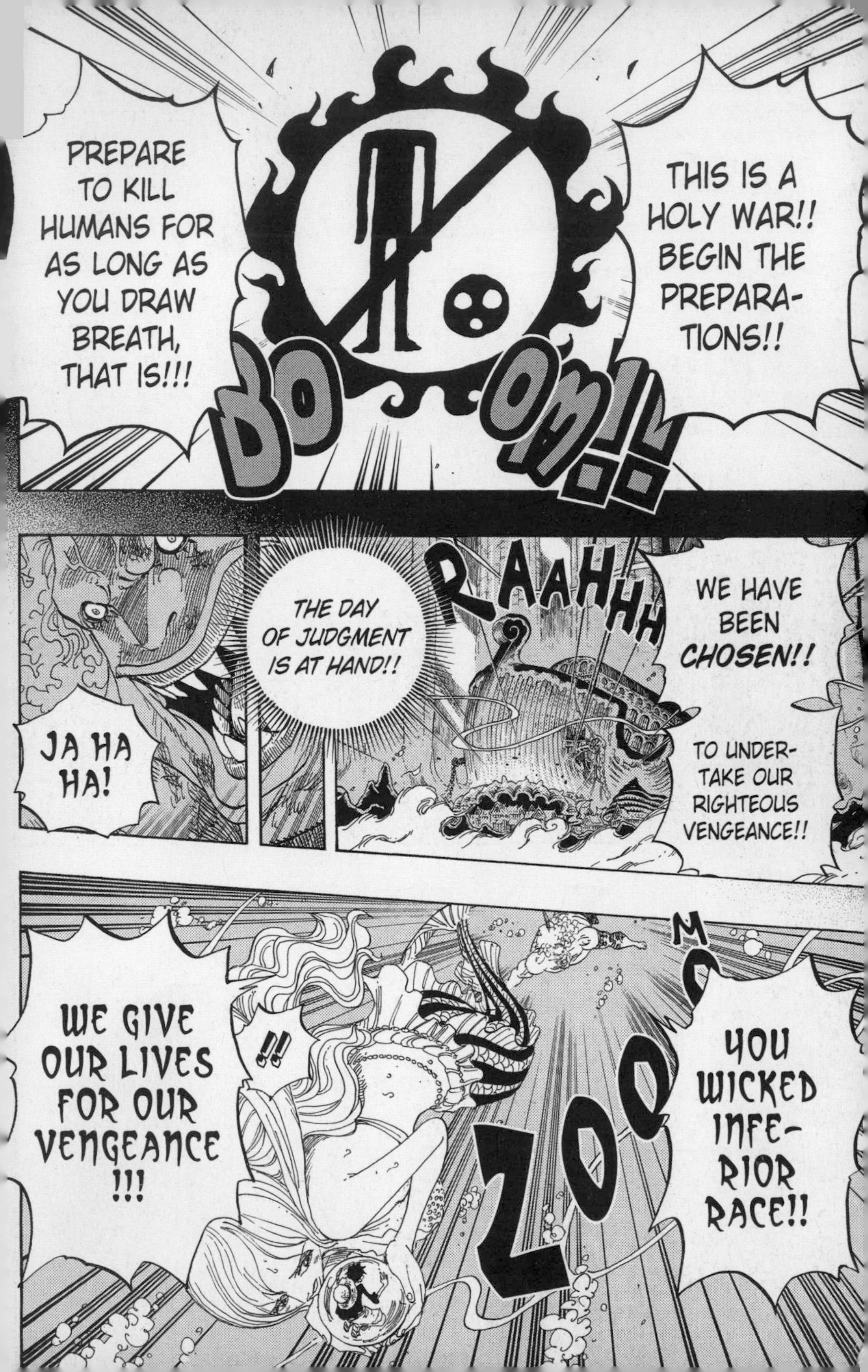
THIS IS A HOLY WAR!! BEGIN THE PREPARA-TIONS!!
BOOM!!
PREPARE TO KILL HUMANS FOR AS LONG AS YOU DRAW BREATH, THAT IS!!!
WE HAVE BEEN CHOSEN!!
TO UNDER-TAKE OUR RIGHTEOUS VENGEANCE!!
RAAHHH
THE DAY OF JUDGMENT IS AT HAND!!
JA HA HA!
YOU WICKED INFE-RIOR RACE!!
ZOOOM
!!
WE GIVE OUR LIVES FOR OUR VENGEANCE !!!

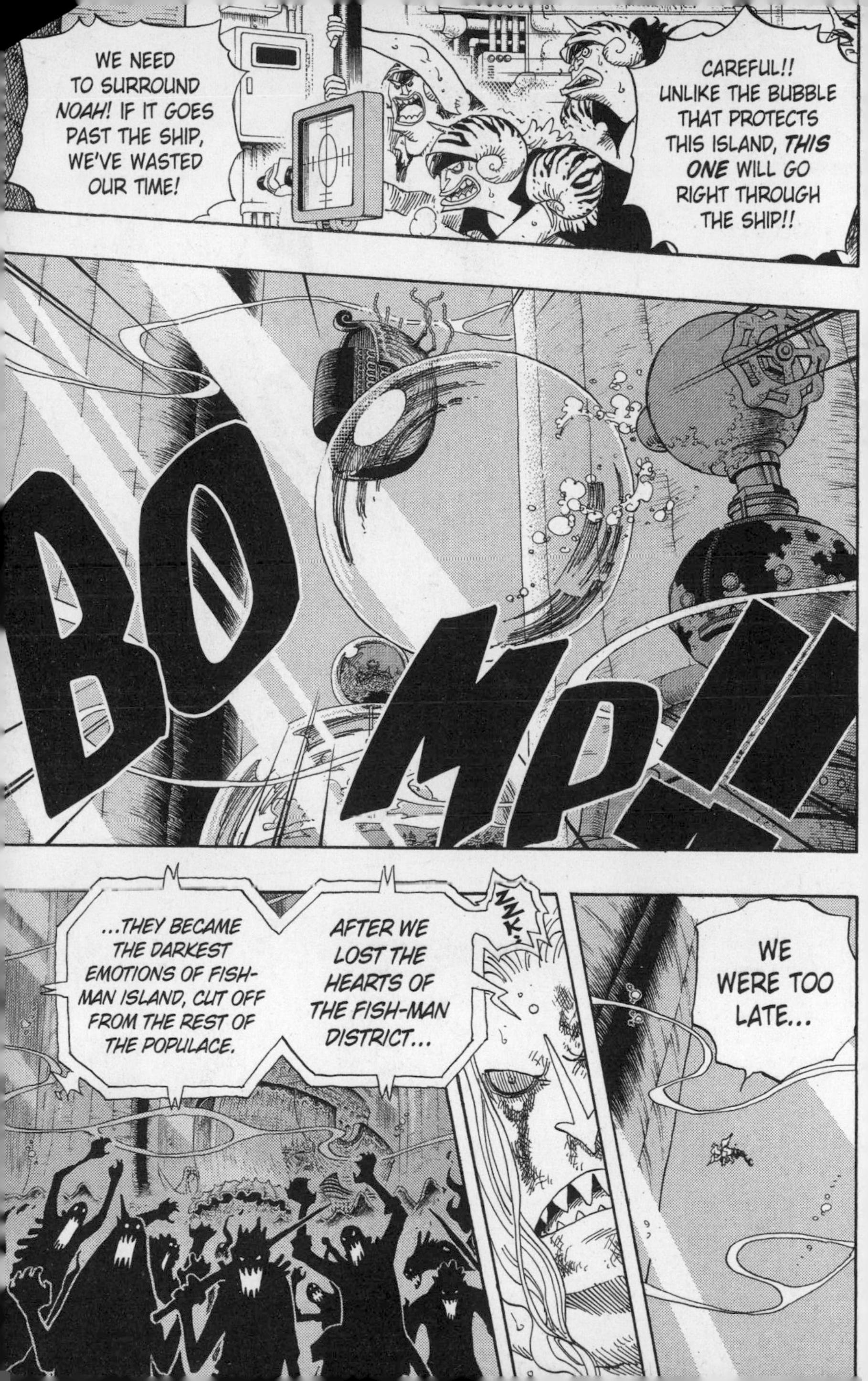
CAREFUL!! UNLIKE THE BUBBLE THAT PROTECTS THIS ISLAND, ***THIS ONE*** WILL GO RIGHT THROUGH THE SHIP!!
WE NEED TO SURROUND *NOAH!* IF IT GOES PAST THE SHIP, WE'VE WASTED OUR TIME!
BOMP!!
WE WERE TOO LATE...
NNK...
AFTER WE LOST THE HEARTS OF THE FISH-MAN DISTRICT...
...THEY BECAME THE DARKEST EMOTIONS OF FISH-MAN ISLAND, CUT OFF FROM THE REST OF THE POPULACE.

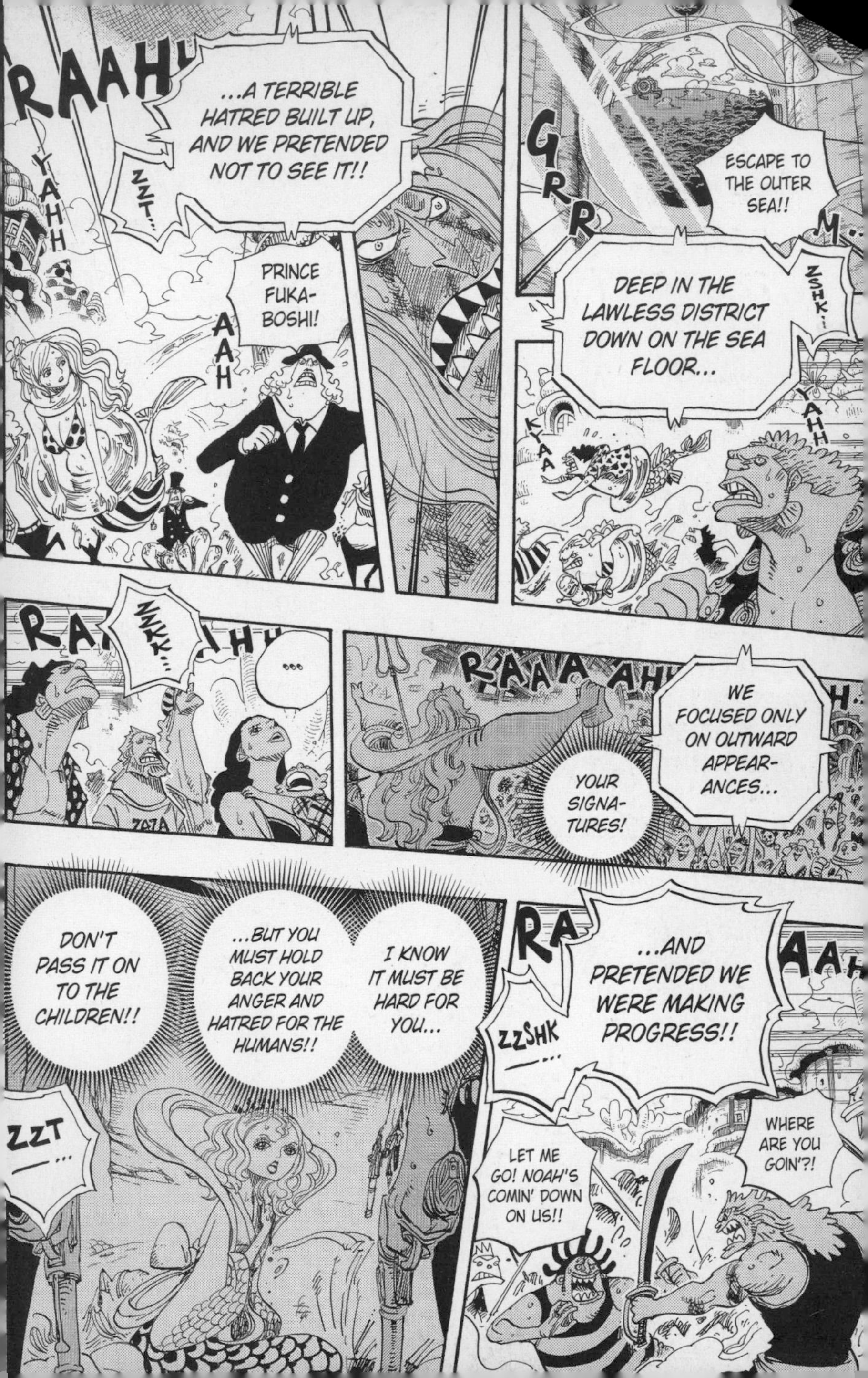
GRRR
ESCAPE TO THE OUTER SEA!!
ZSHK...
DEEP IN THE LAWLESS DISTRICT DOWN ON THE SEA FLOOR...
YAHH
KYAA
...A TERRIBLE HATRED BUILT UP, AND WE PRETENDED NOT TO SEE IT!!
ZZT...
YAHH
PRINCE FUKA-BOSHI!
AAH
WE FOCUSED ONLY ON OUTWARD APPEAR-ANCES...
YOUR SIGNA-TURES!
ZZKK...
...
...AND PRETENDED WE WERE MAKING PROGRESS!!
ZZSHK...
WHERE ARE YOU GOIN'?!
LET ME GO! NOAH'S COMIN' DOWN ON US!!
I KNOW IT MUST BE HARD FOR YOU...
...BUT YOU MUST HOLD BACK YOUR ANGER AND HATRED FOR THE HUMANS!!
DON'T PASS IT ON TO THE CHILDREN!!
ZZT...

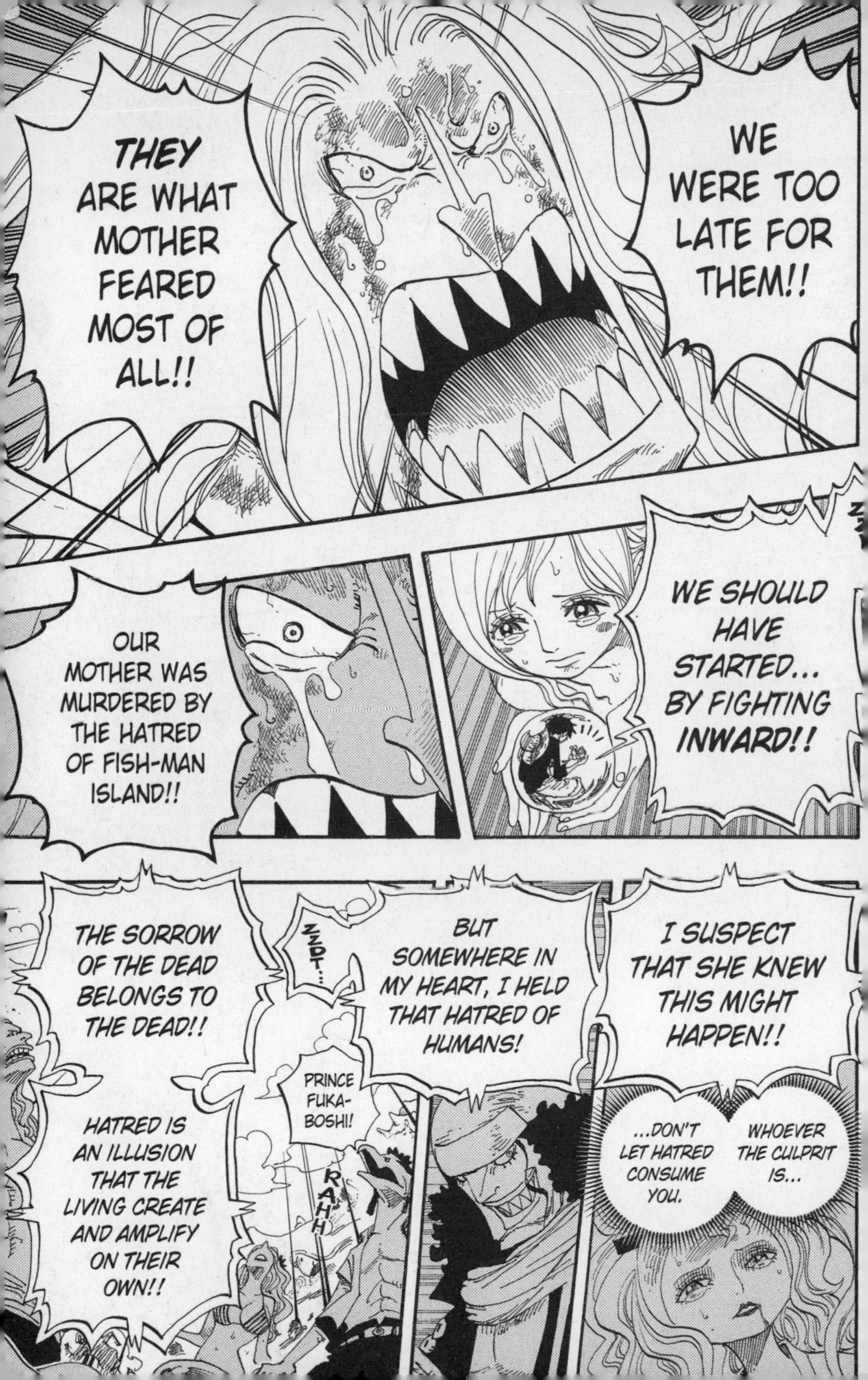
WE WERE TOO LATE FOR THEM!!
THEY ARE WHAT MOTHER FEARED MOST OF ALL!!
WE SHOULD HAVE STARTED... BY FIGHTING INWARD!!
OUR MOTHER WAS MURDERED BY THE HATRED OF FISH-MAN ISLAND!!
I SUSPECT THAT SHE KNEW THIS MIGHT HAPPEN!!
WHOEVER THE CULPRIT IS...
...DON'T LET HATRED CONSUME YOU.
BUT SOMEWHERE IN MY HEART, I HELD THAT HATRED OF HUMANS!
ZZDT...
PRINCE FUKA-BOSHI!
RAHH
THE SORROW OF THE DEAD BELONGS TO THE DEAD!!
HATRED IS AN ILLUSION THAT THE LIVING CREATE AND AMPLIFY ON THEIR OWN!!

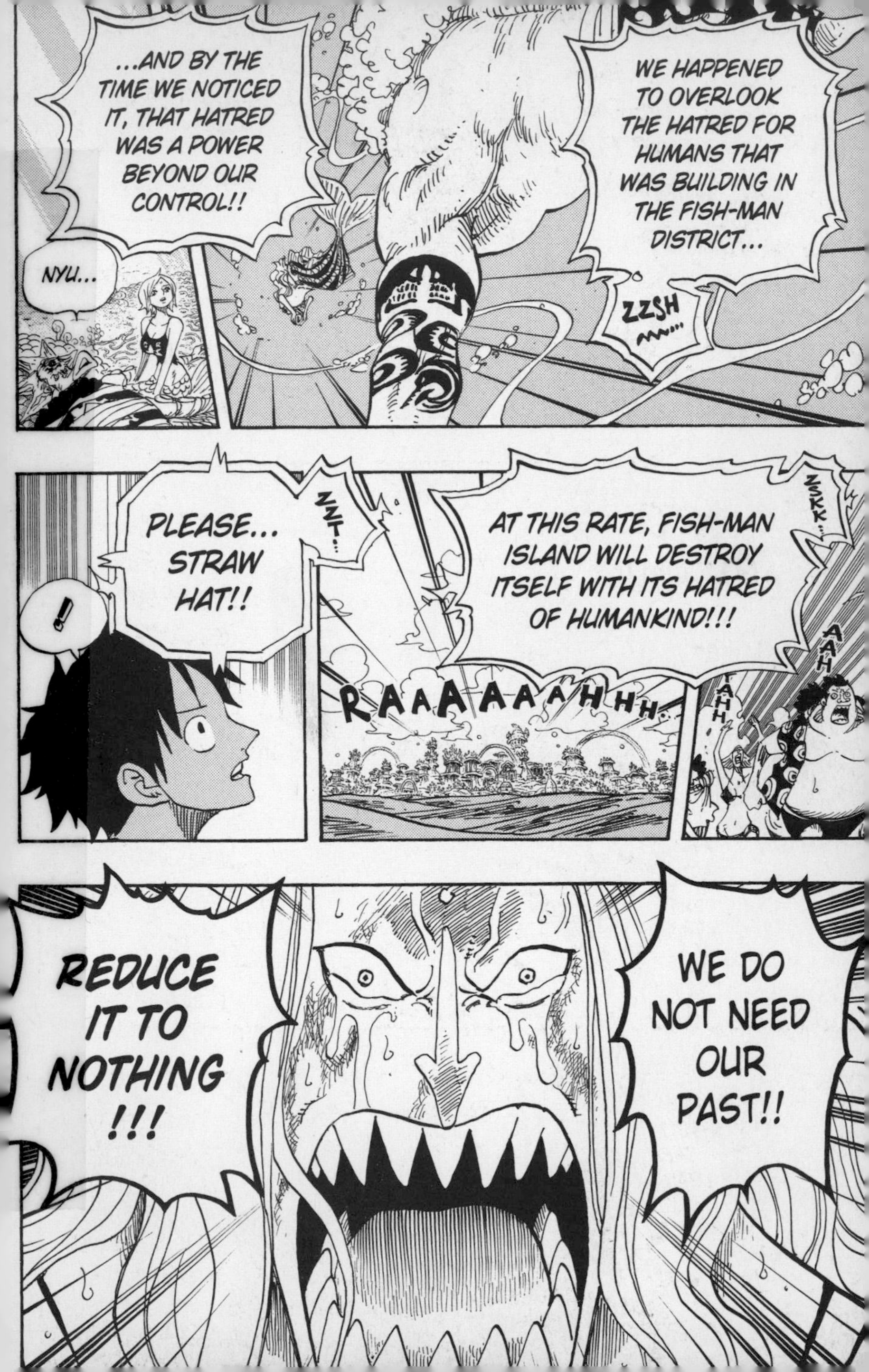
WE HAPPENED TO OVERLOOK THE HATRED FOR HUMANS THAT WAS BUILDING IN THE FISH-MAN DISTRICT...
...AND BY THE TIME WE NOTICED IT, THAT HATRED WAS A POWER BEYOND OUR CONTROL!!
ZZSH
NYU...
AT THIS RATE, FISH-MAN ISLAND WILL DESTROY ITSELF WITH ITS HATRED OF HUMANKIND!!!
ZSKK...
AAH
AHH
ZZT...
RAAAAAAAHHH
PLEASE... STRAW HAT!!
!
WE DO NOT NEED OUR PAST!!
REDUCE IT TO NOTHING!!!

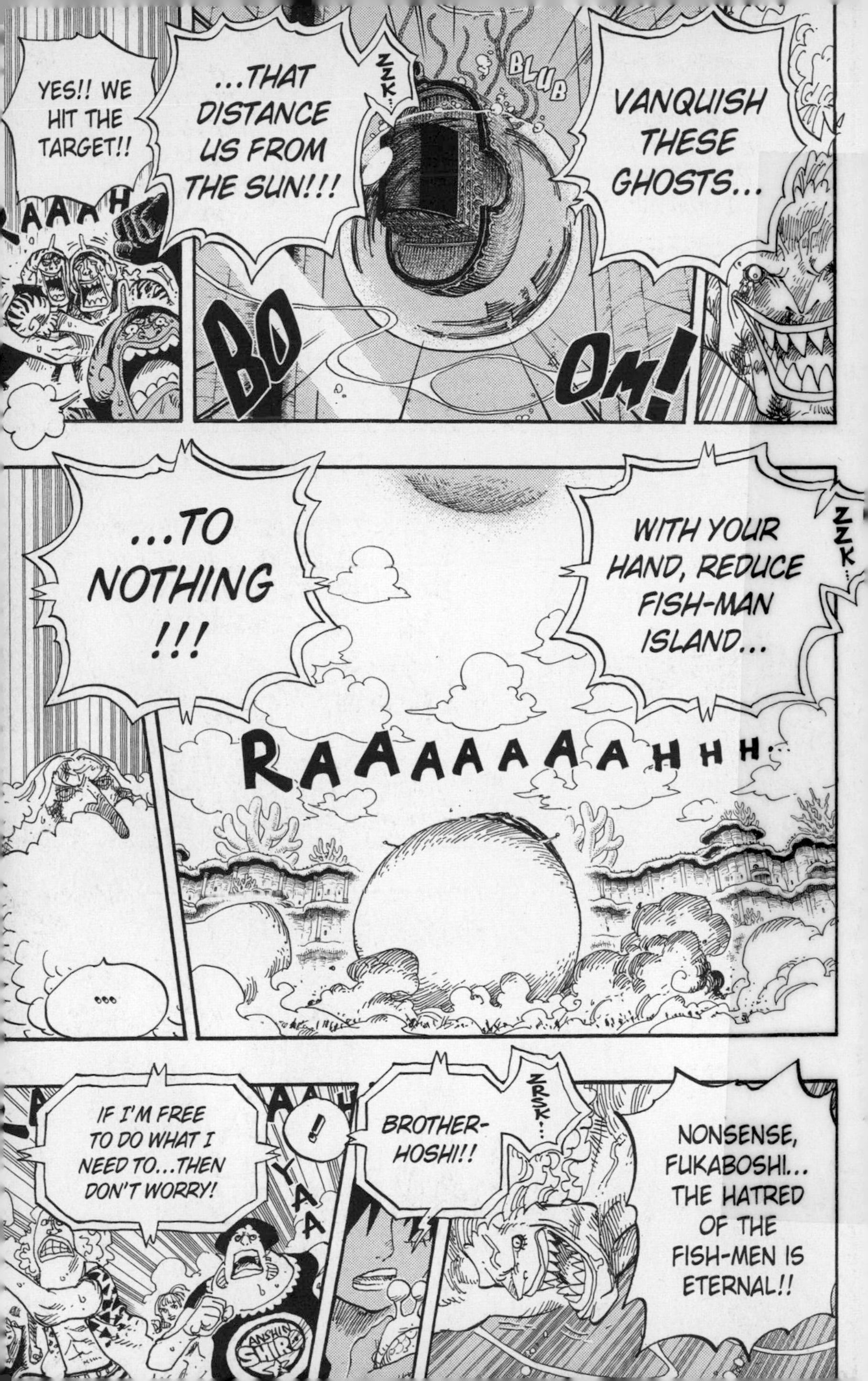
VANQUISH THESE GHOSTS...
ZZK...
BLUB
...THAT DISTANCE US FROM THE SUN!!!
BOOM!
YES!! WE HIT THE TARGET!!
AAAH
ZZK...
WITH YOUR HAND, REDUCE FISH-MAN ISLAND...
...TO NOTHING !!!
RAAAAAAAHHH...
...
NONSENSE, FUKABOSHI... THE HATRED OF THE FISH-MEN IS ETERNAL!!
ZRSK...
BROTHER-HOSHI!!
!
YAAA
AAH
IF I'M FREE TO DO WHAT I NEED TO...THEN DON'T WORRY!

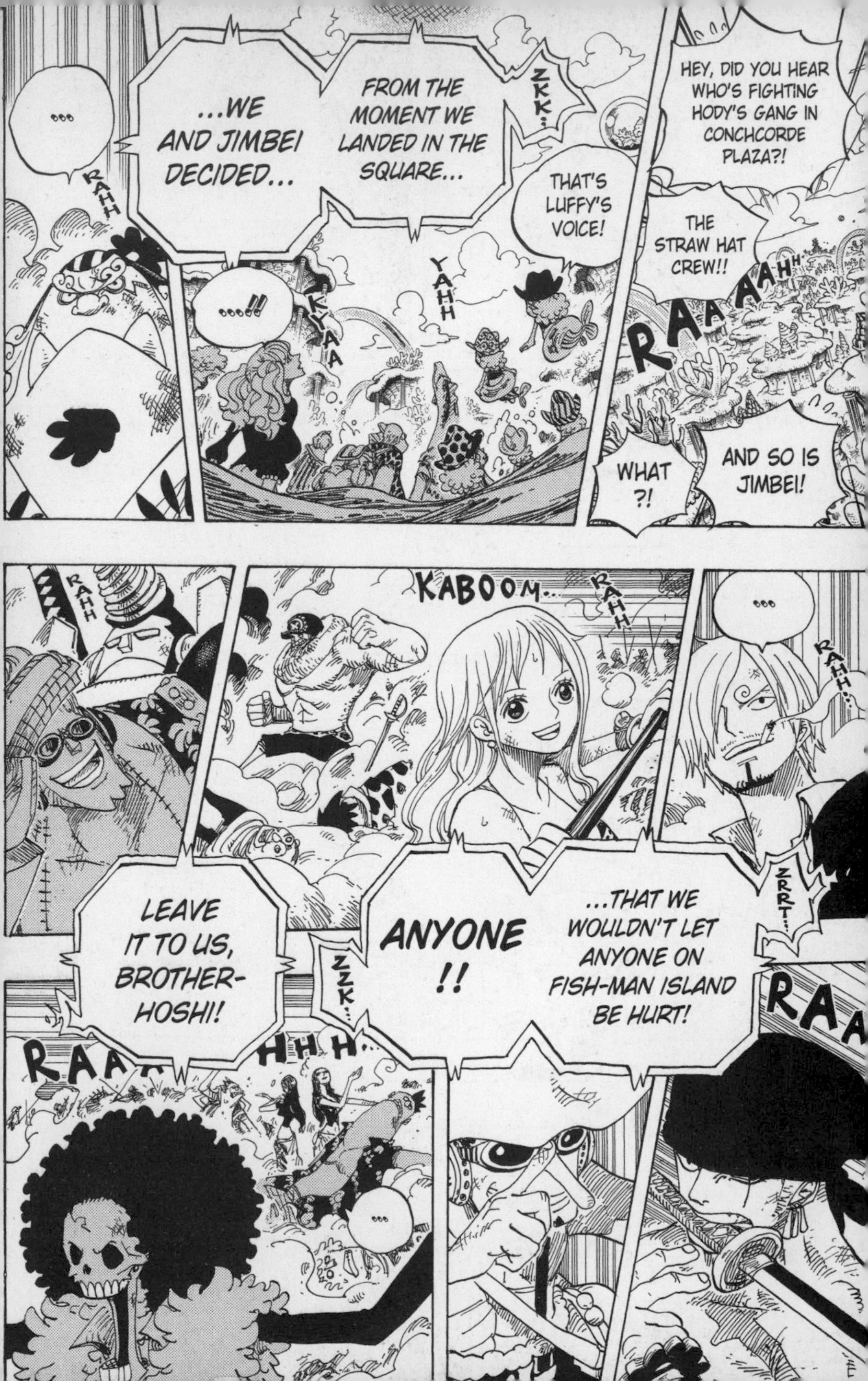
HEY, DID YOU HEAR WHO'S FIGHTING HODY'S GANG IN CONCHCORDE PLAZA?!
THE STRAW HAT CREW!!
RAAAAHH
AND SO IS JIMBEI!
WHAT ?!
ZKK...
THAT'S LUFFY'S VOICE!
FROM THE MOMENT WE LANDED IN THE SQUARE...
YAHH
KYAA
...!!
...WE AND JIMBEI DECIDED...
...
RAHH
...
RAHH...
KABOOM...
RAHH
RAHH
ZRRT...
...THAT WE WOULDN'T LET ANYONE ON FISH-MAN ISLAND BE HURT!
ANYONE !!
ZZK...
LEAVE IT TO US, BROTHER-HOSHI!
RAA
RAAAHHH
...

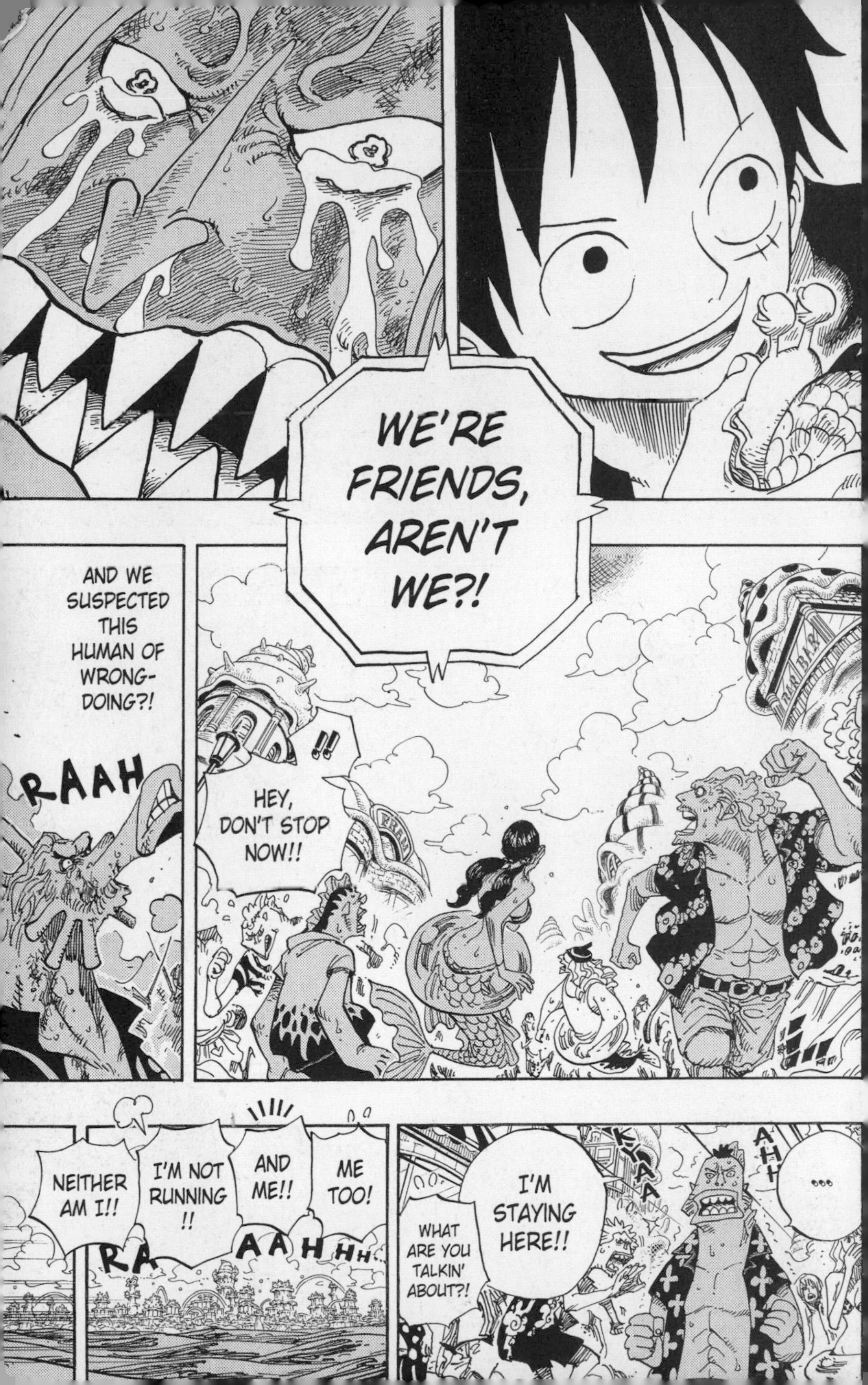
WE'RE FRIENDS, AREN'T WE?!
!!
HEY, DON'T STOP NOW!!
AND WE SUSPECTED THIS HUMAN OF WRONG-DOING?!
RAAH
AHHH
...
KYAA
I'M STAYING HERE!!
WHAT ARE YOU TALKIN' ABOUT?!
ME TOO!
AND ME!!
I'M NOT RUNNING !!
NEITHER AM I!!
RA AAHhh...

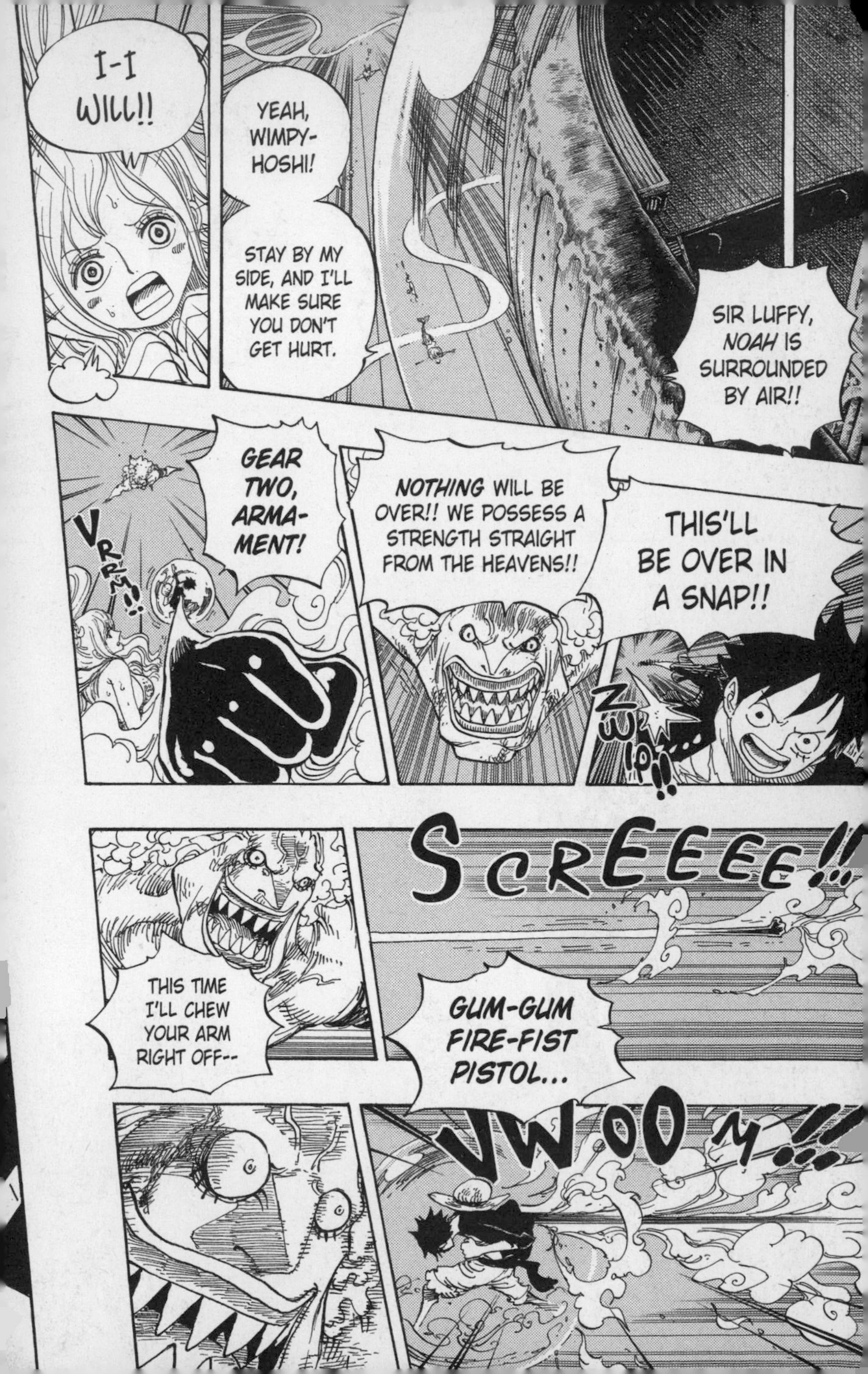
SIR LUFFY, NOAH IS SURROUNDED BY AIR!!
YEAH, WIMPY-HOSHI!
STAY BY MY SIDE, AND I'LL MAKE SURE YOU DON'T GET HURT.
I-I WILL!!
THIS'LL BE OVER IN A SNAP!!
ZWIP!!
NOTHING WILL BE OVER!! WE POSSESS A STRENGTH STRAIGHT FROM THE HEAVENS!!
GEAR TWO, ARMAMENT!
VRRM!!
SCREEEE!!
GUM-GUM FIRE-FIST PISTOL...
THIS TIME I'LL CHEW YOUR ARM RIGHT OFF--
VWOOM!!!

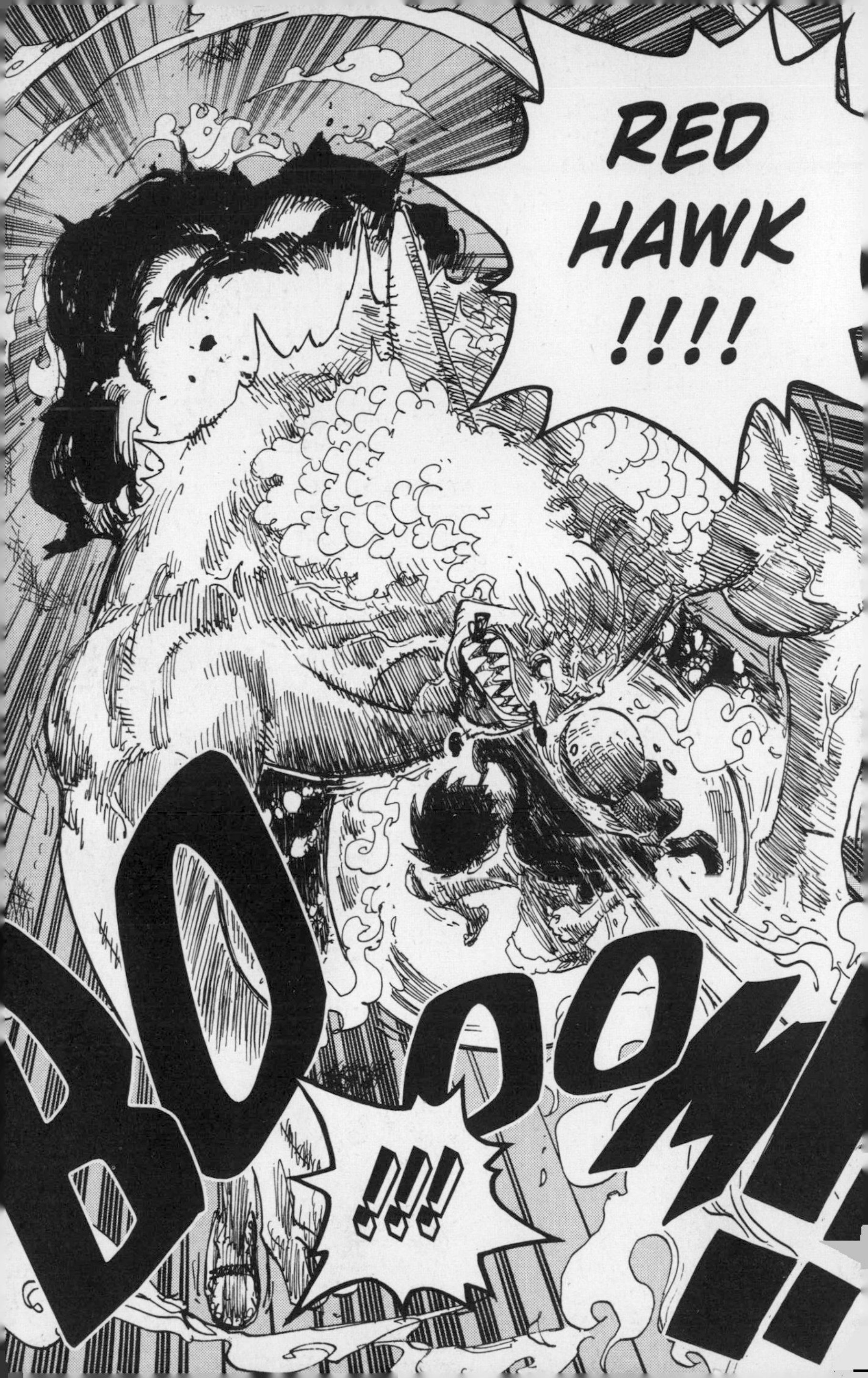
RED HAWK !!!!
BOOOM!!!!

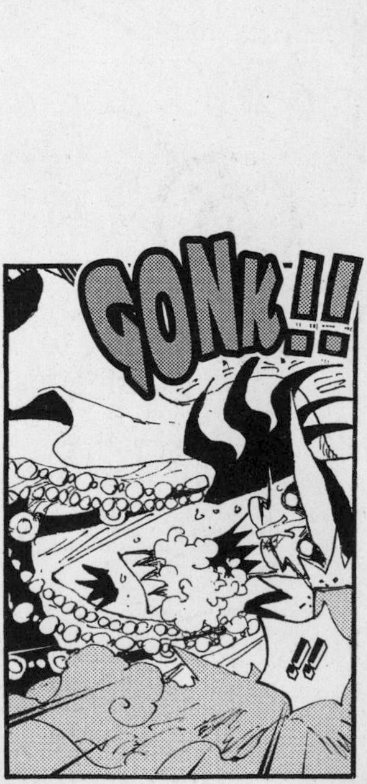
GONK!!
!!

Chapter 645:
DEATH IS ANOTHER FORM OF REVENGE

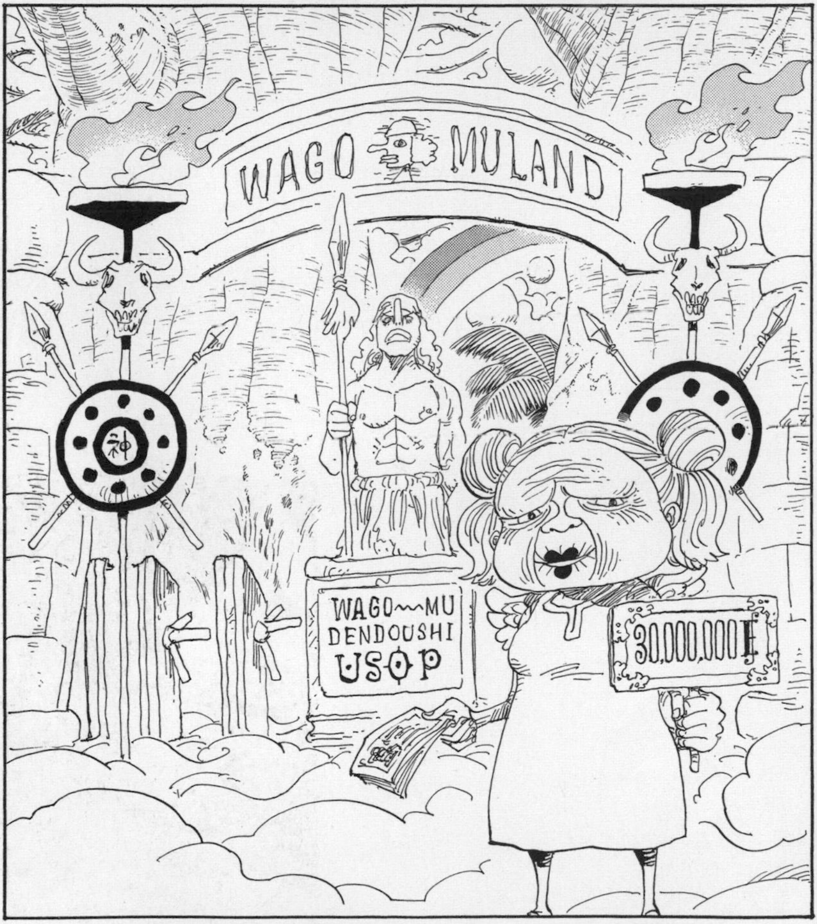
WAGO MULAND
WAGO~MU DENDOUSHI USOP
30,000,000

DECKS OF THE WORLD, VOL. 28: "SKYPIEA–AMAZON SELLS TICKETS TO RUBBER BAND LAND"

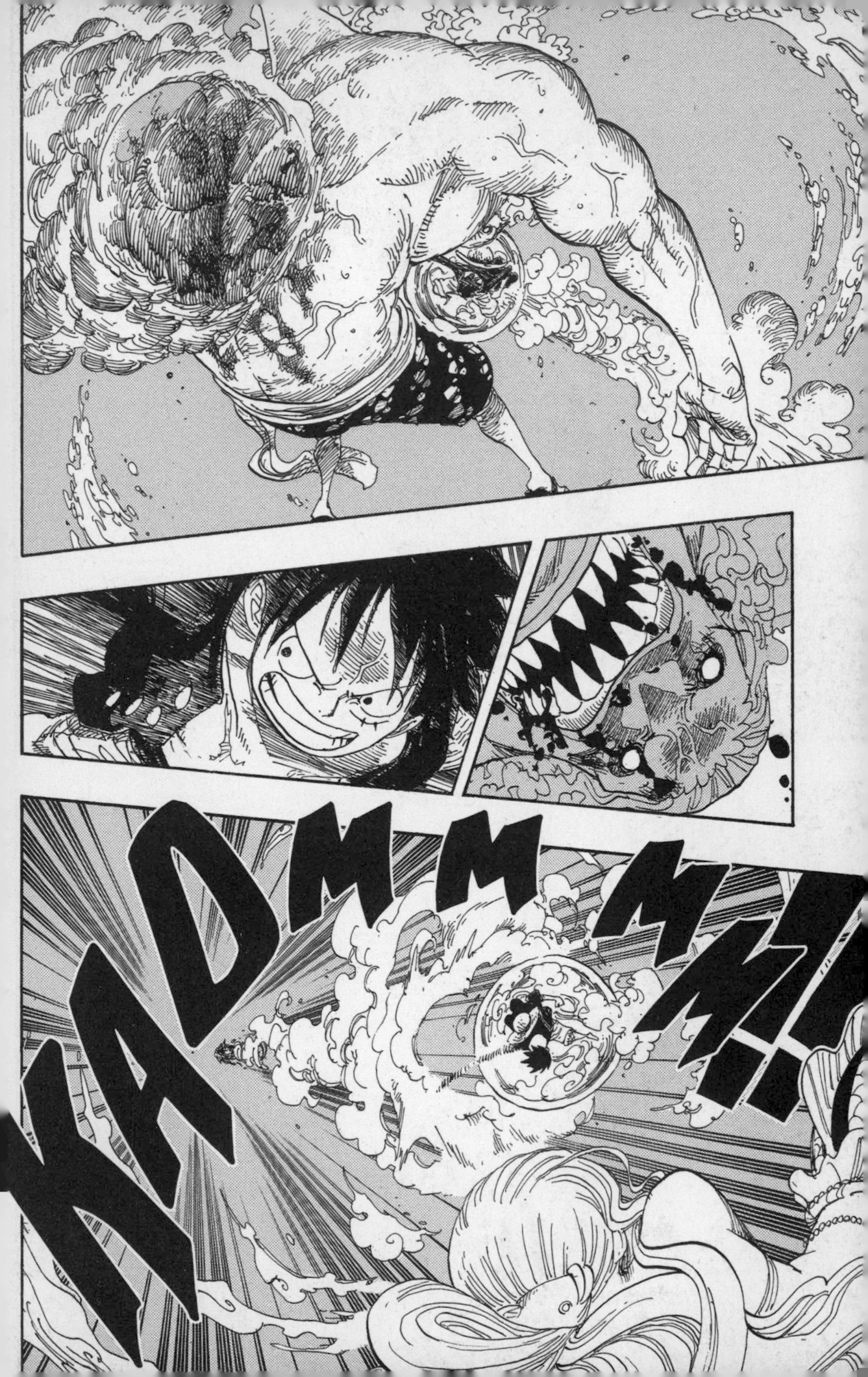
KADMMMM!!

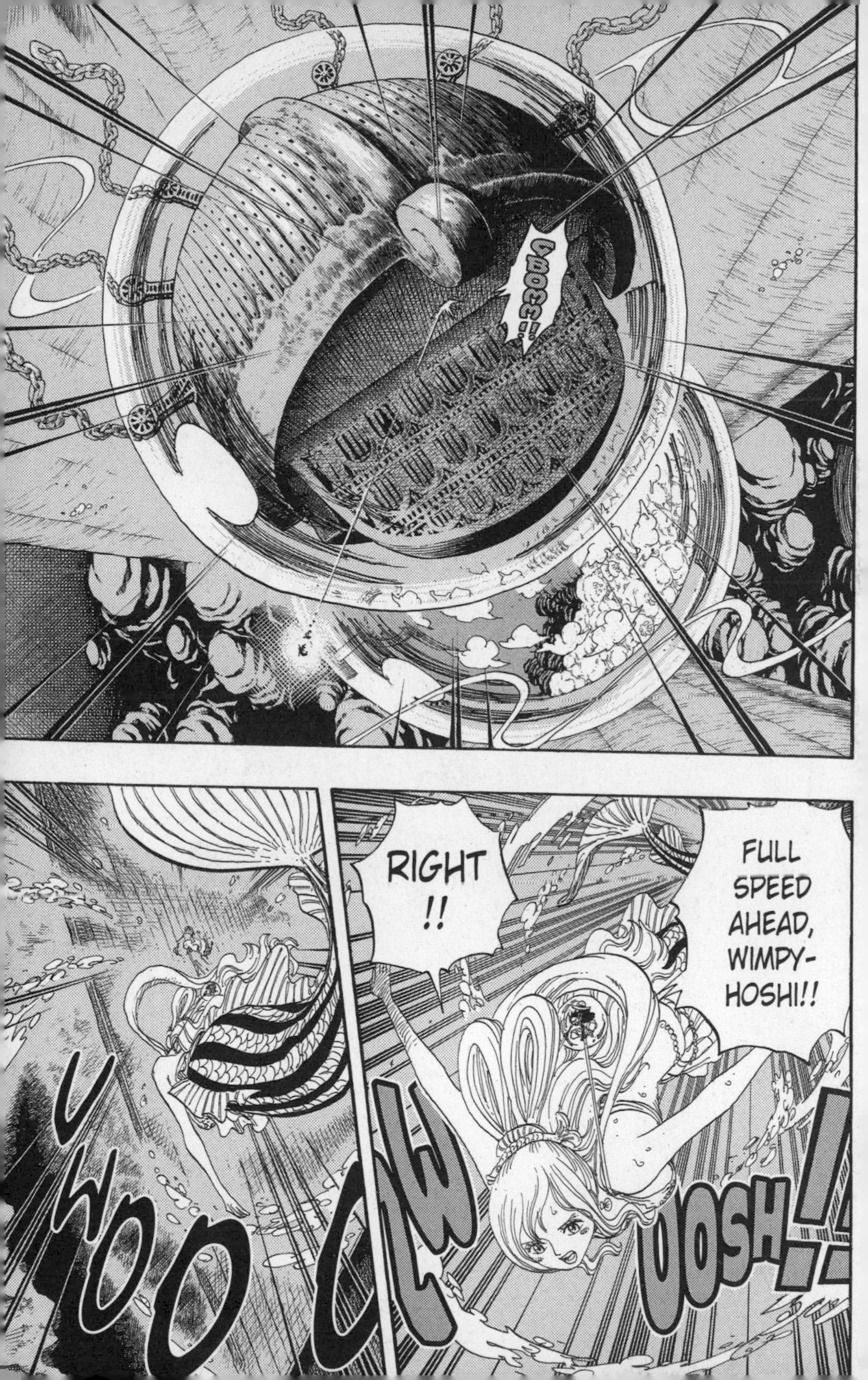
FULL SPEED AHEAD, WIMPY-HOSHI!!
RIGHT!!
WHOOOOSH!!

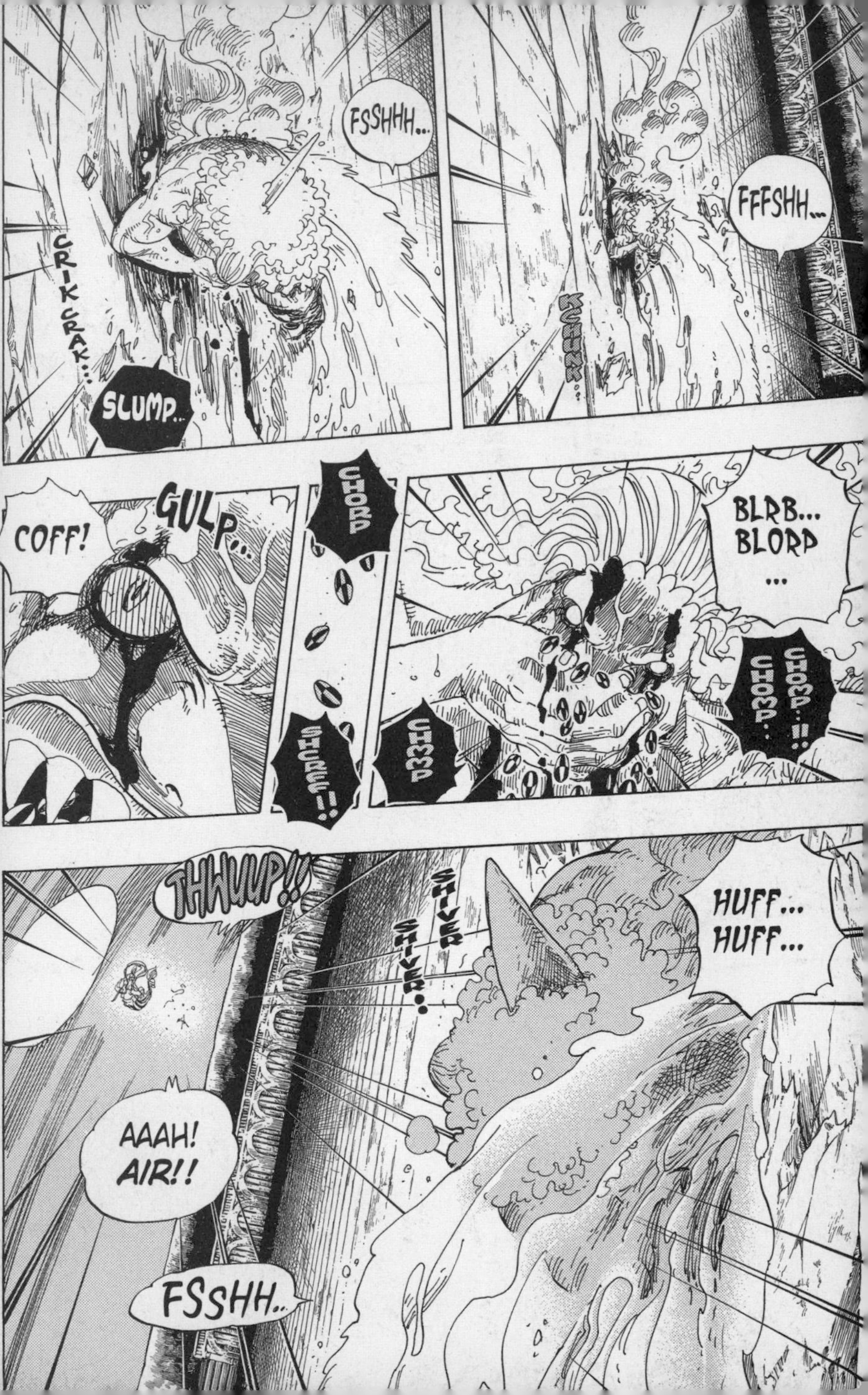
FFFSHH...
KCHUNK...
FSSHHH...
CRIK CRAK...
SLUMP...
BLRB... BLORP ...
CHOMP..!!
CHOMP...
CHMP
CHORP
SHREF!!
GULP...
COFF!
HUFF... HUFF...
SHIVER
SHIVER...
THWUP!!
AAAH! AIR!!
FSSHH...

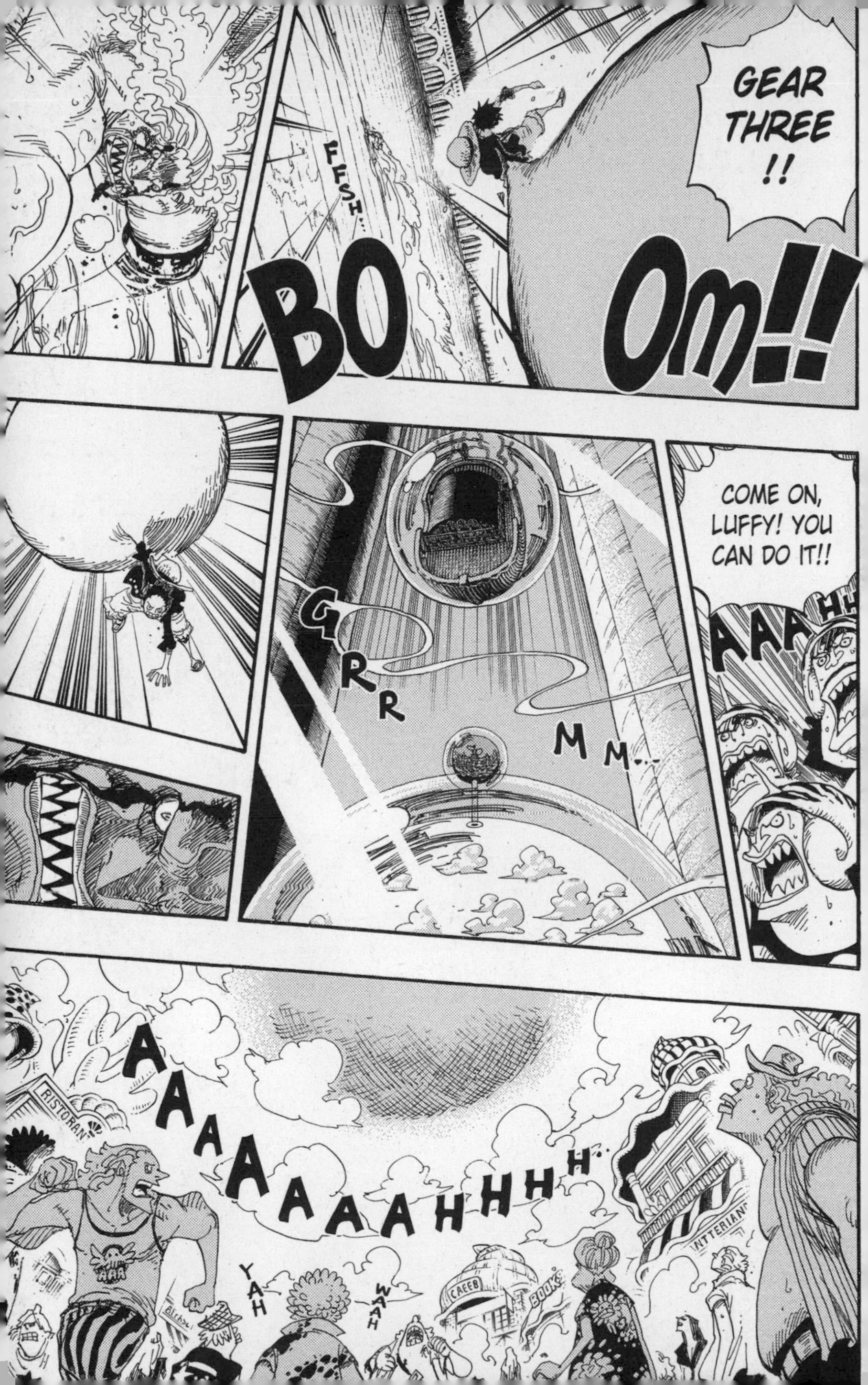
GEAR THREE!!
BOOm!!
FFSH...
COME ON, LUFFY! YOU CAN DO IT!!
AAAHH
GRRR
MM...
AAAAAAAAAHHHH
WAAH
YAH

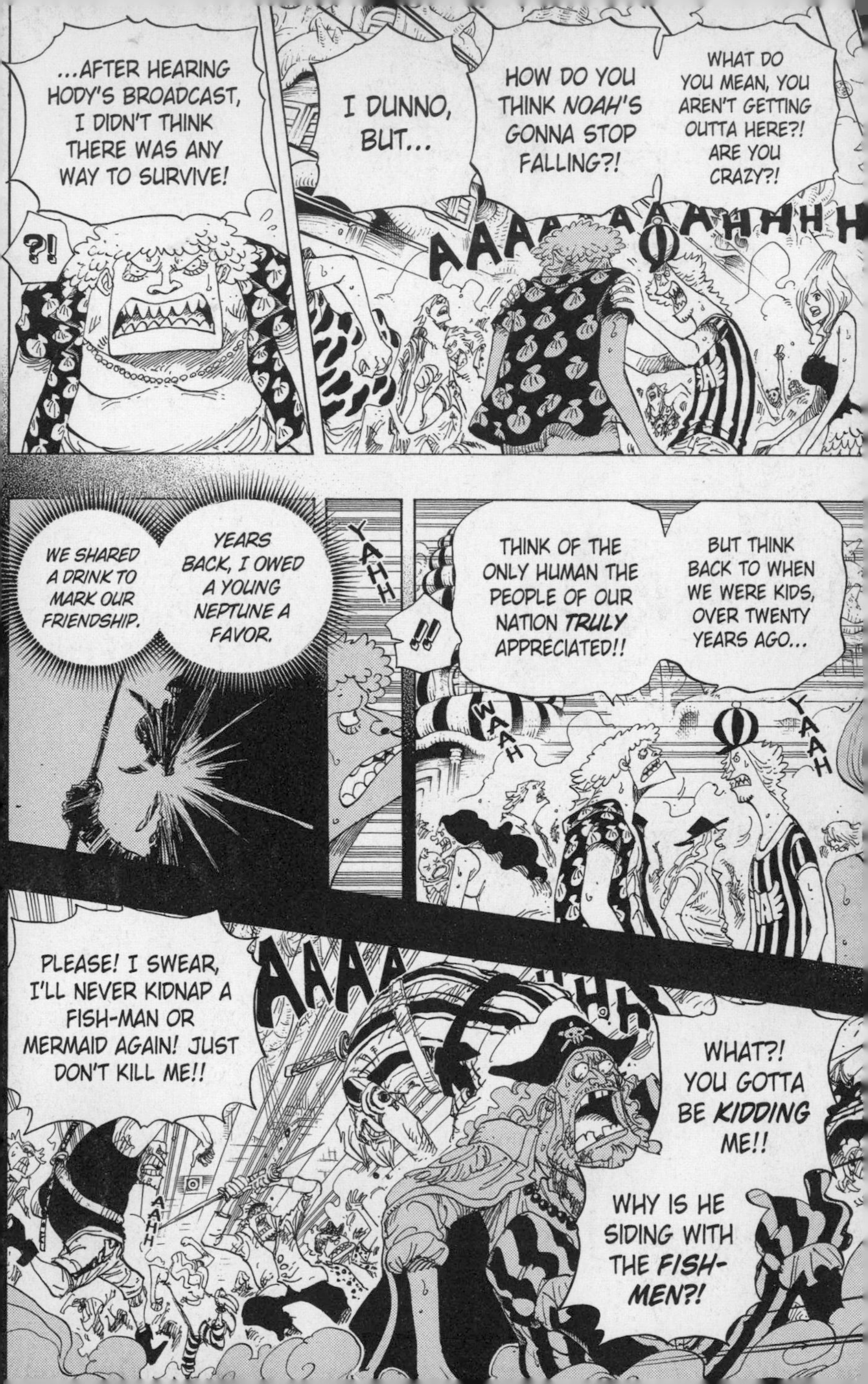
WHAT DO YOU MEAN, YOU AREN'T GETTING OUTTA HERE?! ARE YOU CRAZY?!
HOW DO YOU THINK *NOAH*'S GONNA STOP FALLING?!
I DUNNO, BUT...
AAAAAAAAHHHHH
...AFTER HEARING HODY'S BROADCAST, I DIDN'T THINK THERE WAS ANY WAY TO SURVIVE!
?!
BUT THINK BACK TO WHEN WE WERE KIDS, OVER TWENTY YEARS AGO...
THINK OF THE ONLY HUMAN THE PEOPLE OF OUR NATION ***TRULY*** APPRECIATED!!
YAAH
WAAH
YAHH
!!
YEARS BACK, I OWED A YOUNG NEPTUNE A FAVOR.
WE SHARED A DRINK TO MARK OUR FRIENDSHIP.
WHAT?! YOU GOTTA BE ***KIDDING*** ME!!
WHY IS HE SIDING WITH THE ***FISH-MEN?!***
AAAAHHHH
PLEASE! I SWEAR, I'LL NEVER KIDNAP A FISH-MAN OR MERMAID AGAIN! JUST DON'T KILL ME!!
AAHH

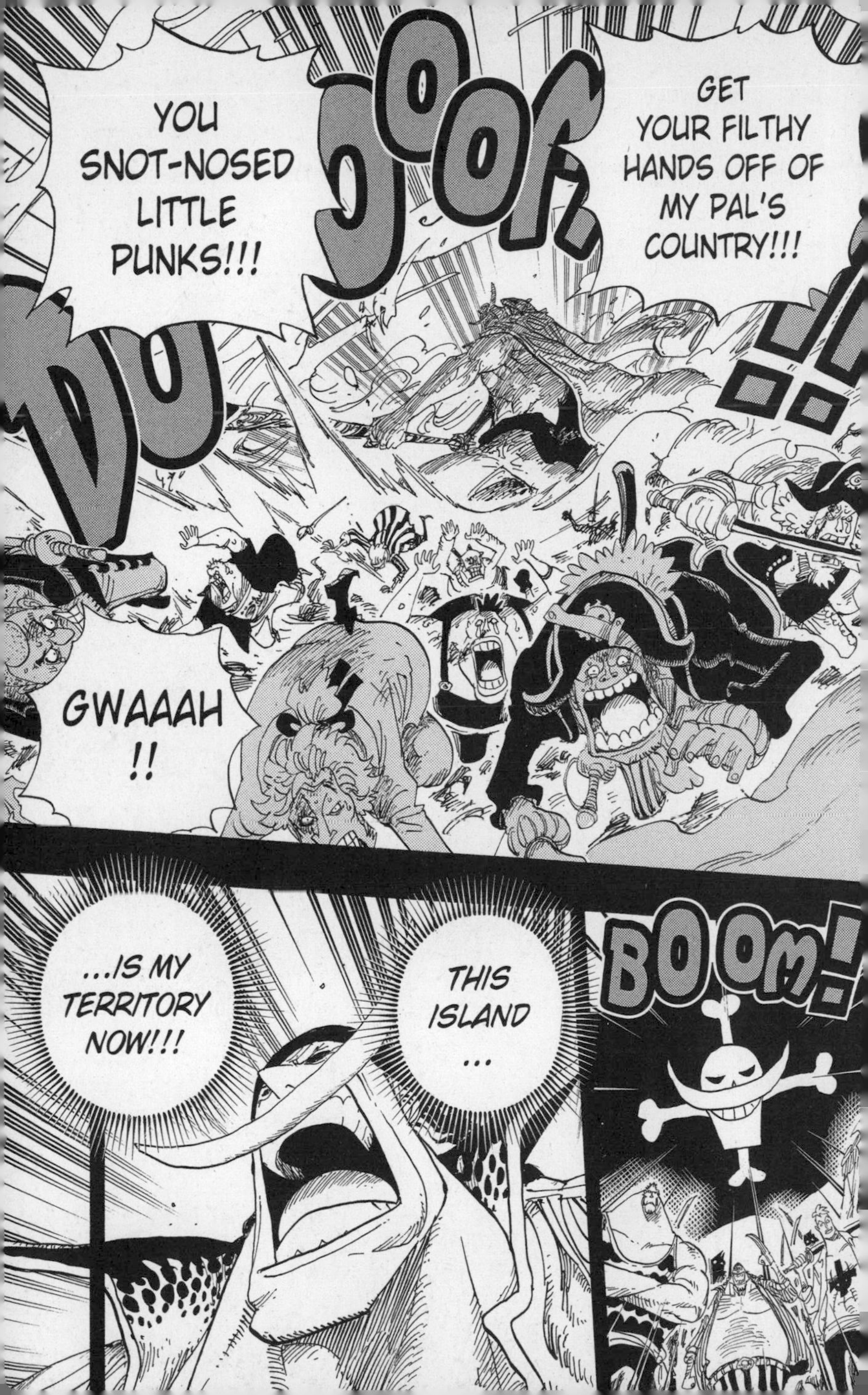
GET YOUR FILTHY HANDS OFF OF MY PAL'S COUNTRY!!!
YOU SNOT-NOSED LITTLE PUNKS!!!
GWAAAH !!
BOOM!
THIS ISLAND ...
...IS MY TERRITORY NOW!!!

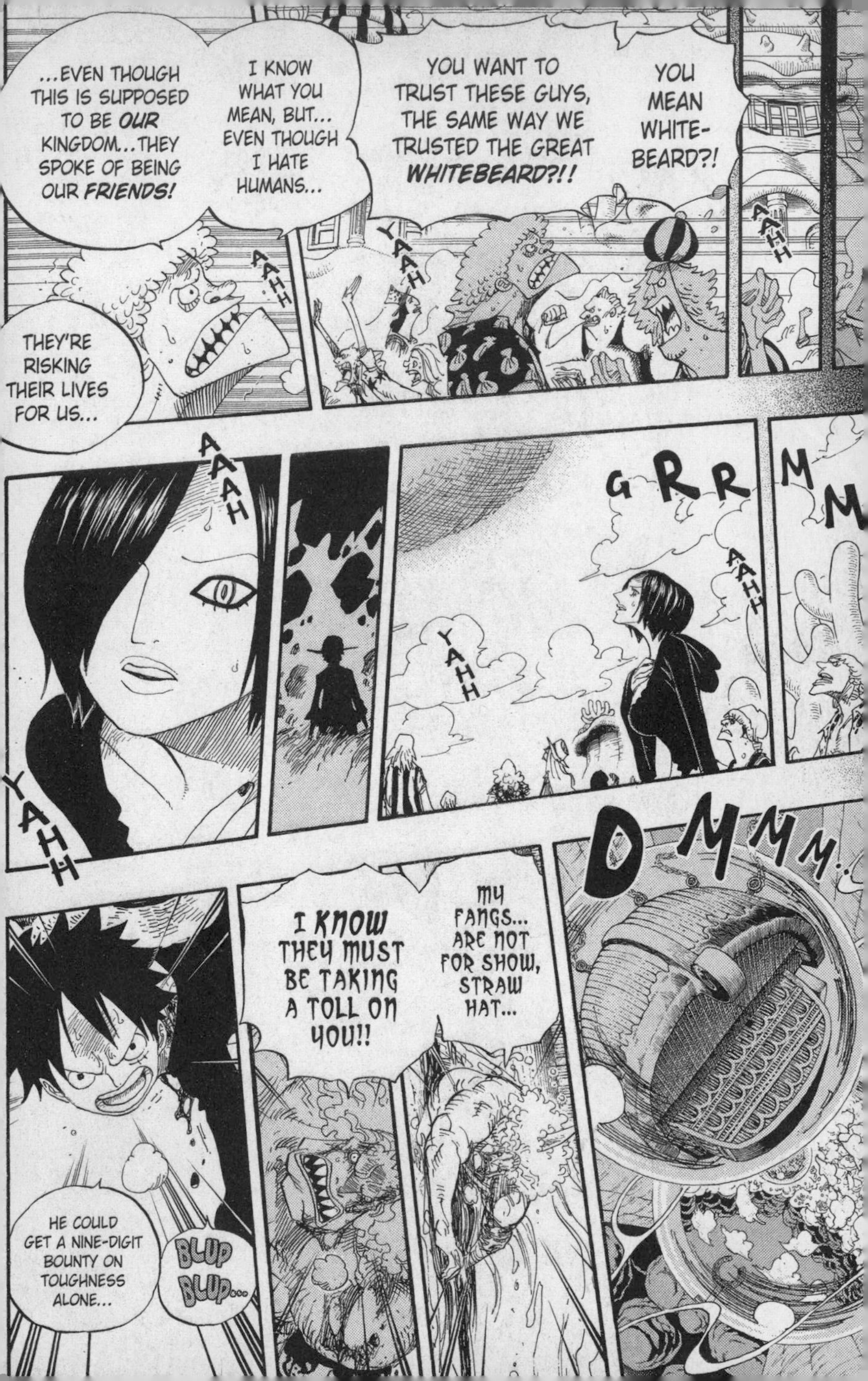
AAHH
YOU MEAN WHITE-BEARD?!
YOU WANT TO TRUST THESE GUYS, THE SAME WAY WE TRUSTED THE GREAT **WHITEBEARD?!!**
YAAH
I KNOW WHAT YOU MEAN, BUT... EVEN THOUGH I HATE HUMANS...
...EVEN THOUGH THIS IS SUPPOSED TO BE **OUR** KINGDOM...THEY SPOKE OF BEING OUR **FRIENDS!**
THEY'RE RISKING THEIR LIVES FOR US...
AAHH
MM
AAHH
GRRR
YAHH
AAAH
YAHH
DMMM...
MY FANGS... ARE NOT FOR SHOW, STRAW HAT...
I KNOW THEY MUST BE TAKING A TOLL ON YOU!!
BLUP BLUP...
HE COULD GET A NINE-DIGIT BOUNTY ON TOUGHNESS ALONE...

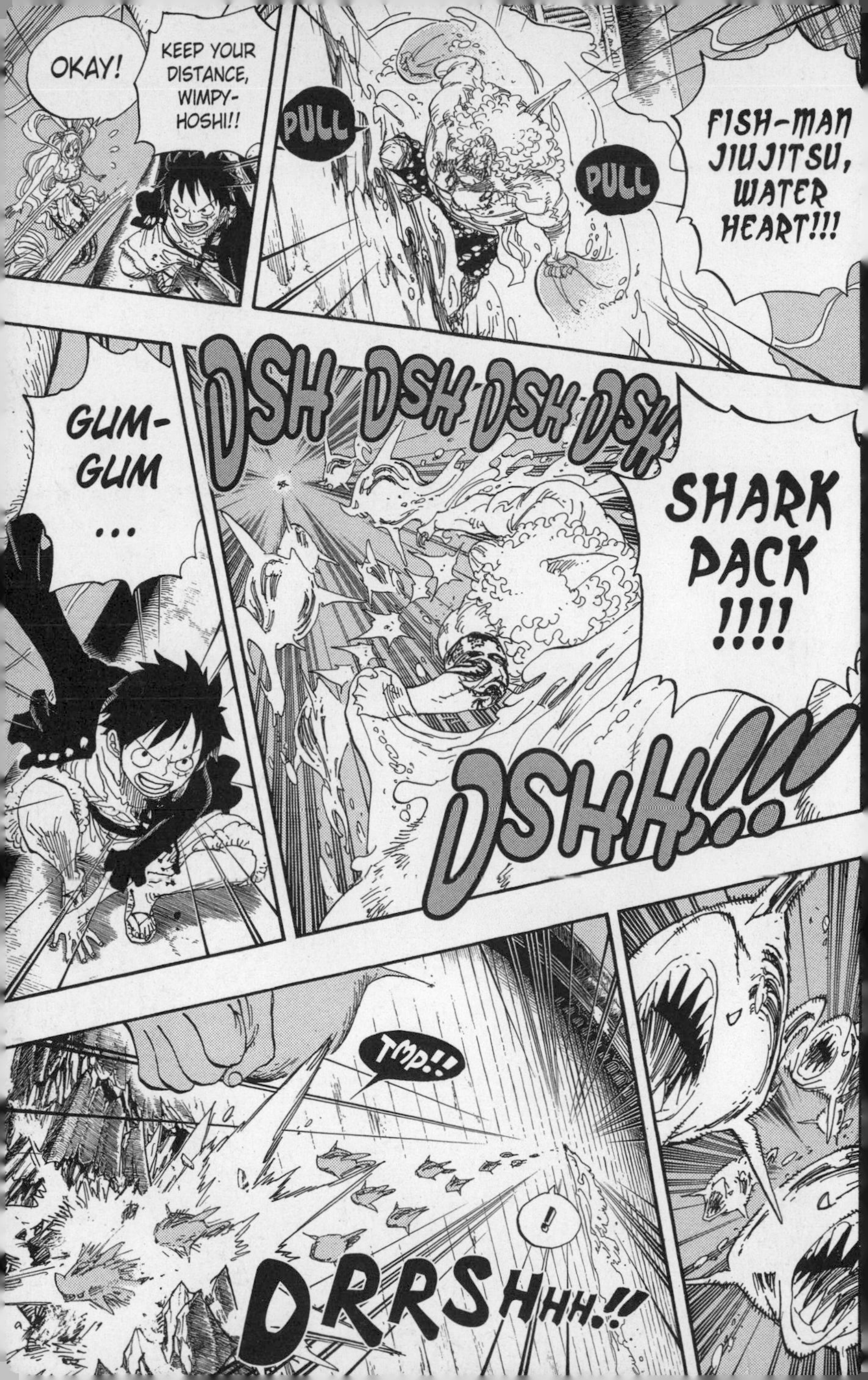
FISH-MAN JIUJITSU, WATER HEART!!!
PULL
PULL
KEEP YOUR DISTANCE, WIMPY-HOSHI!!
OKAY!
DSH DSH DSH DSH DSH
SHARK PACK !!!!
DSHH...!!!
GUM-GUM ...
TMP!!
!
DRRSHHH!!

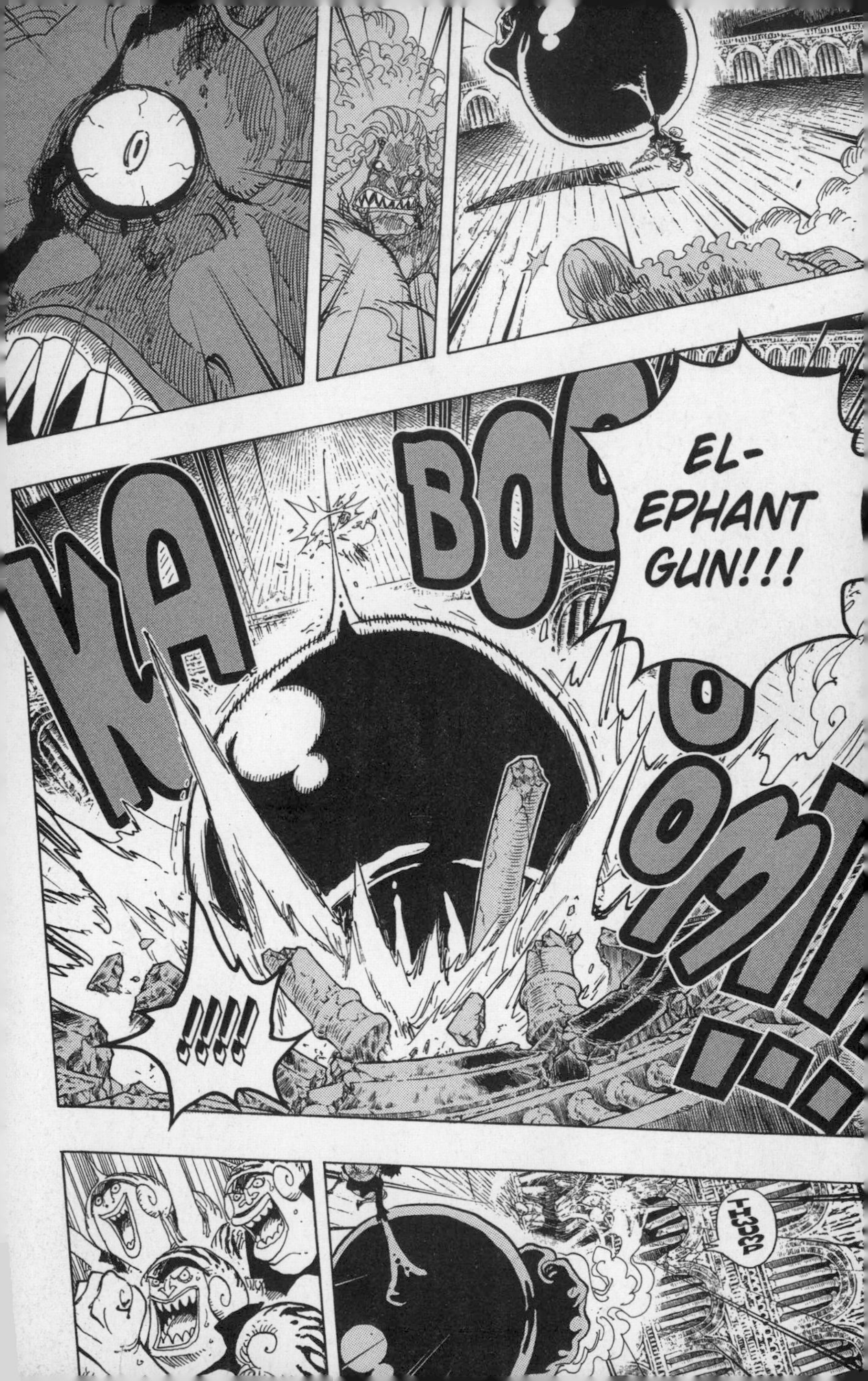
EL-
EPHANT
GUN!!!
KABOOOOM!!...
!!!!
THUMP

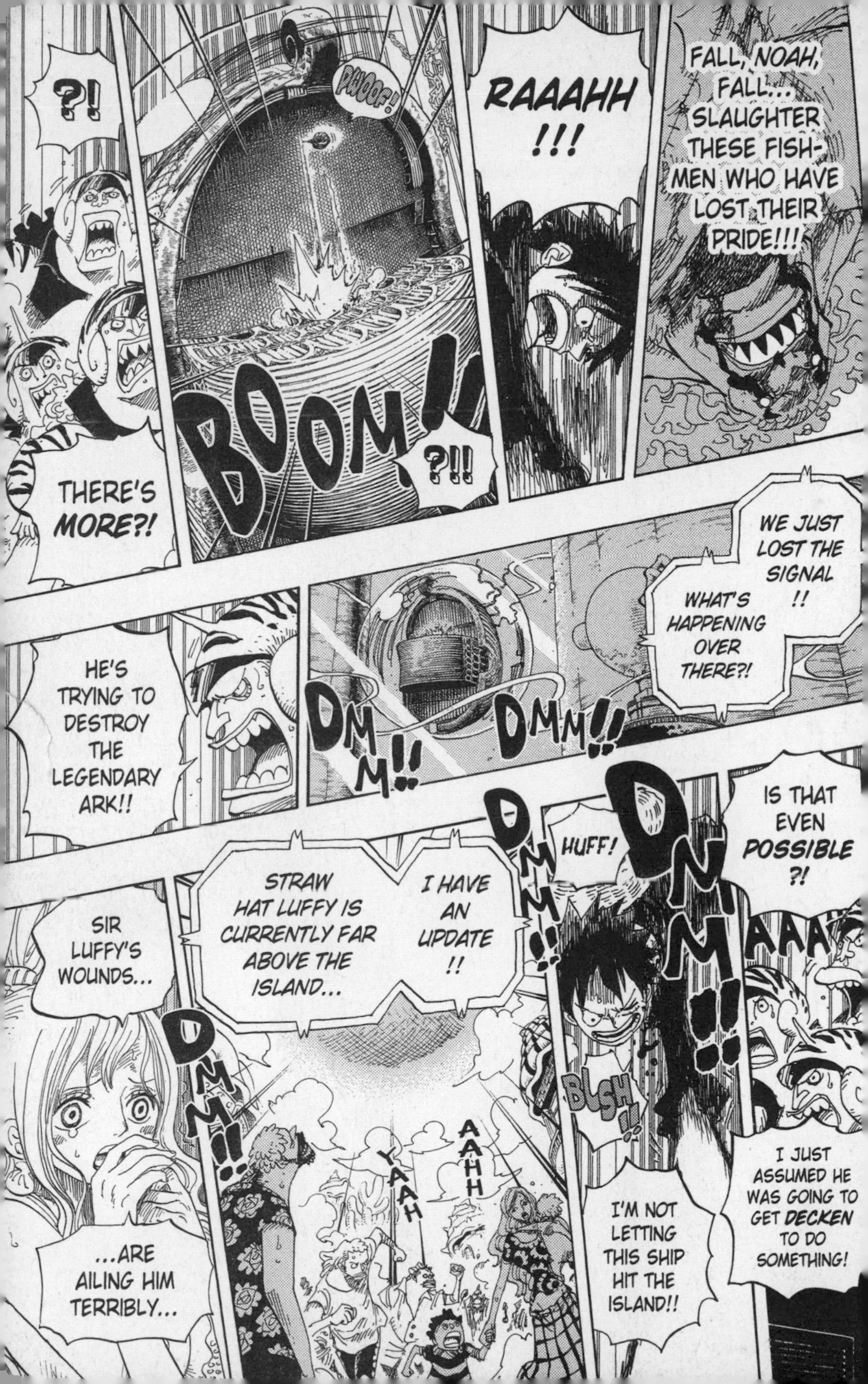

FALL, NOAH, FALL... SLAUGHTER THESE FISH-MEN WHO HAVE LOST THEIR PRIDE!!!
RAAAHH!!!
PWOOF!
BOOM!!
?!!
?!
THERE'S *MORE?!*
WE JUST LOST THE SIGNAL!!
WHAT'S HAPPENING OVER THERE?!
DMM!!
DMM!!
HE'S TRYING TO DESTROY THE LEGENDARY ARK!!
IS THAT EVEN *POSSIBLE*?!
AAAA
DMM!!
HUFF!
DMM!!
BLSH!!
I JUST ASSUMED HE WAS GOING TO GET *DECKEN* TO DO SOMETHING!
I'M NOT LETTING THIS SHIP HIT THE ISLAND!!
I HAVE AN UPDATE!!
STRAW HAT LUFFY IS CURRENTLY FAR ABOVE THE ISLAND...
SIR LUFFY'S WOUNDS...
DMM!!
AAAHH
YAAH
...ARE AILING HIM TERRIBLY...

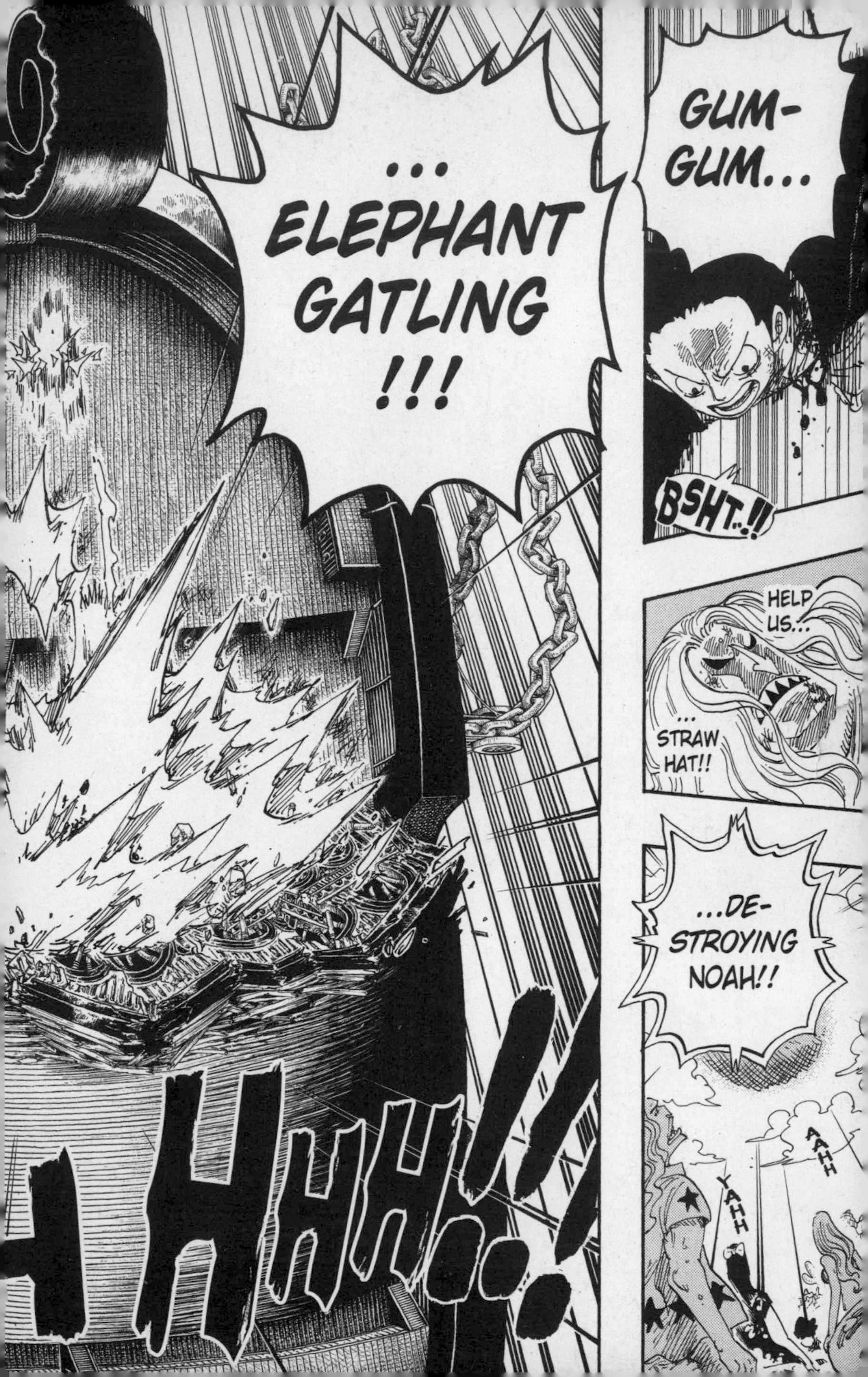
GUM-GUM...
BSHT..!!
HELP US...
...STRAW HAT!!
...DE-STROYING NOAH!!
AAHH
YAHH
...ELEPHANT GATLING!!!

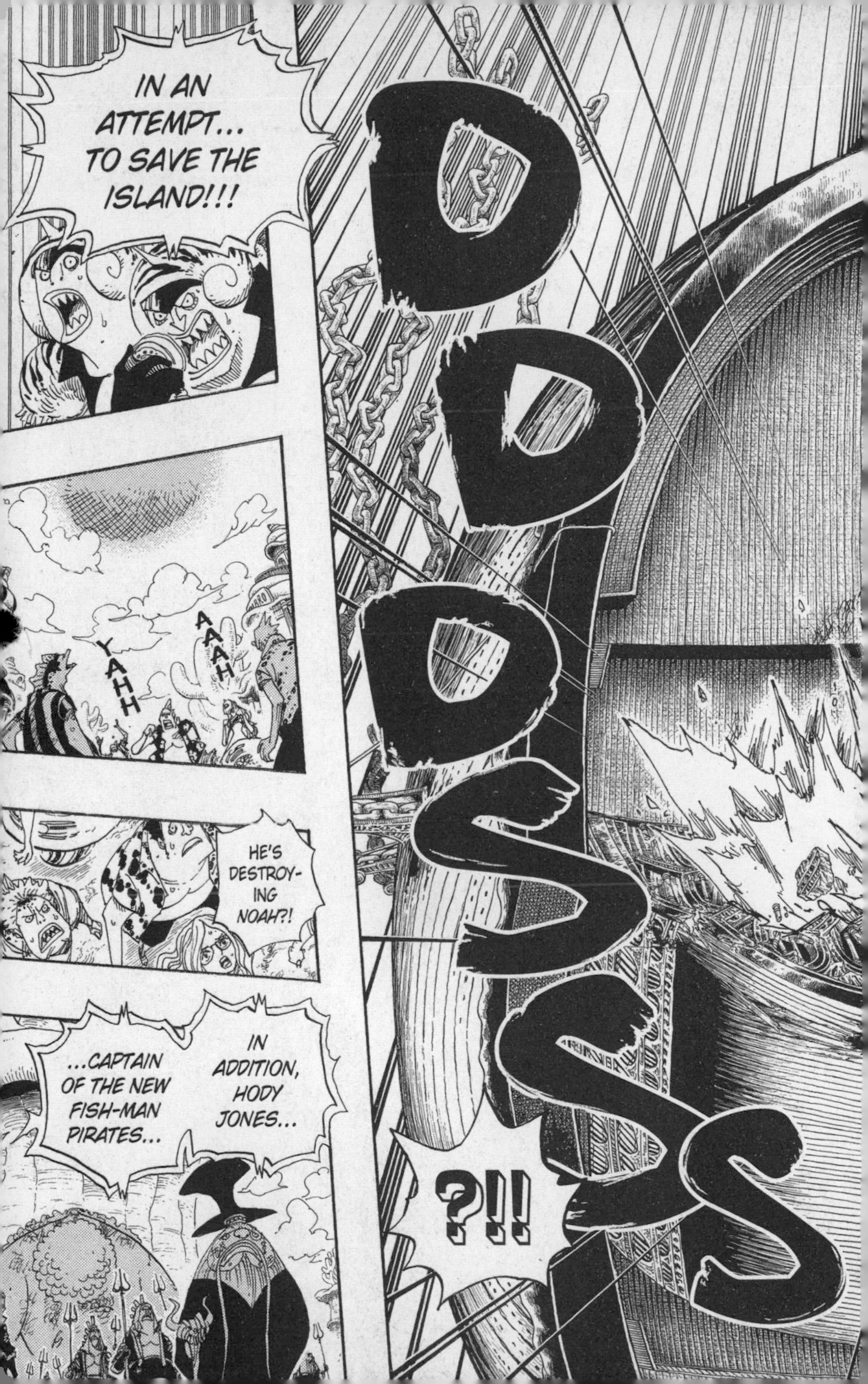
DDDSSS
?!!
IN AN ATTEMPT... TO SAVE THE ISLAND!!!
AAAH
YAHH
HE'S DESTROY-ING NOAH?!
IN ADDITION, HODY JONES...
...CAPTAIN OF THE NEW FISH-MAN PIRATES...

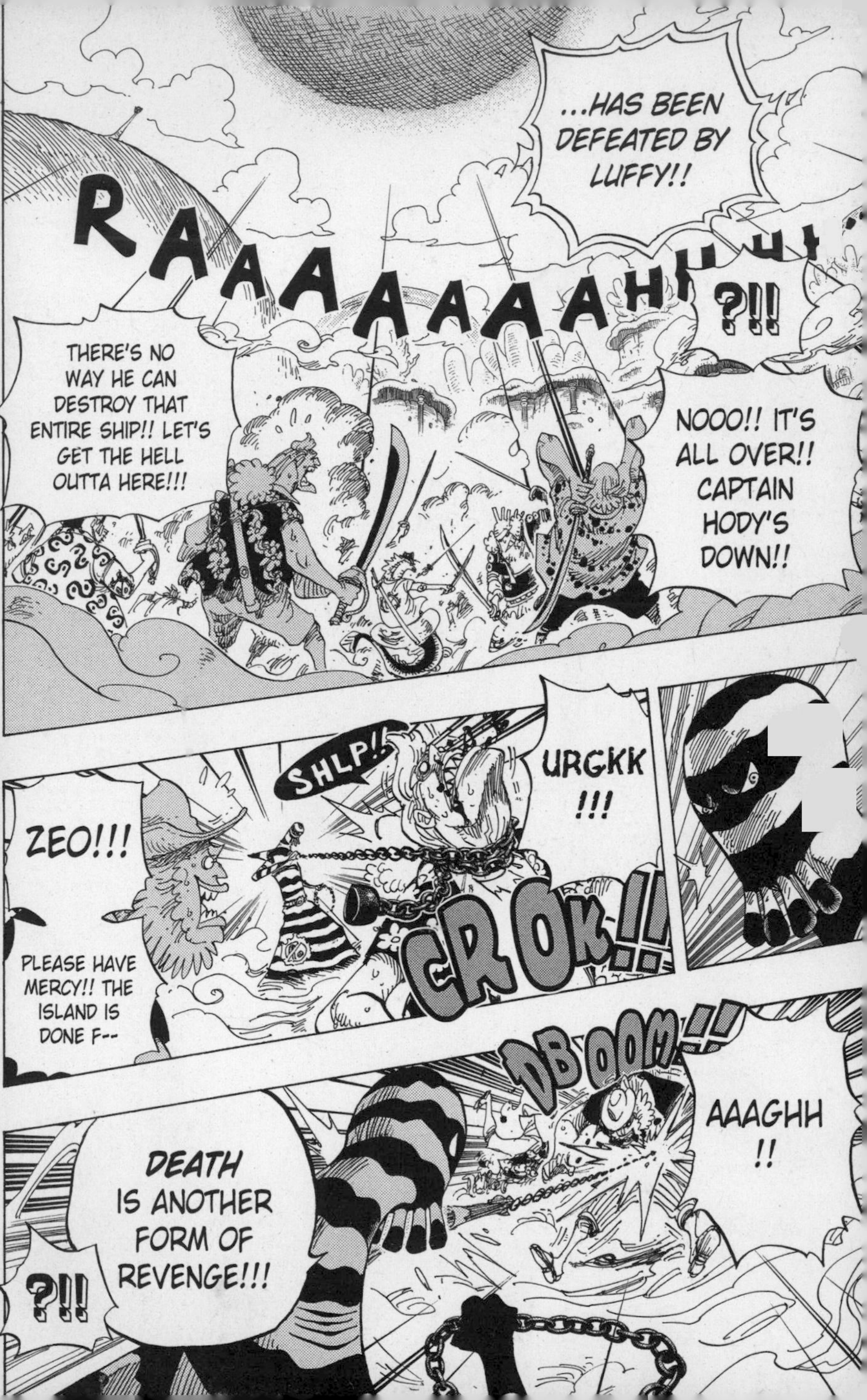
...HAS BEEN DEFEATED BY LUFFY!!
RAAAAAAAAH
?!!
NOOO!! IT'S ALL OVER!! CAPTAIN HODY'S DOWN!!
THERE'S NO WAY HE CAN DESTROY THAT ENTIRE SHIP!! LET'S GET THE HELL OUTTA HERE!!!
URGKK!!!
SHLP!!
ZEO!!!
CROK!!!
PLEASE HAVE MERCY!! THE ISLAND IS DONE F--
AAAGHH!!
DBOOM!!
DEATH IS ANOTHER FORM OF REVENGE!!!
?!!

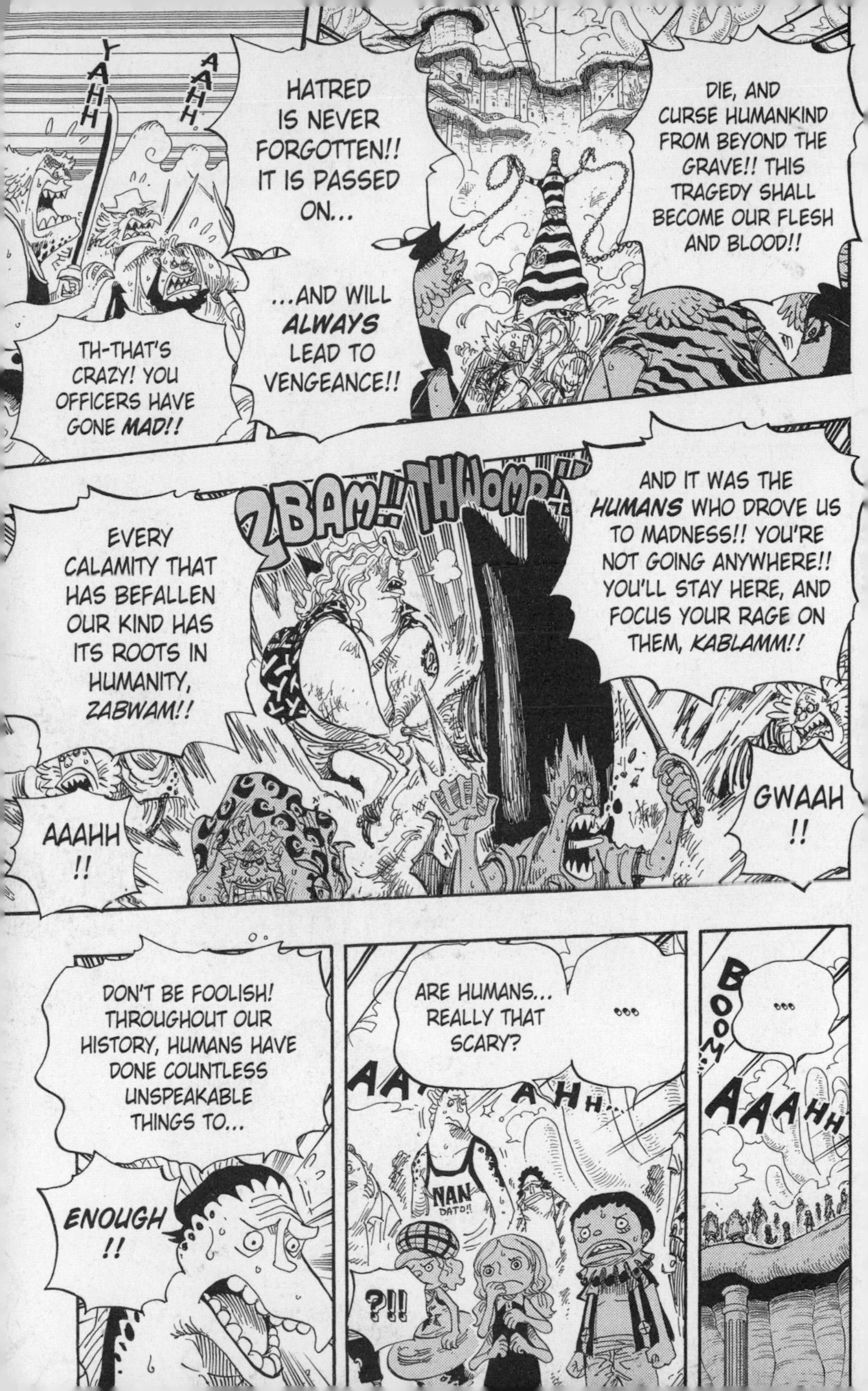
DIE, AND CURSE HUMANKIND FROM BEYOND THE GRAVE!! THIS TRAGEDY SHALL BECOME OUR FLESH AND BLOOD!!
HATRED IS NEVER FORGOTTEN!! IT IS PASSED ON...
AAHH
YAHHH
...AND WILL ALWAYS LEAD TO VENGEANCE!!
TH-THAT'S CRAZY! YOU OFFICERS HAVE GONE MAD!!
AND IT WAS THE HUMANS WHO DROVE US TO MADNESS!! YOU'RE NOT GOING ANYWHERE!! YOU'LL STAY HERE, AND FOCUS YOUR RAGE ON THEM, KABLAMM!!
THWOMP!!
ZBAM!!
EVERY CALAMITY THAT HAS BEFALLEN OUR KIND HAS ITS ROOTS IN HUMANITY, ZABWAM!!
GWAAH!!
AAAHH!!
BOOM
...
AAAHH
...
ARE HUMANS... REALLY THAT SCARY?
AAAHH...
NAN DATO!!
?!!
DON'T BE FOOLISH! THROUGHOUT OUR HISTORY, HUMANS HAVE DONE COUNTLESS UNSPEAKABLE THINGS TO...
ENOUGH!!

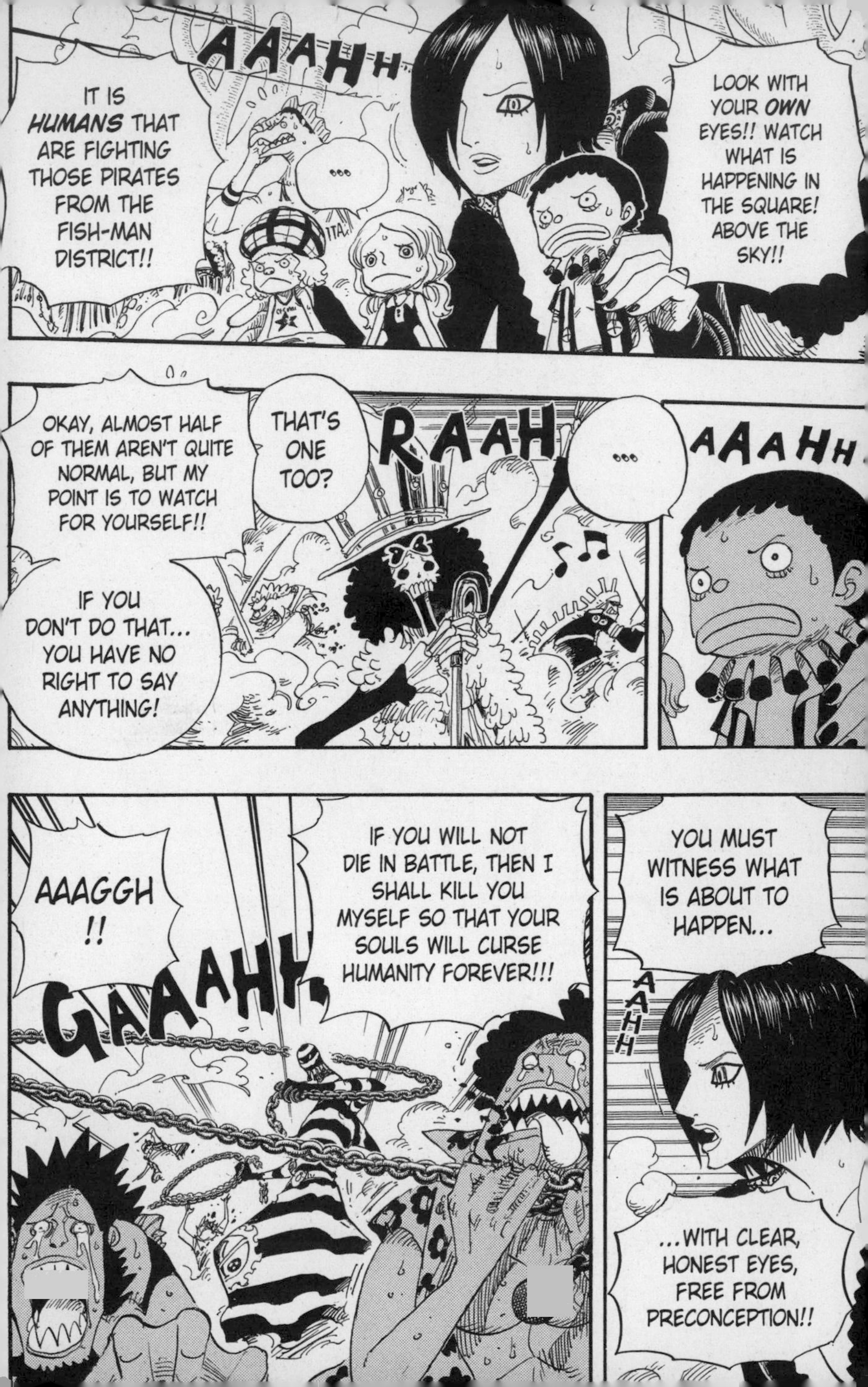
LOOK WITH YOUR OWN EYES!! WATCH WHAT IS HAPPENING IN THE SQUARE! ABOVE THE SKY!!
AAAHH
IT IS HUMANS THAT ARE FIGHTING THOSE PIRATES FROM THE FISH-MAN DISTRICT!!
...
AAAHH
...
RAAH
THAT'S ONE TOO?
OKAY, ALMOST HALF OF THEM AREN'T QUITE NORMAL, BUT MY POINT IS TO WATCH FOR YOURSELF!!
IF YOU DON'T DO THAT... YOU HAVE NO RIGHT TO SAY ANYTHING!
YOU MUST WITNESS WHAT IS ABOUT TO HAPPEN...
AAHH
...WITH CLEAR, HONEST EYES, FREE FROM PRECONCEPTION!!
IF YOU WILL NOT DIE IN BATTLE, THEN I SHALL KILL YOU MYSELF SO THAT YOUR SOULS WILL CURSE HUMANITY FOREVER!!!
AAAGGH !!
GAAAHH

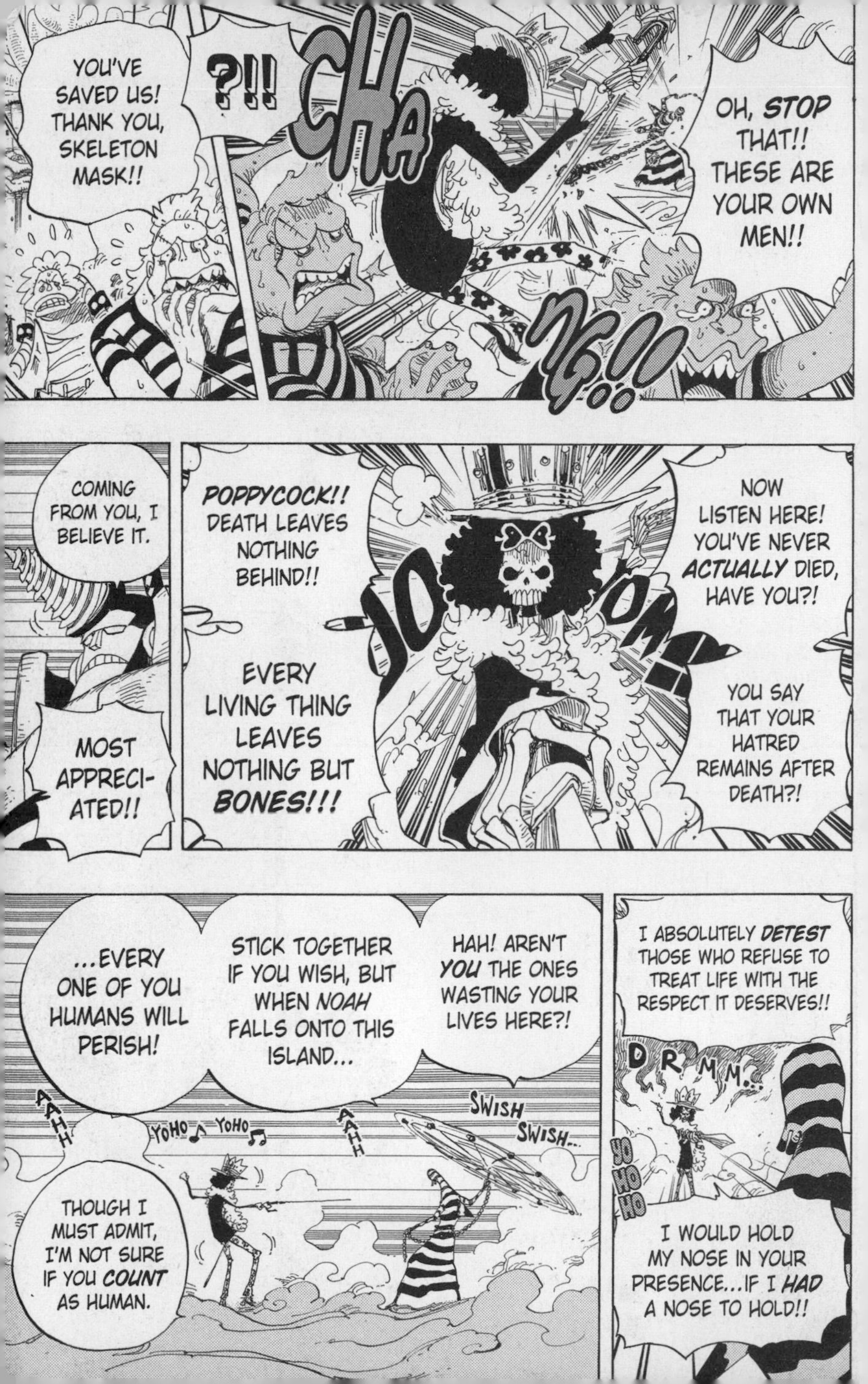
OH, STOP THAT!! THESE ARE YOUR OWN MEN!!
CHA
NG!!
?!!
YOU'VE SAVED US! THANK YOU, SKELETON MASK!!
NOW LISTEN HERE! YOU'VE NEVER ACTUALLY DIED, HAVE YOU?!
YOU SAY THAT YOUR HATRED REMAINS AFTER DEATH?!
JOOM
POPPYCOCK!! DEATH LEAVES NOTHING BEHIND!!
EVERY LIVING THING LEAVES NOTHING BUT BONES!!!
COMING FROM YOU, I BELIEVE IT.
MOST APPRECI-ATED!!
I ABSOLUTELY DETEST THOSE WHO REFUSE TO TREAT LIFE WITH THE RESPECT IT DESERVES!!
DRMM..
YO HO HO
I WOULD HOLD MY NOSE IN YOUR PRESENCE...IF I HAD A NOSE TO HOLD!!
HAH! AREN'T YOU THE ONES WASTING YOUR LIVES HERE?!
STICK TOGETHER IF YOU WISH, BUT WHEN NOAH FALLS ONTO THIS ISLAND...
...EVERY ONE OF YOU HUMANS WILL PERISH!
SWISH SWISH...
AAHH
YOHO YOHO
AAHH
THOUGH I MUST ADMIT, I'M NOT SURE IF YOU COUNT AS HUMAN.

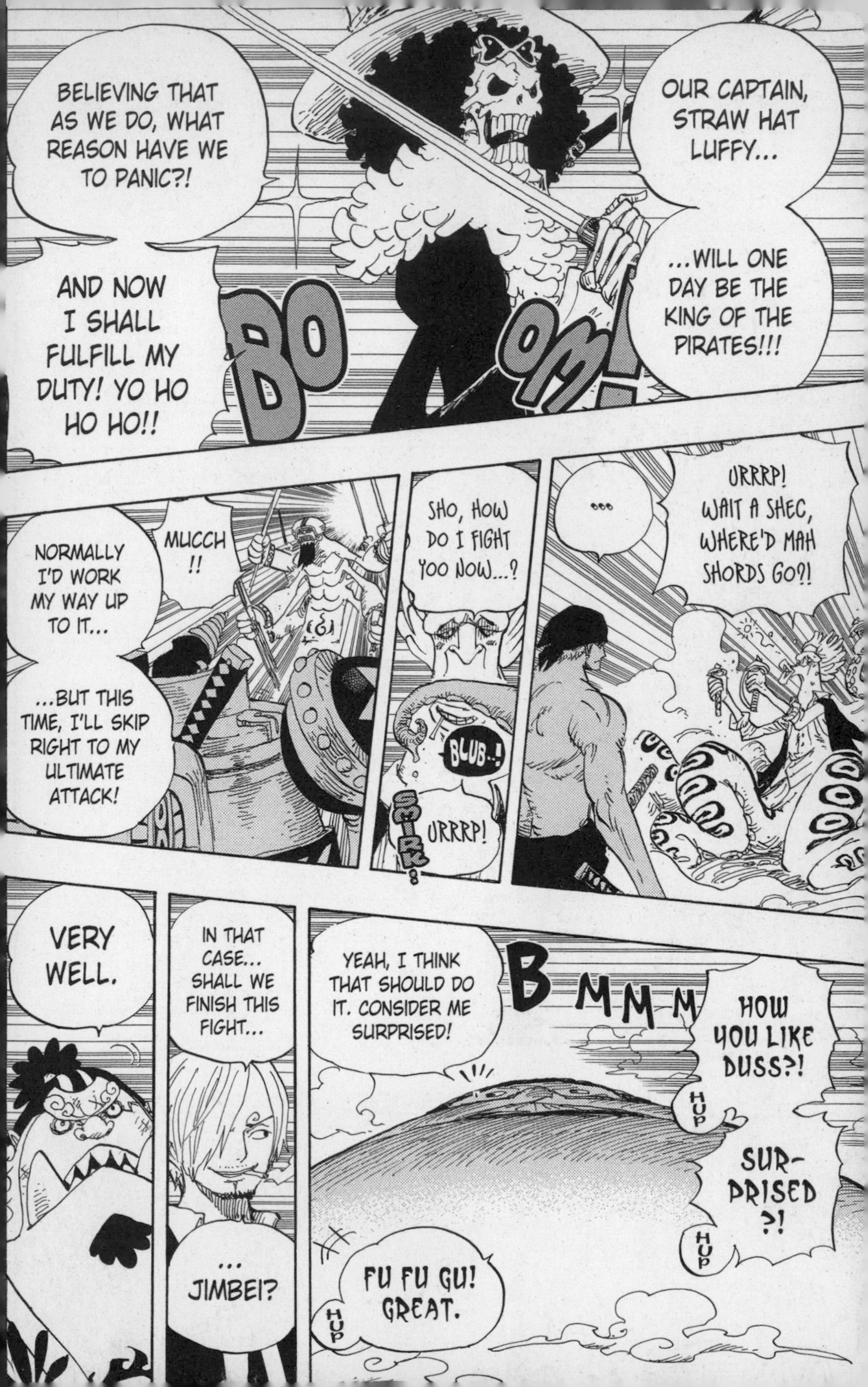
OUR CAPTAIN, STRAW HAT LUFFY...
...WILL ONE DAY BE THE KING OF THE PIRATES!!!
BELIEVING THAT AS WE DO, WHAT REASON HAVE WE TO PANIC?!
AND NOW I SHALL FULFILL MY DUTY! YO HO HO HO!!
BOOM!
URRRP! WAIT A SHEC, WHERE'D MAH SHORDS GO?!
...
SHO, HOW DO I FIGHT YOO NOW...?
BLUB..!
URRRP!
MUCCH!!
NORMALLY I'D WORK MY WAY UP TO IT...
...BUT THIS TIME, I'LL SKIP RIGHT TO MY ULTIMATE ATTACK!
HOW YOU LIKE DUSS?!
HUP
SURPRISED?!
HUP
BMMM
YEAH, I THINK THAT SHOULD DO IT. CONSIDER ME SURPRISED!
FU FU GU! GREAT.
HUP
IN THAT CASE... SHALL WE FINISH THIS FIGHT...
...JIMBEI?
VERY WELL.

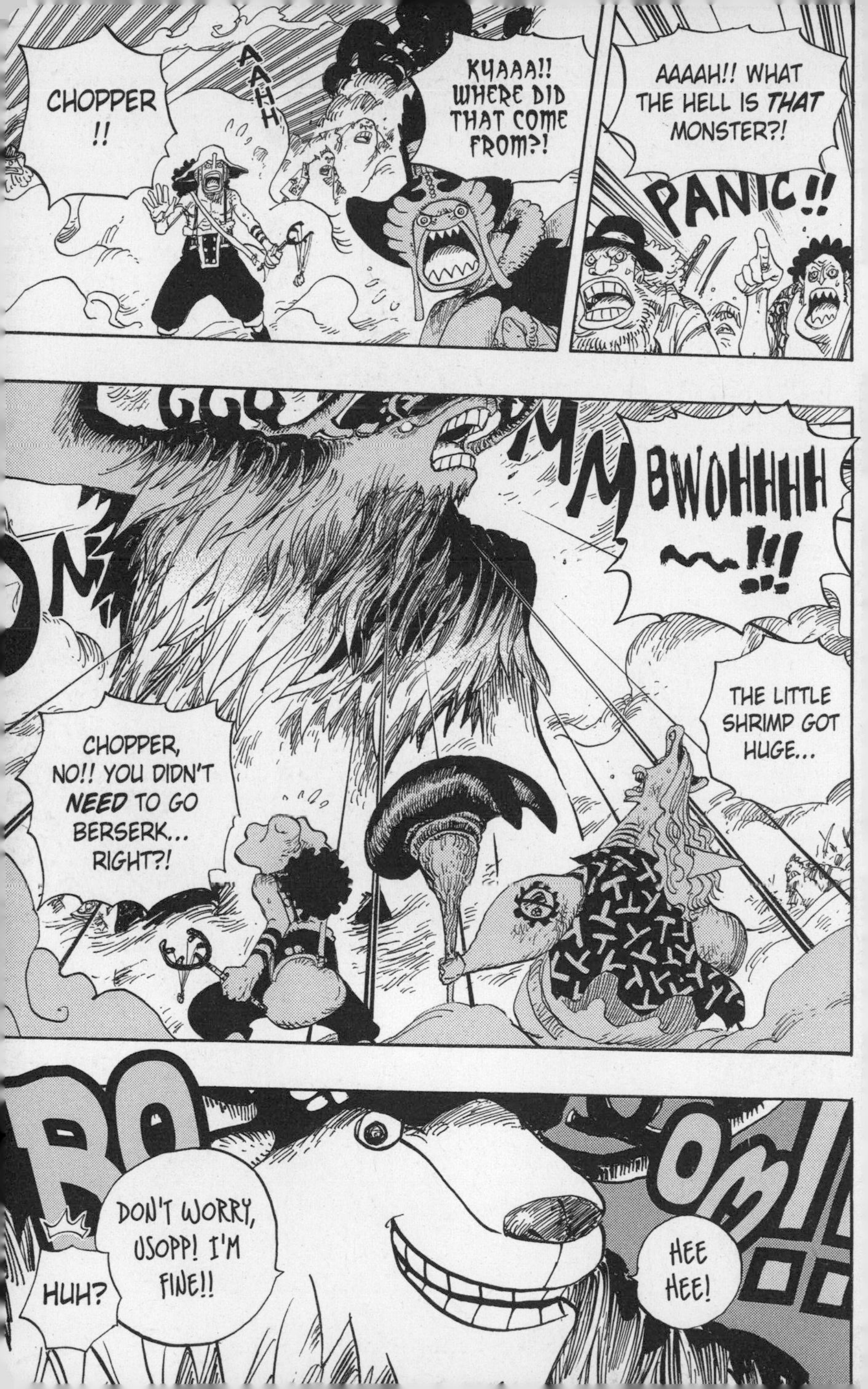
AAAAH!! WHAT THE HELL IS *THAT* MONSTER?!
PANIC!!
KYAAA!! WHERE DID THAT COME FROM?!
AAHH
CHOPPER !!
MMBWOHHHH ~~!!!
THE LITTLE SHRIMP GOT HUGE...
CHOPPER, NO!! YOU DIDN'T *NEED* TO GO BERSERK... RIGHT?!
HEE HEE!
DON'T WORRY, USOPP! I'M FINE!!
HUH?

GR
RM
M

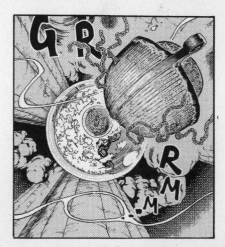

Chapter 646:
FROG

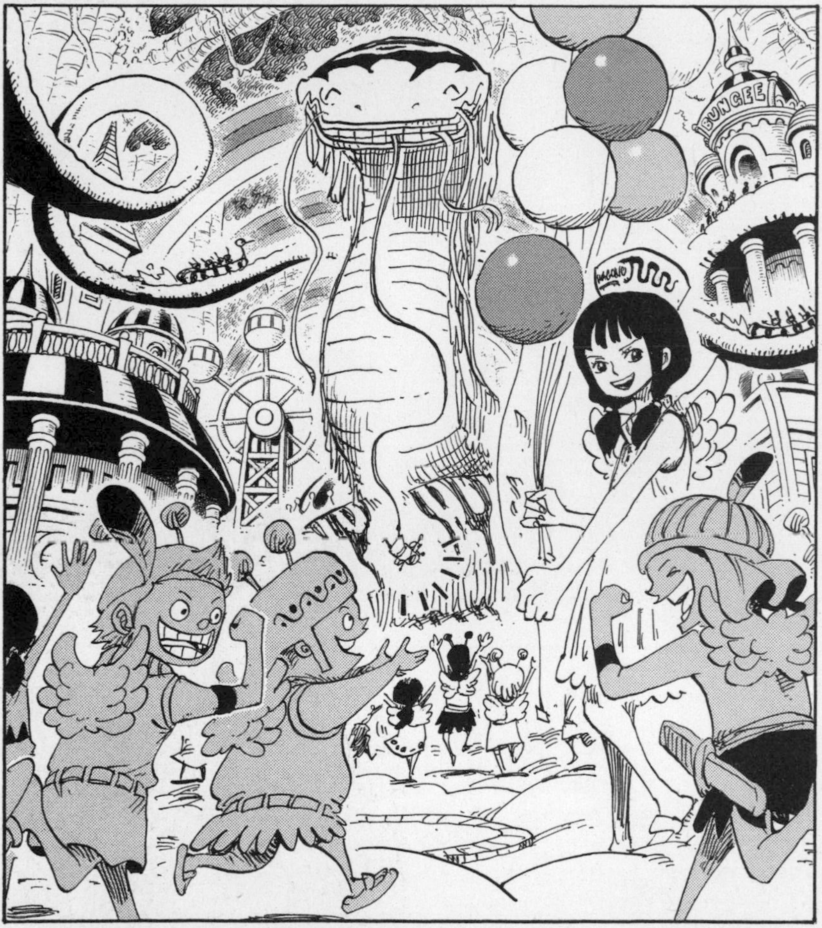
BUNGEE

DECKS OF THE WORLD, VOL. 29: "SKYPIEA–RUBBER BAND LAND ATTRACTIONS: NOLA'S BUNGEE JUMPING & AISA THE SPHERE CLOUD VENDOR"

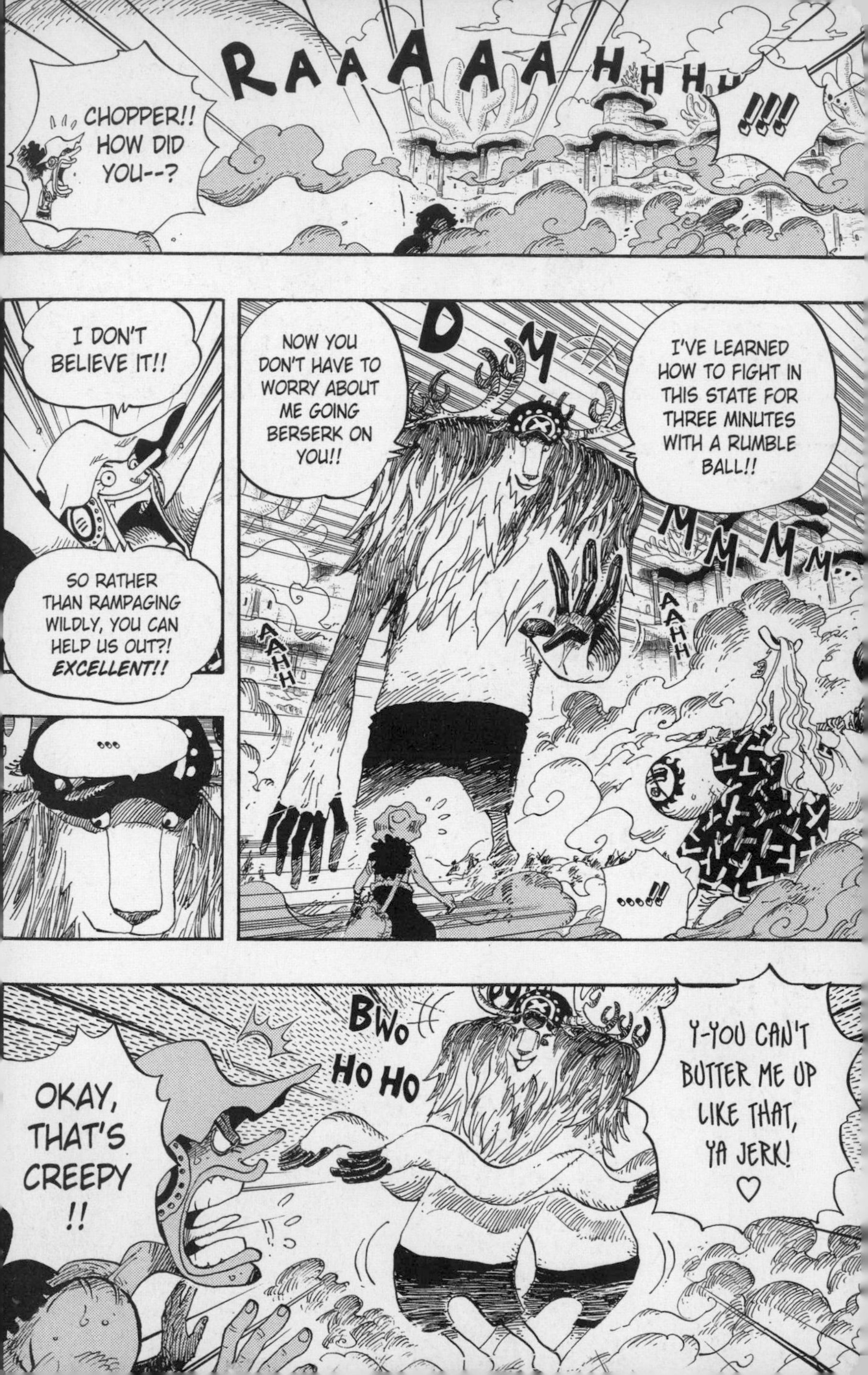
!!!
RAAAAAHHHH
CHOPPER!! HOW DID YOU--?
I'VE LEARNED HOW TO FIGHT IN THIS STATE FOR THREE MINUTES WITH A RUMBLE BALL!!
DMMMMMM
NOW YOU DON'T HAVE TO WORRY ABOUT ME GOING BERSERK ON YOU!!
AAHH
AAHH
....!!
I DON'T BELIEVE IT!!
SO RATHER THAN RAMPAGING WILDLY, YOU CAN HELP US OUT?! *EXCELLENT!!*
...
Y-YOU CAN'T BUTTER ME UP LIKE THAT, YA JERK! ♡
BWO HO HO
OKAY, THAT'S CREEPY !!

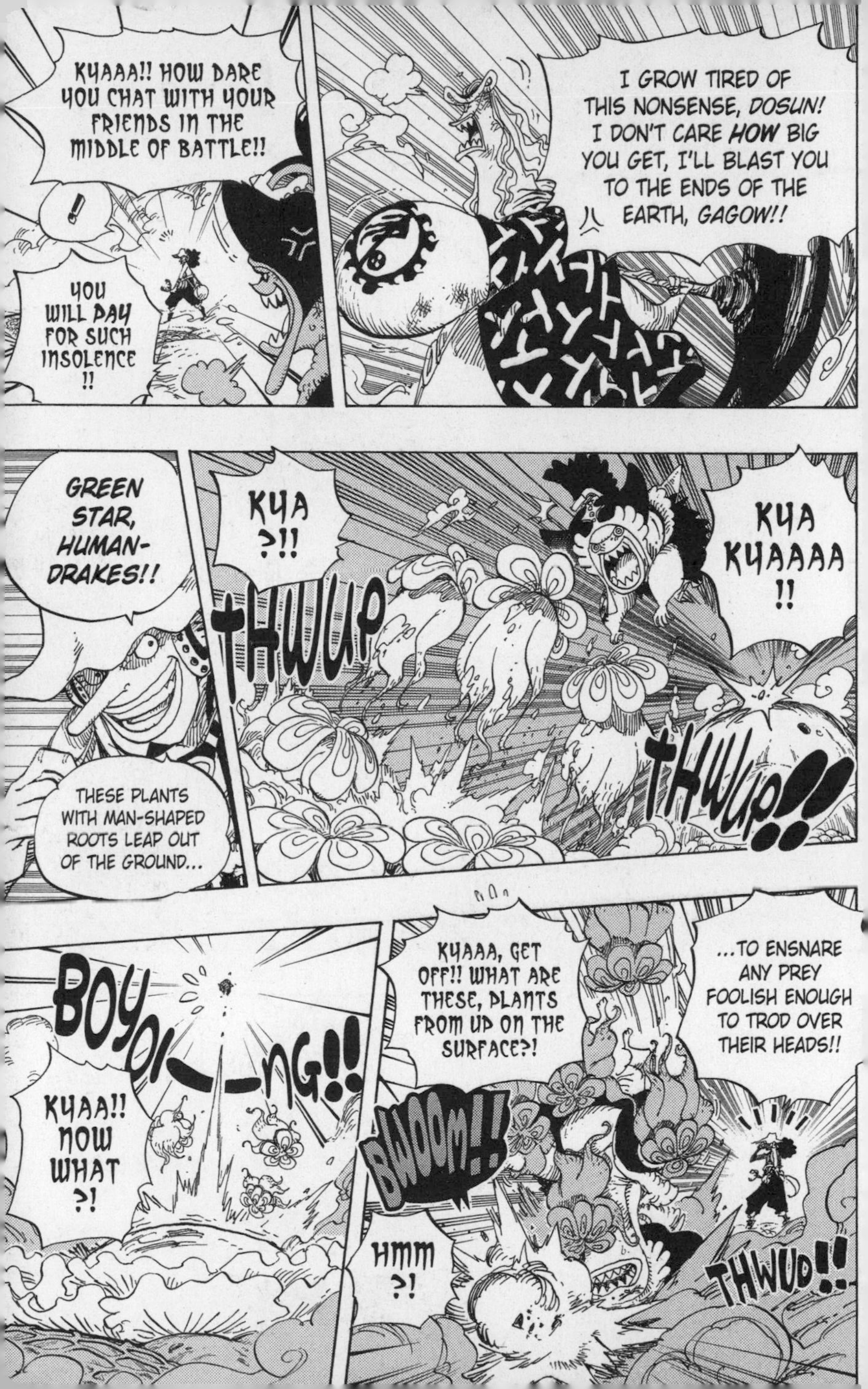
I GROW TIRED OF THIS NONSENSE, DOSUN! I DON'T CARE HOW BIG YOU GET, I'LL BLAST YOU TO THE ENDS OF THE EARTH, GAGOW!!
KYAAA!! HOW DARE YOU CHAT WITH YOUR FRIENDS IN THE MIDDLE OF BATTLE!!
!
YOU WILL PAY FOR SUCH INSOLENCE!!
KYA KYAAAA!!
KYA ?!!
THWUP
THWUP!!
GREEN STAR, HUMAN-DRAKES!!
THESE PLANTS WITH MAN-SHAPED ROOTS LEAP OUT OF THE GROUND...
...TO ENSNARE ANY PREY FOOLISH ENOUGH TO TROD OVER THEIR HEADS!!
KYAAA, GET OFF!! WHAT ARE THESE, PLANTS FROM UP ON THE SURFACE?!
BWOOM!!
THWUD!!
HMM ?!
BOYOI--NG!!
KYAA!! NOW WHAT ?!

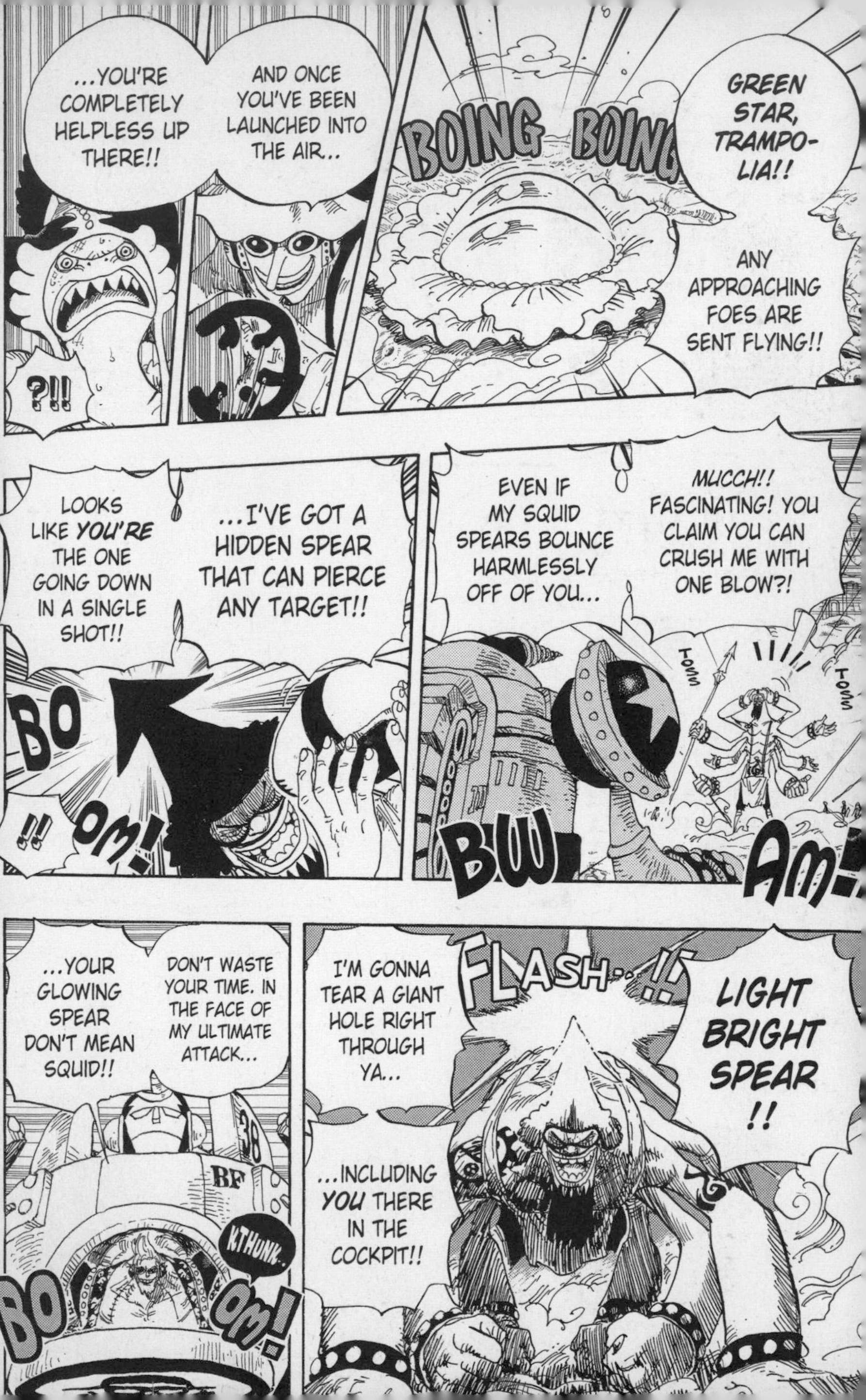
BOING BOING
GREEN STAR, TRAMPOLIA!!
ANY APPROACHING FOES ARE SENT FLYING!!
AND ONCE YOU'VE BEEN LAUNCHED INTO THE AIR...
...YOU'RE COMPLETELY HELPLESS UP THERE!!
?!!
MUCCH!! FASCINATING! YOU CLAIM YOU CAN CRUSH ME WITH ONE BLOW?!
EVEN IF MY SQUID SPEARS BOUNCE HARMLESSLY OFF OF YOU...
TOSS
TOSS
BWAM!!
...I'VE GOT A HIDDEN SPEAR THAT CAN PIERCE ANY TARGET!!
LOOKS LIKE YOU'RE THE ONE GOING DOWN IN A SINGLE SHOT!!
BOOM!!
FLASH..!!
LIGHT BRIGHT SPEAR!!
I'M GONNA TEAR A GIANT HOLE RIGHT THROUGH YA...
...INCLUDING YOU THERE IN THE COCKPIT!!
DON'T WASTE YOUR TIME. IN THE FACE OF MY ULTIMATE ATTACK...
...YOUR GLOWING SPEAR DON'T MEAN SQUID!!
38
BF
KTHUNK
BOOM!

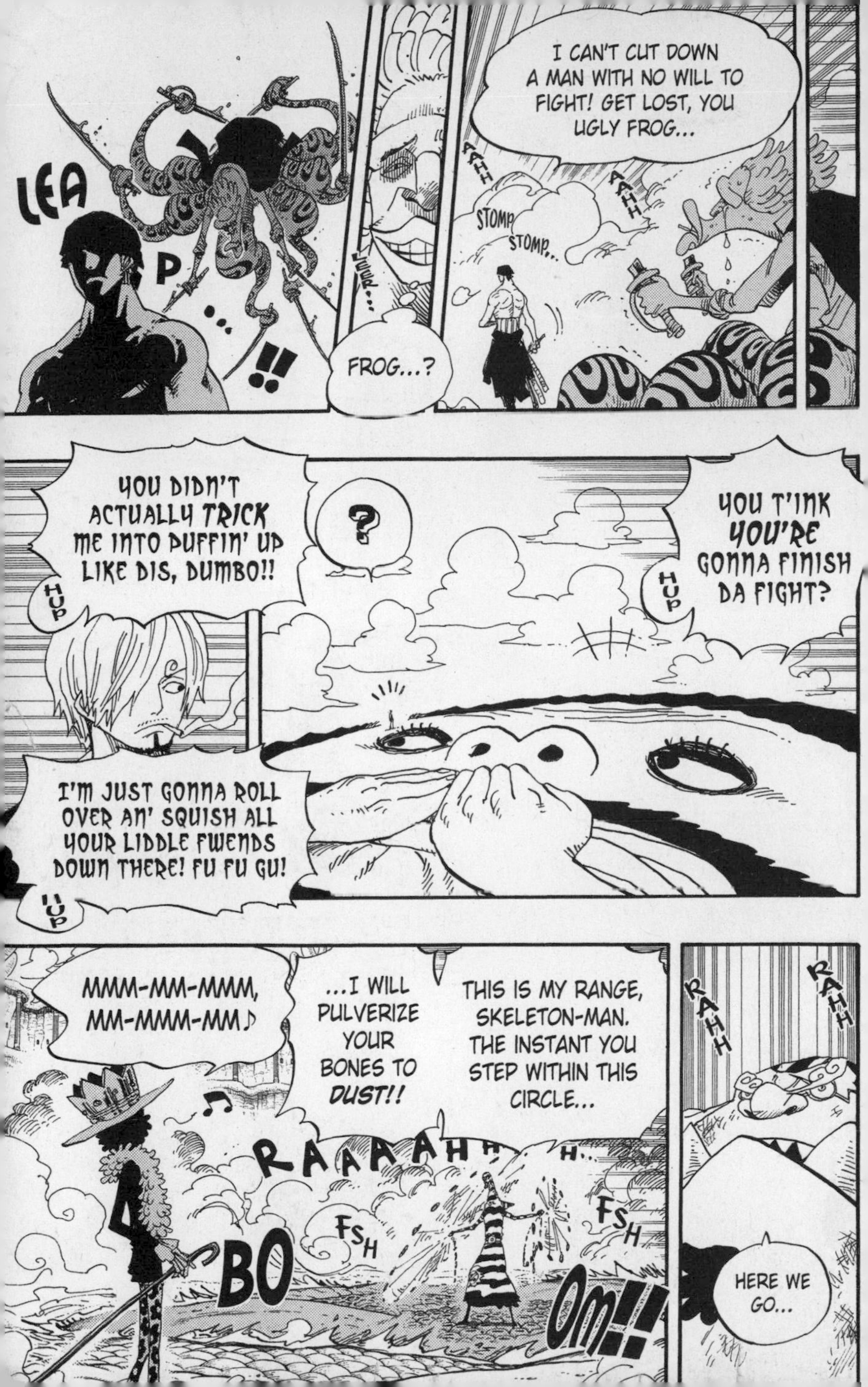
I CAN'T CUT DOWN A MAN WITH NO WILL TO FIGHT! GET LOST, YOU UGLY FROG...
RAHH
RAHH
STOMP
STOMP...
LEER...
FROG...?
LEAP
...!!
YOU T'INK YOU'RE GONNA FINISH DA FIGHT?
HUP
?
YOU DIDN'T ACTUALLY TRICK ME INTO PUFFIN' UP LIKE DIS, DUMBO!!
HUP
I'M JUST GONNA ROLL OVER AN' SQUISH ALL YOUR LIDDLE FWENDS DOWN THERE! FU FU GU!
HUP
RAHH
RAHH
HERE WE GO...
THIS IS MY RANGE, SKELETON-MAN. THE INSTANT YOU STEP WITHIN THIS CIRCLE...
...I WILL PULVERIZE YOUR BONES TO DUST!!
MMM-MM-MMM, MM-MMM-MM♪
RAAAAHHHH...
FSH
FSH
BOOM!!

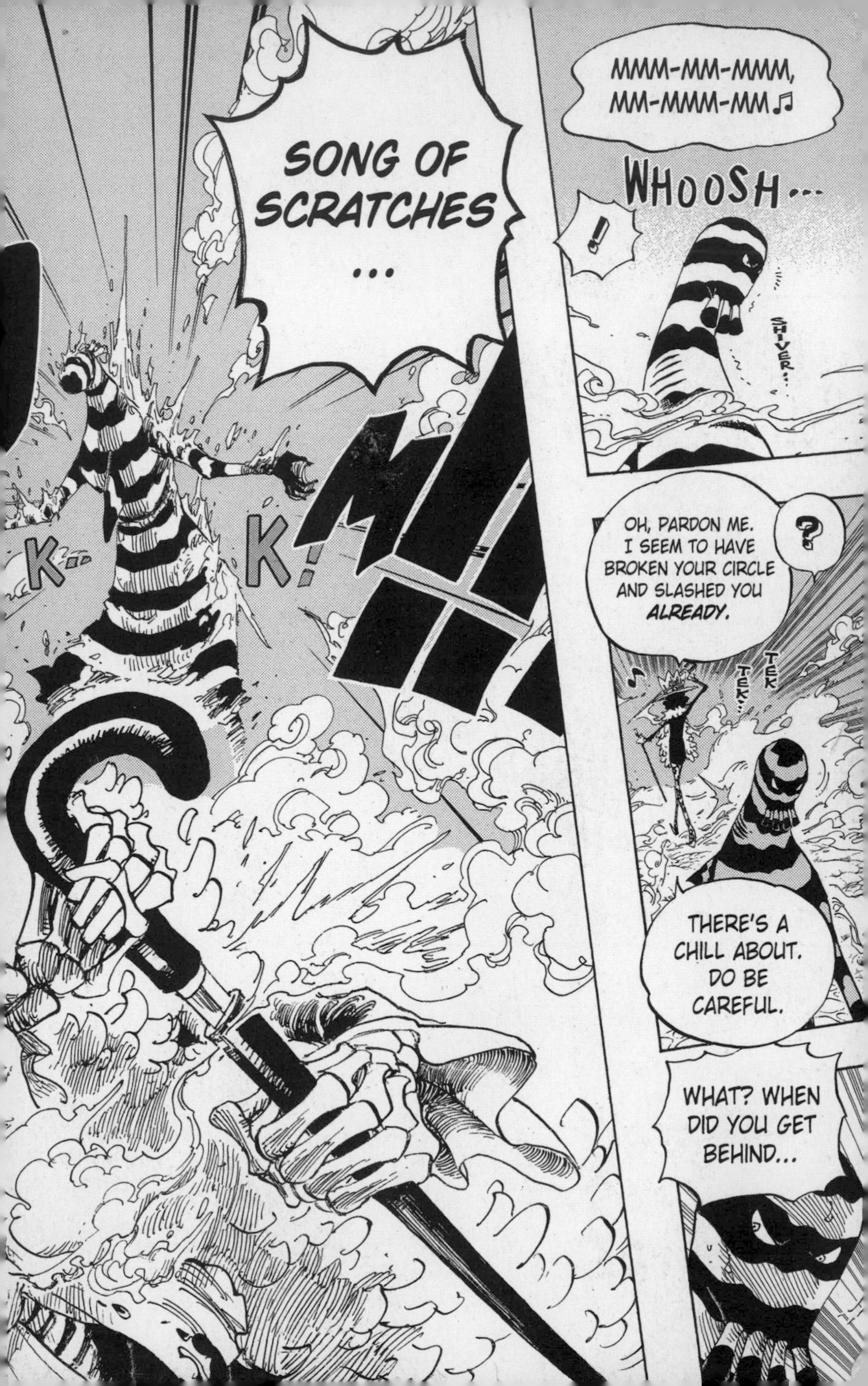
MMM-MM-MMM,
MM-MMM-MM♫
WHOOSH...
!
SHIVER...
?
OH, PARDON ME. I SEEM TO HAVE BROKEN YOUR CIRCLE AND SLASHED YOU ALREADY.
TEK TEK...
THERE'S A CHILL ABOUT. DO BE CAREFUL.
WHAT? WHEN DID YOU GET BEHIND...
SONG OF SCRATCHES ...
K...
K!

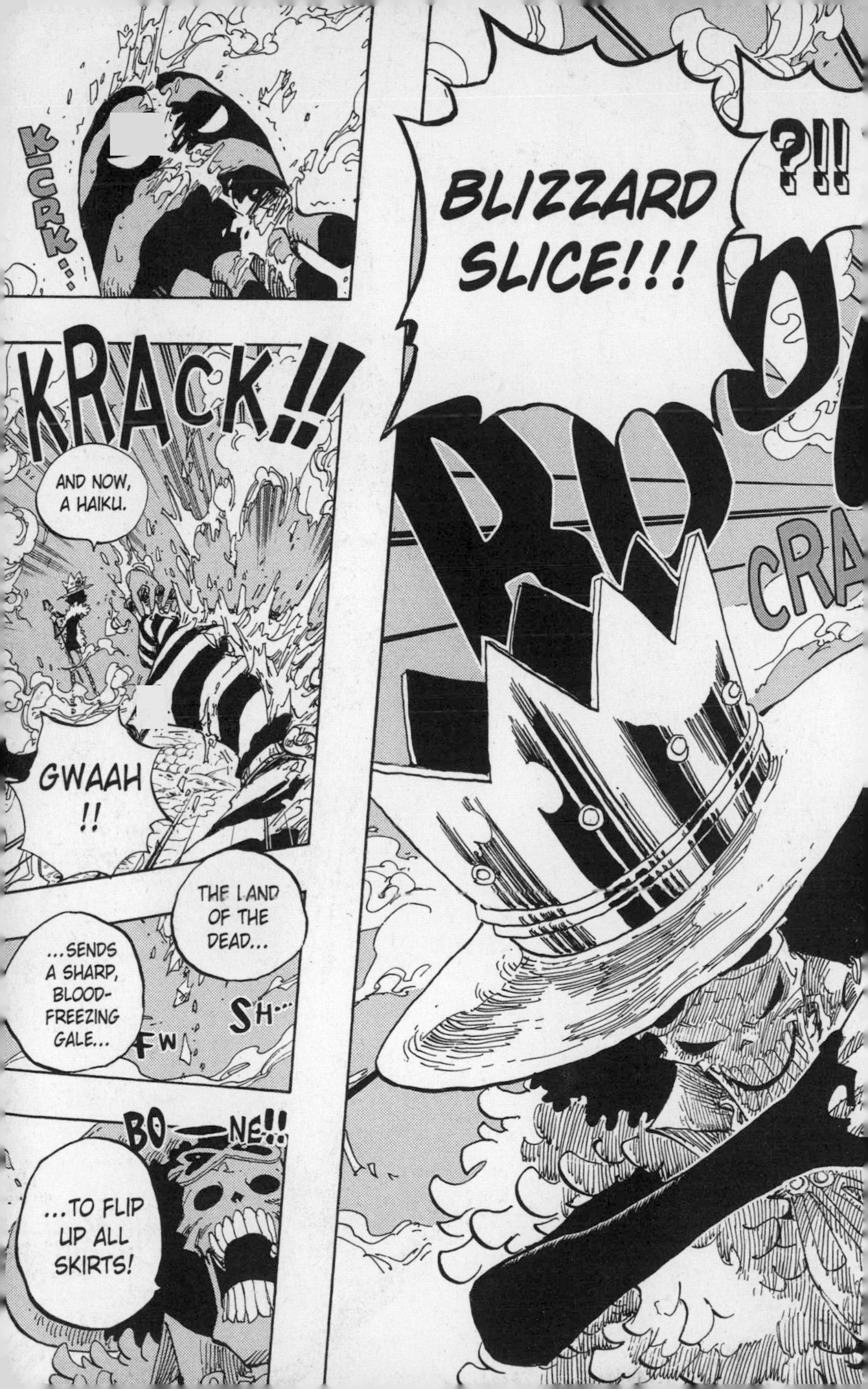
?!!
BLIZZARD SLICE!!!
CRA
KICRK...
KRACK!!
AND NOW, A HAIKU.
GWAAH !!
THE LAND OF THE DEAD...
...SENDS A SHARP, BLOOD-FREEZING GALE...
SH...
FW
BO—NE!!
...TO FLIP UP ALL SKIRTS!

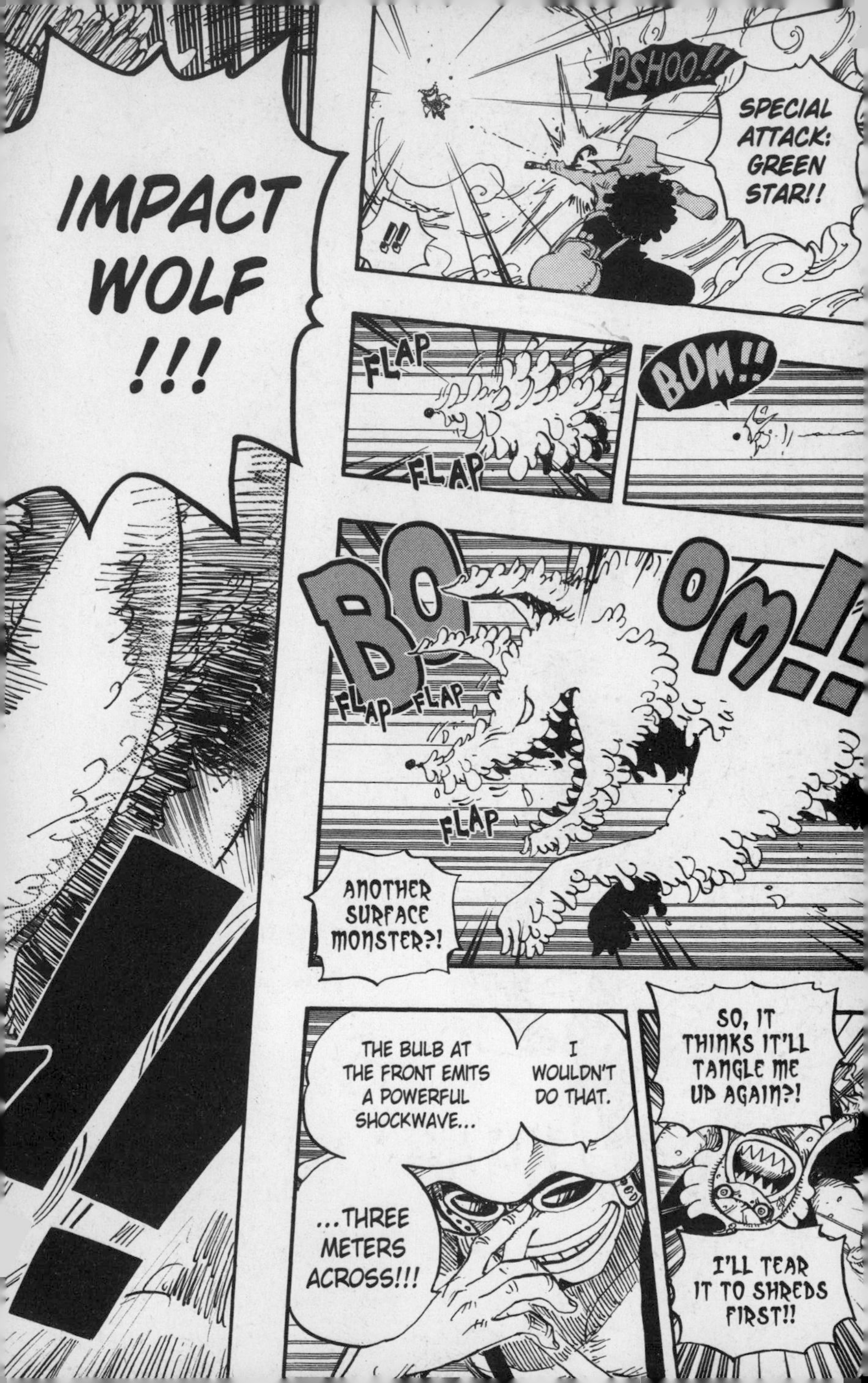
PSHOO!!
SPECIAL ATTACK: GREEN STAR!!
!!
BOM!!
FLAP
FLAP
BOOM!!
FLAP FLAP
FLAP
ANOTHER SURFACE MONSTER?!
SO, IT THINKS IT'LL TANGLE ME UP AGAIN?!
I'LL TEAR IT TO SHREDS FIRST!!
I WOULDN'T DO THAT.
THE BULB AT THE FRONT EMITS A POWERFUL SHOCKWAVE...
...THREE METERS ACROSS!!!
IMPACT WOLF!!!

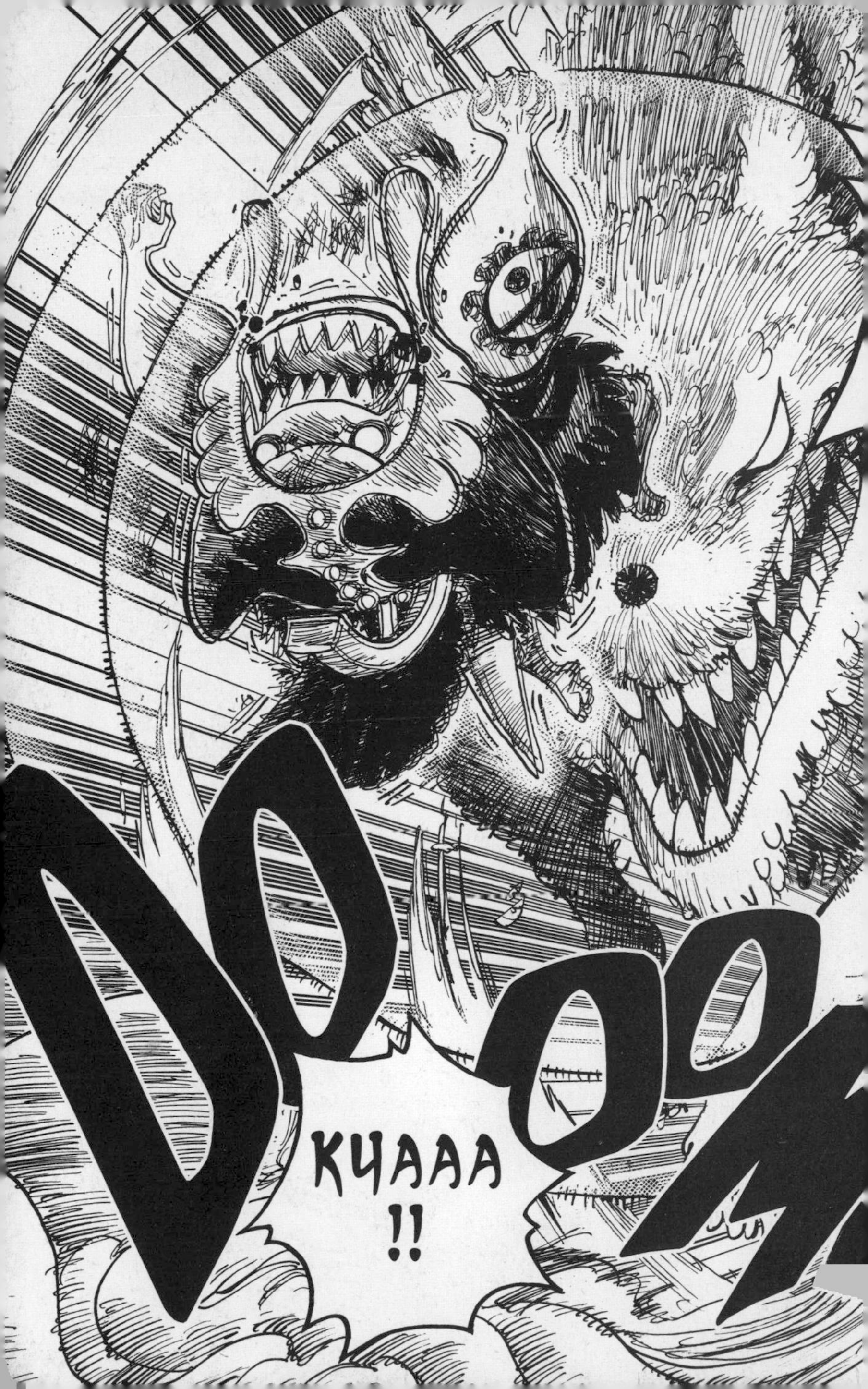
KYAAA
!!

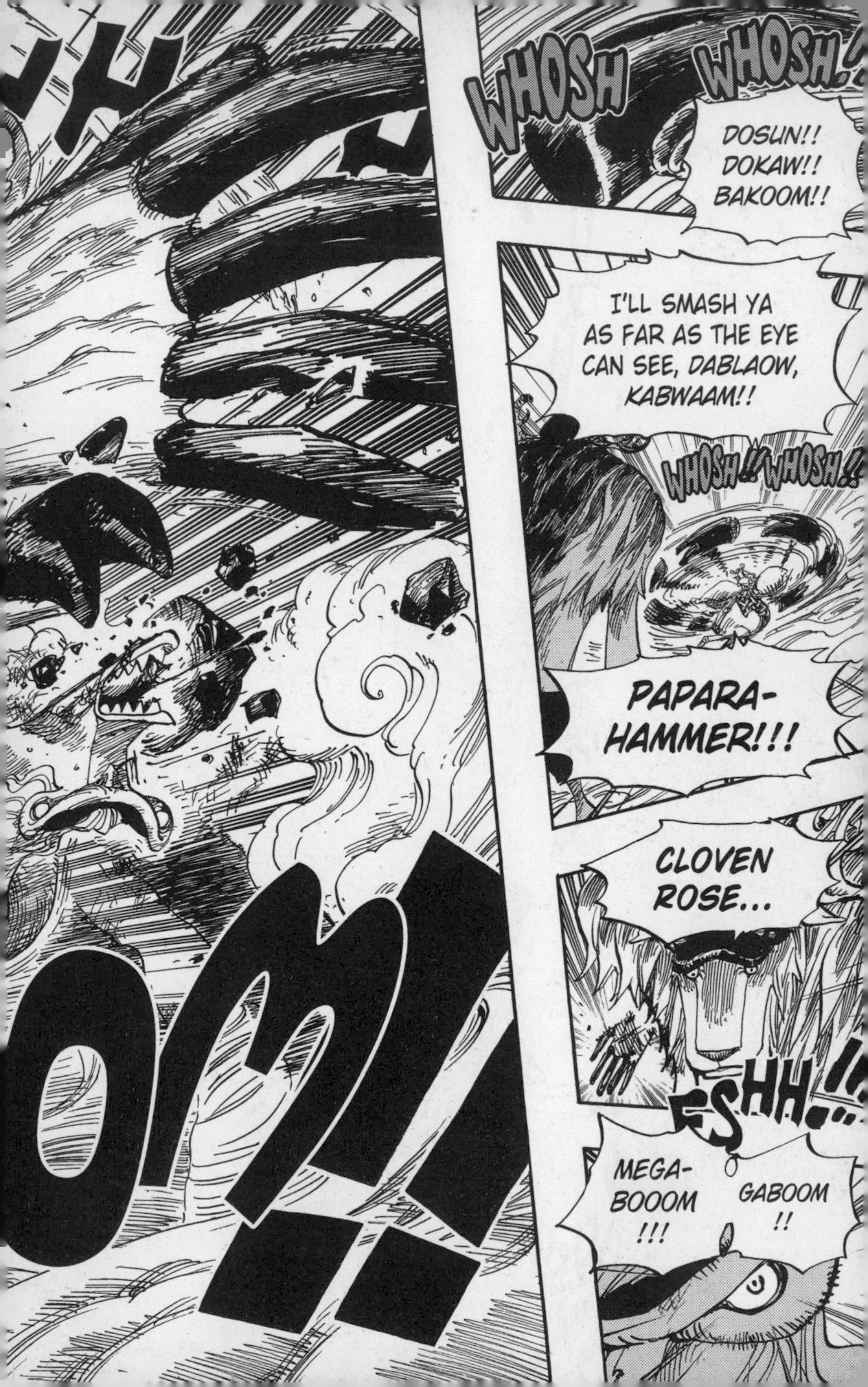
WHOSH
WHOSH!!
DOSUN!! DOKAW!! BAKOOM!!
I'LL SMASH YA AS FAR AS THE EYE CAN SEE, DABLAOW, KABWAAM!!
WHOSH!! WHOSH!!
PAPARA-HAMMER!!!
CLOVEN ROSE...
FSHH!!...
MEGA-BOOOM!!!
GABOOM!!

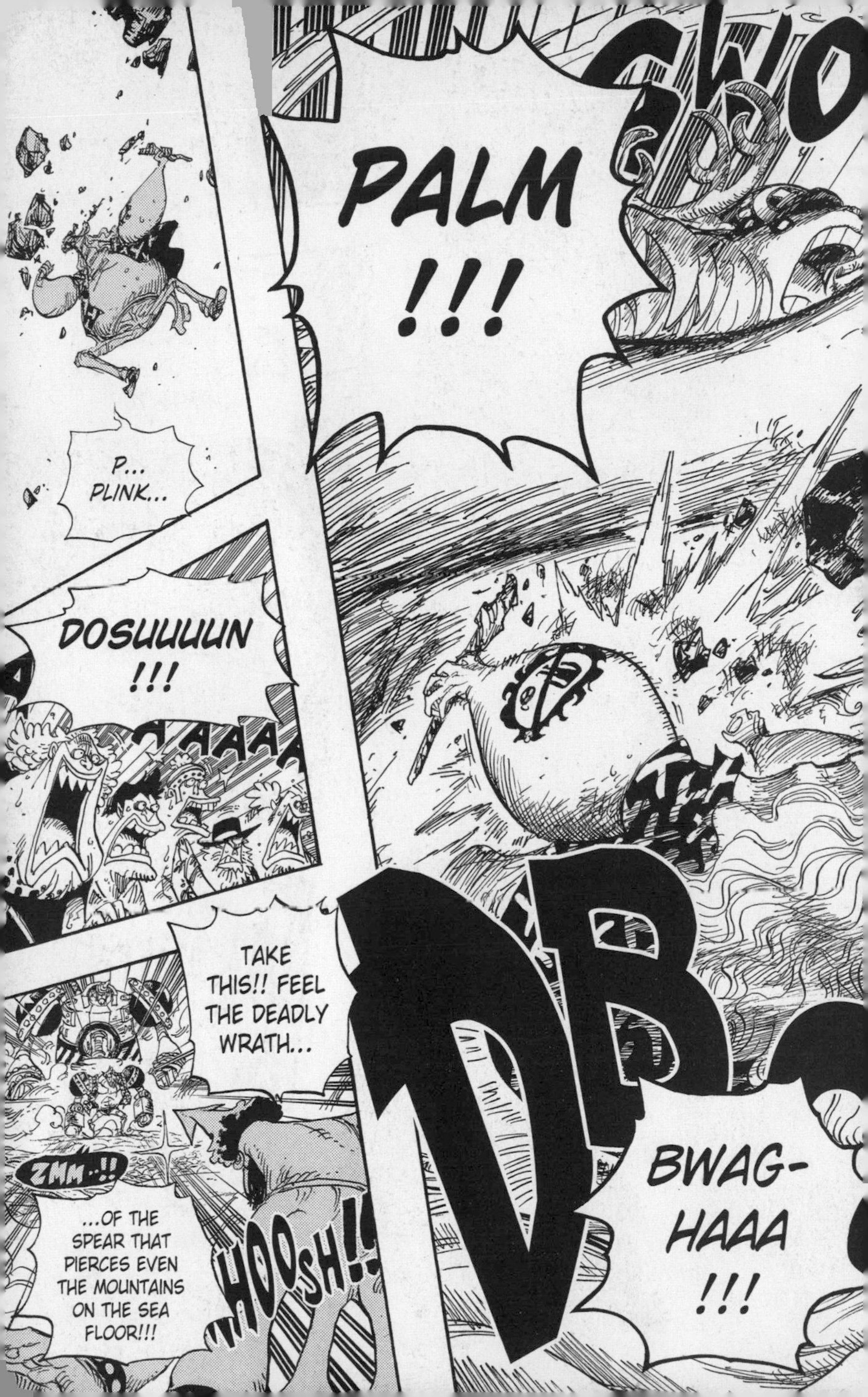
PALM !!!
BWAG- HAAA !!!
P... PLINK...
DOSUUUUN !!!
TAKE THIS!! FEEL THE DEADLY WRATH...
ZMM..!!
...OF THE SPEAR THAT PIERCES EVEN THE MOUNTAINS ON THE SEA FLOOR!!!
HOOSH!!

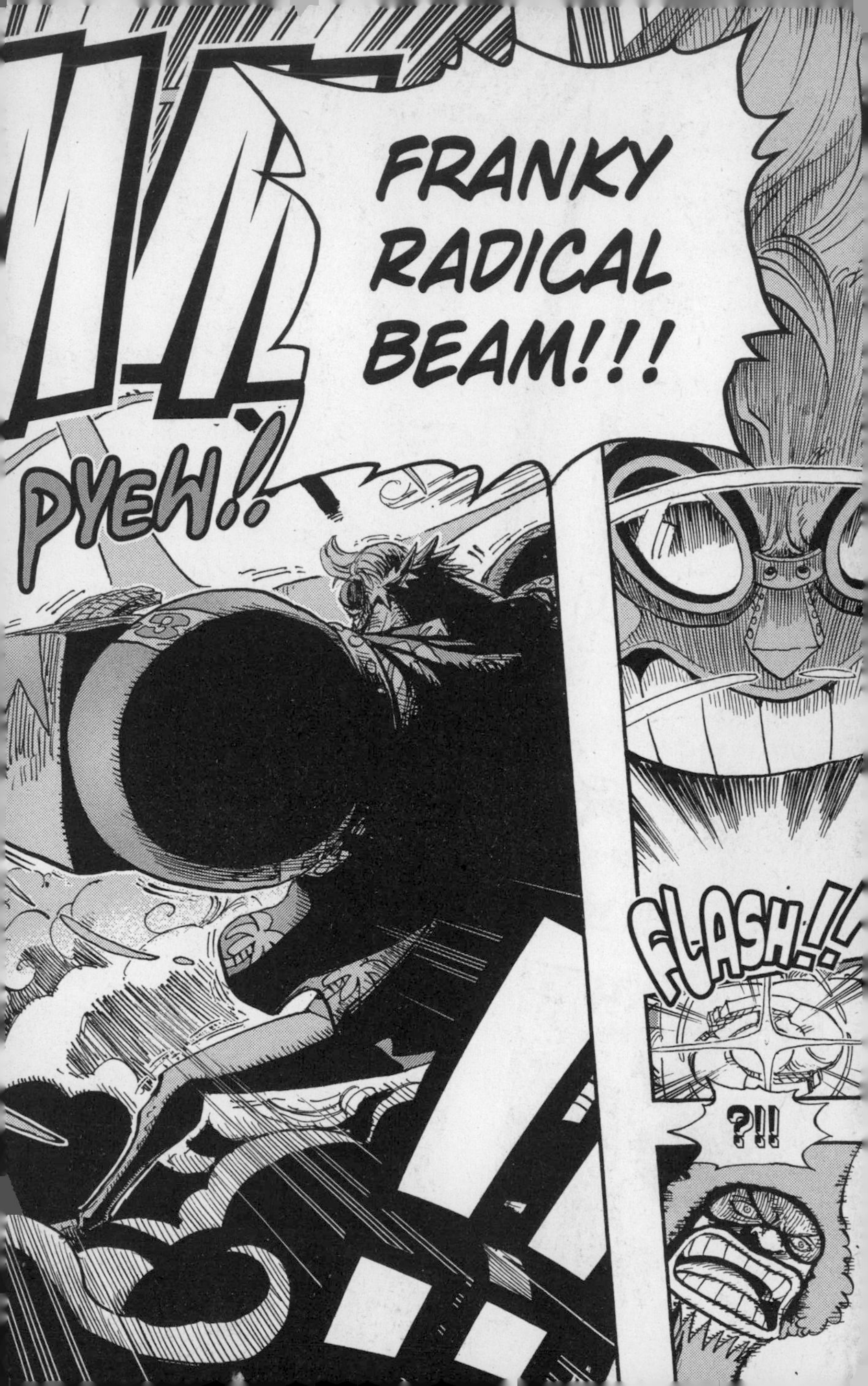
FRANKY RADICAL BEAM!!!
PYEW!!
FLASH!!
?!!

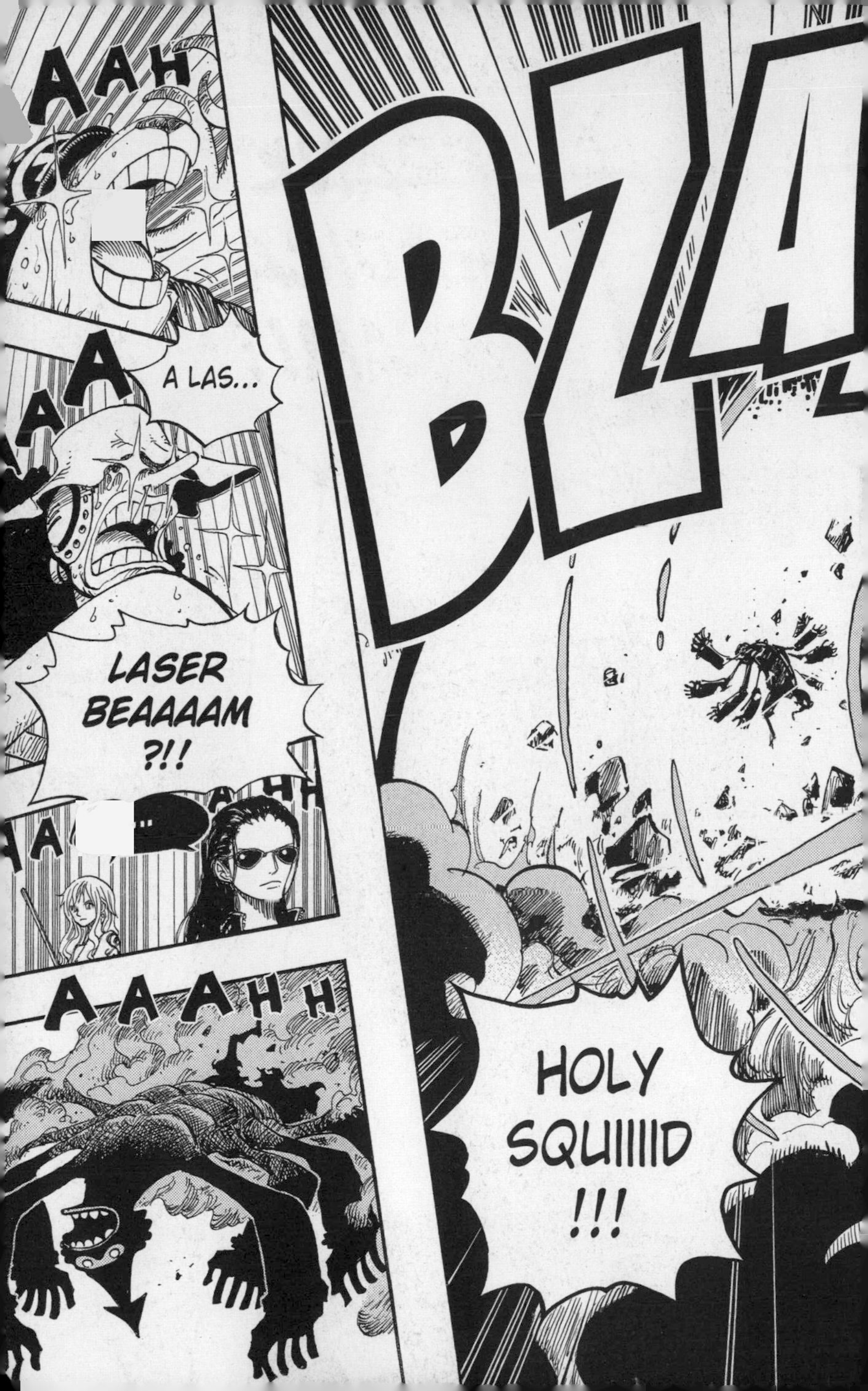

BZA
HOLY SQUIIIID !!!
AAH
A LAS...
AA
LASER BEAAAAM ?!!
AAHH
AAAHH

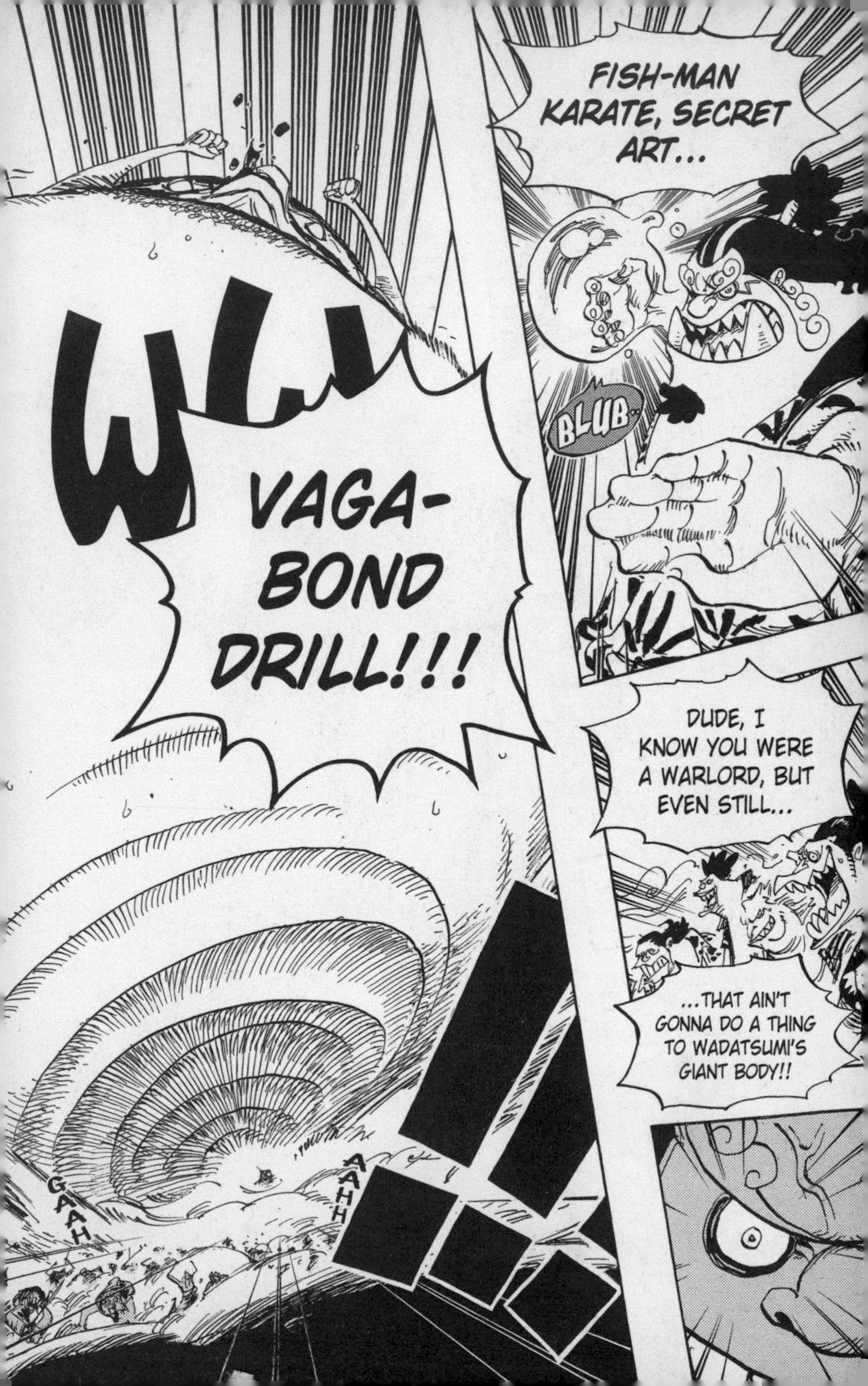
FISH-MAN KARATE, SECRET ART...
BLUB
DUDE, I KNOW YOU WERE A WARLORD, BUT EVEN STILL...
...THAT AIN'T GONNA DO A THING TO WADATSUMI'S GIANT BODY!!
VAGA-BOND DRILL!!!
GAAH
AAHH

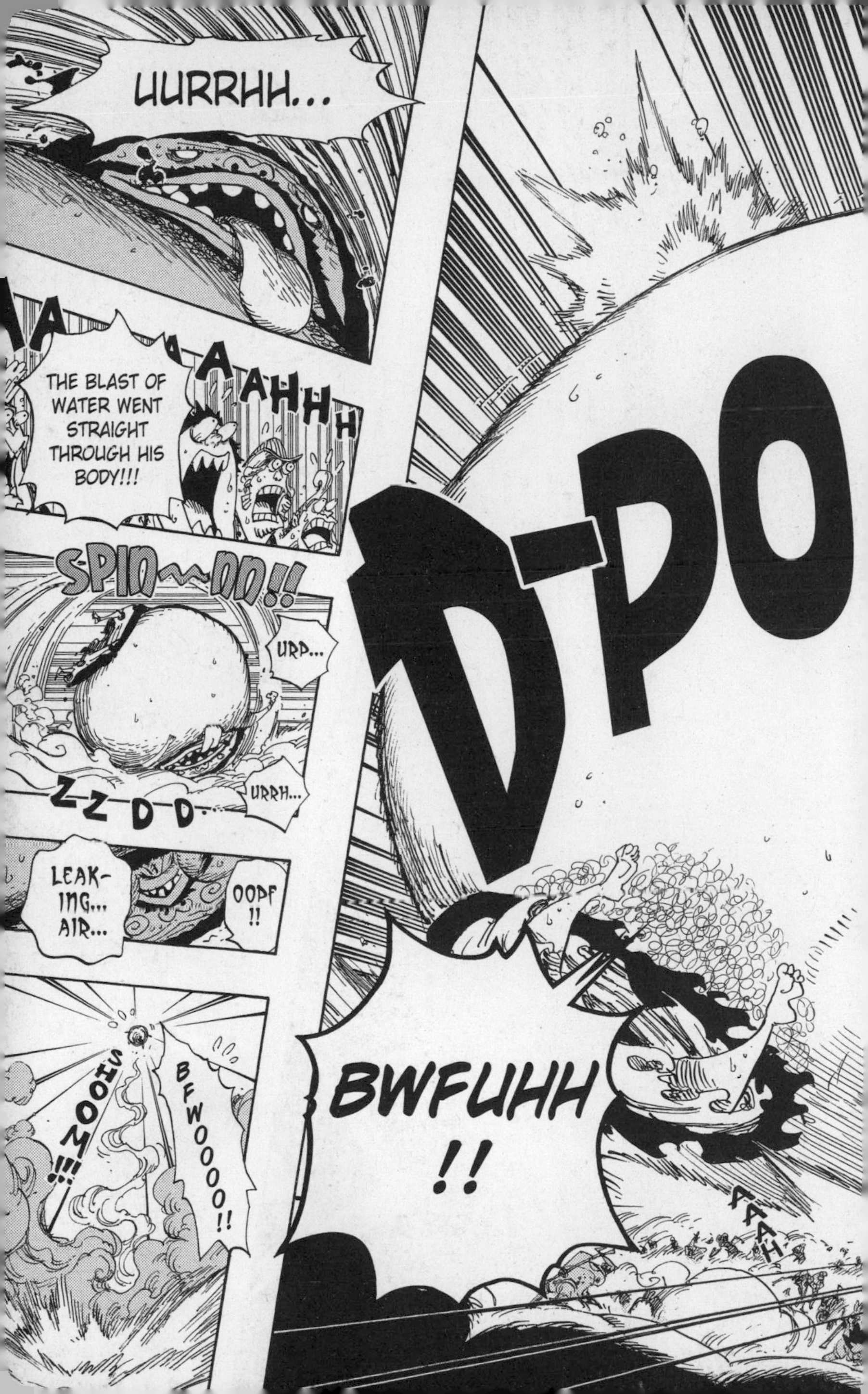
D-PO
BWFUHH !!
AAAH
UURRHH...
AAAAHHHH
THE BLAST OF WATER WENT STRAIGHT THROUGH HIS BODY!!!
SPIN~NN!!
URP...
URRH...
ZZDD
OOPF !!
LEAK-ING... AIR...
BFWOOOOO!!
SHOOM!!!

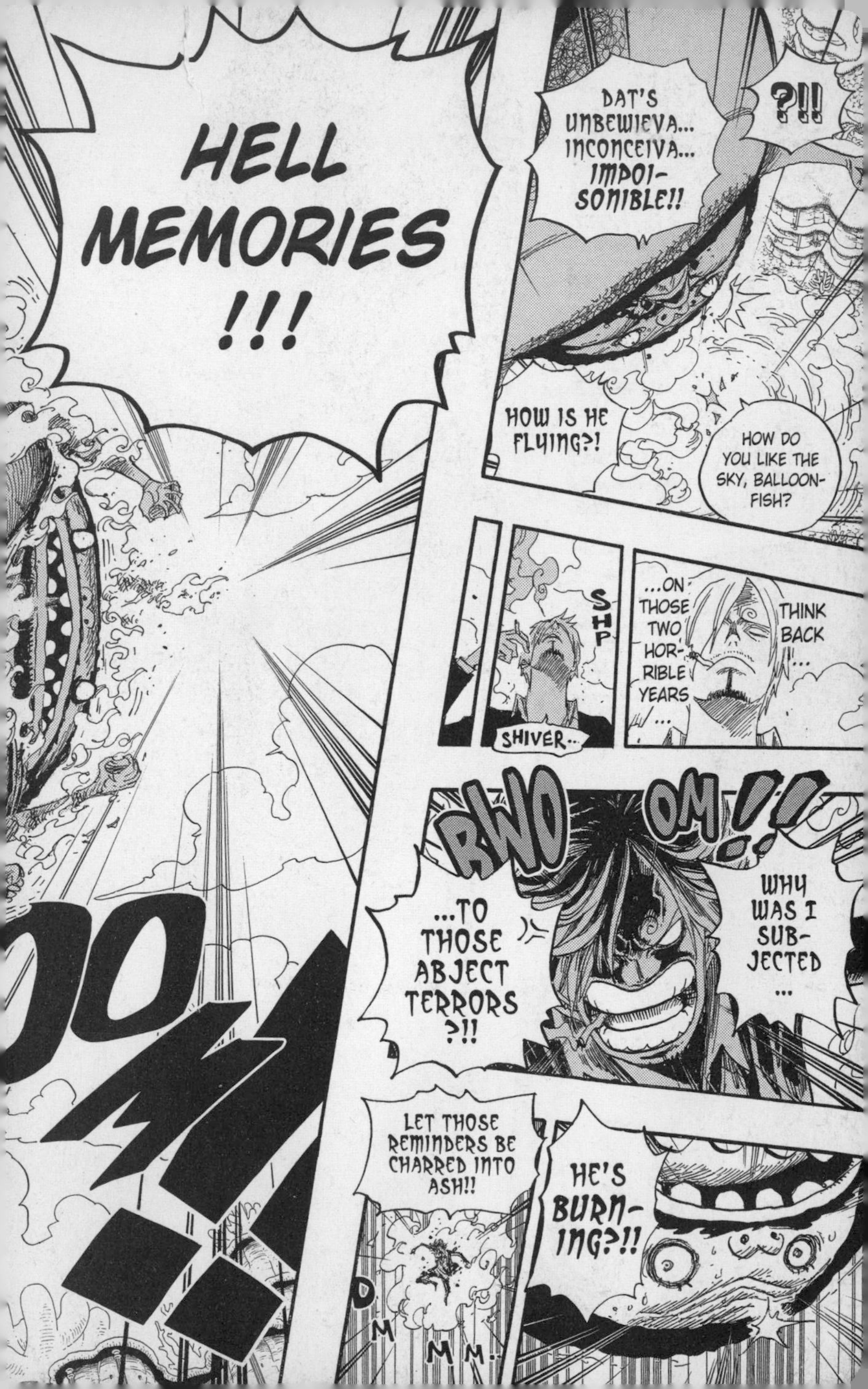
?!!
DAT'S UNBEWIEVA... INCONCEIVA... IMPOI-SONIBLE!!
HOW DO YOU LIKE THE SKY, BALLOON-FISH?
HOW IS HE FLYING?!
THINK BACK...
...ON THOSE TWO HOR-RIBLE YEARS...
SHP
SHIVER...
RWO OM!!
WHY WAS I SUB-JECTED...
...TO THOSE ABJECT TERRORS?!!
LET THOSE REMINDERS BE CHARRED INTO ASH!!
HE'S BURN-ING?!!
DMMM...
HELL MEMORIES!!!
OOM!!

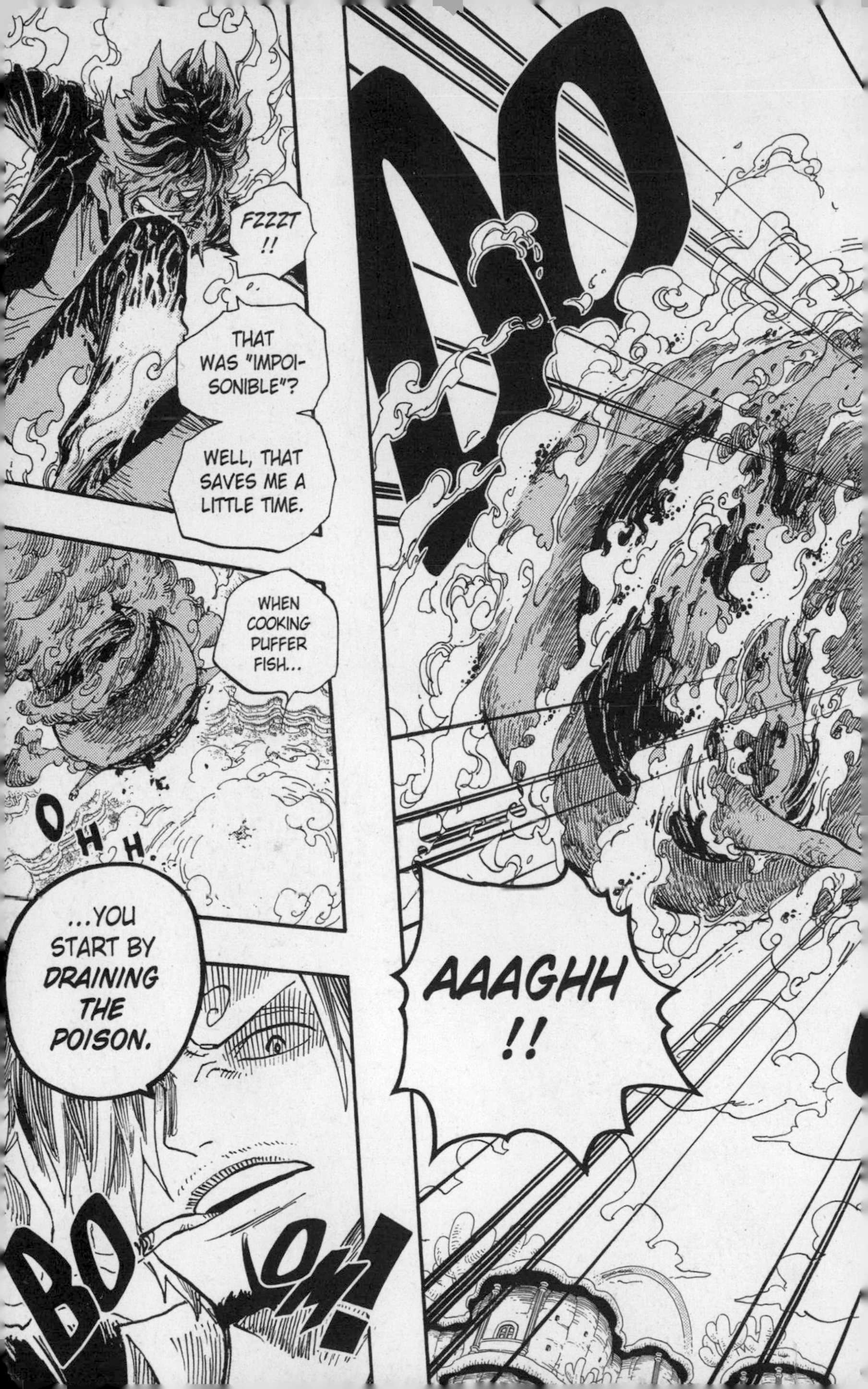
AAAGHH !!
FZZZT !!
THAT WAS "IMPOI-SONIBLE"?
WELL, THAT SAVES ME A LITTLE TIME.
WHEN COOKING PUFFER FISH...
OHH.
...YOU START BY DRAINING THE POISON.
BOOM!

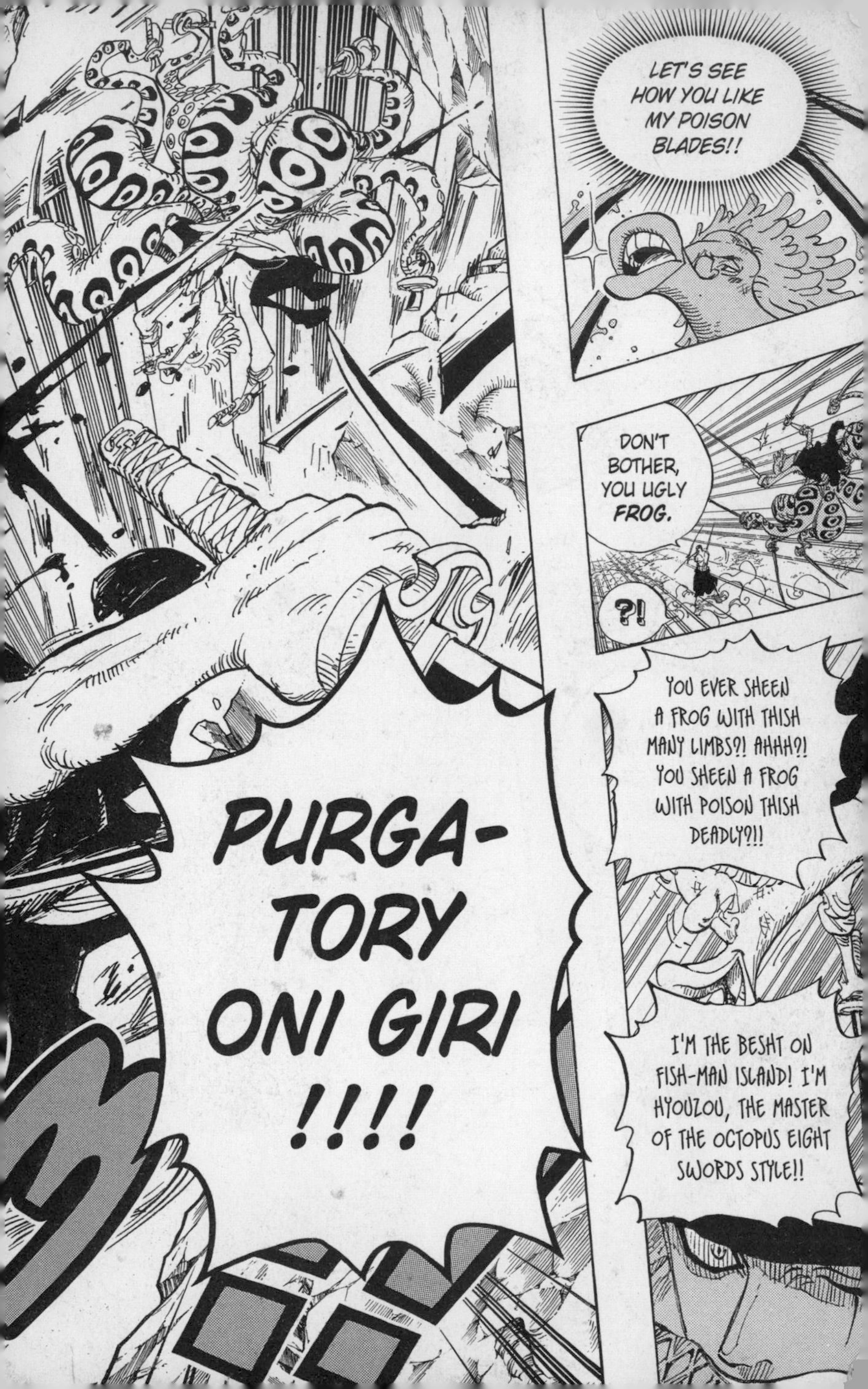
LET'S SEE HOW YOU LIKE MY POISON BLADES!!
DON'T BOTHER, YOU UGLY FROG.
?!
YOU EVER SHEEN A FROG WITH THISH MANY LIMBS?! AHHH?! YOU SHEEN A FROG WITH POISON THISH DEADLY?!!
I'M THE BESHT ON FISH-MAN ISLAND! I'M HYOUZOU, THE MASTER OF THE OCTOPUS EIGHT SWORDS STYLE!!
PURGA-TORY ONI GIRI !!!!

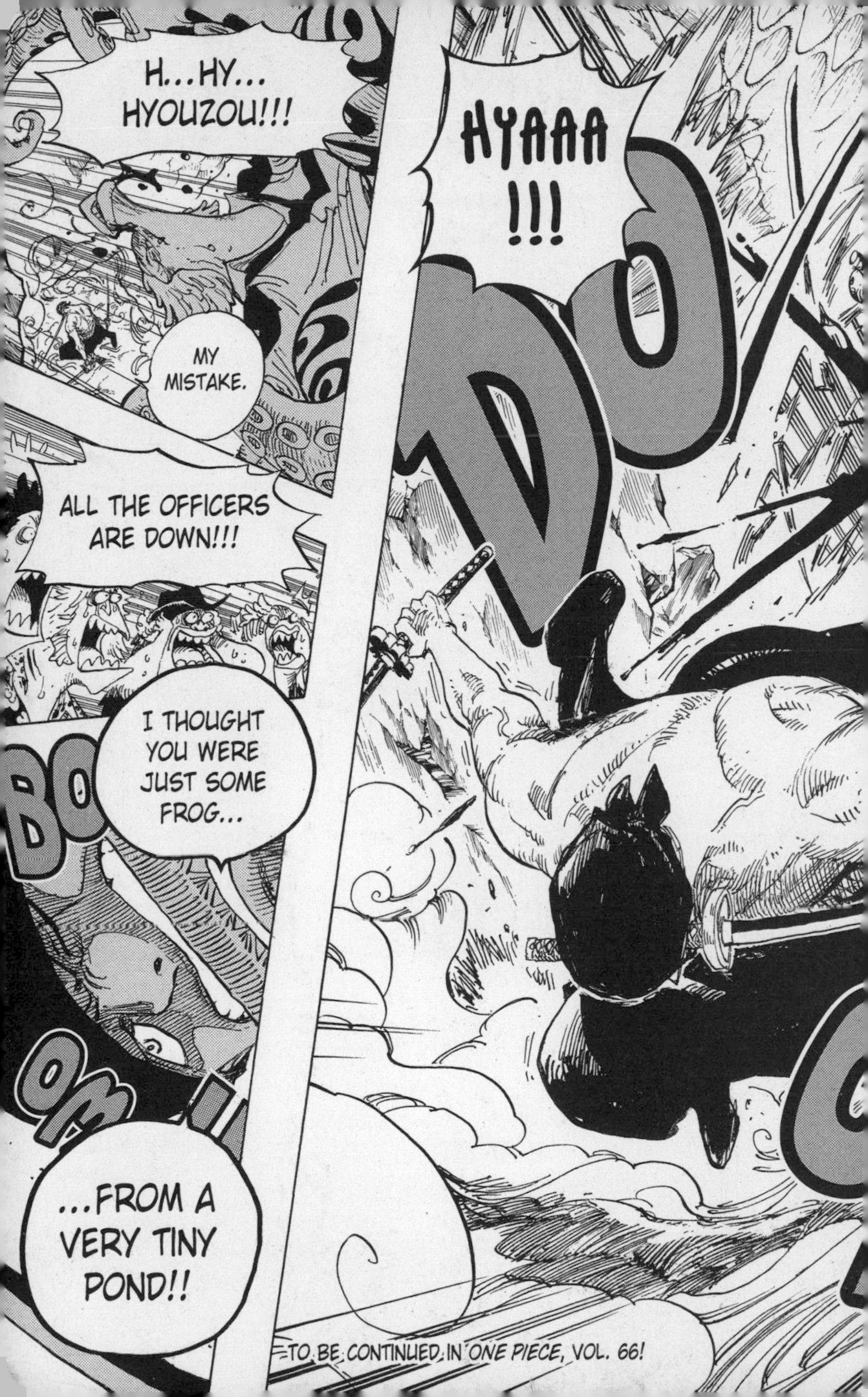
HYAAA
!!!
DO
H...HY...
HYOUZOU!!!
MY MISTAKE.
ALL THE OFFICERS ARE DOWN!!!
I THOUGHT YOU WERE JUST SOME FROG...
BO
OM
...FROM A VERY TINY POND!!

—TO BE CONTINUED IN *ONE PIECE*, VOL. 66!

COMING NEXT VOLUME:

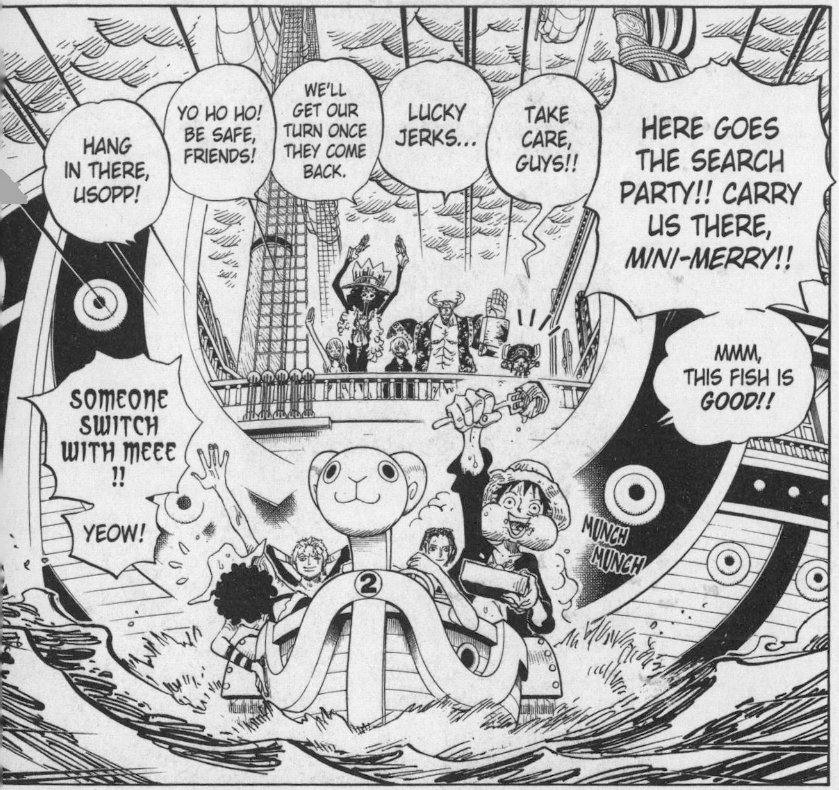
HERE GOES THE SEARCH PARTY!! CARRY US THERE, *MINI-MERRY!!*
TAKE CARE, GUYS!!
LUCKY JERKS...
WE'LL GET OUR TURN ONCE THEY COME BACK.
YO HO HO! BE SAFE, FRIENDS!
HANG IN THERE, USOPP!
MMM, THIS FISH IS *GOOD!!*
MUNCH MUNCH
SOMEONE SWITCH WITH MEEE !!
YEOW!

The Straw Hat pirates may be able to defeat Hody Jones and his minions, but can they stop the destruction of Fish-Man Island itself? When all hope seems lost, a surprising person comes to the rescue. And after the dust settles, the Straw Hats find themselves in all new trouble!

ON SALE MARCH 2013!

⋁I乙MANGA

Read manga anytime, anywhere!

From our newest hit series to the classics you know and love, the best manga in the world is now available digitally. Buy a volume* of digital manga for your:

* iOS device (**iPad®, iPhone®, iPod® touch**) through the **VIZ Manga** app

* Android-powered device (**phone or tablet**) with a browser by visiting **VIZManga.com**

* **Mac or PC computer** by visiting **VIZManga.com**

VIZ Digital has loads to offer:

* 500+ ready-to-read volumes
* New volumes each week
* FREE previews
* Access on multiple devices! Create a log-in through the app so you buy a book once, and read it on your device of choice!*

To learn more, visit www.viz.com/apps

* Some series may not be available for multiple devices. Check the app on your device to find out what's availa

DEATH NOTE © 2003 by Tsugumi Ohba, Takeshi Obata/SHUEISHA Inc.
NURARIHYON NO MAGO © 2008 by Hiroshi Shiibashi/SHUEISHA Inc.
ONE PIECE © 1997 by Eiichiro Oda/SHUEISHA Inc.